AGEING IN EAST AND SOUTH-EAST ASIA

Edited by David R. Phillips (BScEcon, PhD)
Director, Institute of Population Studies
University of Exeter, UK

Edward Arnold
A division of Hodder & Stoughton
LONDON   MELBOURNE   AUCKLAND

© 1992 Edward Arnold

First published in Great Britain 1992

British Library Cataloguing in Publication Data

Phillips, David R.
  Ageing in East and Southeast Asia.
  – (Research studies in gerontology)
  I. Title II. Series
  305.26095

  ISBN 0–340–54367–1

Whilst the advice and information in this book is believed to be
true and accurate at the date of going to press, neither the author
nor the publisher can accept any legal responsibility or liability
for any errors or omissions that may be made. In particular (but
without limiting the generality of the preceding disclaimer) every
effort has been made to check drug dosages; however, it is still
possible that errors have been missed. Furthermore, dosage
schedules are constantly being revised and new side effects
recognised. For these reasons the reader is strongly urged to
consult the drug companies' printed instructions before
administering any of the drugs recommended in this book.

Typeset in Great Britain by Wearset, Boldon, Tyne and Wear
Printed in Great Britain for Edward Arnold, a division of Hodder
and Stoughton Limited, Mill Road, Dunton Green, Sevenoaks,
Kent TN13 2YA by St. Edmundsbury Press, Bury St. Edmunds,
Suffolk and bound by Hartnolls Ltd, Bodmin, Cornwall

CONTENTS

NOTES ON CONTRIBUTORS

Gary R. Andrews MB, BS, FRCP(Edin.), FRACP, FRACMA, FACRM, is Director of the Centre for Ageing Studies of the Flinders University of South Australia. He has been involved at senior levels in clinical geriatrics, health care administration, gerontological and geriatric medicine research and teaching. The Centre for Ageing Studies is a WHO collaborating centre for research on the epidemiology of ageing and Professor Andrews has been responsible for the planning, coordination and reporting of a series of cross-national population-based multidimensional surveys of the health and social conditions of older persons in the Western Pacific, South-East Asian and Eastern Mediterranean regions of WHO including 14 countries in all. He is the current Chair of the Asia/Oceania Regional Executive Committee of the International Association of Gerontology, a member of the WHO global expert panel on health of the elderly, member of the Western Pacific WHO Research Advisory Committee and has been appointed convener for the 16th International Congress of Gerontology to be held in Adelaide, Australia in 1997. In 1989 he was awarded a Special Testimonial by the Secretary General of the United Nations for an outstanding contribution and dedication to the implementation of the UN Programme on Ageing through his international research activities. Professor Andrews has contributed over 80 publications to national and international journals and books including the WHO publication in 1986 *Aging in the Western Pacific – A Four Country Study* and chapters in *Research and the Ageing Population* (J. Wiley and Sons, 1988) and has chapters in *Improving Health of Older People – A World View* (Oxford University Press, 1990).

Cai Guoxuan BPhil, is lecturer in the Department of Social Problem Research, at the Guangzhou (Canton) Academy of Social Sciences. Miss Cai obtained her bachelor degree in philosophy from the Dr. Sun Yat San University in Canton. She has also received advanced training in demography and methods of statistical modelling. Since joining the Academy, she has taken part in over ten social surveys in Canton and its vicinity, including surveys on the value change of youths, the mobility of social classes in Canton, and the Panyu survey co-directed by Dr. Kwong and the Academy.

Hou-Sheng Chan BA, MScEcon, PhD, is Professor of Sociology at the National Taiwan University, Taipei. He received a Special Diploma from the University of Oxford, UK and gained his higher degrees from the University of Wales, UK. He has research and teaching interests in sociological aspects of ageing in Taiwan. He has researched and published on welfare needs of elderly people and changing family structures and has particular interests in their housing, home care and social services in Taiwan.

Paul P.L. Cheung MA, MSW, PhD, is Senior Lecturer in the Department of Social Work and Psychology, National University of Singapore. He is concurrently Chief Statistician of Singapore and Director of the Population Planning Unit. His main interest is in the ageing of populations in Asia and its socio-economic consequences. As principal investigator for a number of major cross-national studies in ageing, he is recognised in Asia for his pioneer work on ageing. He is a member of the Advisory Committee of the UN on Global Population Ageing, and has served as WHO consultant to China on ageing issues.

Sung-Jae Choi MSW, PhD, is Associate Professor in the Department of Social Welfare, Seoul National University in Korea, and Director of Social Service Research Projects, the Social Welfare Research Institute of the university. He received his MSW degree at Washington University in St. Louis, USA, and his PhD Degree at the School of Applied Social Sciences, Case Western Reserve University in Cleveland, USA. He was a visiting scholar in the Tokyo Metropolitan Institute of Gerontology (1990). His major research interests are retirement policy and its impact on pre- and postretirement life, preretirement programmes, domiciliary social services for the elderly, home-help services, housing policy and services, public pension programmes, and perceptions of ageing across adulthood ages. He has been involved in developing home-help services for elderly Koreans provided through HelpAge Korea supported by HelpAge International in England. He is co-author of *Welfare of the Elderly* (Seoul National University Press, 1987) and *Social Welfare Research Methods* (Seoul National University Press, 1988).

Nelson W.S. Chow MBE, JP, PhD, is Professor and Head of the Department of Social Work and Social Administration at the University of Hong Kong. He is specializing in comparative study of social security systems in East and South-east Asian countries and has published a book on *The Administration and Financing of Social Security in China.* He has also carried out research on the issue of community support for the Chinese elderly and has published in *The Gerontologist* and the *Journal of Aging and Social Policy.*

Mark Cleary MA, PhD, is Senior Lecturer in Geography at the University of Brunei Darussalam. He was previously a lecturer in Geography at the University of Exeter. His research interests are in the social and cultural geography of rural areas. He has published on aspects of the rural geography of France and is currently researching on the cultural geography of Borneo.

Hairuni H.M. Ali Maricar BA, MA, is Lecturer in Geography at the University of Brunei Darussalam. Her chief interests are in the demography of Brunei Darussalam, especially questions relating to fertility, mortality, population composition and labour migration. She has published a number of papers relating to demographic trends in Brunei Darussalam and is currently researching aspects of the labour force composition in the region.

Akiko Hashimoto PhD, is an Assistant Professor of Sociology at the University of Pittsburgh. A comparative sociologist by training, her research has focused on ageing in Japan, United States and the Third World. Formerly a research associate at the United Nations University in Tokyo, she directed a seven nation comparative study of ageing in the Third World. Her recent publications include *Family Support for the Elderly: The International Experience* (co-edited with H. Kendig and L. Coppard, Oxford University Press, 1992) and *Living Arrangements of the Aged in Seven Developing Countries, Journal of Cross-Cultural Gerontology* (vol. 6, 1991). She is currently working on ageing in Japan and the United States in comparative perspective.

Graeme Hugo BA, MA, PhD, FASSA, is Professor of Geography at the University of Adelaide. He received his university education at the University of Adelaide, the Flinders University of South Australia and the Australian National University. He completed his PhD in demography (Australian National University 1975) and subsequently took up an appointment at Flinders University as Reader in Geography and Population Studies. He has held visiting positions at the University of Iowa, University of Hawaii, Hasanuddin University (Indonesia) and the Australian National University and has worked with a number of international organizations (a range of United Nations agencies, World Bank, World Fertility Survey, International Labour Office), as well as many Australian and South Australian Government departments and instrumentalities. His doctoral work and much subsequent research has dealt with population issues in South-east Asia, especially Indonesia. He is the author of many books and papers including *Population Mobility in West Java* (Gadjah Mada University Press, Yogyakarta, 1978), *Internal Migration, Urbanization and Development in Indonesia* (United Nations Economic and Social Commission for Asia and the Pacific, New York, 1981) and *Australia's Changing Population: Trends and Implications* (Oxford University Press, 1986). He was joint editor of *Famine: A Geographical Phenomenon* (Reidel, Dordrecht, 1984) and joint author of *The Demographic Dimension in Indonesian Development* (Oxford University Press, Kuala Lumpur, 1987). In recent years he has worked extensively on Australian population issues and problems in particular on issues relating to implications of demographic change for planning the provision of goods and services in the private and public sectors. He is a member of the National Population Council and the Social Sciences Panel of the Australian Research Council and Fellow of the Academy of Social Sciences in Australia.

Paul Kwong BS, MA, DSc, is Lecturer in Sociology at the Chinese University of Hong Kong. He was born in China and educated in Hong Kong and the United States. He has an undergraduate degree in engineering from the University of California at Berkeley, and a doctorate in population sciences from the Harvard School of Public Health. He has been consultant to the WHO and the UN, and has taught courses on demography and sociology in the People's Republic of China. His interests are in the family life cycle and in quantitative methods.

David R. Phillips BScEcon, PhD, is Director of the Institute of Population Studies, a postgraduate research and training institute in the University of Exeter and a World Health Organization collaborating centre for research in human reproduction. He has research and teaching interests in the planning, location and use of health care; service implications of population change and ageing; epidemiological transition and provision of social care and accommodation for elderly people. He has researched these subjects in the United Kingdom and in countries in Asia, Africa and the Caribbean. He has been a visiting researcher at Universities in Hong Kong, the Philippines, Thailand and Jamaica. He is Chairman of the Institute of British Geographers' Medical Geography Study Group and Secretary of the International Geographical Union Commission on Health and Development. His books include *Contemporary Issues in the Geography of Health Care* (Geo Books, 1981), *Accessibility and Utilization: Geographical Perspectives on Health Care Delivery*, with A.E. Joseph (Harper and Row, 1984), *Epidemiological Transition in Hong Kong* (Centre of Asian Studies, University of Hong Kong, 1988), *Home from Home: Private Residential Care for Elderly People*, with J. Vincent and S. Blacksell (JUSSR, University of Sheffield, 1988) and *Health and Health Care in the Third World* (Longman, 1990); co-edited books include *New Towns in East and Southeast Asia*, with A. Yeh (Oxford, 1987).

P.C. Sushama BA, Dip. Social Studies, was a Medical Social Worker with hospitals in the Ministry of Health, Malaysia, before assuming the role of Chief Medical Social Worker, University Hospital, Kuala Lumpur. On appointment as Associate Professor, Universiti Sains Malaysia (USM), Penang, she moved into social work education. Before retiring she helped formulate a module for medical students at the USM Medical School, known as the Community and Family Case Studies, based on a life-span approach. Her interest in health-related issues includes the care of and service developments for the elderly.

S. Vasoo PhD, is Head of the Department of Social Work and Psychology, National University of Singapore. He is actively involved in the improvement of services for elderly people in Singapore. He helped to initiate a number of pioneering community care programmes for elderly. He is Honorary Consultant to the Singapore Council of Social Service, a national co-ordinating body for voluntary social service organizations. He also serves as a member and advisor to various committees on community and social development. He is the author of a number of monographs on social issues and has published various such articles both internationally and locally.

Anthony M. Warnes BA, PhD, is Professor of Geography at King's College, London and Senior Research Associate at the Age Concern Institute of Gerontology. He has been a Visiting Professor at the University of Florida, Gainesville and the University of South Florida, Tampa. From 1984 to 1990 he was Secretary of the British Society of Gerontology and is Review Editor of *Ageing & Society*. His interests in population and housing issues associated with elderly people have developed since the early 1970s through several social surveys, analyses of national datasets and numerous publications. He has recently contributed to a United Nations Population Division international workshop on 'Ageing in the context of the family' and is the Prime Partner for a European Community funded study of the potential of new information technologies to assist older drivers. Among his books are three edited collections of social gerontological research: *Geographical Perspectives on the Elderly* (Methuen, 1982), *Elderly People and Ageing* (special issue, Espaces Populations Sociétés, 1987), and *Human Ageing and Later Life* (Edward Arnold, 1989).

PREFACE

The populations of the countries of Asia's Pacific rim – East and South-east Asia – are all ageing and many at a rapid rate. Whilst the elderly populations in these countries are generally still proportionally relatively small compared with those in the West, these proportions are steadily increasing and, because of the overall numbers of people in many of the countries, the totals of old people are already substantial. Over the next few decades, many of the countries in the region covered by this book will become relatively much more elderly that at present and some, such as Japan, China, South Korea, Singapore and Hong Kong, will have considerably older populations in the early years of next century than at present. Life expectancies are also reaching new records in many parts of the region. This has often been accompanied by increasing economic prosperity and social change, including smaller family sizes.

The social and service provision consequences of this population ageing, rather than demographic ageing itself, are the major concern of this book. What will be the implications for the older citizens and their offspring, as family sizes generally fall, older people live longer, societies become generally more modernized, and the pace of life faster and more expensive? These questions are addressed by experts writing about a wide range of countries in the region. The experts explicitly address the social, housing, health and some economic consequences of the ageing of populations in times of rapid change.

A number of surveys of individual countries in the region and some multi-country studies have been conducted over the past few years, from which results are increasingly becoming available. Many studies point to the emergence of 'problems' associated with ageing but it seems that this region, which has within it some of the most dynamic economies in the contemporary world, has opportunities for addressing and solving many of the so-called problems in new ways. For example, a diminution of the support by the immediate and extended family for its elderly members (which has traditionally been very strong in many of these countries) may be met by policies designed to encourage and enable families to rekindle such support in spite of changing domestic, economic and housing circumstances. Governments in the region, few of which have an extensive history of comprehensive social welfare provision, are now having to face up to new responsibilities for and commitments to elderly persons in a variety of ways. Some initiatives involve financial provision, others involve housing, social and medical services or 'moral support'. Diversity and originality appear to characterize the approaches and solutions in many countries. The economic circumstances of these countries also make comparisons particularly interesting; whilst some countries are still more or less in the category of developing nations, others are strongly industrializing and one, Japan, is a world economic superpower. Yet all are facing the common phenomenon of ageing, at varying rates.

In all the countries of the region covered in this book, care of and respect for elderly family members, especially one's parents, is expected and is sometimes a religious, legal or certainly a filial duty. Perhaps this is being taken advantage of by the authorities in some of the countries, and used as an excuse for delaying or minimizing official action and assistance for elderly people. This may be unwise, however, as in virtually all the countries, circumstances are combining to make it increasingly difficult or unattractive for younger generations to fulfil perceived or felt duties to their elderly relatives. For example, smaller families, fewer children, smaller houses, migration/emigration, increasing longevity and more general aspects of socio-economic change often militate against children successfully caring for parents or elderly family members. The unprecedented number of elderly people who will be alive in the early decades of next century also brings into question whether families will ever again be able to be the main source of care for them, however much they wish to provide it. Nevertheless, the majority of chapters in this book are not unduly pessimistic in their analyses and conclusions and the types of solutions identified are of great interest.

This book is intended to be of interest to a very wide range of disciplines and also to general readers concerned with socio-economic change in this exciting region of the world. Those primarily interested will be in the increasingly cross-disciplinary field of social gerontology, which encompasses the social, economic and demographic conditions of elderly people, but with a particularly applied bent. A major preoccupation of readers will almost certainly be the understanding and improvement of the daily lives of elderly people. They will be as interested in solutions as they are in problems, and as concerned with successes as with failures. The book will thus be of interest to providers of social services and social and medical care, housing specialists, and to people with a range of academic interests including demography, economics, medical geography, sociology and social and physical planning.

The preparation of this book has involved many people and I should like to acknowledge the readiness of all contributors to write so willingly for it. In particular, I should like to acknowledge the advice and help of Professor Tony Warnes in bringing the initial proposal to Edward Arnold, whose staff have dealt very professionally with it and obtained very useful reviews on the book's proposal from a wide range of referees from four continents. Professor Nelson Chow has been a source of advice and encouragement over a number of years in my research into issues involving elderly people in Hong Kong. Professor Gary Andrews was very willing to share his experience of cross-national research projects and to identify research trends and directions in the region. Within the Institute of Population Studies in the University of Exeter, I should like to acknowledge the patience and skills of the secretarial staff, Joan Hodge, Nikki Lamb and Kay Donaldson, in preparing and correcting numerous drafts of chapters and dealing with an array of international communications. Ruth Preist assisted in decoding many types of word-processed contributions and in producing diagrams for Chapter 8. Terry Bacon from the Department of Geography in the University of Exeter produced all the other maps and diagrams with his usual skill and patience. Mrs Jane Hayman assisted with her normal diligence in proof reading. Last, but not least, I wish to acknowledge the patience of my wife Frances who has tolerated my editorial preoccupations over the three years or so during which the book has taken shape. During this time, my family has increased by two daughters, Siân and Carys, and it is to them the book is dedicated. Perhaps, if reading it in years hence, they might feel moved to show sufficient filial devotion to their own ageing parents!

David R. Phillips
Institute of Population Studies
University of Exeter   August 1991

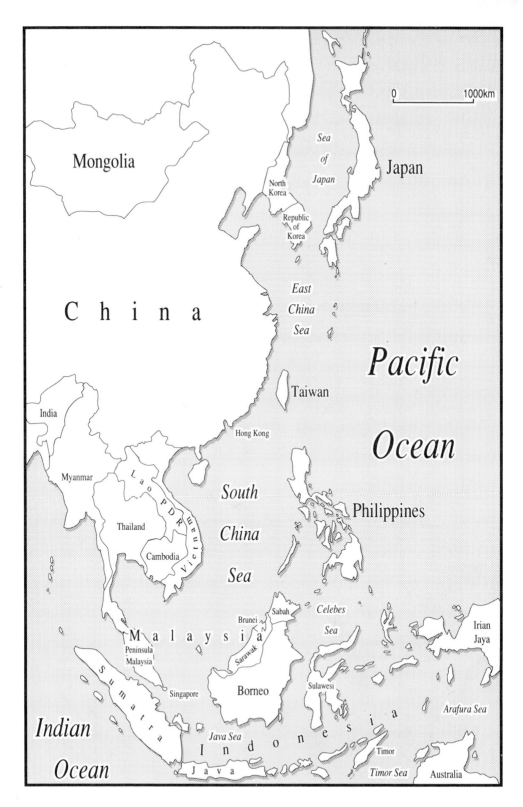

Regional map. East and S.E. Asia.

David Phillips

Institute of Population Studies
University of Exeter

1 EAST AND SOUTH-EAST ASIA: ISSUES OF AGEING IN THE REGION

AIM AND STRUCTURE OF THE BOOK

The underlying aim of this book is to examine the context of elderly people's lives as shaped by provision of services and facilities, including living arrangements and housing, in the region broadly defined as East and South-east Asia. In the developing world, many countries are currently ageing, sometimes rapidly (Kinsella, 1988; Tout, 1989; Chen and Jones, 1989) and, in erstwhile developing countries, population ageing is often now quite substantial. Certain countries of the East and the South-east Asian regions might still be termed developing countries, others are 'maturing' as newly industrialized countries, and one, Japan, is an economic power-house of the region and the world. The region is diverse culturally, linguistically and in socio-economic and geographical terms but it possesses a certain homogeneity of purpose and, in many ways, of outlook on elderly people, their potential and roles.

The contributors to this book come from a wide range of academic disciplines including medicine, population studies, geography, social policy and sociology. Most aspects of the work presented here could conveniently be collated under the title of 'social gerontology'. As outlined by Warnes (1989), gerontology itself is a fairly young field of study in many countries, in North America perhaps better established than in Britain or some other European countries. It is certainly new in this Asian region but it is gathering impetus. Gerontology has generally sought to move from its parent disciplines of medicine, biology and sociology; and social gerontology in particular has a strong applied orientation. It concentrates on the economic, social and demographic circumstances of elderly people, and the ways in which their lives can be influenced by social policies, official stances and community attitudes. Social gerontology is a yet more novel subdiscipline in most of East and South-east Asia; it is a borderline discipline that unites many academics and practitioners from fields which impinge on the study of the social conditions of elderly persons.

Much of the language of the media and even academic writings on elderly people are somewhat negative and assume 'the elderly' (the term in itself implying a group uniformity of conditions and circumstances that is rarely sustained) are a 'problem group'. Warnes (1989) among others, prefers the view that we should respond to the challenge of ageing, putting the problem-assuming perspective under critical examination. This approach seems exceptionally appropriate for the East and South-east Asian region, where ageing was traditionally viewed in honorific terms, with aged people gathering respect and status with their increasing years. Although this optimistic picture has frequently been challenged or been perceived to be eroding with various facets of modernization, it still provides a somewhat more positive starting point for research and policy in the Asian context than that found in many Western countries today.

Perhaps unusually, I shall discuss the structure of the book early in this introduction, since the structure explains the content and coverage of the first two chapters and underpins the presentation of the others. The book is broadly structured into two parts, although it is not formally divided. The first part consists of only two chapters, which deal with issues and research in ageing in the regions. This introductory chapter focuses on the region itself, providing some demographic data for comparative purposes, but stressing that the purpose of the book is to move beyond demographic description and projection. It aims to investigate the research and policy implications of ageing in the region for what is broadly defined below as 'social care'. The second chapter in this first part, by Gary Andrews, specifically addresses research directions in the region. In a clearly structured sequence, he identifies the research approaches to social aspects of ageing that have been adopted so far, and reviews a number of studies now completed (mainly by multicountry agencies such as ASEAN and ESCAP). Various studies by single and multiple countries that are still underway in the early 1990s are also identified. The chapter then considers critically certain methodological issues relating to data and the use of questionnaires of varying levels of appropriateness. Andrews moves on to look at future directions for research in the region, some of which stem from the 1982 United Nations World Assembly on Ageing held in Vienna. Particular types of study are identified as valuable for the future, and certain practical and financial constraints are identified.

The chapter makes two particularly important points. First, there is a need to avoid 'reinventing the wheel' in both research and policy in the region – experiences of other countries can be drawn on and, by implication, intra-regional experiences can be compared. For example, the approaches to housing, care and support in Singapore, Hong Kong or Taiwan might prove to be indicators of what could be attempted in other areas with currently lower levels of aged population. Secondly, there is a high priority in this region, especially in its developing areas, for research which provides information for policy and planning for an ageing population. Results need to be presented in a relevant and convincing manner and there is scope for both encouraging and training research capacity in many of the countries. If this book stimulates regional networks of researchers, this in itself will be a valuable contribution.

The second part of the book is much larger than the first and comprises 11 chapters, each of which is a study of a country in the region, although there are two chapters on Hong Kong reflecting, in part, my interest as editor in this territory, but also both the relatively high level of research undertaken and the interesting service provision attempted there. Likewise, Singapore is the subject of a substantial chapter. For want of a better organizational framework, the countries are sequenced broadly in terms of decreasing percentages of population aged over 65 years in the late 1980s. Editorially, I have attempted to impose a certain degree of uniformity on the presentations in so far as authors have been asked to identify, but not generally to develop in detail, demographic trends and, thereafter, to focus on sources of services, provision and care for elderly people, and to identify strengths and weaknesses in the systems that underpin these. Cultural and socio-economic factors, often pre-eminent, are also considered in this context. Authors were also invited in their chapters to introduce their special research interests which are in many ways indicative of the range of approaches and concerns being adopted by academics in the region. As it would inevitably be repetitious to summarize the major points made about each country or the major features of care in each, I have chosen instead to identify below some specific issues in ageing, referring to certain countries in which these are apparently important. However, first, it is important to consider the region as an entity and in terms of its population characteristics.

THE REGION

The region which is the geographical focus of this book is one of the most economically and demographically exciting in the world today. Massive socio-economic change is being witnessed in the majority of the countries comprising the region, and levels of economic development range from the economic might of modern Japan to the as yet largely untapped or inward-looking potential of certain countries in the southern part of the region such as Burma (Myanmar), Laos and Cambodia. The range of demographic experience is likewise great but a feature common to all countries is the growth in proportion and numbers of elderly people, however defined, in their populations.

There are limitations inherent in imposing a geographical definition such as East and South-east Asia onto the region. This term is somewhat unwieldy, perhaps inelegant, but it is probably more precise than the generalized terms such as Asian Pacific Region, Pacific Asia or Pacific Rim, and wider in compass than South-east or East Asia separately. The term is something of a compromise, describing the region known earlier, in British writing in particular, as the Far East. This book does indeed cover many of the countries which form the foci of a redoubtable journal such as the *Far Eastern Economic Review*. Readers may be referred with confidence to the annual *Asia Yearbook* of this journal (Far Eastern Economic Review, 1991), and to books such as those by Dwyer (1990), Yeung (1990) and Rigg (1991) for further economic and geographical discussions on this region and its components.

A further limitation concerns the countries it was possible to include in this book. The countries have been selected to highlight certain trends, sociocultural features and the like but the levels of research and expertise concerning the countries, in the context of ageing, varies. In some countries, particularly those such as Cambodia, Vietnam and Laos, detailed or comparative information on policies to elderly populations is not readily available, if indeed they have yet been formulated. By contrast, certain of the smaller city-states such as Hong Kong and Singapore now have well-documented research on their elderly populations and on services and provision. Studies on elderly people are also increasingly becoming available in the larger countries such as Taiwan, Korea, Malaysia and Thailand, and are gaining some momentum in the Philippines and Indonesia. There is already much established interest in elderly people, as a group, in China.

Contexts

This section introduces the issue of context of the book and some of the main topics covered. What this book does not fully attempt to do is provide systematic demographic studies of ageing or of population-structure change in the countries concerned. These data are given in most chapters in summarized form although, in some, such as the chapters on Indonesia and Thailand, the changes are of sufficient complexity and import to warrant fuller analysis. There are increasingly recognized limitations to the study of demographic ageing *per se*, not the least of which is that often such studies do little to inform or enlighten policy formulation and practice with respect to elderly people and their care. They tend to be descriptive and to do little other than point to 'problematic' situations of increasing elderly populations. This book, therefore, pays special attention to what is often now being termed 'social care'. This is wider than, say, health-care services alone, but includes the living arrangements, family and community support, formal and informal sectors of care and the like; and their interrelations with health and other welfare needs. There is also growing attention to related matters such as sources of economic support, since these to a considerable extent influence quality of life and options for older people. The editor and authors are by no means denying the importance of the gathering and analysis of population information for developing population policies and programmes. Indeed, they recognize the very real limitations associated with a lack of accurate data on interrelated trends in population and development, and their implications for social care policies and the impact on individuals and on economies at a more macro level (e.g. Economic and Social Commission for Asia and the Pacific (ESCAP), 1990).

Of particular interest and concern is the status of elderly people in the societies of the region and the ways in which this may be changing with modernization. There has been much general support for the contention that the status of aged people diminishes with increasing modernization. A particular proponent of this line of argument, Cowgill, has argued that, whilst it is increasingly apparent that the contention (or even theory) has to be modified in various circumstances, it does appear that 'status' declines with modernization (Cowgill and Holmes, 1972; Cowgill, 1986). Research in many countries of this region seems to lend general credence to the idea of a decline in 'status' in so far as this is reflected in respect, authority and economic role. In Japan, although with some debate as to extent (Cowgill and Holmes, 1972; Palmore, 1975; Palmore and Maeda, 1985), China (Ikels, 1983, 1991), Hong Kong (Chow, 1983; Phillips, 1988b), South Korea (Koo and Cowgill, 1986) and elsewhere, there does appear to be some decline in the traditional reverence in which old age was once apparently held. However, it may be argued that this traditional reverence was often in any case more honoured in the breach than the observance in many of the societies. There have been attempts in Hong Kong, China, Singapore and elsewhere to stimulate the traditional respect for elderly members in particular by encouraging their economic and support roles within families.

Nevertheless, if the traditional familial basis for support is assumed, as is apparent in certain countries such as Muslim Brunei and Indonesia and largely Muslim Malaysia, but the support is actually weakening, then the role of formal sources of support will probably need to be strengthened to supplement or replace it. This may require major changes of official attitudes and resource allocation. As Dwyer (1990) notes, powerful Muslim voices, both from within and outside the region, are now advocating Islam as the determining factor in the lives of citizens and policies in many countries. Malaysia, Singapore, Brunei, the Philippines and Thailand all have significant Muslim populations, whilst Indonesia has the largest Islamic population in the world. Whilst not all these people or governments universally accept all the tenets of Islam, if personal rather than public care for elderly people is advocated, this will inevitably have consequences for such states.

Whether increased state support will occur in practice may be questioned, in particular where economies and systems are not widely geared towards public support of health and welfare services (which, as seen below, is the case in many countries of the region), or where such services are becoming increasingly expensive to provide (as in Japan and countries such as the Republic of Korea and Taiwan). In most industrial societies, retirement from work with some sort of pension support, occupational or otherwise, has become general. This has meant that elderly people have often had more financial and personal independence in recent decades than before. However, in virtually all countries in this region, the economic implications of not working mean reliance on family support or, in some countries such as Hong Kong and Singapore, on the limited state support for the vulnerable or very old. China, by contrast, has a socialist (if overstretched) support system, but one that is very ambivalent to supplementing assumed family support. Japan has evolved a piecemeal social security system, in which public assistance has remained in essence a back-up for inadequacies in various health, pension and employment insurance programmes. In spite of considerable growth, the scale of social security in Japan was, and remains, low in comparison to other developed countries. As Akiko Hashimoto notes in Chapter 3, there was an extended debate on this and other budgetary items at the end of the 1980s.

Care for elderly people has emerged in Japan as a critical element of public and private concern, and this is a precursor for many other countries in the region. Whereas, until the 1980s, Japan had only the relatively small proportion of 9 per cent (1980) of the population aged 65 and over, demographic ageing is accelerating and it is projected that, by 2025, about 23 per cent will be 65+, making Japan's population one of the most elderly on earth. It is ironic that, at the time when other developed nations were experiencing huge cost explosions in the provision of a range of care and support for elderly people, Japan did not seriously have to contend with cost containment, as her age structure appeared to work in her favour. During the decade of the 1990s and early next century, this will be adjusted quite radically. Indeed, there was concern in the 1970s and early 1980s about the proportion of Japanese elderly people alleged to be excessively 'taking advantage' of free health care, which led in 1983 to the introduction of co-payments at the point of service. In addition, epidemiological change, with increasing incidence of cancers and heart disease, has become very evident in Japan, with concomitant increases in care and service costs. This is particularly evident amongst the older group (Martin, 1989a). In Japan, non-hospital alternatives such as nursing homes and community care are poorly developed, and hospitalization rates and lengths of stay are rather high for elderly people (Lawrence, 1985; Powell and Anesaki, 1990). Costs of care and sources of funding are now major practical and political issues in Japan and will certainly become so elsewhere in the next few years.

AGEING IN THE REGION

It has been stated that this book does not propose a detailed analysis of demographic and related trends across the region, nor within specific countries unless of particular significance to social provision and services. However, a basic level of data about, and observations on, comparative trends are essential to an understanding of why ageing is an important regional issue and one likely to become of even greater concern. Traditional census-based analyses or one-off surveys of elderly people (or any section of society) do not, as a rule, provide much depth of understanding of temporal social change in the status and condition of the elderly population and how these will be likely to change. This needs a more sensitive, often ongoing type of work, or research that is replicated at a number of points in time to build up longitudinal pictures.

There are, nevertheless, valuable ways of using census data to look at fixed points and, if more than one census is available, to identify census survival ratios, relative survival of certain groups, and cohort differences in survival ratios. For example, the University of Michigan study of the status of the elderly in several Asian countries (referred to in Chapter 2) contains papers such as that by Hermalin and Christenson (1990) which elaborate such uses of census data to study wider issues than population figures.

Table 1.1 provides an overview of the region in terms of population figures and proportions in the older and younger age groups. Even based on such information there do appear to be quite important differences; broadly speaking these are between the countries in the East Asian part of the region and those in the South-east. The East Asian countries, which include China, Hong Kong, Japan, North and South Korea, Macau and Taiwan, have a distinctly older overall profile, with a sub-regional average of 26 per cent of the population aged under 15 and 6 per cent aged over 65 years. This contrasts with the averages for the South-eastern countries of 38 per cent aged under 15 and 4 per cent aged over 65. Similarly, the countries of East Asia have life expectancies in the region of 69 years (male and female) and above. Often this is much higher for females, reaching over 80 in Japan, Hong Kong and Singapore. Again, the countries of South-east Asia have an average life expectation of around 61 years, although this is increasing strongly in many countries and is already over 70 in Singapore and Brunei and into the upper 60s in Malaysia and in the substantial populations of Thailand and Vietnam.

Such sub-regional differences nevertheless belie the underlying consistency of trends in demographic ageing in virtually all the countries. The point they bring out is that most of the South-eastern group of countries are probably only a few years, perhaps a decade or so, behind the Eastern Asian group in terms of ageing. This makes within-region comparisons even more valuable if, for policy and planning purposes, experiences can be documented and lessons conveyed from one group to the other. This should particularly facilitate what Andrews advocates in Chapter 2, the translation of research effort so that it can inform policy making.

The figures in Table 1.1 provide evidence of contrast in the region (most marked perhaps in GNP per capita, with its concomitant implications for ability to deal with the costs of ageing populations), but also a consistency of trends emerges. What is apparent is that, on the whole, between 3 and 8 per cent of the populations are in the over-65 age group. But there is a greater range, from 20 to 43 per cent, in the under-15-years group, suggesting very different support ratios and very different future proportions of retired to economically active members of the population. For the 'developing' countries of the region, excluding for most part Japan and the first-wave newly industrialized countries (Hong Kong, Singapore, Taiwan and South Korea), there is still time for considered policy adaptation to meet the requirements posed by the ageing of the population. However, even with a small proportion of persons aged 65 and over the numbers concerned are impressive in many of the countries. China, at an extreme, has almost 70 million persons in this age group (considerably more than the total of Europe's most populous countries, Britain, France, Germany, Italy and Spain combined) and will have in the future fewer children to care for ageing parents if the one-child family policy continues to succeed. By the turn of the century, China will have around 90 million persons aged 65 and over, more than double the number in these European countries. It may also have emerging a 4–2–1 population structure; four grandparents, two parents and one

Table 1.1 East and South-east Asia: population data (around 1990).

	Population est. mid-1991 (mill.)	Crude birth rate[1]	Crude death rate[1]	% Population aged under 15	65+	Life expectancy at birth (years)	Per capita GNP (1989) US $	Ageing index nos. 65+/0–14		
								1985	2000	2025
Brunei	0.3	29	3	36	3	71	14 120	–	–	–
Cambodia	7.1	38	16	37	3	49	–	–	–	–
China	1 151.3	21	7	27	6	69	360	17	29	70
Hong Kong	5.9	12	5	22	8	77	10 350	30	45	91
Indonesia	181.4	25	8	37	4	61	490	9	15	39
Japan	123.8	10	7	18	12	79	23 730	46	85	118
Korea (North)	21.8	24	6	29	4	69	1 069	10	14	35
Korea (South)	43.2	15	6	27	5	71	4 400	15	26	67
Laos	4.1	37	15	41	3	50	170	7	9	19
Macau	0.4	17	3	22	6	77	6 877	–	–	–
Malaysia	18.3	29	5	37	4	68	2 130	11	15	44
Myanmar (Burma)	42.1	32	13	38	4	55	195	9	11	22
Philippines	62.3	33	7	39	3	64	700	8	13	38
Singapore	2.8	18	5	23	6	75	10 450	21	33	111
Taiwan	20.5	16	5	27	6	74	6 889	–	–	–
Thailand	58.8	20	7	35	4	66	1 220	9	15	42
Vietnam	67.6	32	9	39	5	63	200(est.)	10	15	33

Sources: Population Reference Bureau (1991); ESCAP (1987); Far Eastern Economic Review (1991).
Notes: [1] per 1 000; – = no data.

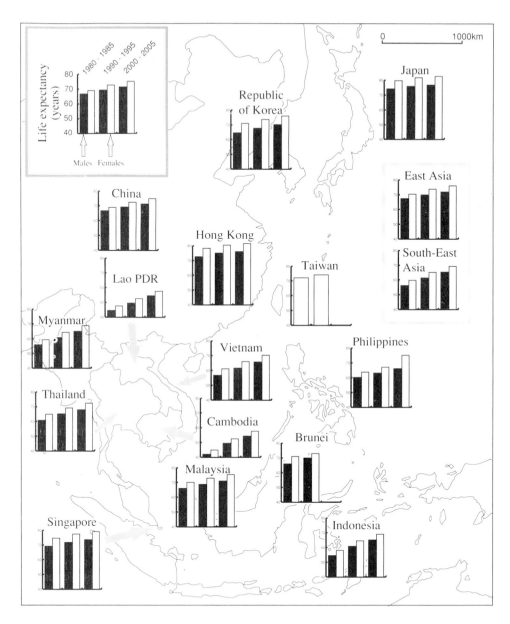

Fig. 1.1 Life expectancy in East and South-east Asia.

child in a family, with concomitant economic and caring burdens on the sole child (Chan, 1991).

Low or reducing levels of fertility in the past few decades have meant that there are proportionally larger numbers of people in the older age group (65 and over) than in the late middle-age group (55 and over) in certain of the countries in this region, notably in Hong Kong, Singapore and China. However, there is set to be a greater percentage increase in population aged 55 and over during the decades to 2020 in many of the countries with large populations, such as Indonesia, the Philippines and Thailand, which means that the numerical importance of older people is bound to increase inexorably during this time. Another way of thinking about this phenomenon, regionwide and indeed in virtually all of the developing world, is to envisage the median age of populations rising, typically by 8 to 10 years or more, over the next three decades (Kinsella, 1988).

Whilst this is not the place for prolonged dwelling on demographic data, an important indicator in addition to median age is an ageing index, defined as the ratio of persons aged 65 and over to every 100 young persons aged under 15 (ESCAP, 1987). Table 1.1 shows that two countries in the region, notably Japan and Singapore, will have more people in the older than in the younger group by 2025. In addition, Hong Kong, China and South Korea will be approaching a balance on this index. By contrast, some countries will, at current projections, still have relatively youthful balances – Laos, Myanmar (Burma), the Philippines, Indonesia, North Korea and Vietnam. Whilst the numbers of aged people in these countries will be much larger, their relative preponderance will be less evident than in the previously-mentioned countries.

To some extent, China and Japan stand apart from the other large countries of the region; China because it is passing so rapidly through demographic transition and Japan because it reached the last currently recognized stage of the transition as long ago as the early 1950s. Today, it has long life expectancy, low fertility and probably the lowest mortality rate in the world. The smaller city-states of Hong Kong and Singapore are also not far behind, demographically and particularly epidemiologically (see below). Several of the other countries in the region are, however, coming close to China in terms of speed of demographic transition. The Republic of Korea, Thailand and to a lesser extent, the Philippines and Peninsular Malaysia, are apparently passing rapidly through the stages of transition. Some UN projections predict that, in view of current trends, Thailand's situation may be comparable to that of China by the end of the century although there may be persistent problems with relatively high levels of infant mortality. Indonesia, however, is rather slower in its transition and greater lags may be expected in Cambodia and some other parts of Indo-China (UN, 1989; Leete, 1987; Kuroda, 1987).

This discussion indicates why, although sometimes tempting, it is largely inaccurate to regard ageing in this region as typical of ageing in the Third World as a wider entity. The region does have a very considerable range of economic development, and many parts are more or less Third World. The economic differentials are, however, unlikely to close as rapidly as the region's demographic and epidemiological profiles, which will tend to conform (ESCAP, 1987; Kinsella, 1988). In regional terms, Africa and parts of Latin America have far lower proportions (around 3 per cent) of people aged 65 and over and lower life expectancy than this Asian region (UN, 1985; Warnes, 1986; Kalache, 1991). Nevertheless, this region is contributing importantly to the overall ageing of the developing world in so far as its constituent countries fall within this classification. On a purely numerical basis, the current world total of some 300 million persons aged 65 and over will be in the region of 410 million by the turn of the century. Much of this increase will be in developing countries and, indeed, by 2020, it is predicted that there will be around 470 million people of 65 and over in developing countries – twice the number as in the now developed world (Davies, 1989). China and India will have contributed considerably to this increase, as will other countries in South-east and East Asia.

ISSUES IN AGEING: IMPLICATIONS FOR POLICY AND SOCIAL CARE

Many academics have been involved in the statistical analyses alluded to earlier of demographic trends and the dynamics of population ageing. Fewer perhaps have successfully translated such efforts into the all-important area of assisting policy or practice, and this point is taken up by Gary Andrews in Chapter 2. However, a number of important issues in ageing have been identified, often of particular relevance either to the more developed or developing countries of the region.

Spatial distribution of elderly populations

One concern has been about the geographical distribution of ageing people, and its implications for both familial support and social care. This has, unusually, taken the form of an analysis of urban–rural differentials in ageing and the distribution of older people. Almost uniformly, during the 1970s and 1980s, the older populations became more concentrated in the urban areas. This may to an extent make the provision of formal care (health care, special housing) easier but, if working family members are to be found in rural areas then this has implications for family support. However, in spite of the increasing urbanization of elderly people throughout most of the region, there are still in most countries absolutely and proportionately more elderly people in rural areas than in towns. This can be because of rural–urban migration of younger folk, or because of reverse migration to the countryside of older people, especially it seems, older men. In some countries, this difference is striking: in the Republic of Korea, for example, some 57 per cent of all men live in cities, but only 39 per cent of men over 55, and 29 per cent of men over 75 are urban residents (Kinsella, 1988). Such rural ageing has implications for agricultural productivity, the maintenance of rural services and the provision of care for rural elderly people. In some circumstances, these might be outweighed, in social terms, by better rural environments, more appropriate housing and better nutrition for older people.

Evidence in Japan suggests that, whilst the percentage of elderly people has been steadily increasing in urban prefectures, it increases much more sharply in rural prefectures, especially 'depopulated ones'. However, in large metropolitan areas composed of urbanized prefectures, the elderly population is expected to increase by more than three times between 1985 and 2020, compared to under twice in the rural prefectures. This phenomenon is largely due to the high numbers of currently young immigrants ageing *in situ* in urban areas (ESCAP, 1989). Therefore, Japan faces a huge urban elderly population early next century and it is highly likely that this trend will be witnessed in other countries in the region.

Epidemiological transition
Epidemiological change is a second crucial feature which often accompanies population ageing and, in many instances, is inseparable in practical terms from demographic transition. The concept and three stages of epidemiological transition are outlined by Omran (1971) and further discussion may be seen in WHO (1984) and Phillips (1988a, 1990) amongst others. In general terms epidemiological transition proposes that, gradually with modernization, the major sources of death will no longer come from infectious pestilences but from chronic and degenerative conditions and so-called 'Western diseases'. It has long been recognized that higher rates of chronic and degenerative diseases (heart diseases, cancers, strokes and musculoskeletal disorders) are almost invariably associated with ageing populations (WHO, 1989). In North America, Verbrugge (1984) and Olshansky and Ault (1986) have gone so far as to discuss a fourth stage of epidemiological transition which involves 'longer life but worsening health'. Older populations may live longer and suffer less from serious degenerative killer diseases but they may be subject to more chronic, non-killer and partially disabling conditions that necessitates adjustments to life-styles and activities. This has obvious implications for health and social care provision in rapidly ageing populations. Some middle-income countries are also experiencing epidemiological polarization, in which degenerative conditions increase and exist alongside infectious and nutritional disorders especially among poorer and younger populations (Phillips, 1988a; Frenk et al., 1989). This can place additional strains on health and social care systems.

For countries in East and South-east Asia, there have been difficulties in developing detailed studies on long-term comparative epidemiological change because of the lack of data covering sufficient time periods. However, even fairly basic analyses show increasing incidence of the more chronic and degenerative conditions in many countries of the region (Phillips, 1991; Martin, 1989a). Detailed data for territories such as Hong Kong suggest very rapid epidemiological change is possible, from an essentially Third World epidemiological profile (high rates of morbidity and mortality from infectious ailments) to a very modern disease profile. This has occurred within as short a time as 20 to 25 years in Hong Kong (Phillips, 1988a, 1990) and has occurred over a similar period, if not to such an extent, in many parts of China. This is true of many other countries in the region: Japan of course, was early identified by Omran (1971) as having experienced an accelerated transition in the postwar period. Data for Japan show in particular a relative increase in heart disease and cancer in people aged over 80 which has occurred between 1950 and the mid-1980s. By contrast, cerebrovascular diseases have relatively declined somewhat in the same period (Martin, 1989a).

The rapidity and generality of epidemiological transition have both academic and policy implications, not all of which have yet been explicitly recognized in many countries of the region. It has already been mentioned that, for a while, Japan was somewhat insulated from the cost and caring implications of its imminent aged-population 'boom'. This came upon it rather suddenly, with the concomitant need for huge public and private investments in care for elderly people. The facts are that whilst many older people are fit and healthy, on average, ageing populations require a changing mix of health and support services, encompassing different health care needs because of the nature of health conditions involved. As Kinsella (1988) notes, there is extensive knowledge in developed countries about, say, proportions of disability and impairment that might be expected among older people (non-institutionalized or otherwise), but much less is known about the health status and health problems of elderly people in the developing countries, particularly the rapidly ageing countries. Indeed, as a rule it seems that the less developed the country, the less is known about health needs and particularly those of the older segments. Some data suggest levels of disability may be similar to those found in developed countries, but this really points to the urgent requirement for appropriate cross-cultural studies.

Social care

Several other issues related to ageing populations are emerging, an important but complex one being a core concern of this book: that of the social care and social support of elderly people. Associated with this are issues of living arrangements, long-term care, family support, kinship systems and family roles. 'Social care' is a broad term embracing more than the formal health care and even social security support available in specific countries and localities. It encompasses the formal and informal, official, voluntary and private networks that provide assistance of many sorts: housing, home helps, mobility, economic support, visiting and moral support. As such, it might be said that the nature, range and sources of social care determine many of the opportunities or disadvantages of elderly people in any particular national setting.

WELFARE SYSTEMS AND PROVISION FOR ELDERLY PEOPLE IN THE REGIONAL CONTEXT

There is a considerable amount of published work which discusses various categorizations and typologies of welfare models and welfare delivery. By and large, these are based on the socio-political orientations of national governments, the ideology of planners and the perceived functions and place of 'welfare' in the society in question. Mishra's work summarizes three basic models of social policy and welfare delivery, ranging through residual, institutional, and structural (socialist) modes of welfare. A fourth mode of occupation-based welfare provision can also be noted (Mishra, 1977, 1981; Titmuss, 1963; Williams, 1989).

There are problems in attempting to impose such a classification onto any particular group of countries; for one thing, there is an implied beneficial progression towards greater state involvement and, for another, an implication of historical progression. Therefore, at any point in time it is reasonable to suppose that a given country's system will be at a particular evolutionary point, and possibly will not fit neatly into a specific category. This difficulty is compounded in the case of regions such as in this book, which cover a wide range of development levels and considerable variety in socio-political orientations.

The field of social planning is relevant in this context. It has been broadly explained as planning for the provision of social welfare services, in the western world in particular. In most developed countries social planning has in fact been directed increasingly towards the planning of social and welfare-related services (Conyers, 1982; MacPherson, 1982, 1987). In many Third World countries and particularly state-socialist societies, there has been a tendency for social planning to become concerned with and integral to development planning. Planning the provision and content of conventional social welfare services forms a part of social planning in such countries, but it has never been more than quite a small part. It often includes many other activities designed to bring broader social change and development, part of the process of comprehensive development planning. The overall economic development of the country thereby becomes paramount, and specific sectoral interests at the time have lower priority. In part, this might explain the inattention given to welfare delivery generally and services for specific groups, such as elderly people, in particular. This may be unfortunate since it has been argued that dependence of elderly persons, particularly the very old, is shaped by public policies, economic conditions and political forces. In many countries, broad economic and public policies have left many elderly people without the means to obtain the help they need. Health-related programmes, for example, need to work effectively and interdependently with other forms of support and particularly with social care. This can prevent unnecessary dependence (Bould *et al.*, 1989). Effective social planning can be the means to achieve this.

Within the four-fold classification noted above, it is tempting to see the majority of countries covered in this book falling into the 'residual' category of welfare orientation. In this, basic, parsimonious, means-tested benefits combined with remedial services might be available to be focused on needy groups and individuals. Hong Kong, Taiwan, Brunei, Singapore, Malaysia, the Philippines and Korea certainly seem to fall more or less into this category because private charities, with varying levels of state subvention, are widely permitted and encouraged. By contrast, few if any of the countries have yet developed the active and thoroughgoing state intervention, fiscal welfare and full citizen entitlement (supported publicly through tax redistributive mechanisms), that the institutional welfare mode implies. Indeed, it may be interesting to ponder that even many Western developed nations during the 1980s and early 1990s moved somewhat away from this, towards greater selectivity and market orientation in welfare. Yet the residual mode, with its laissez-faire underpinnings and lack of government involvement, is often modified somewhat in countries such as Hong Kong, Malaysia, Brunei and even the Philippines, where public sector health care is freely or cheaply available and this inevitably influences elderly people, if perhaps supporting very few of their wider social-care needs. The residual mode here does not always imply the stigma or victim-blaming which is apparent in many Western countries. However, its limited resources often mean that policies such as care in the community end up as care by the family, as there is insufficient investment in formal community support.

At the end of the implied spectrum of welfare types is China, with a structural mode that evolved steadily until the 1980s when greater room for private involvement in a range of welfare-related activities was emerging. Comprehensive coverage has been achieved in many forms of welfare, but the quantity and quality of provision is limited and often dependent on local resources. Very low-cost social housing has, perhaps, been one of the most distinctive features of its socialist orientation. It has had very worthy socialist goals; indeed ideologically it has been relatively more comprehensive and egalitarian in social welfare terms during the 1950s to 1970s than many other socialist states (Deacon, 1983). In practice, however, there has been a huge gap between ideal socialist slogans and the reality of welfare provision in the People's Republic of China (PRC). Chan (1991) suggests that the PRC might be called a 'reluctant collectivist' rather than a classical socialist in terms of welfare policy. It has in reality provided public assistance and welfare services unwillingly and the family and neighbourhood are often the main support for hardship and individual problems. There remains a strong emphasis on self-reliance and a pragmatic socialism which apparently accepts that low levels of welfare provision are inevitable in view of China's socio-economic circumstances. In many fields of social policy there is an almost repressive administrative style evident and priority of economic development over individual rights and welfare (most clearly evident, perhaps, in the 'one child' family planning programme). This is sometimes explained by the state-socialist model or a cultural predisposition to authoritarian and patriarchal rule which Chinese are allegedly accustomed to (Chan, 1991). In China's current transition from state economy to a more market-orientated economy, the issue of welfare reform and its impact on elderly people has yet to be adequately addressed (see Chapter 7).

Elsewhere in the region, welfare policies vary considerably. A country such as Korea, one of the first wave of Newly Industrializing Countries (NICs), has been attempting to develop both public and private pension schemes and old-age allowances, but there is little practical support such as housing and publicly-provided social services. As in many of the other countries, voluntary agencies and charities play an active if limited role. In Chapter 9, Sung Jae Choi explains the Korean government policy which is one of regarding ageing as a personal or family matter, rather than a matter for society. The guiding principle has become 'care by the family first, social security second'. Coupled with the limited public social welfare measures being focused onto poor or low-income people, there is a persistent official neglect of the elderly as a group. The continued emphasis here on family responsibility is regarded as detremental to the development of a welfare policy for all elderly Koreans.

The Philippines has had a traditionally laissez-faire approach to many aspects of welfare and housing policy. Whilst earlier régimes have focused considerably on primary health care, extending a range of services to rural and urban areas, this has to an extent descended to an abrogation of public responsibility to the barangay (parish) level (Phillips, 1986). However, family size in the Philippines is larger than in many other countries of the region and, therefore, family support may remain more realistic than elsewhere for some time to come (Andrews et al., 1986).

In Hong Kong a mixed system has evolved, with considerable public support for health services and certain forms of social welfare, both by direct provision and via whole or part-subvention of charitable organizations. There is also a substantial private sector in health care. For example, in 1990, the sources of hospital beds were approximately 51 per cent public, 38 per cent government assisted and 11 per cent private (Hong Kong Government, 1991). As outlined in Chapter 4, the private sector has become involved in a rapid growth of private homes for elderly people during the 1980s. This reached such a scale that the government introduced a voluntary code of conduct for such homes in 1986 and proposes firmer controls early in the 1990s. Here, a welfare state is unlikely to emerge, and the Hong Kong government has chosen to focus most of its welfare attention onto particular groups or needs. Family care is valued in Hong Kong Chinese families and official policy in the Hong Kong Housing Authority, for example, has wished to stimulate this (Chow, 1983; Phillips, 1988b). The government has, however, particularly emphasized a 'care in the community' policy although it has yet to be demonstrated that sufficiently caring communities exist or are able to provide support for elderly people (see Nelson Chow, Chapter 5). By contrast to the growth of private old people's homes in Hong Kong, Singapore and some other countries of the region, Brunei, with its strong Muslim emphasis on family care, has no private old people's homes and is unlikely to favour their development (see Chapter 13).

LIVING ARRANGEMENTS AND FAMILY SOURCES OF SUPPORT

This brief overview of social policy orientations in the region highlights one major feature which is common to virtually all countries in this book: the family is being regarded almost universally as the principal supporter, carer and home-provider for elderly people and particularly those unable to look after themselves. This imbues the region with a characteristic that is not common in many developed countries where it has become increasingly recognized (if not always fully implemented) that the public sector should provide, or at least underwrite financially, the majority of social care for elderly people. However, it is important to recognize that stress can potentially be placed on families who are expected and called on to provide support for their elderly relatives but who may find this difficult to do (Chen and Jones, 1989). This point is emphasized by several authors in this book.

Belief in the family as the prime source of care can stem from, for example, Chinese, especially Confucian, traditions of filial piety and respect, or from similar Malay cultural attitudes, or from the religious emphases of Islam which, in the Koran and elsewhere, stress the need for children to accept responsibility for the care of their elderly relatives. The influence of Islam is becoming much more important than before in many of the countries in the south of this region, especially in Brunei, Indonesia and Malaysia. As Mark Cleary and Hairuni Ali Maracar discuss in Chapter 13, whilst the state in Brunei might provide important services such as free medical care, education and pensions, actual care for elderly people is regarded differently. The idea that there should be alternative sources of living for elderly people other than within the family (such as the commercial homes in Hong Kong, Singapore and Malaysia, or other hostel arrangements) would, in Brunei, be anathema. Other religions in the region also emphasize responsibilities to older people. Buddhism, the largest religion in many countries, including Thailand, South Korea and Singapore, in addition to respect for living things in general, specifically sets out duties of children to parents and vice versa. Other beliefs, including ancestor worship, appear to give strength to family responsibility to elderly people. However, as many authors stress, in many of the countries of the book the ability and, perhaps, the willingness of the family to care for elderly relatives is often reducing. This means that there is an emerging contradiction through which elderly people might suffer from an expectation of family support (and housing), and a concomitant lack of publicly-funded alternatives.

Public welfare systems in the region are, by and large, serving their older populations only in a 'residual' manner. They provide a barely adequate, or even inadequate, level of services that families cannot give, and the living arrangements of elderly people have therefore come to be a major focus of research and will probably receive increasing policy attention. This is because the place in which elderly people live and the people with whom they live clearly influences their need for specialist accommodation, social carers, meal providers, company and support, and special financial assistance. Elderly people living alone and without families will require their own financial resources from combinations of current income, personal sources and public or private pensions. They may come to need special assistance in day-to-day chores and, if disabled or incapacitated, may require extensive support. By contrast, if cared for in a family home, elderly people often fulfil family roles, and their financial needs may largely be subsumed with those of the rest of their households.

The presence of elderly people with others in a household usually signifies multigeneration living and modernization theorists have often suggested, as noted earlier, that the status and well-being of elderly people are closely associated with their living arrangements. However, family support can be, and often is, given without living under the same roof, but co-residence even under circumstances of good health may be regarded as a kind of insurance (Martin, 1989b). In addition, it is increasingly obvious that, in the process of modernization in towns as much as in rural areas, elderly family members can look after home and children whilst other members of the household are working outside.

Care in the community, as opposed to institutional care, has therefore always been a type of ideal in this region. In its original meaning outlined by Maclean (1989) as care by the community (by informal carers, mainly family members), it has apparently existed in the Asian, and particularly the Chinese, idea of filial piety. Unfortunately, changing demographic, economic and social circumstances in many countries in the region have often reduced this role of families and sometimes reduced co-residence. If state or other formal support does not strongly emerge in such circumstances, then care in the community can become a weak and ineffective option. Many of the countries in this book illustrate this trend and, even if officially-named 'care in the community' policies have not been implemented, care by the family remains a central theme in virtually all of the countries.

Research into the difference between elderly people living with their children and those not doing so has thus become a major area of concern; it may well eventually inform policy as to the wisdom of continued reliance on the family as carers. It appears that as many as three-quarters of Asians aged over 60 may be living with their children although proportions are changing downards in some countries such as Japan. A major source of information has been the mid-1980s four-country study conducted under the auspices of WHO, discussed further by Andrews in Chapter 2. This study of Korea, Malaysia, the Philippines and Fiji, whilst focusing principally on health, gathered valuable data on living arrangements which have been further analyzed by Martin (1989b).

Space precludes detailed consideration of these results, but a number of trends emerge of relevance to the studies in this book. Somewhat surprisingly the older elderly were less likely to be living with children than the younger in all countries except Korea. This is possibly because the children of older people would also be older or perhaps they would be more likely to own their own houses. Years of education and residence in an urban area had no influence except in the Philippines, where co-residence was likely to increase in urban areas. Also surprisingly perhaps, healthiness and abilities to perform activities of daily living (as a measure of health) had no effect on the probability of living with children. Cultural variables do seem to be important. In particular in the three countries for which cultural variables were included, there were ethnic differences in proportions of elderly people living with their children. In Malaysia, being Malay reduced the probability; the Chinese and Indians had similar proportions; in Fiji, being Indian as opposed to Fijian raised the probability of co-residence. In Korea, being religious was associated with a higher probability of living with children. In many countries, being an elderly male significantly raised the probability of living with a spouse which also reduced the likelihood of living with children.

From a policy perspective certain important issues are raised, directly and indirectly, by the findings from this type of survey. For example, ageing populations would generally reduce the likelihood of elderly parents living with children; increased self-support among the Koreans would reduce the probability of living with others, with implications for better-off elderly people in the wealthier countries. Increased migration can also be associated with decreased probability of living with children. A decline in religious affiliations in Korea and a decline in the proportion of Chinese in Malaysia would also lead to a decline in living with children, increasing the probabilities of living alone, with a spouse or with others. However, Martin's analysis does show Malaysian respondents to have significantly different living arrangements from the other three countries, which cautions against drawing uniform conclusions, particularly as differences in family systems are difficult to quantify.

Nevertheless there are many policy implications that may be drawn from the findings of these types of survey which are associated with longer life, greater single survivorship, and less housing being available which is suitable for multigeneration occupation. Males and the young-old were generally more likely to live with their children than females and the older-elderly people. As all the four countries studied are expected to age in the forseeable future and (except Korea) to become more female, so co-residence with children might be expected to decrease if the patterns found continue (Martin, 1989b). This would therefore almost inevitably thrust the responsibility for caring for such people onto sources other than immediate family or children.

Elsewhere in the region, in Japan, there has been a decline in recent decades in the proportion of elderly people (aged 65 and over) living with adult children, from 77 per cent in 1970 to 65 per cent by the mid-1980s. During this time, the percentage of such elderly people living alone increased from 6 to 10 per cent and the proportion living with a spouse only, rose from 12 to 22 per cent (Martin, 1989a). Whilst this may mean more healthy and active older people are living together as couples, the incidence of widowhood also means that the proportions of old and alone will probably increase, unless family care is reinstated or other social care provision is made. Today, both young and old Japanese seem to be less certain than previously about a child's obligation to support parents, which may in fact point to a further decline in the percentage of parents living with and supported by children. Nevertheless, the majority of Japanese elderly people today still prefer living with their children although most elderly men felt they would prefer to be looked after by their spouses if they become physically weak (Martin, 1989a).

In China the government has basically decided that care of elderly people will primarily continue as a family responsibility. The constitution and many articles make this explicit. Chow (1983, 1987) notes that, historically, expectations of reciprocity were explicit in Chinese literature on how parents should take care of their children who, in turn, should provide for them when they are old. This was to an extent translated into a family law in the PRC and is embodied in the high priority accorded to preventive aspects of welfare which include teaching all to revere elderly people and to educate parents and grandparents on child rearing. To a degree, informal family care is thus made obligatory (Yuan, 1990; Zeng et al., 1990). However, a strong reliance on personal and family responsibility is perhaps not consistent with communist ideals, although such ideals have been considerably modified in the PRC, particularly with regard to state provision of welfare services (Chan, 1991).

Ikels (1990, 1991) also notes that families in the PRC are urged to provide care not only on the grounds of filial piety and tradition, but also on the grounds of reciprocity to this particular generation of elderly revolutionaries. However, reference is still made to the fact that childless people and those whose children live away from them will be guaranteed money 'from the collective' plus food and other necessities. The neglect of elderly parents stemming from certain bad examples of 'cultural revolution' images has earlier been condemned (Zeng, 1983). Whilst some communes established retirement homes, the family's caring role is thus still stressed. A recent study in Canton, Guangdong Province, showed that over 50 per cent of current elderly people had three or more children, and only 8 per cent had no children (Ikels, 1991). However, in the future, of course, there will be fewer children and more elderly people with no available child to provide such care. This will inevitably compromise the ability of the immediate family to fulfil its perceived role. Ikels suggests that China is some 10 years behind Hong Kong where private homes for elderly people have been emerging (Chapter 4), and this option may well have to develop in China in the absence of significant state provision.

What the above remarks about living arrangements and attitudes suggest for social care and for official policy is that much more needs to be known about the implications of such changes. Just because family members do not live together, it need not be assumed that practical and emotional support are no longer exchanged. However, it may mean that more formal sources of care or community resources other than the immediate family may eventually be called on. This may impinge particularly on frail elderly people, who have been shown by many studies to have a continuing low status and are sometimes viewed, in overlapping perspectives, as a resource, an impediment, a low priority or a victim (Treas and Logue, 1986; Logue 1990). Processes associated with modernization have exacerbated their plight as potential victims by increasing their numbers and the duration of dependence, and by making solutions more problematic and almost certainly more expensive. Though sometimes tolerated, rarely have frail elderly persons been valued. This has important implications for their future in societies where family care has been, and is, regarded as the norm. In addition, will younger family members be increasingly unhappy or guilty about inability to support frail older relatives in the absence of much official help?

It appears that many elderly people in countries in the region are trying to prepare for their old age by saving and accumulating during their working lives. It seems this is particularly the case for those currently in middle age. However, many people entering or in old age do not have the personal resources to enable their independent retirement, but today family assistance and care may be less readily available than previously. In such instances, state provision is rarely fully formed and is usually only of minimal support. As noted by Graeme Hugo with respect to ageing in Indonesians (Chapter 12), the current elderly groups may be something of a 'transitional generation' who have suffered a decline in family support without yet having benefited from social and economic changes in their working lives. Neither can they expect yet to benefit from emergent state support. In the poorest countries of this region in particular, but also in others, the numbers of elderly people who will be able either to support themselves fully or to receive adequate public support will remain limited for many years to come.

It seems that the above trends will generally increase the role of governments in providing more than a safety net and providing many basic services for elderly people who cannot care for themselves and who do not (or will not) have family support for whatever reason. Much more information is needed to inform policy or persuade policy makers in this area. In particular, housing, pensions, health care, day care and institutional requirements will require approaches probably considerably different to the *laissez-faire*, minimal or residual policies currently being applied in most of the countries covered in this book. In addition, considerable boosts to the family care tradition will need to come from coherent public support of a practical nature if families are to be able to continue their expected roles far into the future.

REFERENCES

Andrews, G.R., Esterman, A.J., Braunack-Mayer, A.J. and Rungie, C.M. (1986). *Aging in the Western Pacific: A Four-Country Study.* WHO Western Pacific Region, Research Report No. 1, WHO, Manila.

Bould, S., Sanborn, B. and Reif, L. (1989). *Eighty-five Plus: The Oldest Old.* Wadsworth, Belmont, CA.

Chan, C. (1991). *The Community-based Urban Welfare Delivery System of the Peoples' Republic of China in the Midst of Economic Reforms: the Guangzhou Experience.* Unpubl. PhD Thesis, Dept. of Social Work and Social Administration, University of Hong Kong.

Chen, A.J. and Jones, G. (1989). *Ageing in ASEAN: Its Socio-Economic Consequences.* Institute of Southeast Asian Studies, Singapore.

Chow, N.W.S. (1983). The Chinese family and support of the elderly in Hong Kong. *The Gerontologist*, **23**, 6, 584–8.

Chow, N.W.S. (1987). Western and Chinese ideas of social welfare. *International Social Work*, **30**, 31–40.

Conyers, D. (1982). *An Introduction to Social Planning in the Third World.* John Wiley, Chichester.

Cowgill, D.O. (1986). *Aging Around the World.* Wadsworth, Belmont, CA.

Cowgill, D.O. and Holmes, L.D. (1972). *Aging and Modernization.* Appleton-Century-Crofts, New York.

Davies, A.M. (1989). Older populations, aging individuals and health for all. *World Health Forum*, **10**, 299–321.

Deacon, R. (1983). *Social Policy and Socialism: The Struggle for Socialist Relations of Welfare.* Pluto Press, London.

Dwyer, D.J. (Ed.) (1990). *South East Asian Development.* Longman, London.

Economic and Social Commission for Asia and the Pacific (ESCAP) (1987). *Population Aging: Review of Emerging Issues.* Asian Population Studies Series No. 80, ESCAP, Bangkok.

ESCAP (1989). *Population Aging in the Context of Urbanization and Industrialization.* Population Research Leads No. 33, ESCAP, Bangkok.

ESCAP (1990). *The Role of Population Information in Response to Changing Population Policies and Programmes for the 1990s.* Population Research Leads No. 34, ESCAP, Bangkok.

Far Eastern Economic Review (1991). *Asia 1991 Yearbook.* FEER, Hong Kong.

Frenk, J., Bobadilla, J.L., Sepulveda, J. and Cervantes, M.L. (1989). Health transition in middle-income countries: New challenges for health care. *Health Policy and Planning*, **4**, 1, 29–39.

Hermalin, A.I. and Christenson, B.A. (1990). *Some Census-based Approaches to Studying Changes in the Status of the Elderly.* Population Studies Center, University of Michigan, Research Report Special Series 90–5.

Hong Kong Government (1991) *Hong Kong 1991.* Government Printer, Hong Kong.

Ikels, C. (1990). Family caregivers and the elderly in China. In *Aging and Caregiving: Theory, Research and Practice*, D. Biegel and A. Blum (Eds), pp. 270–84. Sage, Newbury Park, CA.

Ikels, C. (1991). Aging and disability in China: cultural issues in measurement and interpretation. *Social Science and Medicine*, **32**, 6, 649–65.

Kalache, A. (1991). How old is old in a developing country? *AgeAction*, **3**, 4–5.

Kinsella, K. (1988). *Aging in the Third World.* International Population Report Series P-95, No. 79, Center for International Research, Bureau of the Census, Washington DC.

Koo, J. and Cowgill, D.O. (1986). Health care of the aged in Korea. *Social Science and Medicine*, **23**, 12, 1347–52.

Kuroda, T. (1987). Population aging in Japan, with reference to China. *Asia-Pacific Population Journal*, **2**, 3, 3–22.

Lawrence, T.L. (1985). Health care facilities for the elderly in Japan. *International Journal of Health Services*, **15**, 4, 677–97.

Leete, R. (1987). The post-demographic transition in East and South East Asia: similarities and contrasts with Europe. *Population Studies*, **41**, 2, 187–206.

Logue, B. (1990). Modernization and the status of the frail elderly: perspectives on continuity and change. *Journal of Cross-Cultural Gerontology*, **5**, 4, 345–74.

Maclean, U. (1989). *Dependent Territories: The Frail Elderly and Community Care.* Nuffield Provincial Hospitals Trust, London.

MacPherson, S. (1982). *Social Policy in the Third World.* Wheatsheaf, Brighton, Sussex.

MacPherson, S. (1987). Social security in developing countries. *Social Policy and Administration*, **21**, 1, 3–14.

Martin, L.G. (1988). The aging of Asia. *Journal of Gerontology*, **43**, 4, S99–S113.

Martin, L.G. (1989a). The Graying of Japan. *Population Bulletin*, **44**, 2, 1–42.

Martin, L.G. (1989b). Living arrangements of the elderly in Fiji, Korea, Malaysia and the Philippines. *Demography*, **26**, 4, 627–43.

Mishra, R. (1977). *Society and Social Policy: Theories and Practice of Welfare.* Macmillan, London. Second edn. 1981.

Olshansky, S.J. and Ault, A.B. (1986). The fourth stage of the epidemiologic transition: the age of delayed degenerative diseases. *Milbank Memorial Fund Quarterly*, **64**, 3, 355–91.

Omran, A.R. (1971). The epidemiologic transition: a theory of the epidemiology of population change. *Milbank Memorial Fund Quarterly*, **49**, 4, Pt. 1, 509–38.

Palmore, E.B. (1975). *The Honorable Elders.* Duke University Press, Durham, NC.

Palmore, E.B. and Maeda, D. (1985). *The Honorable Elders Revisited.* Duke University Press, Durham, NC.

Phillips, D.R. (1986). Primary health care in the Philippines: banking on the barangays? *Social Science and Medicine*, **23**, 10, 1105–17.

Phillips, D.R. (1988a). *The Epidemiological Transition in Hong Kong: Changes in Health and Disease since the Nineteenth Century.* Occasional Papers and Monographs Series No. 75, Centre of Asian Studies, University of Hong Kong.

Phillips, D.R. (1988b). Accommodation for elderly people in the newly industrializing countries: the Hong Kong experience. *International Journal of Health Services*, **18**, 2, 255–79.

Phillips, D.R. (1990). *Health and Health Care in the Third World.* Longman, London.

Phillips, D.R. (1991). Problems and potential of researching epidemiological transition: examples from Southeast Asia. *Social Science and Medicine*, **33**, 4, 395–404.

Population Reference Bureau (1991). *World Population Data Sheet.* Population

Reference Bureau, Washington, DC, and Population Concern, London.

Powell, M. and Anesaki, M. (1990). *Health Care in Japan.* Routledge, London and New York.

Rigg, J. (1991). *Southeast Asia: a Region in Transition.* Unwin Hyman, London.

Titmuss, R. (1963). *Essays on the Welfare State.* Allen and Unwin, London.

Tout, K. (1989). *Ageing in Developing Countries.* Oxford University Press, Oxford.

Treas, J. and Logue, B. (1986). Economic development and older population. *Population and Development Review*, **12**, 645–73.

United Nations (UN) (1985). *The World Aging Situation: Strategies and Policies.* United Nations, New York.

UN (1989). *World Population at the Turn of the Century.* Population Studies No. 111, United Nations, New York.

Verbrugge, L.M. (1984). Longer life but worsening health? Trends in health and mortality of middle-aged and older persons. *Milbank Memorial Fund Quarterly*, **62**, 3, 475–519.

Warnes, A.M. (1986). The elderly in less-developed world regions. *Ageing and Society*, **6**, 373–80.

Warnes, A.M. (1989). Responding to the challenge of ageing. In *Human Ageing and Later Life*, A. Warnes (Ed.), pp. 192–208. Edward Arnold, London.

Williams, F. (1989). *Social Policy: A Critical Introduction.* Polity Press, Cambridge.

World Health Organization (WHO) (1984). *The Uses of Epidemiology in the Study of the Elderly.* Technical Report Series No. 706, WHO, Geneva.

WHO (1989). *Health of the Elderly.* Technical Report Series No. 779, WHO, Geneva.

Yeung, Y.M. (1990). *Changing Cities of Pacific Asia.* Chinese University Press, Hong Kong.

Yuan, F. (1990). 'Support for the elderly: the Chinese way'. In *Changing Family Structure and Population Aging in China*, Y. Zeng et al. (Eds), pp. 341–58. Peking University Press, Beijing.

Zeng, S. (1983). China's senior citizens, In 'The elderly in China,' *China Reconstructs, What's New in China*, **4**, 2–12.

Zeng, Y., Zhang, C. and Peng, S. (1990). *Changing Family Structure and Population Aging in China.* Peking University Press, Beijing.

Gary Andrews
Centre for Ageing Studies
Flinders University of South Australia

2 RESEARCH DIRECTIONS IN THE REGION: PAST, PRESENT AND FUTURE

INTRODUCTION

Research on population ageing, of any significant scale, has been undertaken only lately in East and South-east Asia. The present increased efforts are, to a considerable extent, due to the recognition of population ageing in the region. Indeed, the East and South-east Asian region has accounted for a large proportion of the increase in the world's older population in recent decades and will account for an even greater proportion in the future (Kinsella, 1988). In addition there has been evidence of a growing political awareness of the implications of population ageing for social and economic development, as well as an increased understanding of the associated impacts for individuals and communities in terms of health, well being, and lifestyle (Warnes, 1986). None the less the overall amount of research completed thus far is small relative to the region's size and the numbers of its elderly population. There has been greater impetus to undertake ageing research in the few developed or 'newly industrialized' countries of the region but even in these cases the level of activity has been less than adequate in view of the potential social and economic consequences of the phenomenon.

The great diversity of the region in terms of national population characteristics, geographic features, socio-economic development, cultural mores, political systems, languages, traditions, and social support and health systems makes it a particularly rich area for cross-national and cross-cultural research on ageing. Further, it has been widely recognized that Asia is generally undergoing rapid change. Family structure is changing and the traditional attitude of respect and veneration for elders cannot always be expected to prevail (Martin, 1988). Other economic and social changes including urbanization, migration, industrialization and increased female workforce participation are also influencing individual and community responses to ageing in societies throughout the region. The demographic transition and accompanying epidemiologic transition in the context of such changes provide a particularly fertile ground for ageing research at local and national, and regional levels.

This chapter provides a general overview of population ageing research directions in the region. Completed and current regional research projects are reviewed. Some of the limitations of currently employed research methodologies are discussed, new directions are examined, and finally a tentative research agenda is proposed for the region.

APPROACHES TO AGEING RESEARCH IN THE REGION

Taking research in this context to mean any systematic attempt to gather and analyse either primary or secondary data in order to extend our knowledge or understanding of population ageing and its consequences, a very wide range of efforts can be included. The range of research on population ageing undertaken in East and South-east Asia extends from extensive macro approaches using international and national archived data sets to micro studies using in-depth anthropological methods. Studies have been conducted in the region at cross-national, national and local levels. The orientation of these various research efforts has been socio-cultural, demographic, economic, health, be-havioural, ethnographic or some combination of these approaches. As other chapters in this book focus on specific country experience, this review deals principally with research that is multinational and regional in orientation.

Demographic studies
At the broadest level, general descriptive reviews have been undertaken of the demographic characteristics of countries making up the region. For instance, Linda Martin (1988) examined data on health and life expectancy, sex ratios, marital status, living arrangements, rural versus urban residence, labour force participation, retirement, and income for 14 Asian countries using United Nations' sources (UN, 1984, 1985, 1986, and 1987). Martin went on to discuss the implications of the demographic data, drawing upon some more analyticai, principally survey-based, studies. Other efforts at providing regional and country-specific macro data have been published in various forums (Kinsella, 1989; Hoover and Siegel, 1986; Hugo 1988; Myers, 1990). Source data for these types of exercises has generally been accessed from such collections as the United Nations Population Division World Population Projections, the United Nations Data Base on Disability, the World Health Organization Mortality Data and Global Health Indicators, United States Bureau of Census International Division – data on ageing (currently for 25 countries – to be expanded to include others), and other similar sources. Additionally, national census data can, within the limitations of its reliability, be a rich and more direct source for further analysis and interpretation (Martin, 1987).

These macro demographic studies and reports are quite useful in describing population-ageing trends and broad consequences. They also can be particu-larly valuable as a basis for projecting the future size and characteristics of the elderly population, based on alternative assumptions of mortality and fertility and a variety of possible social and economic scenarios. Further, the dis-aggregation and closer analysis of available data can provide more detailed information regarding the increasing heterogeneity of the elderly populations. The extension of demographic studies to include a longitudinal perspective will facilitate improved and more detailed forecasting. However, there are significant limitations to this type of analysis. Ageing is a complex process with substantial interaction among the demographic, socio-cultural, economic, biomedical, environmental and behavioural variables. Thus, more detailed data and qualitative information is necessary in the attempt to avoid the misinterpretation of findings through the application of overly simplistic theoretical models. Trends apparent at the macro level may not reflect the true situation for any particular population group. Ideally the broader data sources should be complemented by information provided by more in-depth research. For the more developed countries of the region, especially Japan, as well as the newly industrialized countries such as Singapore and Hong Kong, this compre-hensive approach is more easily achievable as census-based information is increasingly supported by good quality multidimensional and representative survey research on ageing. Other countries of the region are also making steady progress in this regard including Indonesia, Thailand and China.

Cross-national survey research
In the past decade several multidimensional surveys have been sponsored in the region on a cross-national basis. These studies have been important in providing basic descriptive information on the region's older population from several viewpoints. Generally such multicountry projects have been initiated and supported by international agencies. The principal aims of these studies are to:

- raise the general awareness of policy makers, planners, practitioners and researchers of the emergent issues associated with population ageing in the region;
- provide training opportunities for national researchers in the region and contribute to the development of standardized survey instruments for use in other situations and countries;
- provide relevant quantitative information on demographic, epidemiological, social and economic conditions which affect the health status of the elderly population and which give rise to social and health care needs which may or may not be currently met;
- provide a baseline for simple demographic projections of social, health and economic needs;
- provide baseline surveys for more extensive cross-national and longitudinal studies on ageing;
- identify areas where more in-depth studies may be called for;
- contribute to national, regional, and global data bases on health profiles of elderly populations.

The information generated by recently undertaken population survey research on ageing in the region has usually included some or all of the following elements:

- basic demographic indicators of the population studied, including projections to future decades;
- family structure and living arrangements including family size and patterns of intergenerational support;
- social activities and relationships in the community and the family;
- formal and informal support patterns;
- physical and mental health status including history of chronic illness, impairments, disabilities and handicaps, and self-perceived health status;
- utilization of health and other social facilities in the community, including alternative, traditional health services;
- behavioural habits such as smoking, alcohol consumption and exercise;
- nutrition and eating habits;
- accommodation, housing, and environmental conditions;
- life satisfaction, significant life events, and level of morale;
- beliefs, attitudes and aspirations.

The conduct of internationally sponsored multidimensional and multinational survey research on ageing in countries of the region has significance for the institutional strengthening and training of national personnel in population ageing research methodology. In addition, it contributes to the reinforcement of national capabilities for projecting the developmental impact of ageing population structures and provides data relevant to policy development, planning and programme implementation.

COMPLETED MULTICOUNTRY PROJECTS

Western Pacific four-country study
One of the first of the multidimensional cross-national studies of ageing in the region to be published was the World Health Organization Regional Office for the Western Pacific (WHO/WPRO) four-country study carried out in Fiji, the Republic of Korea, Malaysia and the Philippines (Andrews et al., 1986). This project was carefully designed to provide cross-national comparative data. Reviews of existing country data were undertaken and a household survey of randomly selected samples of the population aged 60 years and over was conducted using standardized survey instruments. The survey data were supplemented by the conduct of a series of case reports on selected respondents. The findings were compared with the selected results from developed countries that had participated in an earlier WHO sponsored 11-country European study. There were notable differences in the findings of the Western Pacific and European studies and also many similarities. In particular, subjects in all four of the Western Pacific countries were much more likely to be living in extended family situations, many with children, than was the case in the European countries. On the other hand many of the classic age-related phenomena of widowhood, declining social participation, loneliness, decline at advanced ages in health and function were similar. These data are now archived and a number of independent analyses have examined such things as patterns of morbidity and function (Manton et al., 1987), living arrangements (Martin, 1989), economics (Agree and Clark, 1991) and family support (Esterman and Andrews, 1991). Based on this experience the author has been responsible for the initiation and coordination of a further set of studies in five countries of the South-east Asian region of WHO (Indonesia, Democratic People's Republic of Korea (DPR Korea), Myanmar, Sri Lanka and Thailand), using methodology similar to that employed in the Western Pacific project.

Association of South East Asian Nations (ASEAN) studies
In 1984 a series of studies funded by the Australian government under the general title 'Socio-economic consequences of the ageing of the population' was initiated as a component project of phase III of the ASEAN Population Programme in five ASEAN countries (Indonesia, Malaysia, the Philippines, Singapore and Thailand). In these studies a core questionnaire was developed to gather information on household structure, housing, economic resources, living support, health and social activities. Some secondary data analysis was undertaken and existing policies and programmes on ageing in the countries were examined and evaluated. The project, which was coordinated from Singapore, gave its main objective as the raising of awareness of policy-makers and planners to the issues of ageing throughout ASEAN. A key finding of this study noted in its cross-national report was the potential stress which could be placed on family members by continued reliance on family support by the elderly population (Chen and Jones, 1989). The authors argued that increased urbanization and social mobility, smaller families, and the tendency for married women to enter the paid workforce all suggest the possibility that parents will not be able to assume that their children will care for them in their old age.

Economic and Social Commission for Asia and the Pacific (ESCAP) studies
The ESCAP secretariat, with financial support from the United Nations Population Fund (UNFPA), initiated a cross-national study in 1986 to examine the impact of population ageing in selected countries (ESCAP, 1989). Countries participating in this series of studies included the People's Republic of China, the Republic of Korea, Malaysia and Sri Lanka. The plan was to collect information in several stages. Data available from censuses and other sources were analysed first. In the second part of the study a sample survey was conducted gathering information from older people and resident care providers. Finally, a review of existing policies and programmes concerning the elderly was undertaken and evaluated. The principal objective was to provide a set of policy and programme recommendations to address the issues of an ageing population as well as the individual needs of elderly people and their carers. Several final country reports have recently been published (ESCAP, 1990a, b and c). The report of a cross-national seminar to review the results notes that most of the problems of the aged identified in the study are related to poverty and decreasing availability of care for the aged (ESCAP, 1989).

UN University study
The United Nations University, based in Tokyo, has been responsible for the planning and initiation of a series of studies on social support systems for the elderly in seven developing nations including the Asian countries of India, the Republic of Korea, Singapore and Thailand. These studies were designed to collect data in several different ways. An historical survey of formal and informal support systems was undertaken; an ethnographic study of communities using participant observation techniques was also included; household surveys covering demographic information, family relationships, current and potential future needs and sources of social support, as well as several other domains, were conducted; and finally, more detailed case study material was also obtained from selected respondents. The overall objective of the project is to delineate the balance of formal, informal and personal resources that may best promote social welfare in countries undergoing rapid social and demographic change. This is to be done at 'an appropriate cost' and taking into account differing socio-cultural settings. In the first cross-national report on findings, Akiko Hashimoto (1991) demonstrates that elderly people appear to maintain co-residence with children despite changing socio-economic and demographic conditions. Variation between different countries was noted in the chosen living arrangements and the extent to which these appeared to be influenced by socio-economic and individual characteristics.

More recent studies
There are a number of more recently initiated projects that are now underway and will provide valuable data in the near future. These efforts are notable for having drawn on the experience of previous studies in the region, generally showing more attention to the cultural aspects of study design, and for the application of newer and potentially useful methods of investigation.

WHO South-east Asian studies
The WHO sponsored four-country study in the Western Pacific has now been extended to the South-east Asian region of WHO where a similar set of surveys have been undertaken during 1990 in Indonesia, the DPR Korea, Myanmar, Sri Lanka and Thailand. Based on earlier experience, the South-east Asian studies have used larger (1200), more nationally representative samples of persons

aged 60 years and over, an extended and improved survey instrument and, in three of the countries (Sri Lanka, Myanmar and Thailand), performance-based measures of physical function have been employed. Greater attention has been given in these later surveys to such questions as the well-being of older persons, intergenerational exchange, contributions of the elderly particularly to family and the community, and the issue of care-giving burden. The first published reports from the findings of these studies are expected in early 1992.

University of Michigan Asian studies
A United States National Institute of Aging (NIA) funded study was commenced in 1989 titled 'Comparative study of the elderly in four Asian countries'. It is co-ordinated by the Population Studies Center of the University of Michigan. The stated goal of this research is to provide a comprehensive, comparative study of the elderly population (defined as persons aged 60 and above) in the Philippines, Taiwan, Thailand and Singapore. More recently the Republic of Korea has been added to the group of countries to be studied. The project will build upon the ASEAN project described above and thus further analysis will be undertaken of the data collected in three ASEAN surveys conducted in 1984–86 (Singapore, Thailand and the Philippines). Other data being analysed include censuses and other official statistics, ethnographic material, a 1989 survey of health and living status of the elderly in Taiwan, and qualitative information from focus group sessions conducted in the participating countries. Now in its second year, the project has published a series of reports including a description of the Taiwan survey (Hermalin *et al.*, 1989), a guide to focus group methodology (Knodel, Sittitrai and Brown, 1990) and a discussion of the use of census-based methods of studying change in the status of elderly people (Hermalin and Christenson, 1990). A series of country-specific and comparative reports is expected to be published over the next few years.

UN studies of developmental implications of population ageing
In 1990 the United Nations Center for Social Development and Humanitarian Affairs, Social Development Division (UNOV/CSDHA) with funding support from the UNFPA embarked upon a 2-year project titled 'Developmental implications of demographic change: global population ageing'. This project aims to identify the specific developmental implications of population ageing, assess the contribution of the elderly to development, and suggest policy options to enhance these contributions. The project plans to accomplish this through 'a research process which synthesizes disparate secondary data and collects primary data in eight developing countries over two years' (UNOV, 1990). The Asian region is represented through the inclusion of Thailand and Sri Lanka. In each country a sample survey of older persons (60 years and over) will be undertaken to determine the economic, social and cultural contributions of the aged at individual, family and community levels. A sample survey will also be conducted of non-aged household members to determine their perspectives regarding the role and contributions of older persons within the family and the community. Semi-structured interviews will be undertaken with key informants, including appropriate ministries, heads of technical departments, non-governmental organizations, professional bodies, older persons' associations and educational institutions, to determine national infrastructure related to the contribution of the aged to development. Finally, a country-level profile of the elderly with respect to their social, economic and demographic characteristics will be developed from secondary data. The

studies in Thailand and Sri Lanka will use the same population samples and will build upon the previous efforts of the WHO-sponsored studies in those two countries outlined above. Fieldwork will commence during 1991 and the project will be completed by the end of 1992.

Beijing longitudinal study of ageing
A study currently being planned for commencement in 1991 in Beijing, China, funded by UNFPA and executed by the Centre for Ageing Studies, Adelaide, will implement one of the first major multidimensional longitudinal studies of population ageing in China. The principal initial focus of this project will be the demographic, socio-cultural, economic, functional and environmental issues associated with population ageing. Through co-operation with the World Health Organization it is planned that a health component will be included in the study design. The project will be undertaken in collaboration with the World Health Organisation Programme for Research on Ageing – Determinants of Healthy Ageing Project which plans to sponsor a series of longitudinal population-based studies around the globe.

METHODOLOGICAL ISSUES
The multinational studies share a number of common characteristics. The stated objectives for each of the studies generally focus on the provision of useful information for policy and planning purposes. At the same time, although the degree of standardization of methods varies, some attempt is made to undertake comparative analysis so that a distinction can be drawn between those universal processes of ageing which seem to be common to people everywhere and those aspects of ageing which are affected by socio-economic circumstances, culture, traditions, beliefs and local practices. To achieve these varied objectives, the studies have generally used a multidimensional approach to obtaining data.

Most studies begin with a review and analysis of existing data. Apart from collection of data using standardized questionnaires, several of the projects have provided supplementary qualitative information usually obtained by selected personal history or case report methods.

A seemingly simple plan to gather descriptive information on ageing populations may involve quite complex issues of conceptualization, definition, measurement and analysis. These problems are compounded many times over when the research is conducted across several languages, cultures and nationalities. The methods used have generally been adopted from Western studies using standardized instruments which have been validated in European and North American research. This approach makes comparison between more developed and less developed countries easier but creates a whole range of other problems. Indeed, even the definition of 'old age' itself cannot be assumed to be uniformly applicable in such diverse settings (Cattel, 1989). Many of the questionnaire items which have been developed, particularly in social and behavioural measurement, are culturally specific. Thus more work is needed in the construction of culturally 'transportable' items.

Many other issues arise, especially in trying to draw policy and programme implications for less developed nations (LDNs) from the comparative findings and experience of the more developed nations (MDNs). Valuable insights can be gained if a 'keen awareness' of cultural factors and especially of one's own culture is maintained as observations are made of others (Binstock, 1986). A related issue is the translation of questionnaires. Serious problems can result from faulty translation or the use of language forms which are inappropriate to the concept behind a particular questionnaire item. Independent back translation is useful and should be done routinely. It is important to remember that survey items which have been widely used and standardized elsewhere may not remain valid in very different socio-economic and cultural settings. Validation of any proposed survey instrument should be undertaken in any new situation in which it will be applied. Test/retest surveys and other methods of reviewing intra- and inter-observer variation should also be routinely employed. The experience of the WHO four-country study revealed quite high indices of reliability for many of the standard questionnaire items in general although some problems were identified with specific items (Andrews et al., 1986).

In recent studies conducted in developed countries, attempts have been made to achieve more objective measures by the addition of standardized biomedical measurements and simple performance-based testing of function. These measures offer the possibility of greater cross-cultural and and cross-national comparability, if they are adequately standardized and observers are appropriately trained (Guralnick et al., 1989).

Difficulty is often experienced in establishing a suitable sampling frame for the conduct of a population survey in developing country settings. Addresses, particularly in rural areas, may be difficult to define and the age given by individuals may be erroneous and difficult to verify. In addition, the categorization of urban and rural areas is increasingly difficult with rapid urbanization and development. Many previously rural areas have become semi-urbanized and do not fit clearly into either category. Thus some arbitrarily agreed definitions need to be established for each participating country at the outset.

A multisponsored seminar on research about ageing in Asia and the Pacific held in 1987 in Singapore attempted to review critically recent survey research on ageing in the region and to explore opportunities for further development of methodology and the promotion of collaborative effort (East-West Center, Honolulu 1987). This theme was further pursued globally at the 14th World Congress of Gerontology (Centre for Ageing Studies, Adelaide 1990). It is apparent from the common objectives, timing, geographic coverage and methods employed in the undertaking of the projects described earlier, that there is substantial scope for a more broadly collaborative effort. Studies on population ageing in the region have been generally conducted under a number of disparate auspices, employed different consultants and different country investigators. There remains substantial scope for a more co-ordinated, incremental and developmental approach to multicountry research sponsored by international agencies and other donor organizations in the region so that the limited resources devoted to these activities can be more effectively applied in the future.

FUTURE DIRECTIONS

The need to identify key areas for future research in health and ageing was highlighted in the Vienna International Plan of Action which arose out of the 1982 UN World Assembly on Ageing (UN, 1982). The recommendations of the Assembly on research remain most applicable to East and South-east Asia. The key sections of the plan of action in this respect are as follows:

Para. 84.   The Plan of Action gives high priority to research related to developmental and humanitarian aspects of ageing. Research activities are instrumental in formulating, evaluating and implementing policies and programmes: (a) as to the implications of the ageing of the population for development and (b) as to the needs of the ageing. Research into the social, economic and health aspects of ageing should be encouraged to achieve efficient uses of resources, improvement in social and health measures, including the prevention of functional decline, age-related disabilities, illness and poverty, and co-ordination of the services involved in the care of the ageing.

Para. 85.   The knowledge obtained by research provides scientific backing for a sounder basis for effective societal planning as well as for improving the well-being of the elderly. Further research is required, for example (a) to narrow the wide gaps in knowledge about ageing and about the particular needs of the ageing and (b) to enable resources provided for the ageing to be used more effectively. There should be emphasis on the continuum of research from the discovery of new knowledge to its vigorous and more rapid application and transfer of technological knowledge with due consideration of cultural and social diversity.

Recommendation 60
Research should be conducted in the developmental and humanitarian aspects of ageing at local, national, regional and global levels. Research should be encouraged particularly in the biological, mental and social fields. Issues of basic and applied research of universal interest to all societies include:

- the role of genetic and environmental factors;
- the impact of biological, medical, cultural, societal and behavioural factors on ageing;
- the influence of economic and demographic factors (including migration) on societal planning;
- the use of skills, expertise, knowledge and cultural potential of the ageing;
- the postponement of negative functional consequences of ageing;
- health and social services for the ageing as well as studies of the co-ordinated programmes and;
- training and education.

Such research should be generally planned and carried out by researchers closely acquainted with national and regional conditions, being granted the independence necessary for innovation and diffusion. States, intergovernmental organizations and non-governmental organizations should carry out more research and studies on the developmental and humanitarian aspects of ageing, co-operate in this field and exchange their findings in order to provide a logical basis for policies related to ageing in general.

Recommendation 61
States, intergovernmental organizations and non-governmental organizations should encourage the establishment of institutions specializing in the teaching of gerontology, geriatrics and geriatric psychology in countries where such institutions do not exist.

Recommendation 62
International exchange and research co-operation as well as data collec-

tion should be promoted in all fields having a bearing on ageing, in order to provide a rational basis for future social policies and action. Special emphasis should be placed on comparative and cross-cultural studies on ageing. Interdisciplinary approaches should be stressed.

Any proposal for a broad agenda for research on ageing in East and South-east Asia, along the lines envisioned in the Plan of Action, must of necessity be tentative. It is important to establish an environment in which research endeavours in the field of ageing will be facilitated. The recent substantial efforts in the region, and elsewhere in the world, in ageing research should be drawn upon so that unnecessary 'reinvention of the wheel' and duplication is avoided. Existing resources and experience, especially that available in the more developed countries of the region, should be fully utilized. Some effective means of monitoring relevant activities and assessing programmes should be established on a regionwide basis but in such a way that scope for innovation and creativity is maintained. Finally, it will be essential for the success of the efforts that research is shown to be relevant to the decision makers at the national level, and that policy formulation, programme development and review considerations benefit from information gained through research efforts. To implement these objectives there is a need to develop more effective mechanisms of regional co-ordination and co-operative effort between the various international agencies involved in ageing research within the region. One way to achieve this would be through a 'consortium' approach to funding of major regional projects.

The nature of the region and the challenges confronting it at present indicate to some extent the research priorities. Any agenda should take cognizance of the special characteristics of the region and the identifiable needs of the elderly within its various populations. Increasing pressures are being experienced in countries of the region as a result of modernization, urbanization, changes in family structure, erosion of traditional cultural values, and housing problems, particularly in urban areas. The continuing importance of the family as a source of support and care for older people is widely recognized none the less, and much of the research which might be carried out on ageing and health in this setting should be interpreted in the context of the traditional role of the family and should include the gathering of data relevant to this aspect of ageing. The agenda proposed here is, therefore, not intended to be exhaustive – it is a starting point, not a conclusion. Nor are the categories of research indicated mutually exclusive. Indeed a multidisciplinary and multifaceted approach, as indicated, yields the greatest potential for fruitful research endeavours.

Some of the relevant areas for future research are outlined below.

Demographic and statistical studies
Analysis of existing data sources should be increasingly pursued, including national censuses, death and morbidity registers, health services utilization records, national surveys, consumer research, and various projections and estimates based on available published reports. This approach requires re-sources to be devoted to secondary analysis of existing data and also for efforts to be made in improving the quality of and access to the primary data available. Mortality and morbidity patterns associated with age can be reviewed and compared cross-nationally. Some economic and social analysis is possible including studies of household composition, urban/rural migration, workforce participation, pension coverage and dependency patterns.

The current (1990) round of censuses in the region will provide a very useful bank of primary data. Effort should be exerted to ensure early and wide access to national census data bases as they become available.

Anthropological studies
Andrea Sankar (1989), in relation specifically to China, has pointed out that ethnography has an important contribution to make in supplementing the large scale surveys commonly being undertaken in many countries. Ethnographic input is important in ensuring that interview questions are culturally meaningful; and to identify the specific cultural and social context of respondents so that their relevance to the wider population can be assessed. Sankar convincingly argues that ethnographic studies are important in their own right. Documentation of the impact of social and economic change can best be achieved by extended participant-observation studies. In this respect repeated longitudinal studies in the same local areas would be particularly useful. The study of cultural practices, meanings and beliefs need further ethnographic investigation if better understanding of ageing and its consequences is to be achieved in Asia.

National and cross-national surveys of health and social aspects of ageing
Much of the multinational effort has been in this category but a great deal remains to be done. Many countries in the region still have only rudimentary information on their ageing populations. A co-ordinated approach using standardized, valid and reliable survey instruments and central analysis of data will be essential if an effective regional data base is to be achieved. The development of research instruments which are culturally appropriate and standardized for use in cross-national investigation is greatly needed. Where feasible, studies should include objective measures and performance-based tests of function as an adjunct to self-reported survey items. At the outset provision should be made for possible follow-up studies to review major outcomes such as hospitalization, morbid events or death.

Longitudinal studies
Longitudinal studies are complex, difficult to implement and costly. None the less a case can be made for conducting such studies where resources and skills are available. Thus far such reported longitudinal ageing research in the region has been largely confined to Japan (Hatano *et al.*, 1988).

Population-based longitudinal studies of ageing which focus upon the determinants of healthy ageing/disability in a representative population should be sponsored within the region. It is possible this could be undertaken in conjunction with the global research programme proposed by WHO/PRA (WHO, 1987). It is only through the collection of longitudinal cohort data that trends over time can be effectively measured. Also, longitudinal studies offer the prospect of better understanding of the impact of structural changes upon the family, and the interaction between social support and subsequent health and welfare needs can be clearly defined.

A case can also be made for mounting, initially on a pilot or demonstration basis, studies which focus specifically on causal factors, efficacy of selected interventions, and the evaluation of services.

In operational terms, specific research areas which could be fruitfully explored include family relationships and support, especially intergenerational support and its impact on health status, stress and coping in different cultural settings, dementia, productivity, work and retirement as related to health and functioning, health behaviours and attitudes. Attitudes to and need (actual and potential) for institutional care form another research area.

CONCLUSION

No brief review can deal comprehensively with all of the issues or activities concerning ageing research throughout East and South-east Asia. Much of the research effort within the region is locally or nationally based and no attempt has been made in this paper to deal with the increasing number of endeavours at these levels, many of which are referred to in the country-specific chapters in this collection. Also, some of the centres in East and South-east Asia, especially in the more developed countries, have undertaken basic biological, behavioural and clinical ageing research as evidenced in proceedings of the regional International Association of Gerontology Congresses in recent years (International Association of Gerontology Asia/Oceania Region, 1980, 1983 and 1987). The extent of this work in the region is generally quite limited and there are few major institutions where such research is the principal activity. When appropriate such endeavours should be encouraged through training fellowships and institutional support. This review, however, has been concerned primarily with research which has regional implications, or which has been conducted cross-nationally within the region. Significant progress has been made recently in these respects and great scope exists for further worthwhile effort. There exists great potential for a range of useful yet varied research on ageing in the region.

Several critical issues relating to population ageing research in the region have emerged in this review. Research which will inform policy and planning for an ageing population is a priority area, especially in developing countries of the region. Greater use could be made of existing data through more extensive secondary analysis and there is a need to present results in a more relevant and convincing manner. Training of researchers in developing countries of the region will be important in terms of strengthening the region's capacity to monitor trends and to explore new directions in population ageing research. Regional networks that could facilitate exchange of information, resource sharing, training opportunities and the more effective dissemination of results will be increasingly necessary. Such networks should be developed by the appropriate international agencies in association with persons at the national level to ensure optimal co-operation and success of research efforts.

One of the most basic challenges facing researchers working in East and South-east Asia is how research effort can inform policy formulation. This is especially important because in the future the region will account for a large proportion of the world's elderly population. Rapid social and structural changes associated with development and modernization have strong implications for the well-being of aged populations in terms of social support, housing, health care and other needs. Countries in East and South-east Asia still have time to assess future needs and demographic projections in order to formulate appropriate programmes and policies. There is, however, a clear need to go beyond past efforts aimed at collecting purely descriptive data and to explore ways of building a developmental dimension into research on population ageing. Such an approach is needed to underpin the development of economically feasible models of support for elderly people as alternatives to Western welfare-state-based arrangements which are unlikely to be sustainable in most countries of the region. Thus research efforts in the region are timely for the development of projections and assessments, and to inform policy and decision makers.

REFERENCES

Agree, E.M. and Clark, R.L. (1991). Labour force participation at older ages in the Western Pacific: a microeconomic analysis. *Journal of Cross-Cultural Gerontology*, **6**, 4, 413–29.

Andrews, G.R., Esterman, A.J., Braunack-Mayer, A.J. and Rungie, C.M. (1986). *Aging in the Western Pacific: A Four Country Study*. World Health Organization, Western Pacific Region, Research Report No. 1, WHO, Manila.

Andrews, G.R. (1988). Health and Ageing in the Developing World. In *Research and the Ageing Population*, D. Everad and S. Whelen (Eds), pp. 17–37. Ciba Foundation Symposium, J. Wiley, London.

Binstock, R.H. (1986). Drawing cross-cultural 'implications for policy': Some caveats. *Journal of Cross-Cultural Gerontology*, **1**, 339–62.

Catell, M.G. (1989). Being comparative: Methodological issues in cross-cultural gerontology. *Journal of Cross-Cultural Gerontology*, **4**, 75–81.

Centre for Ageing Studies (1989). *Report of Post Congress Workshop on Aging Research and Policy, Acapulco Meeting*. National Institute on Aging, Washington.

Chen, A.J. and Jones, G. (1989). *Ageing in ASEAN: Its Socio-Economic Consequences*. Final Inter-Country Report of the ASEAN Ageing Project, Phase III ASEAN Population Programme. Institute of Southeast Asian Studies, Singapore.

East-West Center (1987). *Seminar on Research on Aging in Asia and the Pacific Summary Report*. East-West Center, Honolulu.

Economic and Social Commission for Asia and the Pacific (ESCAP) (1987). *Population Aging: Review of Emerging Issues – report, proposed study design and selected background papers from the Meeting on Emerging Issues of the Aging of Population*. Asian Population Studies Series No. 80, ESCAP, Bangkok.

ESCAP (1989). *Emerging Issues of Population Aging in Asia and the Pacific*. Asian Population Studies Series No. 99, ESCAP, Bangkok.

ESCAP (1990a). *Population Aging in China – Report of a study undertaken in China under the project 'Emerging issues of the aging population'*. ESCAP, Bangkok.

ESCAP (1990b). *Population Aging in Malaysia – Report of a study undertaken in Malaysia under the project 'Emerging issues of the aging population'*. ESCAP, Bangkok.

ESCAP (1990c). *Population Aging in the Republic of Korea – Report of a study undertaken in the Republic of Korea under the project 'Emerging issues of the aging population'*. ESCAP, Bangkok.

Esterman, A.J. and Andrews, G.R. (1991). Southeast Asia and the Pacific: A comparison of older people in four countries. In *Aging and the Family*. H. Kendig and L. Coppard (Eds). Oxford University Press, Oxford (in press).

Guralnick, J.M., Branch, L.G., Cummings, S.R. and Curb, J.D. (1989). Physical Performance Measures in Aging Research. *Journal of Gerontology*, **44**, 141–6.

Hashimoto, A. (1991). Living arrangements of the aged in 7 developing countries: A preliminary analysis. *Journal of Cross-Cultural Gerontology*, **6**, 4, 359–81.

Hatano, S., Matsuzaki, T., Shibita, H., Shichita, K., Haga, H., Maeda, D., Shimonka, Y. and Hayashi, T.A. (1988). A prospective study of Japanese 70 year olds: The Koganei Study. In *Epidemiology and Aging: An International Perspective*, J.A. Brody and G.L. Maddox (Eds), pp. 54–79. Springer, New York.

Hermalin, A.I. *et al.* (1989). *1989 Survey of Health and Living Status of the Elderly in Taiwan: Questionnaire and Survey Design*. Population Studies

Center, University of Michigan, Research Report Special Series 89-1.

Hermalin, A.I. and Christenson, B.A. (1990). *Some Census-Based Approaches to Studying Changes in the Status of the Elderly.* Population Studies Center, University of Michigan, Research Report Special Series 90-5.

Hoover, S.L. and Siegel, J.S. (1986). International demographic trends and perspectives on aging. *Journal of Cross-Cultural Gerontology*, **1**, 5–30.

Hugo, G.J. (1985). Population ageing: some demographic issues in developing countries. Background paper prepared for Program for Developing Country participants, XIIIth International Congress of Gerontology, July 12–17, New York.

International Association of Gerontology, Asia/Oceania Region (1980). *Proceedings of the First Regional Congress (Melbourne 1980).* International Association of Gerontology/Science Centre Foundation, Sydney.

International Association of Gerontology, Asia/Oceania Region (1983). *Proceedings of the Second Regional Congress (Singapore 1983).* International Assocation of Gerontology/Science Centre Foundation, Sydney.

International Association of Gerontology, Asia/Oceania Region (1988). *Proceedings of the Third Regional Congress (Bangkok 1987).* International Association of Gerontology/Science Centre Foundation, Sydney.

Kinsella, K. (1988). *Aging in the Third World.* International Population Report Series P-95, No. 79, Center for International Research, Bureau of the Census, Washington DC.

Knodel, J., Sittitrai, W. and Brown, T. (1990). *Focus Group Discussions for Social Science Research: A Practical Guide with an Emphasis on the Topic of Ageing.* Population Studies Center, University of Michigan, Research Report Special Series 90–3.

Manton, K., Myers, G. and Andrews, G.R. (1987). Morbidity and disability in four developing nations: Their implications for social and economic integration of the elderly. *Journal of Cross-Cultural Gerontology*, **2**, 115–29.

Martin, L.G. (1987). Census data for studying elderly populations. *Reprints of the East West Population Institute No. 214.* East West Center, Honolulu.

Martin, L.G. (1988). The aging of Asia. *Journal of Gerontology: Social Sciences*, **43**, S99–S113.

Martin, L.G. (1989). Living arrangements of the elderly in Fiji, Korea, Malaysia, and the Philippines. *Demography*, **26**, 627–43.

Myers, G. (1990). Demography of Aging. In *Handbook of Aging and the Social Sciences*, R.H. Binstock and L.K. George (Eds), pp. 19–44. Academic Press, San Diego.

Sankar, A. (1989). Gerontological research in China: The role of anthropological inquiry. *Journal of Cross-Cultural Gerontology*, **4**, 199–224.

United Nations (UN) (1983). *Vienna International Plan of Action on Aging – World Assembly on Aging.* United Nations, New York.

UN (1984). *Demographic Yearbook 1982.* United Nations, New York.

UN (1985). *World Population Prospects: Estimates and Projections as Assessed in 1982 (Population Studies No. 86).* United Nations, New York.

UN (1986). *World Population Prospects: Estimates and Projections as Assessed in 1984 (Population Studies No. 86).* United Nations, New York.

UN (1987). *Demographic Yearbook 1985.* United Nations, New York.

United Nations Organization Vienna (UNOV) (1990). *Developmental Implications of Demographic Change: Global Population Aging – Preliminary Research Protocol.* UNOV/CSDHA, Vienna.

Warnes, A.M. (1986). The elderly in less developed countries. *Ageing and Society*, **6**, 373–80.

World Health Organization (WHO) (1987). *Special Programme for Research on Aging – Description of Programme (SPRA).* WHO, Copenhagen.

Akiko Hashimoto
Department of Sociology
University of Pittsburgh

3 AGEING IN JAPAN

INTRODUCTION

Over the last three decades, the number of persons over the age of 65 in Japan has nearly trebled from 4.7 million to 13.8 million as mortality declined and life expectancy increased with unprecedented speed. The concomitant increase in the proportion of elderly persons in the population has been dramatic, rising from 5.3 per cent in 1955 to 11.2 per cent in 1988. Future projections show that population ageing in Japan will proceed further, and at a pace even faster than that of the past. By the year 2015 Japan's older population is expected to more than double, increasing to 30.6 million. As fertility of younger cohorts declines further, this figure implies that 23 per cent of the Japanese population will be aged in barely 30 years from now, in 2025 (Fig. 3.1). This proportion is higher than that currently projected for any other country in the world (Japan Ministry of Health and Welfare, 1989; Martin, 1989).

The increase in life expectancy underlying this trend has indeed been rapid, rising from 59.7 years for men and 63.0 years for women in 1950, to 75.6 years for men and 81.4 years for women in 1988. Yet this longevity has now become a cause for concern because of its consequence on the durability of the social security system, medical and social services and family support, as well as on

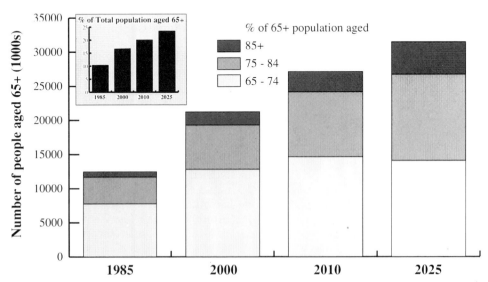

Fig. 3.1 Projections of the elderly Japanese population.

Source: based on data in Martin (1989).

the structure of the future labour market. The reality of limited resources in the face of growing demands is becoming more and more apparent against the background of rising expenditures, greater geographical and occupational mobility, and the growing trend toward smaller nuclear families. There is alarm that current forms of state, community and family support cannot endure, as the number of Japanese elderly increases by millions, and their needs become more complex in nature.

This chapter attempts to shed light on this issue by examining forces of change and continuity, particularly in family support in Japan. As evidenced by the high (but falling) proportion (64.5 per cent) of elderly people living with their children (Okuyama, 1990), the backbone of care for the aged in Japan lies in the family. An inquiry into the antecedent conditions of family care in Japan therefore contributes to the understanding of how care in old age will be affected by the new social and economic environment. Family care will be examined here in relation to structural as well as cultural conditions, with particular focus on its links to the availability of social resources and to normative prescriptions in Japan.

Formal support for the aged
Formal support, defined as institutional, public provision for elderly people, consists of social security pensions, medical care subsidy and social services. The universal pension scheme, instituted in 1961, made participation in one of the eight pension plans compulsory for all Japanese citizens. While the revised universal pension scheme instituted in April 1986 integrated the various pension plans into a consolidated system, the benefits received by the majority of current elderly people in real terms is still determined by the old scheme. Those currently over the age of 78 may receive the equivalent of US $188 per month from the Old Age Welfare Pension (Rorei Fukushi Nenkin) – not part of the eight pension plans – if their income is below a certain threshold, because they were too old to join in the pension plans in 1961. The threshold level varies by household composition. Approximately one-tenth of Japan's current elderly are recipients of this modest pension. Agricultural workers, self-employed persons or persons employed in family business contribute to the National Pension Plan (Kokumin-Nenkin) to receive a flat sum equivalent to $199 per month at the age of 65. A little under half of today's elderly population receive their pension from this scheme. Benefits from the Employee Pension Plan (Kosei Nenkin) are higher and more dependable as a primary source of income ($884 per month), but they are available only for the younger generation of aged persons who have had the employment opportunity and length of time to contribute into the Plan (Ministry of Health and Welfare, 1987; Health and Welfare Statistics Association 1988).

The Medical Subsidy Program for the Aged (Rorei Iryohi Shikyu Seido) is available for those over the age of 70 who require medical attention. This subsidy permitted care at no cost to aged people of most income levels until 1984. The government, however, has since that time attempted to curb rising expenditures by introducing a partial self-payment scheme applicable to all, as mentioned in Chapter 1.

Social service administration for the aged in Japan tends to take a targeted approach rather than a blanket approach. Vital services such as home health care, bathing services, meal services or telephone reassurance are available mostly for a target population, namely those living alone or those bedridden at home. These services often require that recipients satisfy some eligibility criteria determined by age, income, disability and household composition.

This kind of targeting is made possible by the extensive use of local municipal agents (minsei-iin) who locate and monitor the population that is deemed most 'needy'.

Family support for the aged

No assessment of the adequacy of formal provisions in Japan can be made without paying attention to the support resources that are available in the informal, non-institutional support system of the elderly. In Japan, the 'private initiative' remains the primary source of support for elderly people in financial, physical and emotional terms and, in practice, it is found almost exclusively within the family.

The premise that underlies this arrangement in Japan is that the unit of self-sufficiency and of self-help for the aged does not rest with the individual, but with the family. Targeted state interventions of the kind described earlier are designed to provide for persons whose families fail to support their aged members in one way or another. In principle the Old Age Welfare Pension and most formal social services presuppose the family as primary providers by determining the level of eligibility by household composition. This arrangement is also supported by Japanese family law which stipulates legal responsibility for a child to support an elderly parent.

Thus, the life of Japanese elderly people is intricately tied to that of their children. In Japan 64.5 per cent of the aged now live with their children, primarily in three-generation households. Smaller proportions live alone (9.9 per cent) or with spouse only (21.5 per cent) (Okuyama, 1990). The tendency to live with children, particularly the eldest son, is prevalent regardless of age, sex and marital status of the aged, and is a legacy of the primogeniture inheritance practice that operated before the Second World War. There has been a decline in the overall proportion living with children (Table 3.1) but the custom persists, and elderly parents today continue to live with their sons, daughters-in-law and grandchildren. Typically, the financial responsibility rests with the sons, and the caretaker responsibility of the frail elderly at home rests with the daughters-in-law.

Table 3.1 Japan: living arrangements of the population aged 65 and over (non-institutionalized).

	1970	1975	1980	1985
Living with children	77	73	69	65
Living with spouse only	12	16	19	22
Living alone	6	7	8	10
Living with others	6	5	4	4

Source: based on information in Martin (1989).

Consistency and variation in family support

The tendency for the Japanese to live with ageing parents is more pronounced in rural areas (54 per cent) than in metropolitan areas (24 per cent) (Management and Co-ordination Agency, 1983a). A series of five surveys of the aged and their middle-aged children conducted by the Management and Co-ordination Agency in 1974 and 1983–85 reveal no drastic change in patterns of family support over the interim decade for both urban and rural areas (although longitudinal comparison between the surveys require caution since different respondent categories and wordings were used) (Management and Co-ordination Agency, 1974a, 1974b, 1983a, 1983b, 1985). Some difference in attitudes towards support exists, but actual support rendered by the family did not seem to differ greatly between rural and urban areas.

The surveys showed that the rural aged tend to be more traditional in their expectations of support by their children. They were more likely to feel it is a child's duty to support ageing parents financially (69 per cent) than their counterparts in major cities (57 per cent) (Management and Co-ordination Agency, 1974a). The rural aged were also more persistent than the urban aged (45 per cent) in specifically expecting the eldest son and his wife to look after their physical needs when ill (70 per cent). Rural middle-aged children also tended to maintain the more traditional view that it was the natural duty of children to live with ageing parents compared to 58 per cent of their urban counterparts (Management and Co-ordination Agency, 1983a).

In terms of actual support rendered, however, rural/urban differences are less pronounced. The rural middle-aged respondents of three-generation house-holds tended to have less income than those in larger cities (Management and Co-ordination Agency, 1985a). Yet, ageing parents in rural areas received more financial help from their children (53 per cent) than did their counterparts in larger cities (47 per cent) (Management and Co-ordination Agency 1983b). Ageing parents in rural areas who did not live with their children also saw as much of them daily (23 per cent), as did their counterparts in larger cities (28 per cent) (Management and Co-ordination Agency, 1974b). Thus, actual methods of coping with the needs of ageing parents did not differ greatly between urban and rural areas, despite differential expectations towards filial support.

The aforegoing discussion indicates that whilst the normative connotation of family support differs between rural and urban areas, the solutions to the problems of old age remain quite similar. The practice of intergenerational co-residence has persisted consistently in both rural and urban areas in Japan despite drastic industrial development, growing affluence and increasing occupational mobility over the recent decades. This seeming incongruity is indicative of the dynamics of change and continuity in the care for the aged in Japan today.

RESIDENTIAL PATTERNS IN NAKAI TOWN

The crossroads of new and old options of support can be seen more concretely by taking a close look at patterns of adaptation with regard to family care of elderly people found in a town called Nakai. This is a semi-agricultural town of 9 300 inhabitants in an area of 20 km² in the Ashigara Kami-gun district of Kanagawa Prefecture. While the Nakai case study is not a definitive example of a general national pattern, the kinds of socio-economic changes it has experienced over the last decades are far from atypical in Japan. To this extent, it provides a useful case study of modernization and change and their effects on families' ability to care for elderly members.

Nakai is a town that is on the decline as an agricultural community, not because of the geographical mobility of the young, but because the town itself has become more industrial and urban. Today, agriculture offers fewer financial rewards for many Nakai residents who are drawn to wage labour in the newly developed enterprises of cities within commuting distance. Nakai is part of a relatively typical phenomenon in Japan where the need to adapt to changing production and sales activities transforms the agricultural community into a town of mixed occupations. As the proportion of those engaged in primary industry declined in the nation as a whole, so Nakai also grew from being a village of 5 950 inhabitants, of which three-quarters were engaged in agriculture in 1955, to a town of 9 300 inhabitants of which only one-fifth works in agriculture today. Agricultural land now comprises 35 per cent of Nakai, while residences and smaller-scale enterprises occupy 20 per cent of the town area (Ashigara-kami Hokenjo, 1977; Nakai Town Administration, 1983).

The pattern of adaptation among families in this type of community, which is relatively close to urban centres, is one where agriculture was not abandoned by landed households, but was retained by reducing the scale of operations and increasing the division of labour within the household. The residential pattern thereby created is known as the combined-occupation household (Kengyo-noka), where different generations of the family live together on agricultural land, but engage in different occupations. Some members of the family – typically women and the aged – continue in agricultural production, while the more 'employable' engage in wage labour by commuting to cities. In theory, industrial change offers options to younger people in rural areas to pursue non-agricultural occupations either while remaining in their original residence, or by moving out into the cities. In reality, many of the young have opted for the former option, and this Kengyo-noka trend has become prevalent, particularly since the 1960s, alongside agricultural decline in Nakai and nationwide (Hasegawa, 1986).

Thus, younger people in Nakai continue to live with ageing parents in three-generation households while at the same time being employed in city jobs. An extremely high proportion of elderly people in Nakai (approximately 95 per cent) live with their children, typically their eldest sons. Of these older people, 68 per cent only draw pensions from the National Pension Plan or the Old Age Welfare Pension, and 12 per cent receive an additional Agricultural Pension (Nogyosha Nenkin) (Nakai Town Administration 1983). Formal services such as medical examination, meals service, bathing service and senior clubs were as available in Nakai as in the nearby urban centres. However, the targeted nature of formal assistance discussed earlier, which is directed mainly to those without family, was also evident. In this town, financial and physical care for the aged remained very much a family affair, as the high rate of intergenerational co-residence attests.

By comparison, rural communities which are geographically remote from the employment opportunities of larger urban centres (Kaso-chiku) confront a different kind of situation than Nakai does. These agricultural villages have fewer options to turn *Kengyo* to adapt to the changing economy in a country which is no longer an agrarian society. The proportion of the aged tends to be higher in these districts, as more young inevitably move to urban areas. However, the prevalence of intergenerational co-residence still persists at a level comparable to the national average (Okuyama, 1981).

The aged living in metropolitan areas, on the other hand, confront a situation in which potential family resources can be fewer but for different reasons. There is concern over the changing values and structure of the urban family as the number of children declines and the number of nuclear families increases.

Care of the aged, however, is still largely contained within the family when need arises. Younger urban households may not necessarily include aged members while the latter are healthy, but many of these households can take in aged members when they become ill.

More social services of a wider variety are also available to urban elderly people. These, however, tend to constitute supplementary support to the family rather than providing real alternative options to family support (Maruo, 1986). An alternative option such as congregate housing for the elderly may sometimes be widely publicized, not because of its prevalence, but rather because it is a rare phenomenon.

DISCUSSION

Given the rapid social change that has occurred in Japan over the past decades, it is remarkable that the solutions to the problem of old age are still largely found within tradition. Old and new resources may be combined differently from region to region, but the primary source of support rests consistently with the family. Thus, in a town like Nakai, support resources for aged people differ from those of remote villages and those of metropolitan cities not so much in kind, but in degree. According to some estimates, half of Japan's elderly population will still be living with their children at the turn of this century, even if co-residence with children continues to decline at the present rate (Maeda, 1983; Jinko Mondai Shingikai, 1984). The question remains: why does the traditional family support structure remain intact, despite the rapidly changing social environment?

Some factors that sustain family care for the aged can be identified. This is important in order to appraise its continuity and change, and the future viability of such a support system. The first factor relates to the relatively low level of public resources made available to elderly individuals in Japan, which makes the attainment of self-sufficiency and independence from the family difficult. Financial dependence on children is particularly notable for those receiving the Old Age Welfare Pension and National Pension at a low level. A relatively large proportion of Japanese elderly people continue to work beyond official retirement age (55 years of age) to supplement their pension incomes.

In fact 36 per cent of Japanese men over the age of 65 are engaged in full or part-time employment. Comparable figures for other industrial countries are: France 5 per cent, West Germany 7 per cent and USA 18 per cent. However, earnings available from the kind of employment available in old age are usually low, except for senior-ranking people who work in large enterprises. The proportion of Gross Domestic Product (GDP) diverted to social welfare remains relatively low at 15 per cent. However, this is predicted to rise steadily and, by 2025, Japan is expected to spend 27 per cent of its GDP on social expenditure, equal to the proportion spent in Britain, surpassing the USA, but still less than some other developed countries (Martin, 1989).

Secondly, the exchange of support resources between parent and child makes considerable economic sense for the current generation of Japanese, both young and old. Intergenerational households may be construed as the pooling together of limited material resources by different generations. In particular, the high cost of housing is a major consideration for both old and young in this mountainous country of high land prices and high population density. Particularly for the young starting at the bottom of the seniority-based wage system, family housing can be a significant advantage. The earnings curve is also particularly low for the aged who often require financial assistance from children in spite of land and home ownership. The economic rationale of the three-generation household is particularly powerful when the needs and resources of each age group is predictable and cyclical in a highly structured society like Japan.

Thirdly, the persistence of a norm of filial piety as legitimation of family support is evident. The package of mutual obligation between parent and child – centred on property inheritance in exchange for care in old age – has traditionally persisted alongside the normative framework of Confucian ethics that legitimizes this exchange. Changes in the Family Inheritance Law after World War II have done away with the legal basis of this mutual exchange, but the normative framework for reciprocity remains, particularly because the practical need to rely on the informal social security within the family persists.

Finally, the concrete give and take confined within the family under the same roof assures the availability of support resources in times of need, with a high level of certainty. In Japan, much value is placed on the perceived dependability of future care, where illness in old age is largely accepted as a predictable end to one's life cycle. The importance of dependability fosters the preference for establishing an informal but concrete contract with family members in co-residence. Japan adopts a protective approach to care in old age where predicted problems are dealt with in advance, at a cost to the independence and freedom of individual family members.

CONCLUSIONS

Family support in Japan continues to constitute the core of care for the aged for four main reasons:

- Financial independence from the family is more difficult to attain than in other developed countries for the majority of the elderly population. The public and private pensions available for the current cohort of elderly are insufficient to rely on as primary sources of income. Reliance on financial support from children and on continued earnings consequently become a necessity.
- Alternative housing options are few for the old and young alike. Housing comes at a very high price in the densely populated, mountainous nation. Under these circumstances, intergenerational co-residence becomes a cost-effective method of attaining satisfactory housing for all generations involved.
- The traditional ethics surrounding filial piety give legitimacy to filial care. Reciprocity norms entailed within this traditional code, that foster the informal social security system within the family, provide elderly people with a sense of entitlement to care, and children with a sense of obligation of care.
- The Japanese seek a relatively high level of certainty for future security and are more willing than many others to forego independence in exchange for dependable protection. The give and take within the family is more concrete, visible and perceived as more dependable than what is provided by the abstract entity of the state.

If these four conditions sustain family support in Japan in its current form as discussed above, then it should also be predicted that familial support will continue to hold as long as these conditions are present. However, changes in any one condition will also affect the other conditions at the same time, and could bring about change to the overall system of care for elderly people. Normative changes of a drastic nature seem unlikely to occur at the present. Nevertheless, changes of a gradual nature can be expected, as a result of higher pension levels made available to an increasing number of the young old.

The system of social support based on private initiatives and principles of mutual obligation seems efficient and even convenient from the viewpoint of society, as it provides greater security at low economic and social cost. However, the psychological price exacted from individuals of different generations is high because of the conflicts, tensions and compromises that have to be managed within the three-generation households. This price is becoming higher, particularly for the daughters-in-law, as increasing longevity and prolonged illness become more prevalent, and care for frail aged family members becomes more than a full-time job. In the long run, diversification of support resources and increased options of care will become essential, as the intangible and tangible costs of family care become higher for a greater number of Japanese, both young and old.

An earlier version of this article was presented at the International Forum on Aging, Beijing, May 1986, and appeared in the proceedings of the conference (*Aging in China: Family, Economics and Government Policies in Transition.* Edited by Schulz, J. and Davis-Friedmann, D. The Gerontological Society of America, 1987).

REFERENCES

Ashigara-kami Hokenjo (1977). *Nakaimachi Chiku Hoken Katsudo Shiryoshu*, vol. 1, Nakai.

Hasegawa, A. (1986). *Noson no Kazoku to Chiiki Shakai: Sono Ronri to Kadai.* Ochonomizu Shobo, Tokyo.

Health and Welfare Statistics Association (1988). Hoken to Nenkin no Doko, *Kosei no Shihyo*, vol. 35, no. 14. Health and Welfare Statistics Assocation, Tokyo.

Jinko Mondai Shingikai (Ed.) (1984). *Nihon no Jinko, Nihon no Shakai, koreika Shakai no Miraizu.* Tokyo Keizai Shinsetsusha, Tokyo.

Maeda, D. (1983). Family care in Japan. *The Gerontologist*, **23**, 6, 579–83.

Management and Co-ordination Agency, Elderly Affairs Bureau (1974a). *Roshin Fuyo ni Kansuru Chosa*, I and II, Tokyo.

Management and Co-ordination Agency, Elderly Affairs Bureau (1974b). *Chunenso no Roshin Fuyo ni Kansuru Chosa*, Tokyo.

Management and Co-ordination Agency, Elderly Affairs Bureau (1983a). *Chunenso no Roshin Fuyo ni Kansuru Chosa*, Tokyo.

Management and Co-ordination Agency, Elderly Affairs Bureau (1983b). *Katei Seikatsu ni Okeru Rojin no Chii to Yakuwari ni Kansuru Chosa Kekka no Gaiyo*, Tokyo.

Management and Co-ordination Agency, Elderly Affairs Bureau (1985). *Oya o Fuyosuru Tachiba ni aru Monokara Mita Rojin no Chii to Yakuwari*, Tokyo.

Martin, L.G. (1989). The graying of Japan. *Population Bulletin*, **44**, 2. Population Reference Bureau, Washington DC.

Maruo, N. (1986). The development of the welfare mix in Japan. In *The Welfare*

State East and West, R. Rose and R. Shiratori (Eds), pp. 64–79. Oxford University Press, New York.

Ministry of Health and Welfare (1987). *Kokunin Seikatsu Kiso Chosa* (Base Survey of National Life). Health and Welfare Statistics Association, Tokyo.

Ministry of Health and Welfare, (1989). *Kosei Hakusho* (White Paper on Health and Welfare). Health and Welfare Statistics Association, Tokyo.

Nakai Town Administration (1983). *Nakaimachi Yoran*, Nakai.

Okuyama, S. (1981). Noka Koreisha no Shuro to Kazoku Seikatsu (Work and Family of Rural Elderly). In *Koyza: Ronen Shakaigaku II*, Y. Soeda (Ed.), pp. 401–26. Kakiuchi, Tokyo.

Okuyama, S. (1990). Kazoku (The Family). In *Zusetsu Koreisha Hakusho*, F. Miura (Ed.), pp. 34–41. Japan Social Welfare Council, Tokyo.

David Phillips

Institute of Population Studies
University of Exeter

4 HONG KONG: DEMOGRAPHIC AND EPIDEMIOLOGICAL CHANGE AND SOCIAL CARE FOR ELDERLY PEOPLE

INTRODUCTION

Hong Kong is a small territory, a British colony, located on the South China coast. It has evolved from being a relatively minor manufacturing base in the postwar era to be one of the major service, financial and manufacturing centres of this region. Most of its 5.8 million population enjoy a good standard of living, although political uncertainty, focusing on the return of formal administrative control to China in July 1997, has created associated economic and social uncertainty in the years since the mid-1980s.

In Hong Kong various social services which are defined locally to include education, public housing, medical and health care, social welfare, and labour services, have grown rapidly, even spectacularly, since the mid-1960s. Their impact on the lives of most Hong Kong residents is now very considerable. It is suggested by some that true social policy began in 1953 with the initiation of public housing schemes, but it is really only since the mid-1960s that anything resembling a long-term strategy has been devised to guide the coherent development of the social services (Chow, 1985). Indeed, as government involvement in, and the levels of funding of, welfare services have increased rapidly in recent years, the need for ever more comprehensive planning of services has become evident. Hong Kong is fortunate that much of the growth in demand for welfare services and in expectations of what such services provide has occurred during a buoyant economic period. It might be said that its situation is therefore not directly equivalent to those of other countries in the region, except perhaps Singapore and, to a lesser extent, Korea and Taiwan (Chapter 1).

Whilst Hong Kong has developed an impressive array and breadth of health and welfare-related services, based on direct public funding or subvention of charitable and other resources, it has never developed a true 'welfare state'. This is discussed further by Chow in Chapter 5, and it appears to be broadly accepted by the public and administration alike that, as government policy has been 'positive non-interventionist', there is little likelihood that Hong Kong could actually become a fully-fledged welfare state. Nevertheless, many groups and individuals have made generally moderate, but escalating, demands for social welfare reforms and increases, particularly focusing on the more sympathetic treatment of the weak and poor, many of whom are elderly. Much of the territory's help in this direction has in fact been to provide practical assistance in the form of housing, day care, or the like, rather than money to individuals.

However, since Hong Kong's major social welfare success in world terms has been the provision of public housing, it is perhaps surprising that specialist accommodation for the elderly has only relatively recently begun to be developed. Nevertheless, in view of Hong Kong's leading role in public and low-cost housing in the South-east Asian region, its current policies and practices in accommodation for elderly people should be of considerable relevance for Malaysia, Indonesia, Taiwan and Korea amongst others. All of these countries expect to experience pressure from increasing numbers and proportions of elderly people by the end of the century. Hong Kong's nearest comparison, in housing terms, is probably Singapore.

A problem common to all research and projects involved with old people is that of defining the term 'elderly'; it is also apparent in Hong Kong. An age criterion is often chosen but sometimes the criterion is retirement from full-time work. The problem of defining elderly persons in Hong Kong is as great as, or even greater than, elsewhere because varying criteria are used for different purposes. For example, the official retirement age in public service is 55 years; non-means tested old-age allowance was payable at 70 until 1990, when it was lowered to 67 (65 in 1991). The hospital geriatric service caters for those aged 65 years and over, whilst those over 60 are eligible for places in old people's homes and hostels (Ng, 1986; Race, 1982; Chow, 1989). Most of the welfare services are provided for persons of 60 years of age, so many projects have chosen this age as the cut-off point for defining 'elderly' in the Hong Kong context. This chapter conforms largely with this definition since it is primarily concerned with the provision of facilities and care, rather than the financial payments such as old-age allowance and public assistance (Kwan, 1986).

DEMOGRAPHIC AGEING AND EPIDEMIOLOGICAL CHANGE IN HONG KONG

Social and medical care for elderly people, major issues in many Western countries for several decades, have really only become issues in Hong Kong during the past 15 years or so. In most other newly-industrializing countries in the South-east Asian region, this has occurred even more recently and is perhaps not yet recognized in some. In Hong Kong, there are two main reasons for this relatively recent growth of interest. The first is that absolute numbers and proportions of elderly people (however defined) were relatively small prior to the 1960s, whilst now they are growing steadily. The second reason relates to the apparent gradual change and diminution of the tradition of family respect and support for elderly people amongst many Chinese families. A number of writers have pointed out that in Hong Kong, old age was, until the mid-1960s, only a relatively minor cause of need for help in social welfare provision. Today, however, most note the increasing importance of 'old age' as a factor in the demand for, and provision of, care and services (Race, 1982; Kwan, 1986).

The demographic profile of Hong Kong changed quite rapidly after the war, and certain distinct characteristics were noticeable by the mid-1970s. In 1960, Hong Kong was still a very youthful society, living in what was emerging as a rapidly modernizing postwar economy (Phillips, 1986, 1988a; Chan, 1986). A large proportion of the population consisted of migrants, the majority of whom were young men. The population aged 60 years and over had barely changed from the 1920s level of 4 per cent. However, the change between the censuses of 1961 and 1971 brought a new, relatively rapid growth in numbers and proportions of elderly people to public attention. The number of persons aged 60 and over increased from 170 000 (5.4 per cent of the total) in mid-1961 to 301 000 (7.5 per cent) in mid-1971 and 528 000 (10.2 per cent) in mid-1981. The number in the age group was estimated to be 640 000 in mid-1986, about 11.6

per cent of the total population of 5 500 000. The number of elderly people was estimated to be about 737 000 (12.6 per cent) in 1990 and, by the year 2000, it will probably have reached 970 760 people, about 15.5 per cent of the total population.

Both numerically and proportionally, therefore, the incidence of old age is becoming increasingly important. Longevity is also increasing, and the proportion of the very old is growing. For example, in 1961, only 13.8 per cent of the elderly population was aged 75 years or more, but by 1981 this had increased to 19.2 per cent, and by 1986 to 21.9 per cent. This trend is likely to continue because of improvements in medical and social care and nutrition. Indeed, life expectancy at birth in Hong Kong is now amongst the highest in the world: 74.7 years for men and 80.3 years for women (Table 4.1) (Phillips, 1988a; Hong Kong Government, 1991). These factors have important implications for the planning of social welfare and care, because it is widely appreciated that the very old are the most likely to require some kind of residential care and/or other forms of social and medical care.

Epidemiological change is also clearly evident in the emerging causes of ill-health and mortality amongst various subgroups of the population in Hong Kong (Phillips, 1988a). Until the early to mid-1960s, Hong Kong had very much a developing country's epidemiological profile, in which infectious diseases, some malnutrition, and ailments such as tuberculosis, typical of underdevelopment, were major causes of ill-health and death. Today, Hong Kong citizens have a more or less 'modern' epidemiological status. So-called Western diseases proliferate (Trowell and Burkitt, 1981), and the major causes of death in 1990 were heart disease (16.9 per cent), cancer (29.8 per cent), and cerebrovascular diseases (10.5 per cent). These diseases or conditions often cause considerable morbidity and are more prevalent amongst an ageing population. Infectious and parasitic diseases (including tuberculosis) were responsible for only 3.6 per cent of mortality. Age-specific mortality rates indicate that it is the age group over 65 years of age who are most likely to suffer from heart disease (including hypertension), and cancer rates also increase considerably amongst older age groups.

Better detection, improved treatment regimens and social improvements mean that death rates among elderly people from pneumonia are now generally improving. The incidence of deaths from neoplasms (perhaps delayed by treatment) is increasing in the elderly population of the territory. There does, however, appear to be some steadying, or even decline, in deaths from heart diseases amongst this older age group (Table 4.2). This is not the place for a full discussion of epidemiological transition in Hong Kong, but its emergence has important implications for the care of elderly people. Not only are elderly persons more likely than other groups to require community and more formal

Table 4.1 Hong Kong: increasing life expectancy at birth.

Year	Male	Female	Difference
1971	68.0	75.6	7.6
1974	69.1	76.0	6.9
1978	70.6	76.7	6.1
1981	72.4	78.1	5.7
1984	73.2	79.0	5.8
1990	74.7	80.3	5.6

Source: Phillips (1988a); Hong Kong Government (1991).

Table 4.2 Leading causes of death amongst people of 65 years and over, Hong Kong, 1961–1988.

Cause of death	Number of deaths			Percentage of deaths from all causes			Rate per 100 000 population		
	1961	1978	1988	1961	1978	1988	1961	1978	1988
65 years and over									
All causes	4 524	12 223	17 749	100.0	100.0	100.0	4 519.5	4 339.9	3 782.7
• Malignant neoplasms	503	2 421	4 362	11.1	19.8	24.6	502.5	859.6	929.6
• Heart diseases, including hypertensive heart disease	817	2 492	3 517	18.1	20.4	19.8	816.2	884.8	749.6
• Cerebrovascular disease	747	2 082	2 396	16.5	17.0	13.5	746.3	739.2	510.6
• Pneumonia, all forms	435	1 469	1 656	9.6	12.0	9.3	434.6	521.6	352.9
• Nephritis, nephrotic syndrome and nephrosis	88	189	722	1.9	1.6	4.1	87.9	67.1	153.9
All other causes	1 934	3 570	5 096	42.8	29.2	28.7	1 932.1	1 267.6	1 086.1

Source: Director of Medical and Health Services, Hong Kong.

support because of increasing age, but they are also, statistically, increasingly likely to express special health-care needs. Increasingly, too, modern technological developments and social changes in attitudes to ageing mean that not only are treatments better (often involving more expense) but expectations of individuals and their families are much greater too (Swift, 1989; Abrams, 1989; Warnes, 1989). These are important factors to keep in mind when considering demographic ageing; it almost always has associated social, economic and practical outcomes.

MODERNIZATION AND THE DECLINE OF FAMILY SUPPORT FOR ELDERLY PEOPLE?

The question implicit in much of the discussion below is whether Hong Kong society, during, and perhaps as a result of, the process of modernization, has become less caring towards its elderly members. This of course may not be possible to answer definitely. Data are not available with which to measure this, and today's economic and social conditions are not directly comparable with those in past years. Hong Kong society in the immediate postwar period was ostensibly uncaring on many objective measures: public housing and welfare schemes were limited and did not begin to make real inroads into the territory's problems until at least the early 1960s. Today, the same can hardly be said to be the case, at least for most government and many charitable undertakings. It might be argued that the demand for, and development of, a considerable amount of specialist provision for the elderly is not indicative of the breakdown of family caring and support, but merely reflects the unprecedented increase in numbers of elderly people, a result of Hong Kong's demographic and epidemiological transitions (Phillips, 1988a; Chan, 1986). Many of the elderly people may not have a close relative locally and, even of those who do, family members may be in accommodation unsuitable for multigeneration occupation. Therefore, the assumed breakdown of traditional Asian, especially Chinese, family structure and bonds may not be a relevant starting point for research. The following discussion should at least be considered in this light.

The Chinese family has often traditionally been the focus of care for elderly people, who have occupied a respected and valued place in society. Status and authority increased with age, and the significance of family and kinship ties were emphasized, with responsibility remaining with the family for looking after its ageing members. A caring attitude of the community towards the elderly was thereby promoted, and this meant that many old people did not experience the loss of role and disengagement that are so commonly recognized in many Western societies (Chow, 1983). In addition, elderly people often did not 'retire' as such and face the reduced economic circumstances associated with this condition (Choi, 1983). They could often expect to continue to experience reciprocal relationships, in which they could give as well as receive goods, services and affection (Antonucci and Jackson, 1989).

Hong Kong has rapidly modernized both economically and in an infrastructural sense from at least the late 1950s and early 1960s. However, Hong Kong has only really emerged as a major financial centre, a producer of high-quality electronic and textile goods, and a modern gateway to China since the early 1970s. In spite of considerable economic research into this phenomenon, knowledge about the social effects of Hong Kong's modernization process is limited (Wong, 1986), especially in so far as it impinges on the life and aspirations of the majority of the ethnically Chinese residents of the territory.

In the following chapter, Nelson Chow provides an important critical insight into the concept of 'care in the community' as applied in Hong Kong and elsewhere. It appears to depend more on care by families than the community and, therefore, old and alone people will rarely benefit from this mode of care. It is probable that, in spite of rapid and extensive postwar change, the family still remains the fundamental unit of society in modern Hong Kong and continues to perform many of its traditional caring functions. However, it is also argued that these functions have been eroded by the process of modernization, and this seems at least partially likely (Chow, 1983). Wong and others have remarked that it has been almost a standard view among both Western and Chinese scholars that traditional Chinese values are impediments to modernization. However, in Singapore, official and some academic perceptions hold that exposure to Western values and lifestyles, especially through the mass media, is detrimental to the 'positive' Asian concept of the family (Wong, 1986; Lee, 1986), and this will be important if family care is paramount. In reality, in Hong Kong and no doubt in Singapore also, there is not a wholesale acceptance of all that Western-style modernization implies. There seems to be a pragmatic retention of some Chinese practices because they are effective in certain circumstances, concurrent with a selection of certain Western ideas in other circumstances. This is true, for instance, in the choice of medical care in which modern Western or traditional Chinese treatment may be used by many (Topley, 1975; Lee, 1980). There is also considerable persistence of traditional Chinese values such as belief in family solidarity and high priority being given to the familial group.

It thus appears that a general belief still exists in Hong Kong in the maintenance of the family, and that its traditional role of rearing the young and caring for the elderly should continue. It is therefore appropriate to inquire whether modernization has in fact affected the family's efficiency in carrying out such functions. While empirical evidence is relatively limited, it does seem that the practical expression of what the family can achieve, particularly in support of the elderly, is probably less today than it was some two or three decades ago.

Today, far more elderly people are surviving into late old age. Many do not have families or extended kinship networks in Hong Kong because they arrived in the territory as single (mainly male) refugees. Many elderly folk remained single and, being immigrants to the territory, have few or no relations living locally. In addition, with the phase of more advanced industrialization since the 1960s, the nuclear family has become predominant in Hong Kong (Yeung, 1986). In part, this explains why many elderly people are being left to care for themselves.

The nature of Hong Kong's housing provision may also exacerbate the difficulty of housing elderly members within families. By 1990, about one half of the territory's population were living in public housing of some sort, and most families are housed today in self-contained, high-rise apartments. Many of these are small flats of less than 40 square metres in area, which because of size and design are not suitable for multigenerational or extended family co-residence. Similar things may be said of most private-sector housing. In addition, decreasing family size coupled with emigration for political and economic reasons has often reduced the number of children remaining in Hong Kong to care for their elderly parents and, as noted, modern living has tended to promote the idea of the nuclear family.

In 1976, some 60 per cent of households were composed of one unextended nuclear family. This had fallen to 55 per cent in 1981, but the 1986 by-census again showed about 60 per cent of households were nuclear families (Census and Statistics Department, 1986). This trend seems to be increasing, if anything, in some parts of the territory, and Wong (1986) cites studies showing that as many as 77.5 per cent of families were nuclear families in 1985 and only 14.3 per cent were extended families. Indeed, average household size fell from 4.2 to 3.7 persons between 1976 and 1986. An increasing number of families must therefore be living separately from their elderly relatives. These and other changes in family and society have occurred quite rapidly and this in itself presents a problem for the provision of effective care at home. These trends have undoubtedly militated against successful care in the community developing, as Chow discusses in Chapter 5. They may have led to many older folk being institutionalized, particularly in the growing number of private homes for the elderly.

In addition to these factors, the wider network of relatives that has been viewed as a source of help for elderly people in China itself, is often weak or missing in Hong Kong. This can cause concern to many elderly people because, should their children become alienated from them, relatively few sanctions and little public pressure can be invoked to rekindle the children's filial responsibilities. Relatives who, in the village, might have provided additional support and structure to the family are largely absent in Hong Kong. Even in the mid-1970s, Ikels (1983) suggested that the material, ideological, and social facets of Hong Kong life were shifting and contradictory. Independent residence of adult children, increasingly becoming the norm, means that an 'offending child', living elsewhere from his or her parents, will usually be employed and will appear to be a normal, responsible person to peers and neighbours who have no contact with his or her parents. However, the ignored parents will be bereft of the wider social support they could have relied on in traditional Chinese societies. Those without any descendants at all in Hong Kong, such as the elderly single men mentioned above, may be in an even worse position, and ageing in Hong Kong Chinese society is, as a result, increasingly becoming viewed with apprehension (Ikels, 1983). When some of the institutional or community residential alternatives described below are considered, this may hardly be surprising.

Certain other features of industrialization and modernization can also combine to decrease the family's ability as care providers. Unemployment rates in Hong Kong have remained low, even during world recession, with many opportunities for women to work. Female participation rates in the labour force have risen steadily from 44 per cent in 1976 to 51 per cent in 1986 (Census and Statistics Department, 1986). Male participation rates remain at over 80 per cent. As a result, there are increasingly fewer people at home to look after possibly infirm elderly relatives. In addition, in anticipation of 1997 when Hong Kong becomes a Special Administrative Region of China, many families have members training or working abroad, establishing footholds elsewhere. Sadly, too, divorce rates are increasing (by over 25 per cent annually in recent years) and, although these are still at the relatively low levels of around 5 000 divorces per annum in a population of 5.5 million, divorce will be a further disruption to the ability of some families to maintain their elderly relatives at home. Therefore, political, social, and economic factors all seem to be operating to reduce the opportunities for caring for elderly relatives at home. This no doubt makes many families feel uncomfortable and even guilty, but it may be pragmatically regarded as unavoidable.

HONG KONG: SOCIAL AND WELFARE PROVISION FOR ELDERLY PEOPLE

In Hong Kong, social services, including health care and education, are provided from many sources, singly or in combination: by the government (from general taxation and some user charges); by charities; importantly, by government-assisted (subvented) agencies; and by the private sector. The majority of the public sector and charitable providers are members of the Hong Kong Council of Social Service, whose members deliver approximately two-thirds of the social welfare services available in Hong Kong. The Council itself is 80 per cent government funded, the balance coming from charitable sources. Member agencies are subvented according to a formula and according to the types of services they offer, those considered essential usually· receiving full-cost subvention for their staff and services in order to provide a specified standard of service. Hong Kong does not have a system of social security with a compulsory social insurance scheme but, rather, the Hong Kong government has found it more acceptable locally to adopt an approach concentrating on helping the most vulnerable groups, such as disabled and elderly people. Public assistance and special needs allowance schemes enable financial help within certain specified limits to be provided. Indeed, some two-thirds of expenditure on public assistance is directed towards the elderly, and 60 per cent or more of public assistance cases involved aged people (Hong Kong Government, 1985).

As discussed in detail by Chow in Chapter 5, the guiding principle for the planning of services for the elderly has become, as in many other countries, 'care in the community'. This involves the maintenance of elderly persons at home or in small units for as long as possible by means of various support services that encourage families to look after their elderly members. To some extent, this acknowledges the diminution of family responsibilities for their elderly members, but it also involves the encouragement of elderly people who have no close relatives or friends to live alone or with others of a similar age outside formal care settings for as long as possible. The principle of care in the community has, of course, been widely advocated in other countries in Europe and North America, often in association with programmes of deinstitution-alization involving the closure of large hospitals for people in categories such as the elderly, mentally ill, and mentally handicapped. It has recently also become obvious in Hong Kong that, with the increasing number of people surviving into old age and late old age, many elderly people will eventually require more continuous care than can be provided by community support services such as home helps, house visiting, meals, and day care. Therefore, as seen below, a range of residential facilities has also recently been evolved to supplement or even supplant the often unsatisfactory realities of care in the community (see Chapter 5). However, the provision of both community support services and residential services lags far behind demand in quantita-tive and often qualitative terms. Chow (1989) sees little possibility of overall need being satisfied in the foreseeable future, and a Central Committee on Services for the Elderly reporting in late 1988 mainly recommended expansion of services amongst other suggestions. Whilst many of the steps being taken are worthy, the problem of shortage of places and services still remains.

Support services for elderly people
In Hong Kong, a range of government and subvented support services exists to encourage and enable elderly people to live for as long as possible in a 'normal'

setting. Many are local variants of schemes based on the British experience, such as home helps and meal deliveries (Phillips, 1988b). For example, day-care services include social centres, multiservice centres, and day-care centres (see also Chapter 5). By March 1991, nine day-care centres existed, each headed by a registered nurse, and giving assistance with activities such as feeding and bathing, but also providing an opportunity for the elderly to meet together. These centres serve various districts and offer a caring as well as a remedial function. There were also 17 multiservice centres, like the day-care centres non-residential, but also providing food for those unable to cook their usual daily requirements, as well as being a base for home-help teams and the like. Centres range in size from 150 to over 500 members, each of whom pays a small nominal sum per day and can obtain services and facilities such as laundry, bathing and community education. A more informal neighbourhood service is provided in the social centres, which provide a setting for casual meetings for people in the vicinity. By mid-1991, there were over 150 subvented social centres spread through the territory's 19 districts. The social centres range considerably in size, facilities and staffing and are run by subvented agencies, charities and numerous local associations. However, some have experienced financial and supervisory problems, and lobbying from the Council of Social Service led the government's Social Welfare Department to agree in the mid-1980s that an agency operating six or more social centres for the elderly might apply for subvention to support one supervisory post. This post would be based in its headquarters and would assist in the arrangement and co-ordination of centres' functions. By March 1991, there were over 50 home-help teams as support to keep people at home. During 1989, a new form of community support, respite care, was also introduced. An initially small number of places in homes for the elderly were made available to enable relatives to have short-term relief from constant caring, but initial uptake was not encouraging and changes to make the service more attractive were suggested.

Residential services for elderly people
A policy of care in the community, however sincere, can only succeed where a community itself is caring and supportive, and generally where there are vast resources available for community support. In addition, some older folk become too infirm or dependent for care by relatives and friends. It is also accepted that there will be families who cannot take care of their elderly relatives, and there will be elderly folk who have no relatives. A range of residential provision has thus emerged, although in view of Hong Kong's pioneering stance since the mid-1950s in mass public housing, it is perhaps surprising that this occurred only quite recently (Drakakis-Smith, 1979; Phillips, 1981). However, the rapid increase in elderly people has only recently occurred and been widely acknowledged in the territory, which explains some of the lag in provision.

Housing for all categories of elderly people (able bodied, frail or infirm) has been dealt with in the past through a mixture of agencies (including the government's Housing Department and Social Welfare Department), and various subvented agencies. This caused a certain amount of confusion as it has in other fields of social welfare in Hong Kong. However, today's schemes basically divide into two main categories, those for 'able-bodied' elderly persons and those for elderly people in need of care (personal care or nursing care). A particular problem in Hong Kong has been the lack of a reasonable standard of suitable accommodation for single able-bodied elderly people. This reflects the history of general housing shortage in the territory and the inferior housing conditions that would have been accepted by many single people who in the past were predominantly of working age. Housing for single people has not been a high priority in Hong Kong, or in many other places.

In the 1980s and 1990s, many single people are also elderly, either widowed or never married. The principal need of many elderly people is for accommodation only, and a number of schemes have been developed, ranging from those suitable for elderly persons who have families to help them, to those for persons on their own who are independent and capable of self care (Fig. 4.1). These include priority schemes for the allocation of public housing units to families with elderly members; units for single elderly persons in public housing; shared flats in public housing for unrelated elderly persons; and compassionate rehousing.

To encourage families to look after their elderly relatives at home, a priority scheme for families with an elderly member was introduced in late 1982. Families with one or more elderly member were allocated housing one year ahead of their normal waiting time (this incentive was increased to 2 years in 1990). This can be a significant incentive to a family to look after an elderly relative, since the average time on the general waiting list for public housing is some 7 years (although it is much shorter in certain new town estates). This scheme, aimed to foster and rekindle the traditional role of the family caring for the aged in Chinese societies as referred to in Chapter 1, is an interesting and exciting experiment. By 1991, some 5 500 families had benefited from this scheme, which indicates a fair degree of success. However, the length of time that families retain the elderly person with them in their public housing units remains to be seen, and it is possible that some might use the presence of an elderly relative merely to move up the housing waiting list. Since 1990, a new application scheme has allowed young families to apply with their elderly parents or dependent relatives for separate flats in the same public housing block in new towns (Hong Kong Housing Authority, 1990).

Units for single elderly people are part of the singleton units in public housing estates. Able-bodied elderly people, like other single persons, can apply for one of the 300 units allocated annually, although priority is given to residents from the older Mark I and II estates and temporary housing areas.

The Housing Authority has another priority scheme under which elderly couples or single elderly persons applying in groups of two or more will be allocated public housing within 2 years. This enables unrelated elderly folk to join together to apply for public housing units. A group tenancy agreement can be taken out for what would normally be a family flat, and tenants can subdivide it themselves according to normal Housing Department regulations. This scheme was started in 1980 because, at the time, there were no specific units being set aside for single elderly people.

A quota of 300 flats was initially allocated to this type of housing for individuals over the qualifying age of 60. In 1985–86, 1 000 units were set aside, and by 1986 a total of some 4 000 flats had been allocated to this shared-flats category. By 1990, 6 300 flats had been allocated and, by 1991–92, about 15 000 places will have been provided under this scheme. A variety of additional inducements are provided for elderly persons who join in this scheme. For example, applications are accepted from persons of 58 years of age to enable them to be housed when reaching 60. In addition, applicants may have 20 per cent more income than the normal limit for the public-housing waiting list. The 7-year Hong Kong residential qualification may also be waived for elderly persons applying in this category for compassionate housing. Such

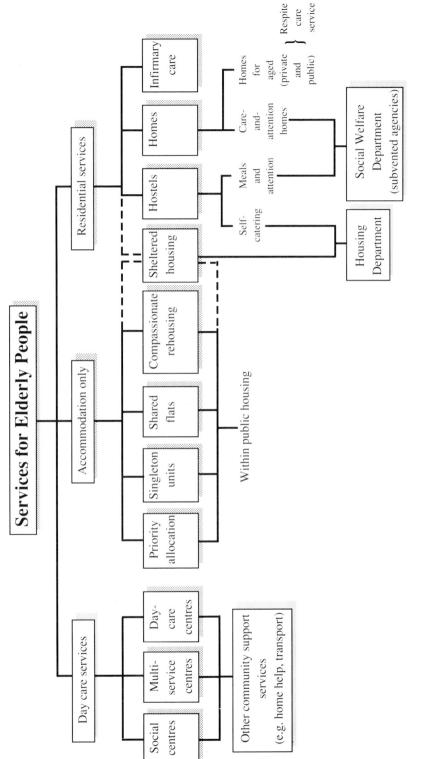

Fig. 4.1

inducements indicate some government commitment to this sector of housing, even if overall numbers accommodated are not vast.

The final scheme comes under a general compassionate rehousing category that exists for entry into public housing, and is not specifically aimed at the elderly. All families in social or other need may apply, and the Social Welfare Department may specially recommend families for such housing. However, the numbers accommodated under this scheme are also limited.

In addition to these schemes there have, to date, been other methods of housing able-bodied elderly people in Hong Kong. One initiative in the early 1980s involved the purchase of flats in private residential blocks and then their allocation to unrelated or related elderly persons. However, in view of various management difficulties and the expansion of the sheltered housing scheme in public housing noted below, the purchase of flats in private housing was discontinued.

Hostels

There are a number of old people's hostels, mainly situated in public housing estates. Hostels have generally set out to provide only accommodation for able-bodied old people but, as their residents have aged, the hostels have often gradually begun to provide meal services, sometimes for certain residents only. Some forms of personal care and group facilities are generally provided, and most of the hostels are run by agencies that are fully subvented by the Social Welfare Department. By the late 1980s, over 3 000 places had been provided in some 20 hostels; about 1 300 places in self-care accommodation and almost 2 000 in sections providing meals. The majority of hostels are located in the new towns in the New Territories, and most are in the size range of 70 to 150 residents. In effect, these hostels offer either a place in a shared room with cooking facilities or a type of bed-and-board arrangement with meals taken in a common dining area.

A new policy to provide sheltered accommodation linked to a warden, on hand for administrative purposes and emergencies, was introduced in 1986 to enable elderly people able to take care of themselves to live in sheltered housing. Under the scheme, in each new public housing estate of over 3 000 flats, premises will be reserved for a sheltered housing unit of some 100 to 150 places, operated by the Housing Department rather than the Social Welfare Department (SWD). The first 138 units became available in March 1987, located in Sha Tin, a new town in the New Territories. This is an exciting development in housing provision for the elderly which, in the future, is expected to become a major form of accommodation for able-bodied elderly people. The second sheltered housing project was opened in 1989 in Tai Po, also in the New Territories, where a similar number of units were allocated to suitable elderly people.

Sheltered housing was initially viewed as a very important aspect of policy for able-bodied elderly people, but actual provision has not lived up to expectations. The sheltered housing scheme is effectively regarded as a housing-accommodation initiative rather than a care initiative. This might be important, since elderly people are thereby regarded as part of the community, rather than a separate group in need of a special welfare focus. The operation of this scheme under the auspices of the government's Housing Department perhaps emphasizes this fact. Able-bodied elderly persons should, in theory, be able to live their own lives in appropriate sheltered housing, existing on their own resources for as long as practical. The sheltered housing scheme, it is hoped, will facilitate their being able to do this and should mean their continued participation in the community for as long as possible, avoiding their being consigned to a care category before absolutely necessary. However, in view of the current relatively poorly-developed community-support network (Chapter 5), this may be over optimistic.

Provision for more dependent elderly people

Even the most caring communities find it hard to support the many elderly people who often become unable to continue to look after themselves, and this proportion generally rises with increasing age in the population. In Hong Kong there are two main types of scheme in operation for the more dependent elderly: homes for the aged and care-and-attention homes. The homes for the aged have developed as a form of group housing for elderly persons who are largely capable of looking after their personal care but who cannot manage the critical business of providing meals, laundry, and household cleaning. In effect, such people could not maintain themselves independently in sheltered accommodation, and they require more services and facilities than are generally provided in the hostels discussed above.

The second main type of provision for elderly people who are increasingly dependent but who are not yet bed-bound or in need of considerable nursing attention is the care-and-attention (C and A) home. The term 'care-and-attention' home is probably special to Hong Kong, and these homes are akin to nursing homes in Western industrialized countries (Chow, 1988; Phillips *et al.*, 1988). Persons are admitted to C and A homes if they are frail or in need of assistance with eating, dressing or bathing but do not suffer from any acute or rapidly progressive medical problem that would require more than $2\frac{1}{2}$ hours' nursing care a week, as such people would in theory be accepted by an infirmary. By 1991, some 3 000 places had been provided in C and A homes. Until 1985, the C and A homes were purpose built but, thereafter, the Housing Department planned to provide homes in new public housing estates with attached care-and-attention units. It is hoped that this will lead to a more integrated approach to care and minimize the removal of frail elderly folk from their familiar environments by enabling within-home transfers.

It is particularly in this sector of care for more dependent elderly people that a major shortfall in provision is increasingly apparent and admitted by the government. C and A homes are currently planned to allow 11 places per 1 000 persons aged 60 and over but, even with proposed generous increases in provision, there are still considerable deficiencies. In 1985, it was estimated that there was a shortfall of over 1 000 places for 1985–86 in C and A homes; recent projections suggest continuing shortfalls. The number of elderly people on the SWD central waiting list who were in need of a place in a C and A home at the start of 1989 was almost 8 000, approximately two-thirds of a total of 12 600 on the list. In recent years the annual percentage increase in demand for C and A home places has in fact been ahead of that for accommodation for the elderly as a whole. This trend of increased demand for C and A places is likely to continue and, with increasing age, a growing proportion of infirm elderly persons already living in these homes will require more than $2\frac{1}{2}$ hours' weekly nursing care envisaged in a C and A home. These people should really be transferred to an infirmary to receive appropriate care but, in this sector also, there is a very considerable shortfall, projected to exist until the mid-1990s. Some infirmary places were created in C and A homes in the late 1980s in an attempt to deal with this impending crisis, by stepping up nursing support rather than upgrading facilities.

Infirmary care

In view of the foregoing discussion, it is appropriate to consider the provision of higher-level nursing and medical care available in infirmaries. The Hong Kong planning norm is for five general infirmary beds per 1 000 of the population aged 65 and over, whilst there is also a standard of one psychiatric infirmary bed per 1 000 of the population of all ages. However, geriatric beds in hospitals are in very short supply. Whilst acute needs are perhaps being coped with, longer-stay beds are scarce and a number of projects are underway to provide beds in various locations in Hong Kong, perhaps an increase of 500 beds by 1990. The government health service is very short of consultant geriatricians, and the service is under great pressure.

This does not particularly help the problems of elderly people who need long-stay medical care and, for most of the 1980s, there was no purpose-built long-stay unit for them in Hong Kong. This is one of the most pressing problems. Only approximately 1 000 infirmary places for elderly people now exist throughout the territory. Some 2 850 infirmary beds will be provided in the early 1990s in health-care projects mainly in the New Territories, but even the trebling of provision by the mid-1990s will still leave a shortfall. The major problem with this type of shortfall, in terms of planning for care of the elderly, is that there are few places in infirmaries to which the more frail elderly from, say, C and A homes can be transferred. This means that people further down in the waiting list who need C and A places cannot be admitted. In personal terms, it suggests that residents in need of higher levels of care (either in C and A homes or infirmaries) may well not be admitted to the types of residence most suitable for them. This may be a source of personal suffering for individual elderly persons and can often be a source of great frustration and worry to staff in homes who are unable, or ill-equipped, to provide the appropriate levels of care needed by some of their residents.

THE PRIVATE SECTOR: THE GROWTH OF PRIVATE HOMES

Many Western countries, even those with developed welfare states, have experienced growth, often relatively recently, in numbers of private-sector homes providing accommodation and various services for elderly people. In Britain, for example, this was a very marked feature of the decade of the 1980s (Phillips *et al.*, 1988), and many of the homes are typically small family businesses based on what might be called a petit bourgeois mode of care (Phillips and Vincent, 1986). Hong Kong has also seen a very rapid development in the private sector of care. Publicly-subvented homes are located mainly in public housing or in purpose-built homes on land granted by government or donated for welfare purposes. They are subject to official scrutiny as well as public finance. By contrast, a private home for the elderly is interpreted as 'a business operation providing residential accommodation with personal and nursing-care service for elderly people in private buildings and charging fees for the service' (Social Welfare Department, 1986). This business orientation and a lack of formal supervision of the sector provide the essential difference between it and the subvented public sector. It is, however, hardly surprising that some elements of care for the elderly have been privatized in view of Hong Kong's mixed economy and its traditional encouragement of the pursuit of profit and of individual entrepreneurship in filling gaps in public provision.

The considerable shortfall in the number of residential places provided for elderly people in Hong Kong, and with demand obviously set to grow considerably in the foreseeable future, made the entrance of private enterprise into this sector of care only to be expected.

Accurate data on the private-homes sector in Hong Kong were initially relatively scarce because there was no obligation for homes to register with an official authority or to seek licences to operate. Social Welfare Department staff often only become aware of new private homes, opening in their districts by the appearance of advertisements for residents or from intelligence gathered by field staff. In Hong Kong no distinctions are drawn, as they are in Britain, between private sector homes that are set up merely to provide accommodation and meals, and those that provide nursing care. This distinction has elsewhere been found to be important because each type of home tends to require different levels of provision of facilities and of medically-trained nursing staff. Therefore, different homes may be better suited to caring for different types of elderly people, and in the nursing homes, residents will be more dependent and in greater need of nursing care. Experience has shown that care for such residents is often not really compatible with the conjoint care for more able-bodied elderly people. In the future, Hong Kong should perhaps consider making a similar distinction, which could help consumers to choose the correct sort of home for elderly relatives, and might help ensure monitoring of appropriate care. The precise definition of C and A homes mentioned above is, in fact, rather misleading because of its emphasis on weekly nursing-care requirements.

The Hong Kong government initially maintained a watching brief over the development of the private sector. It was not eager to introduce compulsory registration and legislation regarding facilities and quality of care (in terms of staffing, space, and the like), apparently because it did not wish to stifle the sector or drive it into clandestine existence. This was perhaps unfortunate, but the authorities in Hong Kong have a long history of tolerance or a *laissez-faire* approach towards such things. They were hesitant to set compulsory standards that presumably many homes would not meet, thereby risking confrontation with this fledgling sector which provides a valuable capacity that the public sector would otherwise have to replace.

During the 1980s the increase in private homes became very evident. It was first really officially noticed in October 1982, and its growth thereafter has been rapid. By the end of July 1986 there were some 3 080 places in some 98 homes. The average number of residents in each home in July 1986 was 27 elderly persons, but the size of homes ranged widely from 10 to 90 residents (although many homes seemed to cater for between 20 and 40 residents). By 1989, there were over 8 000 people living in more than 240 homes.

An interesting regional distribution has emerged within the private-home sector. By 1989, almost 70 per cent of the homes were located in the older urbanized areas of Hong Kong or Kowloon. This suggests that they fill a gap in demand because most other hostel and home capacity is located in the new public housing estates, which are mainly in the New Territories (in the new-town public housing estates in particular), areas that were previously less densely built up. Only about 30 per cent of private homes were in the New Territories, although a much larger proportion of the territory's overall population lives there. This distribution also implies that private homes are providing a service for families who might wish to retain their elderly relatives near to them in the existing older urbanized areas (Phillips, 1988b).

Regulation of the private sector

Two features probably boosted the initial growth of the private homes sector in addition to the existence of unfulfilled demand for places for elderly people. First, Hong Kong property values were at a low point in the years immediately preceding 1984 during the protracted negotiations between Britain and China over the future political status of the territory. This must have enabled many of the early homes to be purchased relatively cheaply. Second, there was a supply of Chinese-trained doctors unable to register their qualifications to practise medicine in Hong Kong. They probably provided key personnel for staffing many homes, since there is generally a shortage of registered doctors and nurses in the territory, in particular those willing to work in this sector.

These two features have increased the need for official regulation of the homes for a number of reasons. Property prices have recovered somewhat and some owners might prefer to sell their homes, having made a quick profit in their real estate as well as an interim income from residents' fees. This suggests that considerable volatility is possible in the sector, which would be most undesirable both for residents and for the sensible planning of care for the elderly. In addition, the quality of staff with no qualifications or who are unable to register is debatable: whilst some may be excellent, others may have little knowledge or experience in the care of elderly people.

In many other parts of the world, and in Britain in particular, the private sector of care has been both profitable and fast growing, but subject to the fluctuations of the wider economy and social care spending. It clearly needs close monitoring, especially with regard to physical factors such as space provision and safety standards (e.g. fire regulations); the quality and appropriateness of care provided; and, by implication, the background, experience and qualifications of staff, and the general atmosphere in homes, including cleanliness, hygiene, and meals. Residents living in private homes for the elderly may often be confused and bedridden and therefore vulnerable to any unscrupulous home owners or staff who might take advantage of them financially or neglect them physically. There is not extensive evidence that this is occurring in Hong Kong homes, but it is undoubtedly the case that the density of occupancy of many homes is higher than would be tolerated in most Western countries, although the same can be said of most forms of accommodation in Hong Kong. Chow (1989), for example, suggests that the living conditions in many private homes are extremely poor.

The government was initially very tolerant and not keen to impose legally-enforceable standards. Whilst there has not been legislation on private homes for the elderly, this will be introduced in the early 1990s, indicative of the growing importance of this sector of care, and concern about its quality. Nevertheless, in October 1986, a voluntary code of practice was introduced with which many homes seemed willing to co-operate (Social Welfare Department, 1986). If adhered to strictly, this code should deal with many of the potential problems outlined above. The 1986 code, and its 1988 revision, sets out detailed recommendations for private homes concerning accommodation and space requirements, safety and fire precautions, staffing, health care services, equipment and furniture, and social care. It is in itself a fairly wide-ranging document, containing ideas from such reports as the British 'Home Life' code of practice (Department of Health and Social Security, 1984). These and other suggestions have been adapted to meet local circumstances. This code will not, however, deal with the 'business aspects' of the homes, related to profit motivation and financial viability.

The voluntary code of practice arguably suits prevailing attitudes in Hong

Kong towards the regulation of welfare provision somewhat better than a legal code, which might imply official interference rather than help. The code does not, however, overcome the problem of the lack of a requirement for all homes to register on a central list and face compulsory inspections. Neither does it clarify for consumers the distinction between homes providing accommodation/care and those that are care-and-attention homes or nearer to being infirmaries. This will almost certainly mean that a very great range of residents in terms of age and physical and mental competence may end up living together in the same home, which can be disturbing for residents and difficult for staff.

Hong Kong's approach to this important phenomenon of rapid growth in the private sector of care for the elderly will undoubtedly provide an important lesson for many other countries in this region, particularly the NICs. It seems that Singapore, too, is going through a similar process of considering the steps to be taken in providing rules or guidelines on minimum standards of care in homes. There, as in Hong Kong, a number of what are termed 'commercial homes' have sprung up, housing from as few as 20 to over 100 residents. Singapore's commercial homes, like Hong Kong's, have a profit-making motive but seem to be concentrating on providing nursing care mainly to upper and middle-income elderly people (Vasoo and Tan, 1985). The level of success that is achieved by voluntary or official regulation, and improvements in the private sector of care for the elderly in both these territories should be of great interest to other countries in the region and should form priority areas for policy-informing research.

CURRENT TRENDS AND FUTURE PROSPECTS

Hong Kong is making some determined efforts to meet the social and residential needs of its fast-growing elderly population. Nevertheless, Chow (1983) suggests that the family needs to be strengthened in its ability to provide support for the elderly, and that elderly persons should be allowed to remain working for as long as their health permits to enable them to earn and feel less dependent. In addition, or alternatively, the potential of elderly people as child carers in the family and of preserving family stability needs to be emphasized so that the elderly receive more attention from their children and are less often regarded as burdensome dependents. The Housing Department, amongst others, has attempted to foster the Chinese tradition of responsibility and for a family looking after its own elderly members. This is unlikely to be a satisfactory solution for a large proportion of cases, and the government and government-subvented agencies are now trying to develop accommodation and care, and at least keep pace with growing demand even if they are not completely satisfying all need. However, as the official effort is directed mainly towards care in the community, the long-term continuation of growth in specialist care and accommodation may be uncertain.

The acknowledged shortfall in provision of places in care-and-attention homes and infirmary care for the elderly will continue in the near future. Almost inevitably, many old people will remain in inappropriate accommodation such as crowded family housing or general hospital wards rather than in specially-designed facilities. What has not been accurately established in Hong Kong, or in any other newly-industrializing country for that matter, is the proportion of old people who will be likely to need specialist accommodation, and the proportion that will be in need of special medical care. An appropriate balance of public and private responsibility for such care has not been discussed either. In this field Hong Kong's experience, as a leader among the NICs, in the growth of elderly population may prove to be invaluable.

Elements of the British model of residential care are developing, in particular the recent rapid growth of private homes. This sector may prove to be of considerable assistance in Hong Kong where there is a tradition of 'self care' or self reliance amongst a substantial proportion of the population. However, the private sector has been seen elsewhere to be notoriously volatile and, if more profitable uses for premises appear, the number of homes may suddenly fall. It will also be unwise for the authorities to place too great a reliance on a legally unsupervised and largely unmonitored private sector, and the moral and practical aspects of 'cash for caring' have to be considered. Nevertheless, the government increasingly recognizes the potential of the private sector and hopes that the voluntary code of conduct and subsequent legislation for the running of private homes for the elderly will successfully raise standards that are often currently lax. The practicalities of monitoring quality of care and of ensuring that capacity is both numerically and geographically appropriately provided for, are, however, considerable.

Further descriptive analyses of Hong Kong's current changing practices in the development of accommodation for the elderly will doubtless prove to be of value to other countries in the region. More detailed research is required of, for example, the dynamics of the private sector and the nature and needs of residents in various types of accommodation including hostels, homes, care-and-attention homes, and sheltered housing. In this way, some sort of 'career pattern' may be established to indicate what elderly people may tend to expect and require in the community and in specialist housing, and how this might be projected into the planning process. Initiatives such as sheltered accommodation for unrelated as well as related persons will bear close monitoring. This has the potential to be one of the most highly demanded and cost-effective means of providing effective and appropriate accommodation for the growing number of able-bodied elderly people who will, it is hoped, live into long and active old age. In particular, the balance of what can be achieved by a 'care in the community' policy or by more formal care needs much wider debate and research in these circumstances. Chapter 5 takes up the realities of community care in detail.

Acknowledgements
Much of the research on which this chapter is based was undertaken during periods when the author was a Visiting Scholar at the Centre of Asian Studies, University of Hong Kong. He wishes to acknowledge the Centre's support, and the help and advice provided by various departments of the Hong Kong government, including the Social Welfare Department and Housing Department. He is also grateful for advice from many official and welfare agencies in Hong Kong and Dr. Nelson Chow of the University of Hong Kong. The author is solely responsible for the interpretation of information contained in this chapter.

REFERENCES

Abrams, M. (1989). 'Third age' lives in the next generation: changing attitudes and expectations. In *Human Ageing and Later Life*, A. Warnes (Ed.), pp. 163–77. Edward Arnold, London.

Antonucci, T. and Jackson, T. (1989). Successful ageing and life course reciprocity. In *Human Ageing and Later Life*, A.M. Warnes (Ed.), pp. 83–95. Edward Arnold, London.

Census and Statistics Department (1986). *Hong Kong 1986 By-Census: Summary Results*. Census and Statistics Department, Hong Kong Government.

Chan, K.L. (1986). Demographic setting of Hong Kong: developments and implications. In *Hong Kong Society: A Reader*, A.Y.H. Kwan and D.K.K. Chan (Eds), pp. 11–44. Writers' and Publishers' Cooperative, Hong Kong.

Choi, K.L. (1983). *Background paper on services for the elderly in Hong Kong*. Hong Kong Council of Social Service, Hong Kong.

Chow, N.W.S. (1983). The Chinese family and support of the elderly in Hong Kong. *The Gerontologist*, **23**, 6, 584–8.

Chow, N.W.S. (1985). Welfare development in Hong Kong – the politics of social choice. In *Hong Kong and 1997: Strategies for the Future*, Y.C. Jao (Ed.), pp. 475–91. Centre of Asian Studies, University of Hong Kong.

Chow, N.W.S. (1988). *Caregiving for the Elderly Awaiting Admission into Care and Attention Homes*. Resource Paper Series, No. 13, Department of Social Work and Social Administration, University of Hong Kong.

Chow, N.W.S. (1989). Social Welfare. In *The Other Hong Kong Report*, T.L. Tsim and B.H.K. Luk (Eds), pp. 215–28. Chinese University Press, Chinese University of Hong Kong.

Chow, N.W.S. and Kwan, A.Y.H. (1986). *A Study of the Changing Life-Style of the Elderly in Low Income Families in Hong Kong*. Writers' and Publishers' Cooperative, Hong Kong.

Department of Health and Social Security (1984). *Home Life: A Code of Practice for Residential Care*. Department of Health and Social Security and Centre for Policy on Ageing, London.

Drakakis-Smith, D. (1979). *High Society: Housing Provision in Metropolitan Hong Kong, 1954 to 1979: A Jubilee Critique*. Occasional Papers and Monographs Series, No. 40, Centre of Asian Studies, University of Hong Kong.

Hong Kong Government (1985). *The Five-Year Plan for Social Welfare Development in Hong Kong: Review 1985*. Government Printer, Hong Kong.

Hong Kong Government (1991). *Hong Kong 1991*. Government Printer, Hong Kong.

Hong Kong Housing Authority (1990). *Annual Report 1989/90*. Hong Kong Housing Authority.

Ikels, C. (1983). *Aging and Adaptation: Chinese in Hong Kong and the United States*. Archon Books, Hamden, Connecticut.

Kwan, A.Y.H. (1986). Social welfare services in Hong Kong. In *Hong Kong Society: A Reader*, A.Y.H. Kwan and D.K.K. Chan (Eds), pp. 155–207. Writers' and Publishers' Cooperative, Hong Kong.

Lee, R.P.L. (1980). Perceptions and uses of Chinese medicine among the Chinese of Hong Kong. *Culture, Medicine and Psychiatry*, **4**, 345–75.

Lee, S.M.C. (1986). Dimensions of ageing in Singapore. *Journal of Cross-Cultural Gerontology*, **1**, 239–54.

Ng, Y.Y. (1986). Geriatrics: an overview. *Mental Health in Hong Kong*, pp. 189–94.

Phillips, D.R. (1981). The planning of social services provision in the new towns of Hong Kong. *Planning and Administration*, **8**, 8–23.

Phillips, D.R. (1986). Urbanization and health: the epidemiological transition in Hong Kong. In *Proceedings of the Second International Seminar on Medical Geography*, C. Palagiano and G. Arena (Eds), pp. 287–99. Edizioni RUX, Perugia, Italy.

Phillips, D.R. (1988a). *The Epidemiological Transition in Hong Kong: Changes in Health and Disease Since the Nineteenth Century*. Occasional Papers and Monographs Series, No. 75. Centre of Asian Studies, University of Hong Kong.

Phillips, D.R. (1988b). Accommodation for elderly persons in newly industrializing countries: the Hong Kong experience. *International Journal of Health Services*, **18**, 2, 255–79.

Phillips, D.R. and Vincent, J. (1986). Petit bourgeois care: private residential care for the elderly. *Policy and Politics*, **14**, 2, 189–208.

Phillips, D.R., Vincent, J. and Blacksell, S. (1988). *Home from Home: Private Residential Care for Elderly People*. Social Services Monographs: Research in Practice, University of Sheffield, Sheffield.

Race, D. (1982). *Residential and Institutional Services for the Elderly*. Resource Paper Series, No. 3, Department of Social Work, University of Hong Kong.

Social Welfare Department (1986). *Code of Practice for Private Homes for the Elderly*. (Revised edition, Oct. 1988). Social Welfare Department, Hong Kong.

Swift, C. (1989). Health care of the elderly: the concept of progress. In *Human Ageing and Later Life*, A. Warnes (Ed.), pp. 135–45. Edward Arnold, London.

Topley, M. (1975). Chinese and Western Medicine in Hong Kong: some social and cultural determinants of variation, interaction and control. In *Medicine in Chinese Cultures*, A. Kleineman, P. Kunstadter, E.R. Alexander, J.L. Gale (Eds), US Department of Health, Education and Welfare, Washington DC.

Trowell, H.C. and Burkitt, D.P. (Eds) (1981). *Western Diseases: Their Emergence and Prevention*. Edward Arnold, London.

Vasoo, S. and Tan, B.H. (1985). *The Status of Ageing in Singapore*. Singapore Council of Social Service, Singapore.

Warnes, A.M. (1989). Responding to the challenge of ageing. In *Human Ageing and Later Life*, A. Warnes (Ed.), pp. 192–208. Edward Arnold, London.

Wong, S.L. (1986). Modernization and Chinese culture in Hong Kong. *China Quarterly*, **106**, pp. 306–25.

Yeung, D.W.T. (1986). The changing family system in Hong Kong. In *Hong Kong Society: a Reader*, A.Y.H. Kwan and D.K.K. Chan (Eds), pp. 231–58. Writers' and Publishers' Cooperative, Hong Kong.

Nelson Chow

Department of Social Work and Social Administration
University of Hong Kong

5 HONG KONG: COMMUNITY CARE FOR ELDERLY PEOPLE

ISSUES SURROUNDING COMMUNITY CARE FOR ELDERLY PEOPLE IN HONG KONG

In caring for elderly people, both the family and the community have long been perceived to be of primary importance (Biegel *et al.*, 1984). Their importance lies in the fact that within these two institutions the elderly are most ready to establish their social relationships. The family and the community have also been seen as 'the contexts in which [ageing] problems arise and in which most of them have to be resolved or contained' (Seebohm Report, 1968). As a result, it is not surprising that a 'community care' approach has often been adopted in countries with a growing ageing population, in which elderly people are encouraged as long as possible to live in the community and with their families. The attraction of this approach is not difficult to see as most countries with an ageing population are finding it increasingly difficult to finance programmes and services to meet the needs of elderly people; and families and communities present themselves as the most viable alternatives to share part of this burden. While acknowledging the desirability of the 'community care' approach, recent research on caring for aged people shows that it is not without its limitations (Quadagno *et al.*, 1987).

As in many other industrial countries, a 'care in the community' approach has been formally adopted in Hong Kong since 1979 as the guiding principle for the care of elderly people in the population (Hong Kong Government, 1979). The principle is reaffirmed in the most recent white paper on social welfare (Hong Kong Government, 1991). Data are thus available for an evaluation of the effectiveness of the approach in caring for the elderly. Apart from that, there are also other reasons which suggest that Hong Kong, among all the countries in the Asian and Pacific region, presents itself as the most appropriate example for an examination of this popular concept of 'community care' (Chow, 1987a). First, more than 98 per cent of the population in Hong Kong are Chinese and certain traditional values, such as respecting the old, are often thought to continue to exist in a Chinese society (Ikels, 1983). Since the 'community care' approach traces its roots to some of these traditional values, the argument goes that this approach should be acceptable in a place where these values are still practised. The validity of this argument has of course yet to be proved.

Together with the above, Hong Kong still possesses a family system that the advocates of the 'community care' approach find most desirable (Yeung, 1990). Despite the indication that, just as in other countries undergoing rapid industrialization, the number of extended families in Hong Kong is decreasing, the percentage of elderly people residing with their married children still remains high. As long as the majority of the elderly are living with their children within the same household, it is assumed that care will be provided by their families to enable them to remain in the community. Whether an elderly person has close kin to live with no doubt determines to a large extent the chances of receiving family care, but the relationship between a particular form of family system and the availability of care has still to be examined (Montgomery *et al.*, 1987).

The last reason why Hong Kong has been seen as ideal for the examination of the 'community care' approach is the fact that Hong Kong has never developed a welfare system comparable to that of the 'welfare states' (Chow, 1986). Many of the 'welfare states' are shedding part of the state responsibility in caring for the elderly onto families and communities by adopting the 'community care' approach, but the approach has never been perceived in this light in Hong Kong. In other words, the 'community care' approach has all along been believed, both by the public and the government in Hong Kong, as being most suitable for the local situation; it has not been perceived as an excuse for the government to neglect its responsibilities (Phillips, 1988). The debates on 'privatization' and 'dismantling of the welfare state', which are so often mingled elsewhere with the adoption of the 'community care' approach, can thus probably be avoided (Walker, 1987).

Notwithstanding the fact that the 'community care' approach to care for the elderly has generally been accepted in Hong Kong, a number of questions have been raised about the concept and its practicability. First, as in many other countries adopting this approach, the meaning of 'community' is only vaguely perceived in Hong Kong and, very often, people are unclear about the networks of social relationships constituting it. Secondly, the exact definition of care and where the burden actually falls is another area about which questions are often asked but which seldom receive an answer. Rather than justifying the 'community care' approach for Hong Kong, the following discussion will attempt to examine the issues raised above by referring to the findings of recent local research on elderly people and their care. It is hoped that the examination will not only serve the purpose of clarifying some of the misconceptions surrounding the approach, but also help to point out the direction that Hong Kong, and perhaps other countries in the region with similar social and economic conditions, may adopt in caring for its elderly (Martin, 1988).

THE DEVELOPMENT OF THE COMMUNITY CARE APPROACH IN HONG KONG

It has been mentioned that a 'community care' approach has been adopted in Hong Kong as the guiding principle to care for the elderly. It was in 1973 that a working party, set up by the government to look into the future needs of the elderly, first acknowledged that there existed in Hong Kong a problem of the aged (Working Party on the Future Needs of the Elderly, 1973). Before that, the government's stand was that the responsibility of caring for the elderly must fall on the 'natural family unit', in particular the children of families, and the government must not do anything to 'accelerate the breakdown of [this] natural or traditional sense of responsibility' (Hong Kong Government, 1965). This stand was changed in 1977 when the government published a policy paper on the future development of services for the elderly, which accepted the recommendations of the Working Party (Hong Kong Government, 1977). This change was partly attributed to the growing number of elderly persons in the population, but more important still, also to the increasing incidence of families failing to meet the needs of their elderly members (Hong Kong Council of Social Service/Social Welfare Department, 1978).

The approach to guide the development of services for elderly people is officially known, as it was first used in the Working Party's Report, as 'care in the community'. As stated in the Report, it means that 'services should be aimed at enabling the elderly to remain as long as possible as members of the community at large, either living by themselves or with members of their family, rather than at providing the elderly with care in residential institutions outside the community to which they are accustomed' (Working Party on the Future Needs of the Elderly, 1973). When the Working Party made its recommendations, what it had in mind was to minimize the necessity of residential care for elderly people. Whether or not the Working Party truly believed that the 'care in the community' approach was a better form of care would be difficult to tell, but the Working Party frankly admitted that they 'looked for solutions which ... would cost less, would make least demand on scarce manpower resources and which could be implemented reasonably quickly ...' (Working Party, 1973). In making its recommendations, the Working Party accepted the fact that the majority of elderly people in the early 1970s were living with their families; it thus assumed that this approach 'makes the best sense from the point of view of the elderly themselves, their families, and the community at large' (Working Party, 1973). It concluded that, as long as some care was provided for elderly people, either by their own families or the community at large, the elderly folk would be content in the environment they knew.

Conceptually, few objections can be raised to the 'care in the community' approach and few will question the general aims of community care policies 'to maintain a person's link with family and friends and normal life, and to offer the support that meets his or her particular needs' (Department of Health and Social Security, 1981). However, as Jones, Brown and Bradshaw point out, 'to the politician, "community care" is a useful piece of rhetoric; to the sociologist, it is a stick to beat institutional care with; to the civil servant, it is a cheap alternative to institutional care ...' (Jones et al., 1978). Hence, the 'community care' approach often promises more than it can actually achieve.

While the 'community care' approach may not necessarily, as argued by Bulmer, 'boil down to care by members of the immediate family' (Bulmer, 1987), governments adopting the approach nevertheless often fail to fulfil their promises and provide families with elderly members with the necessary support of domiciliary services. Little once observed that, 'while lip service is given to the value of community living for the elderly, home-delivered services to supplement family care are in most countries seriously deficient' (Little, 1979). In this respect, Hong Kong is no exception. Although a wide range of community support services noted below and in Chapter 4, such as community nursing, home helps, day care, laundry and canteen services, social and recreational activities, hostel accommodation, and respite care, have been introduced in Hong Kong since the formal adoption of the 'community care' approach in a white paper on social welfare development in 1979, all of these services have been found to be insufficient to meet demand (Hong Kong University, 1982).

In respects other than the inadequate provision of community support services, the 'care in the community' approach itself has also been questioned recently regarding the various assumptions that the Working Party made in 1973. First, as stated in the policy paper published in 1977, the 'care in the community' approach could only succeed when the community was a caring one. No elaboration has, however, been given as regards the meaning of a 'caring community' except that 'these people [the families, neighbours and friends of elderly people] can do a great deal to sustain the elderly's self respect and social integration and thus to enable the elderly to retain a general sense of satisfaction and fulfilment in the latter period of their lives' (Hong Kong Government, 1977). Secondly, the 'care' that can be provided in and by the community has only been assumed and never clearly defined in the recommendation of the 'care in the community' approach. It is therefore open to interpretation. The most common suggestion is that 'care' refers to a whole range of provisions made by the government to meet such basic needs of elderly people as those for subsistence, housing, personal and medical care. Others would have in mind the assistance offered by relatives, friends and neighbours when the elderly are sick and weak. Indeed, the 'care in the community' approach is so vaguely defined in Hong Kong, often implying no more than helping elderly persons to remain as members of the community as long as possible, that it can mean different things to different people (Chow, 1983). To evaluate the approach and put it in its proper perspective, questions such as those that follow might usefully be asked. What constitutes the 'community' in the 'care in the community' approach? What are the networks of social relationships that exist to form the 'community'? What are the factors influencing the functioning of the networks? What is the 'care' offered in 'care in the community' and from whom does it come? How do the different forms of 'care' integrate with each other? Discussions in the following paragraphs are attempts to answer the above questions.

The changing community in Hong Kong
In proposing the 'care in the community' approach as the guiding principle for the future development of services for elderly people, the Working Party in its report referred to the 'community' either as the environment which the elderly knew, or as sources from which elderly people could possibly obtain care and attention (Working Party, 1973). Hence, the 'community' possesses a geographical dimension and at the same time implies a set of social relationships within which help is available. Even if one can accept this understanding of the Working Party on the idea of 'community', one has still to ask: what is the geographical boundary of this 'community'? What are the sets of social relationships that do exist to provide elderly people with care and attention? Do elderly people want to belong to these 'communities'?

In a report of the Barclay Committee, published in the United Kingdom in 1982, 'community' was defined as 'a network or networks of informal relationships between people connected with each other by kinship, common interests, geographical proximity, friendship, occupation, or the giving and receiving of services for various combinations of these' (Barclay Report, 1982). As far as the situation in Hong Kong is concerned, the networks of relationships established between the elderly and other people as a result of kinship, geographical proximity and a giving and/or receiving of services will be most applicable. It has been mentioned that as Hong Kong is a predominantly Chinese society, it has often been assumed that kinship relationships must remain very strong. In the early 1970s, sociologists researching into family structure in Hong Kong had already found that as a result of industrialization, unextended nuclear families had become the norm rather than the exception (Wong, 1975). Furthermore, despite the fact that the majority of elderly people in Hong Kong were living with their families, lonely elderly persons were increasing in number. The policy paper published in 1977 on the future development of services for the elderly mentioned that, in the mid-'70s, 11.3

per cent of those aged 60 and over were living alone, 14.6 per cent with one other person and 3.6 per cent in collective households (Hong Kong Government, 1977).

The more recent figures from the 1986 By-census indicated that 11.5 per cent of those aged 60 and over were living alone, 17.4 per cent with one other person in the household and 3.5 per cent in collective households (Central Committee on Services for the Elderly, 1988). A survey conducted in 1983 to look into life styles of elderly people living in low-income households in Hong Kong, reported an even higher figure and found that about one-quarter of the respondents were living alone (Chow and Kwan, 1986). Of the others in the survey with families, 34 per cent were living with spouses, 74 per cent with children and 55 per cent with grandchildren (Chow and Kwan, 1986). Hence, if kinship relationships are regarded as forming an essential element of the 'community' from which elderly people can receive care and support, then over 10 per cent of the elderly population in Hong Kong, and higher among the low-income groups, are deprived of this 'community'. As for those fortunate enough to have this 'community', it is made up mainly of their spouses and grown-up children.

In addition to kinship relationships, the other network that often constitutes the 'community' is the relationship established between neighbours, as a result of geographical proximity. Nearly all data available on the degree of neighbourliness in Hong Kong, measured in terms of the frequency of contacts between neighbours, indicate that the situation is less than desirable (Chow, 1988a). In the study on the life style of the elderly mentioned above, respondents revealed that when they needed help in their daily life, it came mostly from their children (48 per cent), followed by their spouses (24 per cent); only 11 per cent mentioned their friends and neighbours as their chief source of help (Chow and Kwan, 1986). Though 11 per cent appeared a bit low, a national survey of social networks in adult life conducted in the United States in 1980 reported that '82 per cent of the support networks consisted of family members; only 18 per cent consisted of friends' (Antonucci and Akiyama, 1987). Hence, while neighbours might in future become a more important source of help for elderly people, they can in no way replace family members and, as far as the existing situation is concerned, they only play a minor role and often at times when help from the family is not available (Ngan, 1990).

When the 'care in the community' approach was formally pronounced in Hong Kong in 1979 in a white paper on social welfare development, the government spelt out in no unclear terms that 'services will be expanded on a wide front, with the objective of promoting the well-being of the elderly through care in the community and by the community' (Hong Kong Government, 1979). Though services to enable the elderly to remain in the community have since been introduced or expanded, their supply has fallen far short of the demand, as shown in Table 5.1. The reasons for the continual shortfall of the

Table 5.1 Provision of services for elderly people in Hong Kong.

Service	Provided as of March 31, 1991	Demand	Shortfall
Home help (teams)	56	under review	
Multiservice centres	17	24	7
Day-care centres	9	24	15
Social centres	155	250	95

Source: Hong Kong Government (1991).

services will not be a subject of discussion here, but it explains why the elderly people interviewed in studies conducted in Hong Kong seldom cited such services as the 'community' upon which they could rely for help. For example, in the study on the life style of the elderly, only 9 per cent of the respondents reported that they had ever received services from social welfare agencies (Chow and Kwan, 1986). In a more recent study conducted in 1988 to look into the pattern of caregiving for elderly people on waiting lists for care-and-attention homes (see Chapter 4 for explanation of this term), it was found that among this group of frail elderly, fewer than 20 per cent were recipients of community support services, although the majority of them were benefiting from one type or another of the cash payments provided by the government, including public assistance, the Old Age Allowance and the Disability Allowance (Chow, 1988b). All in all, services available in the community to enable elderly people to remain within it are in such short supply that they can hardly form a caring network for the elderly.

Summarizing the above, the 'community' which presently exists in Hong Kong as a source of help to the elderly is no doubt still the family to which the elderly belong. Neighbours and service networks at best only play a supplementary role for a small number of those who either have no family of their own or who are fortunate enough to obtain help from their neighbours or social welfare agencies. While the family in Hong Kong still provides a 'community' for the majority of elderly people, as in many other industrializing countries, the percentage of elderly people living with their grown-up children is gradually decreasing; this implies that the 'community' which formulates the basis of the 'care in the community' approach is weakening in strength, and so is the approach itself. Furthermore, the average size of a household in Hong Kong now stands at only 3.5 persons and it is also very rare nowadays to find an aunt or another close relative, who are usually very good helpers, to be a member of the household (Central Committee on Services for the Elderly, 1988).

The increasing number of married women employed outside the family is another phenomenon which will further weaken the caring function of the family. Indeed, it is often the simple unavailability of carers within the family, rather than unwillingness, that has posed the most serious threat to the family as a caring institution. In the study of the elderly on waiting lists for care-and-attention homes, the most common reason given for applying for admission into these homes was that there was simply no one at home to look after the elderly person. A survey of residents in private homes for the elderly also revealed that the absence of carers at home was the major reason for admission (Kwan, 1988). Hence, although the family remains as the most important 'community' within which the elderly can obtain care and support, the extent of help available is obviously limited and diminishing in scope. It should also be noted that greater demands to provide care are often made on families which are already under stress, such as those in low-income groups (Payne, 1986). On the other hand, there are no signs at the present moment that neighbours and service networks are emerging as viable alternatives to provide care for elderly people.

FACTORS INFLUENCING FAMILY SUPPORT FOR ELDERLY PEOPLE

As the family still constitutes the most important 'community' for elderly people in Hong Kong, and will continue to do so for many years to come, it would be worthwhile to look at the exact nature of care it provides as well as the factors influencing the performance of its caring role. It should first be noted that a compulsory retirement pension scheme is still absent in Hong Kong (Chow, 1981); as a result, it is not uncommon for elderly people to turn to their grown-up children for financial support. For those who have no children to support them, their last resort would be to apply for public assistance. At present, about 10 per cent of elderly people in Hong Kong are receiving public assistance (Social Welfare Department, 1988). The other form of cash payment for which elderly people are eligible is the Old Age Allowance which is available to all reaching the age of 65. In any event, for as long as a compulsory retirement pension system is not introduced in Hong Kong, it appears that the family will have to continue looking after the financial needs of a substantial number of elderly people, especially those in the low-income groups. However, this task of financially supporting the elderly is admittedly not an easy one. In the study on the life style of the elderly, about 30 per cent of the carers found the obligation of financially supporting their elderly members to be a burden (Chow and Kwan, 1986).

In addition to financial support, the other forms of care most frequently offered by the family (as revealed in the study on the life style of the elderly) included escorting elderly people going out, washing, shopping, cleaning and cooking. However, it should be noted that, even in areas where elderly people most needed help, such as in cleaning and cooking, support was provided to fewer than one-third of the respondents, and they were usually the more aged ones of 70 years and above (Chow and Kwan, 1986). In other words, the majority of elderly people in Hong Kong who live in the community do not actually need a great deal of care from their families. Indeed, in the study on the life styles of the elderly, fewer than 20 per cent of the carers felt that the task of taking care of their elderly relatives had adversely affected their use of time and life in general (Chow and Kwan, 1986).

Rather than putting an immense burden on their family members, the study on life styles revealed that many elderly people were in fact often doing more in the way of providing support for their families than the other way round. Out of the group of elderly people living with their grown-up children, the study reported that 76 per cent helped in looking after the house when other family members went out, 68 per cent helped in doing various household chores and 39 per cent helped in taking care of grandchildren (Chow and Kwan, 1986). Furthermore, those elderly people who provided help in housekeeping and looking after their grandchildren usually maintained a better relationship with other family members. In a review of informal support networks, Walker also concluded that 'we know from research, for example, that the provision of family care is based on reciprocity, exchange, and other interdependence rather than individualistic values' (Walker, 1987).

Research data available in Hong Kong generally confirm Walker's observations. The study on life styles of elderly people revealed further facts. For example, those who were more financially independent and capable of self-care were more likely to be maintaining a better relationship with their family members. What can be concluded from this is that financial support still constitutes an important element of the 'care' received by the elderly in Hong Kong from their families. For those who are deteriorating in health, representing about 10 to 15 per cent of the elderly population (Chi and Lee, 1989), they may in addition require assistance in areas such as cooking and cleaning. Another noteworthy point is that, in spite of much rhetoric about filial piety in a Chinese society, it does not seem that this tradition has been particularly influential in fostering a harmonious relationship between elderly people and their children, and thereby increasing the likelihood that the former are receiving support from the latter. Admittedly, it is difficult to verify the relevance of certain traditional concepts such as respect for the old. But as far as the provision of family care for elderly people is concerned, evidence clearly indicates that certain factors, such as the extent of support that the elderly members manage to provide for their families, are as important, if not more so, than the simple rhetoric of filial piety (Chow, 1987b).

The interrelationship between formal and informal care

In adopting the 'care in the community' approach in 1979 as the guiding principle for the future development of services for the elderly, the government became committed to providing 'a range of community services and improved cash benefits that will encourage families to look after their elderly members, or which will enable old people on their own to live independently, and in dignity, in the community for as long as possible' (Hong Kong Government, 1979). This commitment sounds very much like an objective which the Department of Health and Social Security in the United Kingdom put forward on social care in the 1980s, which states that 'the primary objective of departmental policies . . . is to enable old people to maintain independent lives in the community for as long as possible. To achieve this, high priority is being given to the development of domiciliary provision and the encouragement of means to prevent or postpone the need for long-term care in hospital or residential homes' (Department of Health and Social Security, 1978). The similarity of the two statements is probably not surprising as countries adopting the 'community care' approach often append to it a promise by the government to provide the elderly with the necessary service support so that they can live in the community as members of their families (Secretaries of State for Health and Social Security, 1989).

As discussed above, and as shown in Table 5.1, the promise of the Hong Kong government to provide the elderly with the necessary community support services has not materialized. As a result, many elderly people living in the community are unable to lead an independent life. The inadequate provision of community support services has also produced two effects which were unintended when the 'care in the community' approach was proposed. First, as the services are not available to all who need them, they are thus offered to those perceived to be in the greatest need, who often happen to be frail elderly people without a family. This is clearly shown by a finding of the study on the elderly on waiting lists for care-and-attention homes, in that community support services were usually received by respondents who lived alone. Even among recipients of public assistance, the proportion of lonely elderly is much higher than those living with their families in a ratio of about 9:1 (Social Welfare Department, 1988). This situation is not special to Hong Kong; a national study of caregiving for the frail elderly in the United States reported that 'less than 10 per cent [of carers] reported the use of paid services, and those who did rely on formal care were assisting the most severely impaired elders' (Stone et al., 1987). Although the 'care in the community' approach in Hong Kong also includes as its target of assistance lonely elderly people, particularly the frail, the over-concentration of both cash assistance and community support services on this group implies that most families with elderly members can scarcely obtain any outside help. Furthermore, it is a common belief that elderly people with families should be taken care of by other family members but, as shown above, the caring functions of most families in Hong Kong are diminishing. It has also been observed that 'the potential of the informal sector to take on additional caring responsibilities has been over-estimated' (Phillipson and Walker, 1986). Hence, with the community support services concentrated on lonely elderly people and families increasingly finding themselves unable to look after their elderly members, it is not surprising that the 'care in the community' approach in Hong Kong has often been ridiculed as 'care by the family', or even 'the elderly people caring for themselves'.

Secondly, as families having elderly members to look after often fail to obtain outside support, some inevitably accept the task in a negative manner and this may make elderly people feel unwanted. The study on the life styles of elderly people found that most of the elderly respondents thought rather poorly of themselves. Table 5.2 shows that respondents included in the study were particularly negative about their roles in society and had in fact an extremely poor image of themselves. While it may not be possible to relate this low self-image of elderly people directly to the inadequate provision of community support services, as respondents in the study came entirely from the poorer half of the population, it can still be said of many of the elderly people living with their families, that they can hardly be described as living 'in dignity in the community'.

Table 5.2 Hong Kong: self-image of elderly people in low-income households.

Item	Strongly agree	Agree	Disagree	Strongly disagree	No opinion
Less useful as one grows old	35.0	49.0	10.0	5.0	1.0
Society should take care of me	22.0	59.0	15.0	1.0	3.0
Feel isolated	7.0	44.0	38.0	9.0	2.0
Past experiences are still useful	8.0	43.0	41.0	3.0	5.0
Find present living satisfying	10.0	62.0	23.0	2.0	3.0
Wait for death to come	23.0	43.0	23.0	8.0	2.0

Answers are in percentages.
Source: Chow and Kwan (1986).

There is no doubt that the 'care in the community' approach adopted in Hong Kong has only partially achieved its objectives. The failure is mainly caused by the inadequate provision of community support services which as a result leaves most of the families with elderly members without the necessary support. In other words, community support services are not playing a supplementary role to family support as they are intended to. The two systems of formal and informal support are not therefore complementing each other to form a 'caring community' for Hong Kong's elderly people. While both family support and community support services are needed, they seem to be serving two different groups of elderly people: one with the families and the other without, and there are only rare occasions when the two types of support interact.

STRATEGIES FOR FUTURE DEVELOPMENT OF 'COMMUNITY CARE'

The fact that the 'care in the community' approach in Hong Kong has largely failed to achieve its objectives does not imply that it has to be replaced by another one. The approach recognizes at least that the great majority of elderly people in Hong Kong are living in the community and that most who need care are receiving it from their families. While not excusing the government from its responsibilities, it has to be acknowledged that the inadequate provision of community support services for elderly people is almost universal and is not special to Hong Kong. Indeed, it is questionable whether one should identify formal and informal support as two separate types. Walker once suggested that the rigid division between the formal and informal sectors should be overcome and it is preferable to think more in terms of 'social support networks' which 'may compromise both formal and informal helpers, professional and non-professional personnel'. He further suggested that more research should be undertaken into 'the circumstances in which informal care networks can be successfully stimulated, reinforced, or supplemented by statutory provision without overburdening informal carers' (Walker, 1987). Another researcher into the 'community care' approach also suggested that, in addition to the family, different types of networks – personal, volunteer, mutual aid, neighbourhood and community empowerment – should be built up to provide social support for elderly people (Bulmer, 1987).

The discussion above indicates that, as far as Hong Kong is concerned, it will be a long time before the formal and informal sectors can be fully integrated to enable elderly people to live in the community in dignity. Evidence shows that the needs of the lonely elderly have already far exceeded the capacity of existing community support services and this situation will hardly change in the near future. Hence, for a long time to come, community support services will be unlikely to offer relief to families with elderly members to look after. Under such circumstances, the suggestion of building up 'social support networks' to enhance the caring functions of the family seems to be more realistic than emphasizing the complementary roles of the formal and informal sectors.

Furthermore, it has been shown that the family in Hong Kong is still providing the most important 'caring community' for elderly people and it will hardly be possible for the 'care in the community' approach to achieve its objectives when the 'community' is in fact so limited in scope and diminishing in functions. The provision of formal support will undoubtedly make up for some of the deficiencies of the family system but the help available from neighbours and friends must be further explored. A study conducted in one of the new towns in Hong Kong found that as residents there are further away from their relatives, they tend to turn more to their neighbours for help and assistance and a higher degree of neighbourliness has resulted (Chow, 1988a). Other evidence also shows that people in Hong Kong are now more ready to join in social support networks when they realize the need for them (Chi and Lee, 1989). Indeed, for the 'care in the community' approach in Hong Kong ever to achieve its objectives, it seems that both the formal and informal sectors must be strengthened, with the increase of community support services for the former and the building of various social support networks for the latter.

REFERENCES

Antonucci, T.C. and Akiyama, H. (1987). Social networks in adult life and a preliminary examination of the convoy model. *Journal of Gerontology*, **42**, 5, 519–27.

Barclay Report (1982). *Social Workers: Their Role and Tasks* (Report of a working party under the chairmanship of Mr. P.M. Barclay). Bedford Square Press, London.

Biegel, D.E., Shore, B.K. and Gordon, E. (1984). *Building Support Networks for the Elderly*. Sage Publications, Beverly Hills.

Bulmer, M. (1987). *The Social Basis of Community Care*. Allen and Unwin, London.

Central Committee on Services for the Elderly (1988). *Report of the Central Committee on Services for the Elderly*. Health and Welfare Branch, Hong Kong.

Chi, I. and Lee, J.J. (1989). *Hong Kong Elderly Health Survey*. Department of Social Work and Social Administration, University of Hong Kong, Hong Kong.

Chow, N.W.S. (1981). Social security provision in Singapore and Hong Kong. *Journal of Social Policy*, **10**, 3, 353–66.

Chow, N.W.S. (1983). The Chinese family and support of the elderly in Hong Kong. *The Gerontologist*, **23**, 6, 584–8.

Chow, N.W.S. (1986). The past and future development of social welfare in Hong Kong. In *Hong Kong in Transition*, J.Y.S. Cheng (Ed.), pp. 403–19. Oxford University Press, Hong Kong.

Chow, N.W.S. (1987a). The Urban Elderly in Developing East and South-east Asian Countries. In *Aging China: Family, Economics, and Government Policy in Transition*, J.H. Schulz and D. Davis-Friedmann (Eds), pp. 93–103. The Gerontological Society of America, New York.

Chow, N.W.S. (1987b). Factors influencing the support of the elderly by their families. *Hong Kong Journal of Gerontology*, **1**, 1, 4–9. (In Chinese).

Chow, N.W.S. (1988a). The Quality of Life of Tuen Mun Inhabitants. *The Asian Journal of Public Administration*, **10**, 2, 194–206.

Chow, N.W.S. (1988b). *Caregiving for the Elderly Awaiting Admission into Care and Attention Homes*. Department of Social Work and Social Administration, University of Hong Kong, Hong Kong.

Chow, N.W.S. and Kwan, A.Y.H. (1986). *A Study of the Changing Life-Style of the Elderly in Low Income Families in Hong Kong*. Writers' and Publishers' Cooperative, Hong Kong.

Department of Health and Social Security (UK) (1978). The DHSS perspective. In *Social Care Research*, J.H. Barnes and N. Connelly (Eds), pp. 1–44. Policy Studies Institute and Bedford Square Press, London.

Department of Health and Social Security (1981). *Care in Action*. HMSO, London.

Hong Kong Council of Social Service/Social Welfare Department (1978). *Report of a Study on the Social Service Needs of the Elderly in Hong Kong*. Hong Kong Council of Social Service, Hong Kong.

Hong Kong Government (1965). *Aims and Policy of Social Welfare in Hong Kong*. Government Printer, Hong Kong.

Hong Kong Government (1977). *Services for the Elderly, a Green Paper*. Government Printer, Hong Kong.

Hong Kong Government (1979). *Social Welfare into the 1980s, a White Paper*. Government Printer, Hong Kong.

Hong Kong Government (1991) *Social Welfare in the 1990s and Beyond, a White Paper*. Government Printer, Hong Kong.

Hong Kong University, Department of Social Work (1982). *A Study of the Welfare Needs of the Elderly in Hong Kong: The Needs of the Elderly Living in the Community*. Department of Social Work, University of Hong Kong, Hong Kong.

Ikels, C. (1983). *Aging and Adaptation: Chinese in Hong Kong and the United States*. Archon Books, Hamden, Connecticut.

Jones, K., Brown, J. and Bradshaw, J. (1978). *Issues in Social Policy*. Routledge and Kegan Paul, London.

Kwan, A.Y.H. (1988). *A Study of the Residential Life of the Elderly in the Private Elderly Homes in Hong Kong*. Writers' and Publishers' Cooperative, Hong Kong.

Little, V.C. (1979). Open care of the aging: alternative approaches. *Aging*, **301–2**, 10–23.

Martin, L.G. (1988). The aging of Asia. *Journal of Gerontology*, **43**, 4, S99–S113.

Montgomery, R.J.V., Hatch, L.R., Pullum, T., Stull, R.E. and Borgatta, E.F. (1987). Dependency, family extension, and long-term care policy. In *Critical Issues in Aging Policy*, E.F. Borgatta and R.J.V. Montgomery (Eds), pp. 161–77. Sage Publications, Newbury Park.

Ngan, R. (1990). *The Informal Caring Networks Among Chinese Families in Hong Kong*. Unpublished PhD Thesis, University of Hong Kong, Hong Kong.

Payne, M. (1986). *Social Care in the Community*. Macmillan, London.

Phillips, D.R. (1988). Accommodation for elderly persons in newly industrializing countries: The Hong Kong experience. *International Journal of Health Services*, **18**, 2, 255–79.

Phillipson, C. and Walker, A. (Eds.) (1986). *Ageing and Social Policy*. Aldershot, Gower.

Quadagno, J., Sims, C., Squier, D.A. and Walker, G. (1987). Long-term care community services and family caregiving. In *Aging, Health, and Family, Long-Term Care*, T.H. Brubaker (Ed.), pp. 116–28. Sage Publications, Newbury Park.

Secretaries of State for Health, Social Security, Wales and Scotland (1989). *Caring for People: Community Care in the Next Decade and Beyond*. HMSO, London.

Seebohm Report (1968). *Report of the Committee on Local Authority and Allied Personal Social Services*. HMSO, London.

Social Welfare Department, Research and Statistics Section (1988). *Study of Public Assistance Recipients 1987*. Social Welfare Department, Hong Kong.

Stone, R., Cafferata, G.L., Sangl, J. (1987). Caregivers of the frail elderly: a national profile. *The Gerontologist*, **27**, 5, 616–26.

Walker, A. (1987). Enlarging the caring capacity of the community: informal support networks and the welfare state. *International Journal of Health Services*, **17**, 3, 369–86.

Wong, F.M. (1975). Industrialization and family structure in Hong Kong. *Journal of Marriage and the Family*, **37**, 985–1000.

Working Party on the Future Needs of the Elderly (1973). *Services for the Elderly*. Government Printer, Hong Kong.

Yeung, Sum. (1990). *The Dynamics of Family Care for the Elderly in Hong Kong*. Unpublished PhD Thesis, University of Hong Kong, Hong Kong.

Paul Cheung

and

S. Vasoo

Department of Social Work and Social Psychology
National University of Singapore

6 AGEING POPULATION IN SINGAPORE: A CASE STUDY

BACKGROUND

Founded in 1819 as a British trading station, Singapore has since been transformed into a modern, industrialized city-state and a major economic centre in Asia. Nation building and economic modernization efforts began in earnest after full independence was achieved in 1965. Taking full advantage of her strategic location and human resources, Singapore's economy expanded rapidly. By 1989, Singapore's GNP per capita of $17 910* was the third highest in Asia, after Japan and Brunei. In slightly over two decades after independence, a firm economic base has now been established with manufacturing, services and commerce as the major economic sectors (You and Lim, 1984). With a land area of only about 623 km² and a population of 2.6 million, Singapore's economic future inevitably lies in the further improvement and utilization of her human resources.

In the early years of nationhood, the need to achieve the nation's economic and social aspirations was translated into a number of major social policies. The public housing policy, for example, resulted in 87 per cent of Singapore's population residing in government-built high-rise apartments. With increasing affluence, Singaporeans are aspiring to wider choice and better housing. The educational policy led to the development of a comprehensive and technologically-oriented educational system providing equal opportunities for all. In the case of population planning, the impact of the National Family Planning and Population Programme on population growth is well known: in a single generation, the fertility rate of Singapore dropped well below the replacement level.

INTRODUCTION

A major challenge which will confront Singapore in the future has been identified by the government as the ageing of its population, expressed as the expected dramatic increase in the number of elderly persons and in the relative proportion of the elderly to other age groups. While the aged population in Singapore is relatively small (8.6 per cent) compared to most developed countries (11.4 per cent) (Binstock, Chow and Schulz, 1982), demographers in Singapore have predicted a sizeable increase in the age group of those aged 65 and over in the next 50 years. It is anticipated that this trend, shared by many other newly industrializing countries, will result in a broad-based transformation of the society, requiring adjustments and adaptations at all levels. This would significantly alter the dependency ratio between the young and the old.

* Singapore dollars are used throughout this chapter.

Two implications have received particular emphasis. Firstly, concern is expressed as to whether ageing of the population will increase the dependency ratio on the state for welfare and financial assistance. A related question is whether the traditional caring institutions will remain intact given the rapid social changes that Singapore is experiencing. Secondly, concern is also expressed about the economic implications of population ageing and its potential impact on the economy's future development.

Increasing awareness of the issues related to the elderly in Singapore emerged as early as the 1970s. At least seven studies (Chen, 1982b) were conducted on the elderly during that time. In the 1980s, the number of studies increased significantly. Even before the beginning of 1985, at least ten were known of, one of which, 'Social Policy and the Elderly' (1981), was conducted by the Singapore Council of Social Service. In addition, the appointment of two high-level committees in 1982 and 1988 to review the problems arising from population ageing further reflected this concern. There was also an awareness that the rapidity of the ageing process and its consequences were related to, if not an outcome of, the policies implemented in the past. The two committees, chaired by cabinet ministers and comprised of representatives from various sectors, were therefore given the task of reviewing the policy options and recommending policy changes. These two committees, as well as other initiatives, marked the beginning of Singapore's effort to plan for an ageing society.

The report of the Committee on Problems of the Aged (1984), commonly known as the Howe Report, further opened the gate for public attention and debate on issues facing the elderly.

This paper is a case study of the ageing of Singapore and the policies and measures introduced to moderate the impact of the ageing process.

DEFINITION OF ELDERLY POPULATION: DEMOGRAPHIC PROFILE

Different countries have different cut-off points for defining the chronological age of the elderly population, and these depend on the average life expectancy of the population. In Singapore, where the average life expectancy at birth is over 72 years, it is appropriate to consider the elderly population as comprising those who are 60 years and above. Although there is presently no official retirement age, there appears to be an implicit recognition that the retirement age should be raised from the previous level of 55 years to 60 years.

Population projections prepared by the Singapore government's Population Planning Unit have shown that the age profile of Singapore will undergo a significant transformation by early next century (Cheung, 1988a). The key feature of this transformation will be the dramatic increase in the number and proportion of older persons in the population.

Ageing population

Since independence, Singapore has benefited from a youthful and vibrant population. In 1957, 43 per cent of the population were below 15 years of age, and the elderly population aged 60 years and over constituted less than 4 per cent. In 1989, the age profile reflected a more mature population, with the young constituting only 23.1 per cent and the elderly 8.5 per cent of the population. With the bulk of the population of working age, dependency ratios have been on the decline (Cheung, 1988b). Over the same period, the median age of the population has risen steadily from 18.8 years in 1957, to 19.7 in 1970 in 1970 and to 28.8 in 1988. Projections show that the median age is likely to rise to about 33 years in the year 2000 and to 38 years in 2030 (Chen and Cheung, 1988).

Shift in the age structure – the changing age profile
In a growing population, the increase in the number of elderly persons may not alter the age profile significantly. In a slow-growth population, the increase in the absolute numbers is associated with a corresponding increase in the proportion of the elderly. The relative proportion of the elderly population is therefore a function of the comparative sizes of successive cohorts.

The decline in the population growth rate between 1957 and 1980 that was due to the success of the family planning programme, education, rapid industrialization and increased female labour participation, has affected the age structure of the Singapore population. The effects of the declining population growth rate have resulted in:

- a drop in the young population (0 to 14 years) from 43 per cent to 23.1 per cent,
- an increase in the adult population (15 to 59 years) from 53 per cent to 68.5 per cent,
- an increase in the elderly population (60 and above) from 4 per cent to 8.5 per cent.

Based on the trends of the past 30 years, demographers have predicted a further decline in the proportion of the young population to 17 per cent in the next 50 years. By then, the adult population is expected to be reduced by 58 per cent while the population of aged persons will increase to 25 per cent.

The decline in Singapore's birth cohort sizes is shown in Table 6.1, along with major fertility indicators. The speed of the decline is clearly shown. The Total Fertility Rate (TFR) fell rapidly from 5.76 in 1960 to 3.07 in 1970, a drop of more than 2.5 children per woman over a 10-year period. Since 1975, Singapore's fertility has fallen below replacement level and a historic low was reached in 1986 when the TFR fell to 1.44. The number of births also declined from about 62 000 in the 1960s to about 42 000 in the 1980s. Table 6.1 also shows the rebound in the number of births in 1987, 1988 and 1989, after the announcement of the New Population Policy.

Table 6.1   Demographic indicators, 1960 to 1989.

	Number of live births	CBR	TFR	Rate of natural increase
1960	61775	37.5	5.76	3.5
1965	55725	29.5	4.66	2.5
1970	45934	22.1	3.07	1.7
1975	39948	17.8	2.07	1.4
1980	41217	17.1	1.73	1.2
1985	42848	16.6	1.62	1.1
1987	43616	16.7	1.64	1.2
1988	52957	20.0	1.97	1.5
1989 (estimated)	47735	17.8	1.78	1.3

Note: CBR (Crude Birth Rate)
       TFR (Total Fertility Rate)

DEFINITION OF ELDERLY POPULATION: DEMOGRAPHIC PROFILE 79

Based on a long-run average TFR of 1.8, projections prepared by the Population Planning Unit have shown that the proportion of persons aged 60 and over will increase from 7 per cent in 1980 to about 26 per cent in 2030. With one out of four Singaporeans aged 60 and over, Singapore by 2030 will be a truly 'mature' society.

The need to maintain a balanced age structure was one of the main objectives of Singapore's New Population Policy, announced in 1987 with the slogan 'have three or more if you can afford it' (Cheung, 1989). The policy offers a number of incentives to encourage parents to attain a family size of three or more children. The stated goal of the policy is to return the TFR to replacement level. Over time, by raising fertility gradually, the policy hopes to stabilize the population structure with a more even distribution across the age groups. If this is achieved, the proportion of the elderly will stabilize at about 20 per cent. Before this occurs, however, the proportion of the elderly is likely to rise beyond the 25 per cent level.

Is it possible to bring the targeted 20 per cent even lower to bring about a rejuvenation of the population structure? This is possible in the long run if a higher than replacement population growth rate is adopted by the government as a policy objective and is eventually achieved. In view of Singapore's limited land and water resources, there is an absolute upper limit on the carrying capacity of the island. Sustained high population growth may bring about a younger age structure, but the adverse effects of over-population may be serious. Moreover, in modern Singapore, small family size has been internalized by many parents during the 'antinatalist era'. This norm may not be easy to overcome. Thus, it appears that a population structure with 20 per cent to 25 per cent of the population being elderly may have to be accepted as inevitable for Singapore. The socio-economic impact of this change in age profile will be fully felt within the next 40 years.

Size of the elderly population

Attention to overall population structure as presented, however, tends to mask the social implication of growth in actual numbers. If one were to compare the actual number of elderly persons over time, the rate of growth of the elderly would have increased even more drastically. The increase in the number of elderly persons in Singapore is and has been rapid. In 1970, there were about 118 300 persons aged 60 and above. The number increased by 47 per cent to 173 600 in 1980. In 1984, there were about 193 900 persons aged 60 and over which, by 1989, had increased by 18 per cent to 229 700. By the turn of the century, the number will rise to about 332 000 and to 835 000 by 2030 (Table 6.2). The number of elderly persons will therefore increase by about 300 per cent from the present level to the year 2030.

The rapid increase in the number of elderly persons is due to two factors. The first arises from the ageing of the postwar baby-boom cohorts. At present, these cohorts are in the 20 to 39 age range. By 2030, they will be in the age range of 70 and above. With the passage of the baby-boom cohorts in the next century, the number of elderly persons will subsequently decline because of the smaller cohorts born since the 1960s. The second contributing factor is the increase in the life expectancy of the population, resulting in more persons surviving to older ages. Life expectancy at birth has been increasing steadily over time. In 1957, the life expectancy of an average Singaporean was only 64 years. In 1989, it was 74 years. Life expectancy at the age of 60 has also increased: in 1989, it was 17 years for men and 20 years for women.

The change in the population structure in Singapore will result in a gradual

Table 6.2 Actual and projected elderly population in Singapore, 1980 to 2030.

Age Group	1980 no.	1980 per-centage	1990 no.	1990 per-centage	2000 no.	2000 per-centage	2030 no.	2030 per-centage
Total population	2413.9	100.0	2716.0	100.0	2995.0	100.0	3214.0	100.0
60 to 64	59.7	2.5	81.8	3.0	111.7	3.7	196.3	6.1
65 to 69	49.3	2.0	58.0	2.1	81.7	2.7	213.0	6.6
70 to 74	33.3	1.4	43.4	1.6	60.0	2.0	183.3	5.7
75 to 79	18.6	0.8	30.1	1.1	35.6	1.2	118.1	3.7
80 and above	12.7	0.5	25.7	0.9	43.4	1.4	124.7	3.9
All 60 years and above	173.6	7.2	238.9	8.8	332.4	11.1	835.3	26.0

Notes: Projections based on 'medium' fertility assumptions
Numbers in thousands

shift from the burden of child dependency to old dependency. With a fall in the birth rate, the age distribution is affected in such a way as to lower the overall economic dependency ratio. There will be a shift in the composition of the dependant population as elderly dependants make up a larger proportion and youth a declining proportion. Demographers have established through this ratio that there will be fewer adults to support the increasing number of the elderly. In 1957, the old dependency ratio was 0.07. In 1980, however, it had increased to 0.11 and, with the forecast growth of the aged persons from 7 per cent in 1980 to about 26 per cent in 2030, the old dependency ratio will increase to 0.46.

THE COMPOSITION OF SINGAPORE'S ELDERLY POPULATION

Singapore's development over the past few decades will not only have a lasting impact on the numerical dimensions of the elderly population. Their socio-economic characteristics are also changing, mirroring the social transformations that have occurred (Chen and Cheung, 1988).

Literacy
The average educational attainment of the elderly is expected to increase as the younger, better-educated cohorts move into old age. In 1980, 71 per cent of the elderly men and 93 per cent of the elderly women had no formal education. By 2030, these poportions will be reduced to about 18 per cent for men and 35 per cent for women. The elderly with secondary and higher education will increase from about 4 per cent in 1980 to about 20 per cent in 2030. The gain in educational advancement among elderly women will be particularly noticeable, reflecting the educational advancement of women over the last 20 years.

Economic status
In 1970, the male labour-force participation rate for the age cohort of 60 to 64 was 56 per cent. It then declined to 53 per cent in 1980 and to 48 per cent in 1989. A similar trend may be observed for those aged 65 and over. The participation rates for elderly women have been much lower than for elderly males (Table 6.3). The relatively small percentage of elderly people in the workforce suggests that there is a lot more room for elderly people to work or to continue working. Increasing affluence in Singapore and the rising demand for leisure could have reduced the elderly's commitment to work. Lack of

Table 6.3 Labour-force participation rate of older persons by sex and age, 1970 to 1988.

		1970	1975	1980	1988
Male					
	55 to 59	73.9	73.6	70.7	65.1
	60 to 64	55.6	54.2	52.5	47.3
	65+	31.7	31.7	28.6	21.2
Female					
	55 to 59	16.2	14.2	14.5	17.4
	60 to 64	13.4	14.0	11.3	11.9
	65+	6.5	6.4	6.4	4.7

appropriate employment opportunities and some employers' discriminatory hiring practices have also hindered greater participation. The steady decline is likely to continue if obstacles to continued employment are not removed. On the part of the government, appropriate incentives have to be given to both employers and potential elderly employees to induce them to remain in the workforce.

In terms of age, there are significantly more younger elderly workers than older elderly workers. The distribution for both males and females within each age group is quite similar. A majority (84 per cent) of the working elderly are employed in sales, service and production lines (National Survey on Senior Citizens, 1983). The large percentage of working elderly in these three areas suggests that there is either no mandatory retirement age or that there is a high demand for workers for these jobs. Only a small percentage (5 per cent) are engaged as salaried professionals, managers and administrative workers.

Country of origin
Due to Singapore's demographic history, 75 per cent of the elderly population in 1980 were foreign-born. This proportion is expected to decline gradually to about 20 per cent by 2030. The increase in the number of indigenous elderly people also implies greater generational depth and a firmer grounding for families ties in Singapore.

Demographic characteristics
It is common knowledge that women tend to outlive men and, in Singapore, the difference in life expectancy is about 5 years. In 1989, there were about 122 200 women and 107 500 men aged 60 and older, giving a sex ratio of 0.88. In the future, older women will continue to outnumber men, especially in the oldest age group. There are also sex differences in the incidence of widowhood among the elderly. In 1980, 80 per cent of the elderly men were married and only 14 per cent were widowed. The pattern was reversed for elderly women, with 37 per cent married and 57 per cent widowed. This pattern is likely to persist into the future as men continue to marry women younger than themselves and women continue to outlive men.

ECONOMIC AND SOCIAL LIFE

The economic and social well-being of elderly people is of interest and concern. As the population structure changes, it will inevitably bring with it changes in their economic and social life. Some major features are now considered.

Retirement
Like most other people, elderly people want to be independent. In the National Survey on Senior Citizens, most elderly people indicated that they favoured the idea of extending the retirement age. In fact, 85 per cent of the respondents indicated that they had no intention of retiring. Of those not working, only a small percentage (16.3 per cent) indicated that they stopped work because of reaching retirement age. Most of these elderly people indicated domestic reasons and ill-health as the main reasons for not continuing to work. These findings certainly demonstrate that the elderly are keen to be financially and socially independent rather than a burden on the community. Extension of the retirement age is thus a wise move, allowing the elderly to work as long as possible to ensure a sense of financial independence. This would then provide them with the means to live an economically viable life and to remain active in the community. Although a delayed retirement is desirable in view of the increased life expectancy, it could affect firms that want to employ younger and more educated workers. At the same time, it might limit job openings and delay promotions for young and middle-aged workers. Consequently, some friction between the young and old workers should be expected.

An interesting question to ask is: will inducing the elderly to work or continue working deprive the young of valuable jobs in the tight labour market in Singapore? The Howe Report (1983) asserted that the young would not be deprived of valuable jobs for three reasons:

- the small family size of Singaporeans will reduce the number of younger entrants into the labour force,
- young people are expected to join the labour force at a later age because of extended educational opportunities and National Service,
- foreign unskilled workers will be gradually phased out.

The National Survey on Senior Citizens indicates that financial problems and boredom are foreseen by elderly people as the most pressing issues during retirement.

Interestingly, retirees or those not working do not appear to be eager to re-enter the labour force. The National Survey on Senior Citizens found that relatively few of the elderly people surveyed wanted to return to the labour force. This phenomenon is also compounded by a reluctance of most firms to re-employ retired workers. In order to provide an incentive for firms to be more ready to employ older workers, it may be necessary to either waive or reduce Central Provident Fund (CPF) contributions for both the older workers and the employers. The suggestion that there should be a reduction of wages with increasing age may also help to encourage employers to employ or retain elderly workers.

Social security
Personal income is the most basic form of social security for elderly people and, in Singapore, personal income is negatively correlated with age (National Survey on Senior Citizens, 1983). This happens because the tendency to stop work grows with age. A higher proportion of elderly females than males is without any personal income. This difference is accounted for by the difference in the labour-force participation between the male and female elderly.

Household income is an important source of social security for the economic life of Singapore's elderly people. The National Survey on Senior Citizens (1983) revealed that 13 per cent of those surveyed had a household income of less than $500 per month. This percentage is quite close to the national percentage of low-income households in Singapore. This group of elderly people is, however, more vulnerable than others to risk and social problems. An interesting finding is that more elderly people who are not working but who are looking for work come from the lower-income household group. This suggests that they are eager to maintain financial adequacy.

The National Survey on Senior Citizens (1983) reveals that the majority of elderly people (84 per cent) do receive financial and material support from their immediate family members and other relatives. These forms of support are significantly more pronounced for those who do not have a source of income than for those who have. Similarly, more than 80 per cent of elderly people receive support in kind. These findings indicate that elderly persons in Singapore generally have a source of financial security in their families or relatives. The findings also imply that there is still a sense of filial piety and family obligation among many Singaporeans towards their aged parents. Few elderly people receive contributions in cash or in kind from non-relatives or from voluntary organizations. However, among those who might need such support, it is not surprising that many do not seek support because of the possible social embarrassment brought both on themselves and their family members.

Only a small percentage (7.2 per cent) of the elderly surveyed have Central Provident Fund (CPF) as a form of social security (National Survey on Senior Citizens, 1983) although the 1984 Labour Force Survey indicated that 25 per cent of elderly people are CPF members. Males outnumbered females in having CPF as a reserve fund. This is because many females have never worked and therefore have never been CPF members. The reserves in the CPF for elderly people are however generally low because of the low rate of contributions during their working years. Nevertheless, it is envisaged that with the current CPF rates of 40 per cent and higher wages, the CPF is likely to become a critical source of reserve funds in the future, especially for those who are currently below 45 years old. Those above this age are unlikely to benefit much as most of their CPF funds would be tied up with repayments of housing loans leaving very little for old age.

While the CPF scheme may ensure a sense of financial security for those who are about to retire, there are still groups of workers who are not covered by the CPF scheme. These groups include the self-employed, employees who are casual or family labourers, and employees who work outside permanent employment relationships. A social insurance scheme for these workers should be seriously considered to ensure their financial independence in retirement.

Another form of social security for elderly people is the pension given upon retirement. Major developments in the course of the CPF's evolution, however, have drastically reduced the number of people with pensions. While pensions act as an important source of income for retired persons, mostly government civil servants, there is some suggestion that adjustment to the amount paid should be made commensurate with rising inflation and cost of living.

The social support system of elderly people

The family has been a potent source of support for both young and old through the ages. To what extent is it still playing a supportive role for the elderly in Singapore today? The National Survey on Senior Citizens found that a high percentage of elderly people is confident that they can depend on their family members when they fall ill (88 per cent) or when they need to confide in them (78 per cent). Although there are no past data to make accurate comparisons, it is our contention that there may actually be a slight drop in family support for the elderly. This drop could be attributed to the rapid industrialization and modernization, the assimilation of Western educational-system values and philosophy, and the government's resettlement programme which encourages the formation of nuclear families. In order to allow the family to be a continuing source of support for elderly people the government should continue its policy of giving priority public housing to young couples who apply for flats on a joint basis with their parents (see also Chapter 4). At the same time, efforts should be made to help young couples obtain flats that are close to the homes of their parents.

Of those elderly people living separately from their children, about 60 per cent are visited by their children at least once a week. The survey also reveals that elderly people who live alone or with non-relatives receive far fewer visits. In accord with Asian culture the eldest son was likely to be the most frequent contact or visitor for elderly parents, although on the whole daughters tend to visit elderly parents more often than sons do. Interestingly, children who contact their elderly parents most frequently are not likely to be the ones providing the most financial support in cash or in kind.

Overall, the findings generally suggest that most of the elderly who have immediate family members would have little problem in getting help and assistance in times of need. Many elderly people have maintained meaningful interaction and contact with their children. This provides the basis for their confidence in securing help from their children in times of need.

Spending habits
'Modest' would be the word to describe the spending habits of elderly people in Singapore. The National Survey on Senior Citizens found that 80 per cent of the elderly spend less than $500 (US$250) per month, with 37 per cent spending less than $100 per month. Because of their higher rate of labour-force participation, males tend to spend more than females. An interesting question relating to the spending habits of the elderly is: whether their income is adequate to cover their monthly expenses? According to the National Survey of Senior Citizens, 93 per cent of elderly people reported that they have sufficient income to cover monthly expenses. Only 7 per cent have to draw on their savings and CPF or rely on other means to meet their monthly expenditure.

An adequate standard of living among the elderly – at least until recently – can be attributed to rapid economic growth during the past two decades. The period of economic growth following the independence of Singapore, despite spells of instability, facilitated the foundation of economic support for most elderly people. However, when the economy hits a downturn, it might be expected that a higher proportion of elderly people would find it difficult to meet their monthly expenditure.

HEALTH STATUS OF ELDERLY PEOPLE

In order to achieve and maintain a viable economic and social life, it is important that the elderly maintain a good and healthy life. In the following section we discuss the health status of elderly people in Singapore.

Perception of health status
Perceptions of health are critical to how elderly people feel about life and to how they behave. The National Survey on Senior Citizens reveals that more than two-thirds of the elderly people surveyed perceived themselves to possess good health. People who perceive themselves to have good health tend to be

happier, more satisfied, more involved in social activities, less anxious and less lonely (Verbrugge, 1983). Although the causal relationships among these factors are still unclear, it is not unrealistic to expect life to be much more pleasant for those elderly people who feel healthy than for those who feel unhealthy.

It is very likely that the elderly people in the National Survey on Senior Citizens compared themselves to their own contemporaries, including friends who had died. Hence their health assessments are more positive than if they were to compare their health with that of younger adults or with their own health during younger days. If residents in institutions were included in the survey, the findings of poor health amongst the elderly would no doubt increase. This is because those in institutional care have generally poorer health than those outside it. The study also establishes that the elderly's perception of poor health increases with age. Differences between the sexes in the perception of their health status, however, were not analysed.

Mortality
Standardized death rates of elderly people in Singapore dropped by 30 per cent between 1957 and 1982, suggesting an improvement in the health of the elderly. Between 1974 and 1989 mortality rates for elderly males were higher than for females (Department of Statistics, 1989). This is true for all age categories of 59 years and above. Although large sex differences in health and mortality persist, the reasons for such differences are not fully understood. Various authors have attributed the differences to genetic factors, risks acquired during life, and from attitudinal effects of illness perception and curative behaviour. None the less, it is a fact that men's health risks are higher than women's. Life expectancy figures also reflect a higher risk for elderly males. For example, men who were 60 in 1980 could expect to live for another 9 years compared to 14 years for women. Between 1957 and 1980, the increase in life expectancy was higher for females than for males (Ministry of Health, 1982).

The main causes of death for elderly people in Singapore have not changed much. The trends over the years show heart disease, malignant neoplasms and cerebrovascular disease to be the major causes of death. Death due to senility, which was once the most common reason, has declined significantly as a result of better death certification from qualified personnel. Slight differences exist between the sexes; for example, while there are more males dying of heart disease and tuberculosis, more females die of cerebrovascular disease (Ministry of Health, 1982).

Morbidity
An analysis of hospitalization rates reveals that there is an increasingly high proportion of total admission for the elderly, rising from 12 per cent in 1977 to 14.2 per cent in 1988. The increase in hospitalization rates seems to suggest that the health of elderly people is getting poorer. However, it should be pointed out that this need not necessarily be so. Indeed, it may suggest that elderly people are either more health conscious or that there are more ailments being reported as a result of more and better medical services. There are also suggestions that some doctors may induce admission of their clients even when it is not absolutely necessary.

In the National Survey on Senior Citizens, the hospitalization rate among elderly people was found to increase with age – 6.6 per cent, 9.9 per cent and 11.6 per cent for the 55 to 64, 65 to 74, and above 74 age groups respectively. Longitudinal records from government hospitals further reveal that the number

of admissions among the various age groups of the elderly increased significantly by 168 per cent in 1982 (Ministry of Health, 1982). The above data
clearly points to the vulnerability of the people in the oldest age group who are
more susceptible to illness and poor health.

According to the National Survey of Senior Citizens, the most common
reasons for admission of elderly people to hospital are diseases of the
respiratory system followed by heart disease. This finding closely corresponds
to the statistics on major causes of death, although the ranking order is slightly
different due to possible differences in classification.

Mental health

With regard to mental health, the National Survey on Senior Citizens shows
that 3.7 per cent of elderly respondents exhibited some degree of maladjust-
ment. More elderly females are found to be less well adjusted than males. Only
a small minority (0.2 per cent males and 0.5 per cent females) are reported to
need urgent psychiatric treatment. As with other health indicators, mental
well-being is found to deteriorate slightly with age. Analysis of the mental
health of elderly people by ethnic group reveals that Indians have a higher
mental health risk while Malays appear to be the best adjusted.

Sensory and dental status

In terms of vision and hearing, the results indicate a deterioration of vision and
hearing ability with age. However, it should be noted that a higher proportion
of elderly people indicate that they can 'hear well' (95 per cent) than say they
can 'see well' (68 per cent). This certainly suggests a need to prevent further
deterioration of the eyesight of the elderly. Although differences between sexes
were not analysed in the study, research elsewhere has established that elderly
women may have more vision problems than men (Verbrugge, 1983).

The National Survey on Senior Citizens also establishes that many elderly
people do not have good dental health. About two-thirds of the elderly are
found to be without any teeth or with fewer than 14 teeth. Again, the status of
dental health deteriorates with advancing age. Elderly people of Indian origin
are found to have better dental health than other ethnic groups.

Personal care

An important indicator of health status is the ability of elderly people to attend
to their own personal needs. In Singapore, a majority of elderly people are able
to attend to their personal needs independently; only about 1–2 per cent of
elderly people were found to need help in feeding, bathing and dressing. The
ability of elderly people to attend to their daily needs, however, declines with
advancing age (National Survey on Senior Citizens, 1984).

Mobility

According to the National Survey a very high percentage of the elderly people
in the community (95 per cent) are completely mobile. Only 4.2 per cent
require some form of assistance from time to time. A very small percentage (0.6
per cent) are bedridden; this percentage increases with age from 0.2 per cent
among those below 75 years to 2.1 per cent for those in the 75 and above age
group. In a survey on Homes for the Elderly in Singapore (1985), it was found
that 37 per cent of the elderly in the homes are either semi-ambulant or
non-ambulant.

One can conclude from the above discussion that the health status of the elderly in Singapore is generally good. This gives a sound basis for the encouragement of policies for care in the community.

THE NATIONAL INFRASTRUCTURE FOR POPULATION AGEING

The national infrastructure for dealing with population ageing will be considered in two aspects: policy formulation and programme implementation. Three general features of the infrastructure deserve special mention at the outset. First, population ageing and its implications have been accorded high political emphasis. The ruling political party, the People's Action Party, has explicitly mentioned population ageing as an important issue in its agenda for national discussion. As a result, efforts in policy formulation and programme implementation have benefited from such political patronage. Second, Singapore is a relatively small place and an extensive network of government and non-government organizations are already in place. Thus, it is possible to exploit what is already in existence to create a support infrastructure for the aged. Third, the growing affluence of Singapore makes it possible for the government and society in general to divert resources to programmes and services for elderly people, leading to a rapid expansion of the formal support network.

Policy formulation

In the 1970s, concern for the welfare of the immigrant aged led to the establishment of a number of services catering for the special needs of this group. Such services were formulated by the then Ministry of Social Affairs in conjunction with the Singapore Council of Social Service. Although they attracted much attention, planning efforts were essentially sectoral and services were treated as an extension of the existing social welfare schemes. In the 1980s, the concern broadened as the implications of population ageing were recognized. The fact that the problems and needs of the aged will not disappear with the passage of the group of immigrants, often destitute in old age, led to serious reviews of the issue. In June 1982, the appointment of a high-level 13-member committee marked the beginning of the government's efforts to understand the implications of population ageing and to implement appropriate measures.

The Committee on the Problems of the Aged was chaired by the then Minister for Health. In its deliberations, the Committee took the problems of old age beyond the realm of humanitarian and social welfare concerns. It took note of the long-term impact of population ageing and its ramifications. As a result, the Committee stressed the potential contributions of the elderly to society and the importance of incorporating them in socio-economic development, while concurrently acknowledging and meeting their special needs. They were thus moving away from looking at elderly people solely as a 'problem'. To assist in its deliberations, the Committee commissioned the National Survey on Senior Citizens in 1983, providing updated information from an earlier study conducted in 1976 (Chen, 1982a). The survey report was released in 1983. The National Survey on Senior Citizens was conducted jointly by the then Ministry of Social Affairs, and the Ministry of Health for the Committee on the Problems of the Aged in 1983. The Survey was based on 5 538 persons aged 55 years and above and who were living in private households.

The report of the Committee was finalized and released in March 1984.

Several controversial policy recommendations such as raising the proportion of aged people eligible for provident fund withdrawal, and legislation on filial piety led to much public outcry and discussion. However, the bulk of the Committee's recommendations were accepted. The major ones included the change in provident fund contribution rates for older persons to generate employment for older workers; legislation on minimum standards for homes for the aged; increased aged dependants' relief under the Income Tax Act and measures to foster family and intergenerational cohesion.

To implement the report's recommendations, several committees were established with members drawn from relevant ministries, statutory boards, institutions of higher learning and non-government agencies. The Co-ordination Committee to implement the Report on the Problems of the Aged was set up in August 1985 under the Ministry of Community Development (formerly the Ministry of Social Affairs) to evaluate and oversee the imple-mentation of the report's recommendations. The Committee to Co-ordinate the Development Programmes and Activities was formed in January 1986 by the Ministry of Community Development to promote, direct and supervise the implementation of the report's recommendations with respect to health and recreational needs, social services, and institutional care by government and non-government agencies. The Committee on Public Awareness on Ageing to spearhead a public education and awareness programme was set up by the Ministries of Community Development, Communication and Information to educate the public with a view to projecting a more wholesome image of senior citizens. The Public Awareness Programme on Ageing was launched in November 1987 and a tripartite Task Force on the Employment of the Elderly was established by the Ministry of Labour. The task force comprised em-ployers, and government and union representatives and studied the need to provide counselling for and retraining of older workers.

Recognizing that population ageing is also a demographic matter, in 1984 the government established an Inter-Ministerial Population Committee (IMPC) to undertake a comprehensive review of Singapore's population trends and to make recommendations on policy measures to arrest the declining fertility rate and to bring about the desired population size and composition. Chaired by the Permanent Secretary of the Ministry of Health and reporting to the First Deputy Prime Minister, the members of the IMPC comprised Permanent Secretaries of relevant government ministries. Following the IMPC's recommendations, Sing-apore's population policy was revised in 1987. The Committee, assisted by the Population Planning Unit, continues to monitor population trends in Singa-pore.

In June 1988, the Advisory Council on the Aged, headed by the Minister for Home Affairs, was formed to undertake a comprehensive review of the status of ageing in Singapore. Its terms of reference include, amongst other things, the review of programmes and services now available to aged people; the examina-tion of premises, assumptions and policy recommendations contained in the 1984 Report on the Problems of the Aged; to suggest ways to enable the aged to work beyond the age of 55; and finally to examine how families can be helped to look after their aged dependants.

The Advisory Council appointed four committees to look into the specific issues of concern. The four committees were: a Committee on Community-Based Programmes for the Aged; a Committee on Attitudes Towards the Aged; a Committee on Residential Care Programmes for the Aged, and a Committee on Employment for the Aged. The members of the Advisory Council and the committees included experts from government ministries, statutory boards and voluntary organizations concerned with the provision and planning of services for elderly people.

In September 1988, the reports of the four committees were reviewed by the Council and subsequently submitted for the consideration of the government. One of the key recommendations proposed by the Council was that a National Council on Ageing should be set up, with the character and authority of a statutory board to effectively plan and co-ordinate policies and programmes for elderly people. Other proposals included raising the retirement age from 55 to 60, as continued employment provides a sense of worth, dignity and financial independence for elderly people; adjusting the seniority-based wage system so that more elderly people will be employed; expanding and strengthening public education programmes on the aged and ageing so that the 'right' attitudes towards the aged could be inculcated; making land available for voluntary organizations to set up homes for the aged; lengthening the leases for homes; studying the feasibility of providing health and medical services for frail elderly people living in their own homes; and increasing the dependency tax rebate for families who look after aged people.

A national policy on ageing in Singapore is therefore taking shape after these successive policy reviews. Two characteristics are worth noting in the policy formulation process. First, these committees have the benefit of representation from various sectors. This has the advantage of receiving diverse inputs and making implementable decisions. Historically, cross-sectoral representation has worked well in the local context and it is a standard feature of the Singapore government's problem-solving approach. Secondly, the committees were given much publicity. Public awareness of the issues was heightened, especially when controversial recommendations were made. Enhanced public discussion on policy changes places increasing emphasis on social care for elderly people in Singapore. Public input thus became an important considera-tion in the committees' deliberations.

Programme implementation
The programmes and activities for elderly people are co-ordinated through three principal organizations: the Ministry of Community Development, the Ministry of Health and the Singapore Council of Social Service. The two ministries, in addition to the provision of direct services, provide overall guidance in planning for welfare and health services respectively. The Singa-pore Council of Social Service plays a co-ordinating role among non-government organizations and helps in representing their views to the govern-ment. A total of 26 voluntary and religious organizations affiliated to the Singapore Council of Social Service are currently providing services to elderly people. In addition, other ministries or statutory bodies may also be responsi-ble for certain schemes concerning the elderly, such as the Housing and Development Board. Taken together, the services offered by the government and non-government organizations are comprehensive (Vasoo and Tan, 1985). Basically, provision of social services for elderly people can be categorized into formal and informal care. Formal services for elderly people in Singapore include community-based services and residential care. Informal services are support given by the family or friends of the elderly people. The provision of social services for elderly people is particularly important in view of the rising number of old people in the community, the smaller size of the family and the greater number of women entering the labour force. The routine of the family can be greatly disrupted when an elderly member becomes weak and requires regular attention. In addition, the large number of elderly people (11 044) who

live in one-person households (Census of Population, Release No. 6, Household and Houses, 1980) suggest the vulnerability of this group in times of need and sickness.

Family support services

Traditionally, and to a large extent today, elderly people have been informally cared for by their immediate family or kin members. However, with industrialization and modernization, the capacity to look after elderly people has been reduced. This reduced capacity stems in part from the resettlement programme, in which large extended families living either in the same household or nearby kampongs have been separated and relocated to units in different housing estates. Associated with this is the tendency of young couples to form nuclear families. The breakup of the extended family, together with the tendency to form nuclear families, inevitably leads to a shrinkage in family size which reduces the capacity to support elderly people. The reduced capacity of the family to care for its elderly members is further affected by the increase in number of married women now entering the labour force, particularly the more educated women. Their increased participation in the workforce to improve family income or for self fulfilment has meant a reduction in a traditional source of support for many elderly people during the larger part of the day. With the influence of individualistic and 'Western' values and the general acceptance of these values by the younger generation, the scope for care of some elderly people is expected to be further eroded (see also Chapters 4 and 5 for a discussion of this issue).

Neighbours and friends have also been known to be important sources of informal care for certain elderly people. However, this source of care givers seems to be diminishing as Singapore modernizes and as people are resettled into new housing estates. Not only have some elderly people been separated from old and familiar neighbours, they may also have an uphill task making new friends in the new environment.

Community-based services

Ambulant old people constitute the majority of the elderly population in Singapore, so community-based services play an important role in enabling them to function adequately in their own homes and communities. This overriding principle has been adopted in both the 1982 and 1988 reviews of services for the elderly. In response to the probable inability of the family to provide for elderly people, and the need for community care for them, various community-based services are gradually springing up to help elderly people remain independent in the community. Currently the types of community based services available include:

- *Home nursing services*, in which frail and infirm elderly people are provided with basic nursing care within their own homes. Many of the requests for nursing care arise from recently discharged hospital patients and as referrals from outpatient clinics or general practitioners.
- *Befriending service*. As the name suggests the befriending service involves mobilizing volunteers to befriend elderly people in their own homes as well as in institutional homes. Some of these volunteers, however, go further and assist elderly people with household chores and cleaning. There are presently 41 constituencies with a befriender's service managed by the Ministry of Community Development in conjunction with grassroots organizations. In addition to government initiatives, a number of voluntary

welfare organizations are also involved in befriending elderly people.

- *Senior citizens' or retirees' clubs.* In order to meet the needs of the increasing number of elderly people both now and in the future, the People's Association, Residents' Committee; Citizens' Consultative Committee and voluntary organizations have recently established about 166 senior citizens' clubs with a membership of 47 600 elderly people. Most of the activities organized by these clubs are social, educational and recreational in character. The People's Association also provides employment services to retirees who wish to be re-employed through its retirees' club.
- *Day-care centres.* Establishing a day-care centre is one important way to help elderly people remain independent in the community. At present, there are four such centres which provide physiotherapy and/or basic nursing treatment. These centres are instrumental in maintaining and improving the mobility functions of certain elderly people. There are two other day-care centres which are oriented towards social and recreational activities.
- *Meal services.* There are about three voluntary agencies providing meal services to elderly people. In this service, meals at low prices are either provided for elderly people from low-income families in the premises of an agency or delivered to their residence.

With the exception of the home nursing service, most of the other community-based services have yet to be fully developed. For example, the significant increase in the number of senior citizens' clubs has resulted in some teething problems for the clubs in attracting members as well as organizing appropriate programmes for them. As with the senior citizens' clubs, the befriender's service run by the government has a short history. The provision of low-priced meals in the agencies' premises appears to be quite successful as it is patronized by many elderly people. The meal delivery scheme, however, is still trying to establish its clientele and resolve manpower problems. Nonetheless, it is envisaged that with the expected rise in the number of elderly people in the future, the meal delivery scheme may become an important service. This scheme could perhaps best be undertaken by Homes for the Elderly which have the infrastructure to provide and deliver meals to isolated elderly people living in neighbouring housing estates.

As for the day-care centres, there are currently very few with therapeutic functions; it is not generally convenient for elderly people who live far away from these centres to utilize their services. However, as there is a general agreement among policy makers and academics that elderly people should remain as long as possible in the community, more therapeutic day-care centres should be set up in public housing estates. This is necessary to make the service more accessible to the elderly people who are mainly housed in these estates. A plan by the Home Nursing Foundation to establish ten community health centres in public housing estates to provide direct therapeutic, rehabilitative, medical and educational programmes is certainly a positive step to support the independence of old people.

While existing services should be developed further, other forms of services for elderly people should also be explored and possibly introduced in Singapore to provide a broad-based service. Several of these services which merit consideration include:

- A telephone contact service which could be set up to get in touch with old people who are living very much on their own. This service would help to ensure that these elderly people are safe while they are on their own.

- Home-help service to assist with household and domestic chores. Volunteers or paid staff could help those elderly people who need such a service.
- A neighbourhood mobilization scheme in which neighbours who are not working could be approached to lend a helping hand with those elderly people who require assistance during the larger part of the day when their children are at work.
- Pre-retirement courses, which although they have been conducted by the People's Association and by certain companies, are mostly carried out on an ad hoc basis or are based on the interest of a few companies. There is no single body to co-ordinate pre-retirement courses to benefit a broader spectrum of people who are approaching retirement age.
- Health Centres, which once set up would screen the health of elderly people, educate them on health matters and identify risk factors so that early prevention against ill-health can be taken.
- Support for family care-givers because as family members are expected to play an important role in providing care for sick and disabled elderly people it would be useful to initiate a self-help group for them. This self-help group could be a source of encouragement in giving support and advice to families who are faced for the first time with having to care for sick or disabled elderly people.

Residential care
In addition to the community-based services, formal services for elderly people are also provided by various Homes for the Elderly. Admission into a long-term institutional care facility is generally discouraged unless the elderly person, for reasons of physical and/or mental infirmities, cannot be cared for at home. At present, homes for the aged cater primarily for the destitute aged. As of 31 December 1989, there were 70 institutions providing a total of 5 040 beds. Three government-run homes provided a total of 1 525 beds for the destitute aged. The non-government homes, of which 43 were voluntary and 24 were commercial homes, had a capacity of 3 515 beds. There were 1 390 residents in the government homes and 2 788 in non-government homes at the end of 1989.

The aged home was initially established to house destitute elderly migrants in need of assistance and to provide help with meals, housekeeping and other self-maintenance functions. The home normally accommodates more than 80 elderly people in large dormitories and they are usually situated in isolated areas far away from the activities of community life. To meet the changing needs of the elderly population, aged homes managed by voluntary welfare organizations have gradually been opened to a small number of ambulant elderly people who for various reasons are not staying with their own family members.

A close relative of the aged home is the nursing home. In addition to incorporating the general functions of the aged home, nursing homes provide various levels of medical and nursing care to their residents who have health problems. Unlike the aged homes, nursing homes have special provision for admitting semi-ambulant and non-ambulant elderly.

Sheltered care in the form of community homes provides elderly people with the basic necessities of life such as shelter and a sense of security. Unlike the institutional home, the community home provides a certain amount of freedom for elderly people to look after themselves. The home is intentionally located in a public housing estate to allow elderly people in these homes to mingle with the residents in the community. Another form of sheltered care is the temple home which is generally situated away from the mainstream of society. In contrast to community homes, in which residents are encouraged to be involved in the activities of the community, the activities of the residents in temple homes are mainly confined within the home itself. Commercial homes are distinguished from the other types of home by their profit-making motive. The size of commercial homes varies from as few as 20 to over 100 bedspaces. Most commercial homes provide nursing care for their elderly residents.

In a study of 45 homes for the elderly in Singapore (Singapore Council of Social Service, 1985), it was found that 70 per cent of residents were 70 years and above, and 37 per cent were semi-ambulant or non-ambulant. As most of the homes admit mainly ambulant clients, the findings certainly suggest the need for the homes as a whole to prepare for changes so as to meet an expected increase in the number of infirm and sick elderly. Without such preparation, many elderly residents will have to be transferred to other homes with nursing care facilities when they become ill and less mobile. To encourage the transfer of infirm elderly people to other homes with medical facilities and care is probably an unwise option as it may dislocate the social and psychological bearing of such elderly people.

The Council's study also revealed that there was a waiting list of some 287 for the homes. Of these, 58 per cent were waiting to be admitted to homes which provided some form of nursing care. This finding clearly suggests that the demand for care of infirm and weak elderly people will be high. However the demand for care of healthy elderly people is small and insignificant. In view of the expected lack of demand for care of the healthy elderly, aged homes should perhaps consider changing their admission policies to include the semi-ambulant and non-ambulant elderly people as well as incorporating nursing programmes. Alternatively, the aged homes should plan for a change in direction of services, perhaps providing supportive services such as day care and community-based programmes to meet the needs of elderly people in the community. In developing such supportive services, the aged homes would also provide a link between the home and elderly people in the community.

One pertinent question is: will the homes for the elderly be able to cope with the demand for bedspaces? The answer is 'yes'. By looking at the current vacancies (774) and the number of bedspaces planned for the next 5 years (467), it appears probable that demand will be met. Any additional plans to build new homes in the next 5 years should therefore be carefully considered. By building more new homes, unnecessary bedspaces will be generated as a result of an excess supply (Singapore Council of Social Service, 1985). There is therefore also a need to monitor the number of bedspaces and vacancies and the waiting lists in the homes to prevent a situation whereby supply exceeds demand.

One interesting observation about the homes for the elderly is that most of the homes which are managed by voluntary organizations mainly admit the poorer section of the community, while commercial homes mostly admit from the middle and higher income groups. The lower-middle income group hence becomes sandwiched as not rich enough to afford entry into commercial homes nor poor enough to qualify for homes operated by voluntary organizations. Homes should perhaps review their services and provide some openings to serve the often neglected lower-middle income group.

In addition, hardly any homes provide short-term convalescent services to those elderly people who are either recuperating from illness or recovering from disability. Such a service is needed for those elderly people who have working children who, for various reasons, are not able to look after their ailing parents. It is our contention that a short-term convalescent service will be not only of help to ailing elderly people recovering from their illnesses, but it will also cushion the stress that may arise if the working children were to look after elderly people at the critical stage of recuperation.

To ensure that there is a good standard of care in the increasing number of homes for the elderly, the Singapore Council of Social Service and the government have drawn up guidelines on minimum standards of care for these homes (see also Chapter 4). This move is a positive step in protecting the interests of the elderly residents of the homes, as well as ensuring that the homes provide a better service to their clients.

Financial support services
A public assistance scheme under the Ministry of Community Development provides monthly allowances ranging from $140 for single-person households to $400 for four-person households. At present, about 2 833 persons aged 60 and above are receiving direct financial assistance. In addition, voluntary organizations also render assistance in cash and in kind to financially distressed elderly people. Churches, temples, charitable foundations and various community-service groups provide ad hoc aid such as Hong Bao and food to needy elderly people during the festive seasons. However, the various financial schemes lack co-ordination to ensure efficient and effective distribution of financial resources.

Old-age financial security for Singaporeans is provided principally through the CPF scheme, whereby monthly contributions are made by both employees and employers. At present, the rate of contribution is 17.5 per cent for employers and 22.5 per cent for employees. The scheme is run by a statutory board and guaranteed by the government. Contributors can also draw on the fund for approved purposes, such as the purchase of property, payment of medical expenses and other investment ventures. The principal sum plus interest can be withdrawn at the age of 55, except for a sum of $30 000 which can only be withdrawn after the age of 60. This is to provide an added protection for financial well-being in old age against the squandering of savings. Part of the CPF is channelled into a Medisave account which can only be drawn on for medical expenses. At present, the cap for the Medisave account is set at $15 000.

FAMILY SUPPORT AND SOCIAL SUPPORT

In Singapore, with only 2 per cent of elderly people living in institutions, the family's role in ensuring the well-being of the elderly is of paramount importance. In a rapidly changing society such as Singapore, the family is also subjected to numerous competing demands that might affect its capability and willingness in the provision of care. In this section of the chapter, the present and future trends in living arrangements and family support are reviewed and assessed (Chen and Cheung, 1988).

Living arrangements
The National Survey on Senior Citizens (1983) showed that about 5 per cent of non-institutionalized elderly people lived alone, with the remainder living in households mainly with immediate relatives. The finding was reaffirmed in a 1986 survey noting that elderly people tended to live with immediate family members. This Survey on the Aged Living in the Community was conducted by the Ministry of Health in 1986. The survey was based on 1 013 persons aged 60 and over who were living in private households. The same survey also showed that the elderly enjoyed reasonably good accommodation with 98 per cent

living in satisfactory living conditions in terms of sleeping arrangements, accessibility to facilities and cleanliness. It was also found that home ownership was high and two-thirds of elderly people lived in households with a monthly income exceeding $1 000.

Questions were asked in both surveys about preferred living arrangements. It was found that there was a distinct and overwhelming preference among elderly people to live with their children, in particular their married children. The choice of co-residence appears to be culturally influenced: the Chinese and Indians preferred to live with their married sons, while the Malays preferred to live with their married daughters. The surveys also found an overwhelming reluctance amongst elderly people to stay in old folks' homes, as was expected.

Family support
Findings from a number of studies have shown that most elderly people with immediate relatives (spouse, children and grandchildren) would have few problems in obtaining support in times of need (Chen, 1982a; Cheung, 1988c). They were also found to be engaged in meaningful interactions with the children they lived with and maintained frequent contacts with children who were living apart. The respondents were also confident that they could rely on their family for help when they were ill or when they had other problems. Table 6.4 shows the profile of care givers who tended to the elderly who were ill or who needed care. The prominence of family members as the care givers is clearly shown.

This pattern is really not surprising as the family has always been the primary care giver for its aged members. No evidence has been found in Singapore to suggest that the family, as an institution, is shirking its responsibilities. However, several changes could restrict the effectiveness of the familiy as the primary source of care in the future. First, the increasing involvement of married women in the labour force could reduce the availability of care givers within the family. In 1980, the labour-force participation rate of married women in the 30 to 40 age group was 33 per cent. This increased to 46 per cent in 1988 and, with the shrinking of family size, there are thus likely to be fewer people to share in the responsibility of care. In the 1960s, a woman tended to have about 6 children in her life time. This had fallen to about 4 children in the 1970s and to about 2.5 in the 1980s. There is also concern that the younger generation may not be as filial towards their ageing parents. The decline in family size, coupled with increasing external commitments and possible value changes of the family members, could erode the capability of the family to cope with the care of an aged, and particularly a sick, relative. These changes suggest that the formal support system may have an increasingly important role to play in the future.

To encourage the family to care for its elderly members to the fullest possible extent, the Singapore government has introduced measures which include intergenerational co-residence, income tax relief, a moral education programme, community-based services and legislation.

In the intergenerational co-residence scheme, married children and their parents are allowed to apply for adjoining Housing and Development Board flats. Their applications will also be given priority in allocation. As a financial incentive, a person who is caring for an elderly dependant may be given $3 500 income tax relief from Year of Assessment 1991, provided that the latter is not earning more than $1 500 a year. Moreover, children can claim tax relief of up to $6 000 a year for the equivalent sum of money they have contributed to their parents' CPF account.

Table 6.4 Care providers for the elderly when ill or needing care, by sex, age and marital status.

Care provider	Sex		Age group				Marital status			Total
	Male	Female	60 to 69	70 to 79	80 and above		Widowed	Married		
Self	11.0	15.1	14.0	12.9	8.3		15.7	10.1		13.2
Spouse	47.9	9.2	32.5	22.8	6.4		0.2	47.9		27.3
Son/daughter-in-law	16.9	38.8	23.6	33.9	43.9		43.9	18.6		28.6
Daughter/son-in-law	8.3	19.6	13.2	15.8	15.9		21.6	9.0		14.3
Grandchildren	0.5	3.4	0.4	2.2	14.0		4.4	0.5		2.1
Others	2.3	3.2	2.9	2.4	3.8		2.7	1.7		2.7
No need	13.1	10.7	13.5	10.0	7.6		11.5	12.1		11.8

Source: Survey on the Aged Living in the Community (1986).

Using the moral education programme, the government has initiated changes in the school curriculum to strengthen traditional family values and inculcate filial piety and respect for elderly people. An annual senior citizens' week is being organized to promote the contributions and status of elderly people. A family-life education programme has also been implemented to promote harmonious family living. In support terms, in order to help reduce the burden of care on the family, services such as home visiting, day care and respite care are being offered. The government has also launched various initiatives to promote as much community involvement in these services as possible. Two objectives are emphasized. First, elderly people should be kept fit and healthy, capable of full participation in the mainstream of community life. Second, aged sick people are to be provided with supportive services which will enable them to live with their families for as long as possible.

The Committee on the Problems of the Aged recommended that laws be passed to impose on children the obligation to care for their elderly parents. No legislation has yet been instituted and the Advisory Council on the Aged has subsequently advised against it. However, the government is prepared, if necessary, to institute legal protection for the welfare of elderly people if families appear, in the future, to be abrogating their responsibilities.

Are these measures likely to be effective in fostering greater family support? These measures reflect to a large extent a cultural emphasis on the importance of the family and they are therefore consistent with general sentiments. However, these are essentially passive measures designed to maintain rather than to foster family ties. The moral education programme is therefore special as it takes a proactive role to inculcate specific filial attitudes. Whether such intervention can help to stem the influence of 'Westernization' remains to be seen. However, education of this nature may help prepare the young to accept the challenge of caring for their aged parents.

COMMUNITY PARTICIPATION AND INVOLVEMENT

A major planning principle put forward by the Committee on the Problems of the Aged is the recognition of the potential contribution of elderly people to society and to their own welfare. This principle came through clearly in the committee's report and was again endorsed by the Advisory Council on the Aged. If in the future Singapore is to have a quarter of its population aged 60 and over, it is clear that this vast human resource must be tapped if Singapore is to maintain its economic prosperity. Harnessing the contributions of the elderly population is, however, easier said than done. Age-old prejudices often cast elderly people in a poor light and the emphasis is mainly placed on their problems rather than their potential contributions. The developmental emphasis of the government's approach is therefore encouraging. Recognizing that contribution is possible only through participation, the two national planning committees have given prominent attention to three aspects of participation: health maintenance, community activities and gainful employment. Each of these will be discussed in turn.

Health maintenance
Health is often the critical factor in a person's adjustment in old age. While old age is not necessarily a time of ill health and disability, a variety of chronic illnesses do occur more frequently among elderly rather than younger people. In Singapore, the large majority of elderly people enjoy reasonably good health and lead independent lives. However, they are also disproportionately large

consumers of medical care. In 1986, elderly people accounted for 18 per cent of all admissions into government hospitals, while forming only 8 per cent of the population. In absolute numbers, the admission statistics showed an impressive rise of 79 per cent from 23 000 in 1977 to 40 000 in 1986. It is projected that, by the end of the century, their admissions will increase to at least 30 per cent of total admissions. To reduce the level of morbidity among elderly people, the role of primary health care has been emphasized. Three aspects, namely health education, health screening and self-help groups, have been promoted thus far.

It is felt that an elderly person must take the first step towards good health through a healthy life style and a balanced diet. In this regard, the Training and Health Education Department of the Ministry of Health has conducted regular health education classes for elderly people. These are often conducted in public housing estates and public libraries to ensure easy accessibility. The Singapore Sports Council has also assisted in planning physical education for elderly people and the Council has so far trained a number of trainers to conduct exercises for this group. These are held at venues of easy access.

Secondly, health screening is provided for elderly people through a network of screening centres. Early detection often ensures speedy recovery. Currently, there are 38 regular health screening centres located across the island. In addition, there is a network of general practitioners providing outpatient care and general medical advice.

Thirdly, encouragement is given to the formation of self-help or support groups constituted either by type of ailment or by locality. Such groups are commonly found in day-care centres, especially those with rehabilitative activities. In the future, the establishment of community hospitals, which are intermediate-level care facilities with community involvement, will further help foster the formation of these groups. The first community hospital to be built in a public housing estate is expected to be completed by 1991.

Community activities
Participation in community activities is arguably an indication of an elderly person's integration into society, beyond the confines of the family. Greater involvement in the community, especially in age-integrated activities, also signifies a respectable status being accorded to elderly people. Conversely, social isolation of elderly people may reflect a poor image of the elderly as a group among the younger generation.

Community participation of elderly people can be grouped into two types: age segregated or age integrated. The former is far more visible in Singapore. With the encouragement of the government, the proliferation of senior citizens' clubs has been rapid. These clubs offer recreational programmes, health screening, keep-fit activities and opportunities for community services. As the name implies, these clubs are open only to senior citizens. At present, there are 166 such clubs with a membership of about 47 600, run mostly by government or paragovernment organizations. Among the few non-government-run clubs, the Singapore Action Group of Elders (SAGE) is the largest, with a membership of about 1 500.

Such age-segregated clubs meet certain needs of the elderly population. They provide a contact point for meeting and making friends and a forum for the exchange of opinions and experiences. Unfortunately, they also segregate elderly people from the other age groups. The establishment of a network of senior citizens' clubs may therefore heighten awareness of the elderly as a distinct social group. Thus far, these clubs are not linked to form a larger organizational base. The National Council of Ageing, proposed by the Advisory

Council on the Aged, could conceivably provide the linkage to these clubs, effectively organizing them into a potentially potent self-interest group.

To what extent are elderly people involved in age-integrated activities? This is difficult to assess, as empirical evidence is scarce. In a 1987 survey (The Transition of the Support Systems for the Aged in Singapore, 1987) on the support systems of elderly people, sponsored by the United Nations University, it was found that the most common avenue of participation was through religious activities. Apart from these, the study found that the higher the educational attainment, the greater the involvement in formal organizations. By and large, however, such involvements were not extensive, suggesting very strongly that avenues have to be developed for elderly people to be more involved in age-integrated activities. Reasons cited for non-involvement included being too busy with household chores, lack of interest, and lack of opportunities.

The potential for elderly people to participate in community services in Singapore has yet to be realized. This group clearly possesses varied experience and talents that could be tapped by the community for specific projects. At present, elderly persons are involved largely in ad hoc community activities. More people could be encouraged to join in community services such as child care, home nursing, crime prevention, befriending, teaching and home help. The Volunteers Development Programme of the Singapore Council of Social Service is currently exploring the recruitment of elderly volunteers.

Economic participation
The government has emphasized that elderly people should be encouraged to work for as long as possible in order to maintain mental alertness and financial independence. Moreover, in labour-short Singapore, the elderly constitute an important source of labour supply. However, as noted earlier, there has been a gradual decline in their labour-force participation rates over the past 5 years. The Advisory Council on the Aged, in its deliberations, was aware of the urgent need to promote greater economic participation of elderly people and arrived at four broad recommendations: raising the retirement age; changing the wage system; increasing employment opportunities; and training and retraining.

The Council was of the view that the customary retirement age of 55 should be raised to 60. This increase should be done through negotiations between employers and employees, taking into consideration the special needs and circumstances of each economy or job. However, the government has since indicated that such negotiations may be too slow to bring about changes in retirement age. In spite of the government's urging, only 65 per cent of unionized companies and 25 per cent of non-unionized companies in the private sector had changed their retirement age in 1990. The employers were apparently concerned with the unsuitable nature of the work, the high cost and lower productivity of employing older workers. In a survey on retirement policy conducted by the Labour Relations Department of the Ministry of Labour in 1988, it was found that 47 per cent of the companies with a retirement age below 60 reported that it was impractical to revise their retirement age. The survey was based on 711 unionized companies and 36 unions; among them, 56 per cent gave the reason of unsuitable work and about a third each indicated high cost, lower productivity and less feasibility in employment as reasons. The Ministry of Labour, therefore, announced in March 1989 that the retirement age will be raised to 60 by 1992. The 3-year period of grace is to allow companies to make necessary adjustments.

The Council also noted that wages in Singapore are largely based on seniority. Consequently, the wage bill for an older worker is far greater than for a new entrant, even if they are employed in the same job. As an inducement to encourage employers to retain older workers, the government has reduced the rate of provident fund contributions for older workers. To further facilitate the expansion of employment opportunities, the Council advocated fundamental adjustments in the wage system, taking into account considerations such as the salary being tied to the worth of a job, salary scales being shortened, costly fringe benefits tied to seniority being reduced and staff being rewarded through one-off bonuses rather than through basic wage increments. To increase the employment opportunities, the concil urged employers to allow greater options such as part-time work, flexi-time work, working at home or working on alternate days. The Ministry of Labour's Employment Service Department will provide special assistance to older workers in job placements.

The Council recognized that one obstacle in continued employment for older workers is that their skills might be inadequate or outdated. It urged the Skill Development Fund, a statutory body financing skill training, to develop special schemes for older workers and to provide special subsidies to employers to retrain their older workers. It is foreseeable that, in the future, training programmes for older workers will be developed by various local training institutes.

Will these measures taken together halt the decline of the labour-force participation rate of elderly people? The answer to this question is contingent on a number of factors. First, it is clearly essential that these measures are fully implemented. While the government can take steps to encourage the employment of older workers, employers themselves must see the advantages of hiring them. Reluctance on the part of the employers will not help generate work opportunities. Secondly, the attitudes of the older workers may be changing such that leisure is increasingly valued over continued employment. If this is the case, then Singapore may follow the example of many developed countries in which the participation rates of older workers drop steadily, regardless of employment opportunities.

REGIONAL AND INTERNATIONAL CO-OPERATION

As a member state of the United Nations, Singapore has benefited from the regional and international seminars and workshops on ageing organized by ESCAP, CSDHA and UNO. Links with the Ageing Units of the CSDHA and the Institute of the Ageing in Malta have also been established. Singapore is also one of the participating countries in a cross-national research project on support systems for elderly people co-ordinated by the United Nations University.

As noted in Chapter 2, from 1984 to 1988, a major collaborative ageing project at the regional level was launched as a component project of the phase III ASEAN population programme. The project, 'Socio-economic Consequences of the Ageing of the Population', was funded by the Australian government under the ASEAN Australian Economic Co-operation Programme and co-ordinated by Singapore. The major activities undertaken in Singapore during the project years included the conduct of three surveys on the elderly living under different environmental settings, an update on population projections, and a review of the current services available for aged people. The three surveys conducted by the Ministry of Health were the Survey on the Aged Living in the Community (1986), the Survey on the Health Care Needs of the Elderly Sick Living in Their Own Homes (1986) and the Survey on the Aged and Aged Sick Living in Institutions (1986). A national seminar was also convened to disseminate the project's findings to the public, policy makers and planners.

Certain other cross-national research activities are referred to in Chapter 2. Such activities in Singapore include participation in workshops conducted by the National Academy of Sciences of the United States and other professional bodies, and involvement in the major four-country comparative study on social change and ageing, launched in 1989 and funded by the National Institute of Ageing of the United States and co-ordinated by the University of Michigan. A number of international seminars have also been held in Singapore. These include the Seminar on Research on Ageing in Asia and the Pacific in 1987, and the Workshop on the Transition of Support Systems for the Elderly in 1988.

The Singapore Council of Social Service has regular exchanges with major international voluntary organizations on issues related to ageing. These organizations include the International Council of Social Welfare, HelpAge International and Age Concern. It is also affiliated to the International Federation of Ageing. Similarly, the Home Nursing Foundation and other social service agencies maintain contact with their counterparts in other countries.

CONCLUSION

This study has briefly described Singapore's experience in planning for an ageing society. As a country, Singapore has taken clear steps in meeting the challenges arising from the dramatic increase in the number and proportion of elderly people in the population. Given the current set of demographic characteristics of elderly people, specific areas of their economic and social life have been examined. The staggering fact that there will be an increase in Singapore's elderly population from 4 per cent in 1957 to 25 per cent in 2030 implies that there will be a shift in the pattern of consumption of goods and services among the population. This might well have serious implications for businesses and entrepreneurs.

The emerging national policy on ageing unequivocally emphasizes both humanitarian and developmental concerns. In considering humanitarian concerns, the needs of elderly people are to be met largely by the family with support from the state. The family, however, is expected to remain as the cornerstone of the support network for elderly people. Generally, the elderly are well supported. This shows that the sense of filial piety and family obligation among adults is still strong in Singapore. The government has an important role to play in encouraging and fostering strong ties among intergenerational families through its implementation of appropriate social policies. With respect to developmental implications, elderly people themselves are encouraged to be as fully involved and participative in the community as possible. Economic participation will be assisted through a variety of initiatives. Participation in community and health activities, already widespread, is vigorously promoted. In addition there is scope for the expansion of current services to meet the needs of those elderly people who are isolated from the mainstream of societal life, who require short-term convalescence, who are at high risk of episodes of severe illness and who are often enduring chronic illness and disabilities.

A large number of elderly people are currently left untapped by employers; only 22 per cent of elderly people are in the labour force. If this trend continues, there is a likelihood that issues relating to employment will become contentious. In particular, there will be a need to examine ways of inducing employers to employ and retain older workers. The finding that elderly people in Singapore want to be independent also points to the importance of addressing the future employment needs of the elderly as a group. One issue which will be critical in maintaining the independence of elderly people is the contribution made to the CPF. With the changes in the CPF, there is a need to review how it will affect the future social security of elderly people.

In terms of health status, this chapter shows that elderly people in Singapore are generally in good health. However, in anticipation of a drastic increase in the number of elderly people in the future, one would expect an increased need for preventive and curative medical programmes. This would also mean that there would be an expected increase in the future health expenditure.

What Singapore has done should greatly prepare her to face the uncertainties of an ageing society. What remains uncertain however, is whether elderly people themselves will take their future into their own hands and remain as productive and participative as possible. With at least one-fifth of her population projected to be aged 60 and above by the next century, Singapore's future is inexorably tied to the character and predisposition of her elderly population.

REFERENCES

Binstock, R.H., Chow, W.S. and Schulz, J.H. (1982). *International Perspectives on Ageing: Population and Policy Challenges*. New York: United Nations Fund for Population Activities.

Chen, A.J. and Cheung, P. (1988). *The Elderly in Singapore*. Phase III ASEAN Population Project, Socioeconomic Consequences of the Ageing of the Population, Singapore Country Report.

Chen, P.S.J. (1982a). *The Elderly in Singapore*. Unpublished survey report, Ministry of Health.

Chen, P.S.J. (1982b). *Survey of Sociological Study in Singapore Society*. A project sponsored by the Faculty of Arts and Social Sciences, National University of Singapore.

Cheung, P. (1988a). *Household and Population Projections, 1990 to 2030*. Singapore: Ministry of Health, Population Planning Unit.

Cheung, P. (1988b). *Population Trends: The Ageing of Singapore*. Singapore: Ministry of Health, Population Planning Unit.

Cheung, P. (1988c). *The Transition of the Social Support Systems for the Aged in Singapore: Emerging Patterns and Policy Options*. Report presented at the Second International Workshop on the Social Support Systems in Transition, Singapore.

Cheung, P. (1989). Beyond Demographic Transition: Industrialization and Population Change in Singapore. *Asia–Pacific Population Journal*, **4**, 35–38.

Department of Statistics, Singapore (1980). *Census of Population 1980: Administrative Report*.

Department of Statistics, Singapore (1980). *Census of Population Release No 6. Household and Houses, 1980*.

Department of Statistics, Singapore (1989). *Yearbook of Statistics*.

Ministry of Communications and Information (1990). *Singapore 1990*, Singapore.

Ministry of Community Development, Singapore (1989). *Annual Report*.

Ministry of Health, Singapore (1982). *R and E Monitor and Morbidity among Elderly in Singapore*.

Ministry of Health, Singapore (1984). *Report of the Committee on the Problems of the Aged*.

Ministry of Labour (1984a). *Report on the Labour Force Survey of Singapore*, Research and Statistics Department, Ministry of Labour, Singapore.

Ministry of labour (1984b). *Singapore Yearbook of Labour Statistics*, Research and Statistics Department, Ministry of Labour, Singapore.

Ministry of Social Affairs, Singapore (1983). *Report on the National Survey on Senior Citizens.*

National University of Singapore (1987). *The Transition of the Support Systems for the Aged in Singapore: Emerging patterns and policy options.*

Research and Statistics Department (1984). *Report on the Labour Force Survey of Singapore.* Ministry of Labour, Singapore.

Research and Statistics Department (1984). *Singapore Yearbook of Labour Statistics.* Ministry of Labour, Singapore.

Singapore Council of Social Service (1984). *Social Policy and the Elderly in Singapore*, Report of the Study Group on the Elderly, Singapore.

Singapore Council of Social Service (1985). *A Survey on Homes for the Elderly in Singapore.*

Vasoo, S. and Tan, B.H. (1985). *The Status of Ageing in Singapore.* Unpublished manuscript, Singapore Council of Social Service.

Verbrugge, L.M. (1983). Women and men: mortality and health of older people. In *Ageing in Society: Selected reviews of recent research*, M.W. Riley, B.B. Hess and K. Bond (Eds). Lawrence Erlbaum Associates, New Jersey.

You, P.S. and Lim, C.Y. (Eds.) (1984). *Singapore: Twenty-Five Years of Development.* Nan Yang Xing Zhou Lianhe Zaobao, Singapore.

Paul Kwong

Department of Sociology
The Chinese University of Hong Kong

Cai Guoxuan

Department of Social Problem Research
Guangzhou (Canton) Academy of Social Sciences

7 AGEING IN CHINA: TRENDS, PROBLEMS AND STRATEGIES

INTRODUCTION

The concern over China's ageing problems is in part a by-product of her success in bringing down fertility levels since the early 1970s. There is a debate, in and out of China, about the future direction of China's population policy. Opponents to the official 'one-child' policy cite the high speed of population ageing as a reason to go slow with fertility control. Supporters of the policy, however, point out that 'the future' will be a distant one, and that China must rapidly develop her economy so that it will be able to afford the high cost of solving the ageing problem. The speed of population ageing versus the speed of economic development are now the two key variables in the population debate.

The future course and speed of China's economic development (Di and Li, 1990) will not be emphasized in this chapter, as it is covered in journals such as Renkou Yanjiu and Renkou yu Jingji. Rather, the focus is on the demographic indicators of population ageing and especially on many related social issues. A description of the type of organization of social services for elderly people in China will be followed by a discussion of social attitudes and policies. Compared to all the writings on China's fertility and population control there are only a few monographs on her ageing problems (Davis-Friedmann, 1985; Parish and Whyte, 1978; Whyte and Parish, 1983; Tian, 1988; PISAP, 1988; CASS, 1988).

POPULATION CHANGE: A SUMMARY

Overall population size
The 8 years following 1950 were the formative years of the People's Republic of China. Her population increased by almost 100 million during that period, from 552 million in 1950 to 647 million 1957. The next 4 years saw the disastrous Great Leap Forward Movement which ended with a net loss of a million people, 660 million in 1958 to 659 million in 1961. Population growth resumed in force after 1962 and in the next 10 years annual growth rates were very high and fluctuated between 2.5 per cent to 3.3 per cent per year. As a result, China's population stood at 872 million in 1972, as compared to 692 million in 1963. Much of this enormous increase of 180 million people is attributed to the 'catching-up' growth of the population after the Great Leap, and to the breakdown of official control during the Cultural Revolution in the late 1960s and early 1970s.

The family planning programme
A significant change in China's growth rates came in 1973 when, for the first

time with the exception of 1958–1961, her crude birth rate fell below 3 per cent. The previous year marked the start of China's drive to bring down her fertility rate through a rigorous family planning programme. At this beginning stage, the family planning slogan was 'wan (later marriage), xi (longer child spacing), and shao (fewer births)'. Before 1972 population control was a taboo topic in academic circles because Chairman Mao Zedong was alleged to oppose family planning in China. After 1972, the State Family Planning Commission was established which co-ordinated the Ministries of Health (health personnel devoted to family planning), Commerce (supplies of contraceptives), Education (propaganda), and Public Security (registration of people) in a concerted effort to persuade the broad masses to accept the family planning policy.

Speed of growth
The results after a decade of hard work have been spectacular. By the early 1980s China's population growth had been brought under control and her total fertility rate had declined from 2.6 to 2.2 children. This level was significantly smaller than the 6.0 to 6.4 of the 1950s and the 1960s. The proportion of children under fifteen years of age declined from 41 per cent in 1964 to 30 per cent in 1985 (Zhongguo shehui tongji ziliao [Data on Social Statistics of China], 1990). During the same period, the crude birth rate fell from a peak of 3.34 per cent to 1.78 per cent, and the natural rate of increase fell from 2.58 per cent to 1.12 per cent. It took 5 years to increase China's population from 705 million in 1964 to 807 million, and another 5 years to 906 million by 1974. At that speed, the 1 000 million mark would have come at about 1979, but it actually came in 1981–82 (China, State Statistical Bureau, 1990). Though somewhat slower than before, the rate of expansion of 100 million people per decade still exerted a very heavy burden on China.

Population projections
Table 7.1 presents three of the many population projections made by Chinese demographers during the mid-1980s when strict fertility control was still feasible. Projection 1 assumes that the Total Fertility Rate (TFR) will decline from 2.6 in 1982 to the 'replacement level' of 2.1 in the year 2000. It was assumed that after the year 2000 it will be held constant at that level. In this case, China's population would continue to grow beyond 2050 when it would reach 1 547 million. Projections 2 and 3 assume that the TFR will drop below the replacement level to 1.8 in the 1990s. Projection 2 assumes that TFR will slowly rebound to 2.1 by 2010, and Projection 3 this by 2025.

In the light of the 1990 census figures, all three projections proved to be over-optimistic. Almost all official projections underestimated the population in 1990 by about 10 million or more. It is therefore necessary that new sets of projections be prepared by the authorities when details of the census age distribution and the fertility patterns become available. Since the release of the 1990 census data, debates on the future fertility policy of China no longer centre around the official population target of 1 200 million people by the year 2000. Most projections now start at 1 300 instead (Kwong, 1991). According to the 1982 census, the population aged 60 and over was 76 640 000, accounting for 7.6 per cent of the total population. By year 2000, this group will increase to about 10 per cent of the population (Table 7.1).

In terms of the longevity of the population, male life expectancy is projected to rise from 66.4 years in 1982 to 69.1 years in the year 2000, whereas for females it will be from 69.4 to 72.7 (Table 7.2). Decline of mortality and fertility will have a joint effect on the speed of population ageing in China. By the year

Table 7.1 Projections of population aged 60 and over, China, 1985–2050. Models assuming different fertility levels.

Model assuming fertility to be:	Total national population (million)					Old age dependency ratio population 60+/population 15–59					Old age population as per cent of total population (%)				
	1985	1995	2000	2025	2050	1985	1995	2000	2025	2050	1985	1995	2000	2025	2050
High	1049	1197	1270	1498	1547	0.129	0.150	0.160	0.287	0.363	8.2	9.7	10.2	17.6	21.4
Medium	1049	1183	1242	1437	1453	0.129	0.160	0.160	0.309	0.390	8.2	9.8	10.4	18.4	22.5
Low	1049	1183	1242	1380	1287	0.129	0.160	0.150	0.305	0.438	8.2	9.8	10.4	19.2	25.4

Source: Yao, S. (1986).

Note: On the basis of the 1990 census results and the recent trends of fertility, we project the population of China to exceed 1 300 million in the year 2000. So the projected figures of this table reflect a faster pace of aging than the actual pace.

Table 7.2 Expectation of life of males and females, China, 1982–2050.

Current year	Male life expectancy (years)	Female life expectancy (years)
1982	66.4	69.4
2000	69.1	72.7
2025	70.3	74.0
2050	71.8	75.5

Source: Yao, S. (1986).

2025, the proportion of the old (60 and over) will rise to 17.6 per cent and to 20 per cent by the year 2050. The more aggressive birth control is in China, the faster the population's ageing process will be (Table 7.1).

The aged population
Whichever trajectory China's population growth takes, the increase of the elderly population will be much faster than the total population as a whole (Table 7.3). The indicator of ageing used in China is: if people aged 65 and over constitute fewer than 5 per cent of the total population, then the population is called 'young'; if 5–10 per cent are over 65 it is 'maturing'; and if over 10 per cent are over 65, then the population is 'old age'. Accordingly, China will probably enter the 'old age' stage shortly after the year 2000, rapidly approaching the 'accelerated old age' stage during 2020–2025. She will reach the 'super old age' stage by year 2025 when her elderly population accounts for 20.4 per cent of the total population. If the fertility level declines faster, these

Table 7.3 China: relative growth of the total population and the aged population (60 and above), 1985–2025.

Period	Range of projected % increase of total population	Range of projected % increase of the aged population
1985–2000	18 to 21	50 to 55
2000–2025	11 to 21	105 to 121

Source: Yao, S. (1986). Using various models of fertility increase which give ranges of increase.
Unit: % increase.

Table 7.4 China: population age distribution, 1985–2050.

Year	Age groups	
	0–14 as % of total population	65+ as % of total population
1985	29.1	5.3
1990	25.4	6.0
2000	23.9	7.5
2020	16.9	12.6
2040	14.2	23.1
2050	14.1	23.8

Source: Jiang Zhenghua and Zhu Chuzhu (1985).

ageing stages will appear sooner. However, current prospects point to a slower speed of ageing than previously expected due to higher than expected birth rates.

A consequence of China's rapid ageing is that her age structure will evolve from a 'pyramid' shape to an 'inverted cross' (Table 7.4). The sheer size of the elderly population will be staggering. By 2025 the population aged 60 and above has been projected to lie between 264 million and 298 million, larger than the total population of the United States.

THE PROBLEMS OF POPULATION AGEING IN CHINA

Demographic transition
Unlike most Western countries which have taken 50 to 100 years to go through a 'demographic transition' process through which a country changes from a state of high fertility and high mortality to one of low fertility and low mortality, China took only 20 years to do so. One result of this rapid transition in China is that in the 1990s the proportion of children in the population will decline. The relative number of working adults will increase rapidly. This should be favourable to capital accumulation for economic development, but the problem is whether China can provide adequate employment opportunities for them all in time. Another problem is whether the productivity of the workforce will improve fast enough to be able to support the establishment of a viable social security system such as a superannuated scheme, rather than the current 'pay-as-you-go' scheme.

Judging from the erratic record of economic growth in the last 20 years, the answer to the last two questions seems to be at best doubtful. Productivity has been low in general except for some foreign joint ventures in the 'open economic zones' and 'open cities'. For less than a decade after 1979, there was a time when many small-scale companies were heralded as models of efficiency and reservoirs to absorb excess rural labourers. Sadly, however, many of these 'productive' factories are heavy polluters and the heavy costs of the externalities associated with them are now beginning to be felt.

Abject poverty is still prevalent in many inland provinces and in rural and hilly areas in coastal provinces. Even in the better times of the mid-1980s, when more optimistic income projections had been made, per capita GNP was forecast to be between US$800 and US$1 000 in the year 2000. At this low income level – largely a result of the huge denominator (population) – it is hard to imagine how the state will be able to afford to institute a social security system fashioned after those in the West.

Financing of social security
There exists a system of payment of 'old-age security' to staff working in state enterprises in the cities and towns of China. The problem with this scheme is that the money comes from the current revenues of the enterprises, rather than from a superannuation fund. Each year an enterprise sets aside from its current income before tax, a large sum of money to pay retirees of the enterprise. The amount paid for this purpose in 1979 was Renminbi (RMB) 3.3 billion (one RMB is about one-tenth of a pound sterling), for the benefit of 6 million retirees. By 1985, when the number of retirees rose to 16.4 million, the payment jumped to RMB 14.6 billion. The rate of increase of such payment over the 7 years was 35.6 per cent per annum! (Table 7.5).

By the year 2000, the number of retirees will be about 40 million, and the

Table 7.5   Number of retirees and amount of retirement payment, China, 1979–1989.

Year	Retirees in year (million)	Retirees as % of current employees (%)	Retirement payment (billion RMB)	Retirement payment as % of social security and welfare expenditure (%)
1979	6.0	6.0	3.3	44.7
1980	8.2	7.8	5.0	53.7
1981	9.5	8.7	6.2	56.5
1982	11.1	9.9	7.3	57.3
1983	12.9	11.2	8.7	58.2
1984	14.8	12.3	10.6	59.9
1985	16.4	13.2	14.6	63.7
1986	18.1	14.1	16.9	65.6
1987	19.7	14.9	20.4	64.6
1988	21.2	15.6	27.0	66.0
1989	22.1	16.1	31.3	—
Change over last year (%)				
1980	36.9	30.0	55.1	
1981	16.4	11.5	23.6	
1982	17.2	13.8	17.3	
1983	16.1	13.1	19.4	
1984	14.4	9.8	21.5	
1985	10.8	7.3	37.2	
1986	10.4	6.8	16.1	
1987	8.9	5.7	20.1	
1988	7.6	4.7	32.3	
1989	4.2	3.2	16.0	
Annual growth rate (%)				
1979–81	26.6		35.6	
1981–85	14.9		23.4	
1985–89	7.4		20.0	

Source: Calculated from Data on Labour and Wage Statistics of China (Zhongguo laodong gongzi tongji ziliao) (1990) and Data on Social Statistics of China (Zhongguo shehui tongji ziliao) (1990).
Units: Persons, Renminbi (RMB).

payout will be as much as RMB 40 billion. It is obvious that this burden will be heavy on enterprises, and that it will have adverse effects on the economy as a whole. Unless there is a thorough overhaul of the social security system for retirees, the current scheme of financing will soon break down because enterprises will simply go bankrupt under the ever-heavier burden of retirement payments alone.

According to the projections of the State Statistical Bureau, the size of the labour force will continue to increase through the middle of the next century. There is not a problem in the supply of the number of people in the workforce. However, ageing of the workforce will pose a problem. In 1982, 57 per cent of the labour force were aged 15–34 but, by the year 2000, this will decrease to 48 per cent. In the meantime, the percentage of workers in the older age group of

35 and over will rise from 43 per cent to 52 per cent. If the projections were to continue to 2050, the under-35 group would constitute only 35 to 39 per cent of the labour force, while the over-35 group will have risen to within the range of 61 to 66 per cent. Among male workers, the proportion aged over 55 will be double that of 1982 (10 per cent) at 21–23 per cent; female percentages will be similar (Table 7.6).

In all events, the current pay-as-you-go retirement systems in both state and collective enterprises are severely strained. Concern for productivity and preservation of the environment certainly render vulnerable any serious reforms in the social security systems. Alternative systems such as the indigenous arrangements emphasizing the roles of the extended, if not nuclear, family are being investigated.

The most acute problems of population ageing will appear in the rural areas where living standards are much lower than in the urban areas. At the end of this century there will be about 100 million old people living in the country-side where benefits such as retirement payments and subsidized medical care are covered only to a limited extent in some townships. There is rarely coverage in administrative levels below the townships, for instance in the former 'commune' or 'brigade' levels. In millions of villages, old villagers, especially females, do not receive a fixed income as do their urban counterparts. The main source of financial and social support comes from their own extended family members. According to the 1987 national sample survey of people over 60, 72.5 per cent of respondents in rural areas were cared for by the family, and of these 67.5 per cent were looked after by their children (Tian, 1988).

Recent social and economic changes in the rural communities have caused fundamental changes in the elderly care system. First, since the abolition of the commune-brigade economy during 1983–1985, the burden of caring for the old has been largely switched from the collective to the families. Truly homeless and childless elderly people are still supported by the local government and the collectives. However, the load on the collectives suddenly increased after 1985 as the 'responsibility system in the rural areas' firmly took hold. This system had, by the mid-1980s, redistributed all collective property such as land and tools to individual families. Each family must sign a contract with the state to produce certain crops or pay certain levies to the collective and the state, and

Table 7.6 Age distribution of the labour force by sex, China, 1982–2050.

Sex	Age group (%)							Total
	15–19	20–24	25–29	30–34	35–54	55–59	60+	
Male workers								
1982	15	13	16	13	33	5	5	100
2000	8	11	14	15	40	5	7	100
2050	6–7	9–10	10–11	10–11	37–40	8–10	14–19	100
Female workers								
1982	20	15	17	14	25	4	4	100
2000	11	13	16	17	34	5	4	100
2050	9–11	12–13	12–13	12–13	32–34	7–8	10–14	100

Source: Yao, S. (1986)

to take care of the property and tools allocated. So, as the collective's power to produce goods is weakened, the quality of life of old persons is no longer guaranteed as it was in theory during the collective-farming years. Children of ageing parents in poor families might easily treat their parents as a burden; while those in better-off families are able to treat their parents much better because the elderly people can be counted on to relieve the adult children by doing simple tasks such as child care and household chores.

Family planning and urbanization
Apart from the changes in political economy of household production, demographic changes within the family have brought to the fore the problem of the *dependency ratio.* A consequence of China's successful family planning programme for household composition is that the number of children has rapidly declined. Fewer children mean that in future there will be fewer working adults per family to support parents and other kinsfolk. According to a 1987 survey of rural families in Guangdong Province, the number of children belonging to currently married couples was 2.5, whereas among their parents (i.e. people of the previous generation), the number was 5.6 children per couple (Table 7.7). If the official fertility-control policy were to be continued 'successfully' for a sustained period of time, then there will be fewer than two children in every family (Kwong, 1991; Banister, 1988). It has been projected that the dependency ratio will be 32 per cent in the year 2025 if the one-child policy continues, and 51 per cent if a two-child policy is implemented. However, the percentage of old people in the population will be 60 per cent with a one-child policy and 41 per cent with a two-child policy (Banister, 1988).

Table 7.7 Average number of children in two generations, Panyu County, Guangdong Province, China, 1987.

Generation of	Sample maximum no. of children	Sample minimum no. of children	Sample average no. of children
Respondents' parents	12	1	5.6
Respondents	6	0	2.5

Source: Authors' survey conducted in the summer of 1987.

Rural economic development will also entail the release of excess workers to cities. In urbanization, most rural urban migrants are young and, since many will never return to the villages, the net loss will mean fewer children available in the villages to care for the elderly. Some aged parents will therefore be abandoned (Zeng and Vaupel, 1989). This could also happen in cities because, when China's economy is liberalized, urban workers will be able to move to other cities looking for better economic opportunities. Parents of such mobile workers will be likely to be abandoned like their rural counterparts. By necessity, therefore, the collective, and ultimately the state, will have to shoulder an increasingly heavy load of this kind of 'left over' burden (Hu, 1988). Yet, as noted above, the collective and the state will be less and less able to fill the gap. If so, this bodes ill for the old, especially those in the rural areas.

SOCIAL SERVICES

The basic philosophy of China's social welfare system is a combination of traditional values and socialist principles. Deeply ingrained in the Chinese mentality is an ideal social system which has been described in the classic Confucian text, Li-yun Da-tong Bian (Universal Brotherhood); a society in which 'the old are to be taken care of' (lao you suo yang). As a socialist country, the Chinese authorities give this adage a socialist-humanistic interpretation. Specifically, the term 'yang' (care) is expanded to include four more items: entertainment (le), meaningful work (wei), learning (xue), and health care (yi) (Zhou, 1988). Admittedly, in her 'early stage' of socialist development, China has been unable to afford to provide all these for everyone. Only a very small proportion of the state enterprises and localities can do so.

Types of social services

Income security

There are three types of income security programme in China. The first is implemented in cities and towns but rarely in the rural areas. It caters for state (ministry) civil servants and workers in local (cities and towns) enterprises. Retired ordinary workers receive a monthly retirement payment which is the equivalent of between 60 and 80 per cent of the final month's salary. It has been estimated that fewer than 10 per cent of China's old people are eligible for a pension (Martin, 1988). Retired middle and high-ranking cadres (so-called lixiu cadres who are supposed to be merely taking a leave of absence to rest or convalesce) enjoy not only full salaries, but also many additional benefits that vary according to rank. The total number of retirees and lixiu cadres was 22.1 million in 1989 and a total of RMB 31.3 billion was paid out that year (Table 7.5).

The second type of income security programme caters for ageing widows and widowers. In cities, the welfare payments are from the state or local government and the money is distributed via publicly-run retirement homes and social welfare institutions (SWI). Between 1980 and 1988, there was a rapid increase in the number of such organizations in the cities (from 669 to 870 over the 8 years), and per person, expenditure rose from RMB 854 to RMB 2209 per annum (Table 7.8). At the end of 1988, there were 76 710 persons of different age groups housed in SWI, of whom 41.4 per cent or 31 760 were old people.

In the rural areas, ageing widows and widowers with no close kin are generally supported by the local collectives (economic co-operatives) through the 'Five Guarantees Household (FGH)' system which provides for their food, clothing, shelter, health care, and burial expenses. Those who can carry on some household duties receive voluntary home-making services from members of the community. In 1988, 2 million out of 2.8 million elderly people eligible for FGH were supported. On an average, each supported person received RMB 303 that year. There has been a marked decline since 1985 in the proportion of eligible elderly people being supported by the FGH system (Table 7.9), and the reasons for this trend are discussed below. Rural old folk who are too feeble to live alone are housed in village-run elderly homes called Jinglaoyuan. By the end of 1988, there were 36 665 rural elderly homes in China which housed 434 000 old persons each supported at the cost of RMB 547 per annum (Table 7.10). The most remarkable trend is, that while there has been a rapid rise in the total expenditure on Jinglaoyuan homes, the share borne by the state has dropped by over one-half since 1984. About one-eighth of all counties have

Table 7.8 Social welfare institutions (SWI) in cities of China, 1979–1988.

Year	No. of Urban SWI (Units)	Average no. of residents (thousands)	Expenditure per SWI resident (RMB)
1979	606	40	699
1980	669	41	854
1981	691	40	980
1982	684	39	1225
1983	709	40	1402
1984	743	41	1674
1985	752	42	1782
1986	797	44	1973
1987	844	46	1995
1988	870	47	2209

Source: Data on Social Statistics of China (Zhongguo shehui tongji ziliao) (1990).

Table 7.9 The 'Five Guarantee Households' (FGH) in the rural areas of China, 1979–1988.

Year	Eligible elderly persons (no.)	Supported elderly persons in FGH (thousands)	Per cent supported (%)	Expenditure by the rural collectives (million RMB)	Average expenditure per supported person (RMB)
1979	3 150	2 678	85.0	126	47
1980	2 944	2 539	86.2	172	61
1981	2 899	2 595	89.5	204	79
1982	2 989	2 690	90.0	285	108
1983	2 951	2 838	96.2	339	123
1984	2 961	2 691	90.9	419	152
1985	3 008	2 238	74.4	529	215
1986	2 932	2 204	75.2	505	228
1987	2 876	2 190	76.1	600	273
1988	2 826	2 072	73.3	646	303

Source: Data on Social Statistics of China (Zhongguo shehui tongji ziliao) (1990).

achieved the status of being able to establish one such unit in every sub-county district (xiang).

The last and most common form of income security is based on support by the family members. About 80 per cent of families are in rural areas and the great majority belong to this type of support system. The income that the elderly people receive naturally varies widely with the income of the supporting children. In cases of extreme poverty, the household income of the sons is supplemented by a small grant from the state or the collective. In 1989, according to the Statistical Yearbook of China (p. 810), 34.5 million persons (all household members young and old) received this form of assistance which is called 'Welfare to Hardship Households' (pinkunhu).

Table 7.10 Old age homes (Jinglaoyuan) in China, 1979–1988.

Year	Old age homes (no.)	Old age persons (thousands)	Expendiure (million RMB)	Funding source		Average expenditure per person (RMB)
				Subsidized by the state (%)	From the collective (%)	
1979	7 470	106	18.4	36.8	63.2	174
1980	8 262	112	27.1	34.4	65.6	249
1981	8 544	115	30.0	31.0	69.0	264
1982	10 586	138	42.0	35.6	64.4	332
1983	14 047	169	66.5	37.3	62.7	433
1984	21 190	246	116.1	37.8	62.2	560
1985	27 103	309	134.6	24.9	75.1	485
1986	32 792	368	183.0	19.9	80.1	541
1987	35 015	407	226.4	18.2	81.8	584
1988	36 665	434	230.1	17.0	83.0	547

Source: Data on Social Statistics of China (Zhongguo shehui tongji ziliao) (1990).

Health care services
As part of the employment benefits, a free and comprehensive health-care system is available to employees of State and collective enterprises in cities and towns. Patients can choose the hospitals they like, and almost all expenses are covered by the State. City residents who are close relatives (parents or children, for instance) can also enjoy free health care benefits or substantial discounts. According to the national population sample of old people aged 60 or above, over one-half of the elderly population in cities and towns benefits from free or subsidized health services (Liang, Tu and Chen, 1986).

In the rural areas, however, 90 per cent of older people must pay something for health-care services. This trend began in the early 1980s when the Old People's Commune system was gradually phased out. The once world-famous 'barefoot doctors' became private practitioners and began to charge fees. In some places, these paramedical professionals engage in group practices which are collectively funded by certain insurance schemes. Elderly people joining the scheme pay a small premium in return for reduced charges for the medical services received.

As regards hospital services, the government requires the hospitals to reserve beds, where possible, for elderly people; to schedule consultation hours for them; and to give them priority over younger patients in dispensing drugs. Home-care of elderly patients is also available in some cities. For those elderly people who prefer residential care, the community clinics at the district level arrange the so-called 'home geriatric beds' which are supported with periodic check-ups by visiting nurses and paramedical personnel. In a few large cities, there are geriatric hospitals that serve only old people. With 50 to 100 beds, these hospitals specialize in the treatment of chronic geriatric illnesses. For example, the 75-bed Yishou Geriatric Hospital in Guangzhou (Canton) provides outpatient, home-visiting, on-call, and family bed services (Canton Almanac, 1990). These hospitals are funded by business organizations, including health-insurance companies, and are run by medical professionals.

Urban social services
Several services are provided for elderly people in the cities who live alone or away from their children. One type is the 'guaranteed-care' (bao hu) service which is provided by neighbourhood communities. The services 'guaranteed' are such household chores as shopping, house cleaning, and doing the laundry. Additional tasks include bathing, accompanying the elderly people to see doctors, and assistance in physical rehabilitation. The actual social organizations running these services are the neighbourhood branches of the Women's Federation, the Communist Youth League, and the Old Age Association. Free of charge and staffed by young or old volunteers, these services are co-ordinated through neighbourhood (street) administrative units called the Street (Neighbourhood) Committees.

A further form of social service is the 'elderly people's apartments' with single or shared rooms in each apartment (15 to 30 m^2 each). Facilities in large apartment complexes include canteens, recreational facilities, libraries, and clinics. These apartments are usually experimental (temporary) programmes run by non-government organizations. For instance, the Linghai Yilao Club in Canton established an elderly apartment which was built with foreign investment and local capital raised by elderly women. Though welcomed by those who could afford it, these programmes serve only a few wealthy clients. None the less, this marks a significant beginning of private enterprise becoming involved in elderly services.

Elderly schools exist which are sponsored by the government and operated by the Old Age Association, the Ministry of Education, the labour unions, and private elderly associations. At an elementary level the schools offer courses on such subjects as psychology, calligraphy, drawing and personal health care. At college level, 2-year diploma courses are taught by retired professors and specialists in the cities. The earliest 'elderly university' was established in 1983 by the Red Cross Association in Shandong Province. In China there are 20 elderly schools and 85 elderly universities, serving a total of 45 000 persons (Wang, 1986).

Entertainment for elderly people is a required service of all state-run organizations. At the provincial and city levels 'elderly activity centres' are established, while at the county level there are only 'elderly activity rooms'. Day care, health check-ups, libraries, sports, and counselling services are provided. In some centres where retired specialists are found, technical consulting and mutual aid activities are organized. For example, the Chongqing Retired Engineers Association (in Sichuan Province) was established in 1979 and had a membership of over 500 within 5 years. It serves almost 600 small enterprises in the city as well as in the rural area. It has trained some 2 000 technicians and unemployed youths in recent years (Hu and Wang, 1988).

In spite of the many services described above, China's annual budget allocated to social services for her older population is rather small. The entire budget for social welfare in 1987 was 5.6 per cent of the national income (Table 7.11). Within this figure, three-fifths was spent on retirement benefits. What was left for welfare services was obviously limited. For the great majority of elderly people, the main source of support is still the family.

Table 7.11 Labour insurance plus social welfare expenditure as a percentage of national income, China, 1980–1988.

Year	Labour insurance payment (billion RMB)	Social welfare payment (billion RMB)	Labour insurance payment (%)	Social welfare payment (%)
1980	9.6	8.7	2.6	2.4
1981	11.0	9.0	2.8	2.3
1982	12.8	9.5	3.0	2.2
1983	15.0	11.1	3.2	2.4
1984	17.7	12.4	3.1	2.2
1985	22.9	15.5	3.4	2.2
1986	25.8	20.2	3.3	2.5
1987	31.6	23.3	3.4	2.4
1988	40.9	28.8	—	—

Period	Growth (%)	
1980–85	138.9	176.8
1985–88	79.0	186.4

Source: Data on Social Statistics of China (Zhongguo shehui tongji ziliao) (1990).
Units: Renminbi (RMB), %.

THE ORGANIZATION OF SERVICES FOR ELDERLY PEOPLE

The organizational principle of China's social welfare system is as follows. On the basis of the family support system, the government and the local enterprises contribute limited financial resources, co-ordinate activities and enforce the family-care norms of elderly support. The family is required by law to care for its elders financially and socially; local work units are responsible for providing partial retirement allowances and old age welfare; and the government ministries are to co-ordinate and provide essential welfare services. The whole neighbourhood community is expected to provide free visits and household services for single (deserted) elderly people.

The government plays a very important role in the maintenance of elderly care in society because there are only a small number of private-care institutions in big cities. In the more backward cities or in the rural areas, the government shoulders the responsibility for sheltering all the old people on welfare. Five government departments serve different clients as shown in Table 7.12.

In China, the labour union is a tightly-controlled government organization, which has vertical branches down to the enterprise and neighbourhood levels. Its role is to mediate between retired workers and the government's labour and personnel departments, and in many instances, provide direct services to the workers. Indeed the 'elderly university', the 'elderly activity centres (rooms)', and the rehabilitation programmes mentioned above are organized by the labour unions with financial contributions from the enterprises and fee-paying individuals. With so many different parties taking different roles in care provision, conflicts of interest and duplication of efforts naturally arise.

In order to reduce wastage, the State Council approved the establishment of a national organization, the China National Committee on Ageing (CNCA), in 1982. Its role is to co-ordinate the activities of various agencies, to improve interagency relations, to study problems related to service provision, and to

Table 7.12 Division of responsibilities among government agencies concerned with elderly care and service provision.

Organization	Target clients	Services provided
Old Cadres Bureau	Senior cadres	Rehabilitation, entertainment, re-education
Personnel Dept.	Civil servants, staff	Administration of fund for retirement
Labour Dept.	Retired workers in state enterprises	Administration of fund for retirement
Social Welfare Dept.	• Totally dependent elderly (no kin) • Some old workers	Comprehensive welfare coverage (food, clothing, shelter, health care, burial benefits)
Health Dept.	All elderly people	Medical and health services, consultation and health advice.

devise collective strategies. All provinces and big cities in China have established CNCA branches headed by local senior officials and staffed by from 4 to 10 full-time specialists. Local branches of CNCA are 'think tanks' where regulations and measures to deal with ageing problems are formulated. In Shanghai, for instance, the CNCA drafted a set of provisional ordinances for elderly care for the Shanghai legislature (People's Congress) in 1987 (Xiao, 1988).

The China Old Age Fund (Zhongguo Lao-ling Jijinhui) was established in 1986. It is a mass organization that raises funds from official and private organizations. It invests in money-making businesses such as selling products for elderly people (special food, health-care aids, and the like), sponsoring exhibitions, and providing medical and social services. As noted earlier, for a socialist country, a private enterprise such as this is a bold undertaking. The government accepts this because it effectively complements its regular services. China is continuing to carry out profound political-economic reforms in her social institutions. There will no doubt be more innovative schemes along these lines and in the general direction of privatization which appear in the 1990s.

SOCIAL ATTITUDES, LIVING ARRANGEMENTS, DECISION MAKING AND STATUS

In respect of power and control at home and in the work place, age grading has traditionally been very important in the social attitudes of the Chinese people. Yet, in the last decades, rapid social and economic changes have brought many young technical people to assume important posts in government and industry. The so-called seniority effect is gradually receding in cities and modern enterprises. None the less, in the rural areas, the making of major decisions by the eldest person in the family is still the norm. The Institute of Psychology of the Chinese Academy of Science surveyed a sample of people aged 55 and above and found that 86 per cent of elderly people said that they had experienced 'no change' on entering old age. The ratio of 'happy incidence' to 'anxiety-inducing incidence' was 41 per cent to 15.4 per cent. Most respondents rated themselves highly on a score of satisfaction. Only 14 per cent worried about, or were troubled by, their ageing problems. What bothered them, rather, were social problems such as housing shortage and crime.

Most elderly people in China live in families with their children, many with grandchildren as well, and this may have contributed a great deal to their state of well-being. The reason is that, apart from the deference by society, a multigenerational home environment provides aged people with much-needed emotional support. According to the 1987 (first ever) national sample survey of elderly persons aged 60 and above, 82 per cent of China's senior citizens lived in households with two or more generations. Furthermore, 53 per cent of the respondents lived in households with three or more generations (Tian, 1988). In cities, the role of the aged at home is one of intergenerational mutual assistance in daily life: grandparents supervise grandchildren with housework and homework, and adult children reciprocate by providing for the ageing parent's material and health care needs (Wu and Xu, 1988).

As to the pattern of living arrangements in the rural areas, the authors conducted a survey in Guangdong Province in 1987 in which it was found that 75.3 per cent of the elderly people in the sample lived with their children. In case of illness, 92.8 per cent were looked after by children, children-in-law, or grandchildren, and only 7 per cent by neighbours or the collective. Although in past decades, there has been a gradual rise in the proportion of nuclear families among all households, the trend toward the so-called 'nuclear family pattern', which is characterized by the isolation of old people living far apart from their children, is not so marked. The proportion of families with two or more generations that live apart in separate households is generally higher in large cities than in towns or rural areas. This proportion was in any case quite low: it was 17 per cent in Tianjin, 20 per cent in Shanghai, 19 per cent in Beijing, and 24.7 per cent in Guangzhou (Canton). Living apart by no means implies isolation from social and emotional contacts. In our survey, we found that many children regularly visited their parents and gave money to them (Table 7.13).

Decision making
Concomitant with the slow change in the patterns of living arrangements and social relationships, there has been a slow change in the pattern of decision making in the family. For centuries, older Chinese parents in the family have been portrayed in countless novels and folk stories as symbols of authoritarian despotism. Under socialist rule, which abolished private ownership of land and major properties, the material basis of authoritarianism was severely undermined. Over four decades, the Chinese population has been taught in a communist system of education that cherishes egalitarian ideals. This has contributed somewhat to a weakening of the grip of authoritarian rule in the family. Nevertheless, older people in China today still wield considerable influence in decision making at home. In a 1984 survey of older people in Tianjin by the Tianjin Academy of Social Sciences and the municipality government, it was reported that 49.5 per cent of old respondents made the major decisions for the family. In the 1987 study, cited above, by the Chinese Academy of Science (CASS), 50 per cent of elderly people in the sample rated themselves very authoritative.

It is interesting to note that the degree of self-rated authoritativeness of elderly people in rural families is far lower than that in urban families. For example, according to the 1987 CASS survey, 49.7 per cent of rural elderly people did not have decisive power in economic matters (CASS, 1988), only a small proportion did. The reason lies in the crucial urban-rural differences in the mode of production. In cities where wage earning is the norm, housing and

Table 7.13 Frequency of visits and financial sources of livelihood, Panyu County, Guangdong Province, China, 1987.

Frequency of visit	% of cases	Financial source of livelihood coming from	% of cases
Several times per month	45.5	Parents themselves	34.8
Once a month	0.8	Children who live apart	62.1
Not regular	51.5	Relatives	1.5
Never	2.3	Other sources	1.5

Source: Authors' survey. The sample size of the survey was 440 persons, and the cases here were those who did not live with their parents.

social benefits are bestowed on the younger family members through the ageing parents. So long as the parents are alive, retired or not, this protective umbrella remains in effect. The higher the political and economic position of the parents, the stronger this dependency in fact becomes. To illustrate this point, no other item is more important in the cities than low-cost housing which is heavily subsidized by the enterprise. In a great majority of cases, children are allowed to stay and, in a sense, 'inherit' the apartment on the death of the parents, under whose name the unit was originally allocated. Viewed in this light, the elders' power in the cities, and the deference that they achieve, is derived from this peculiar socialist system of allocation.

The same cannot be said for the rural areas where farming households generate income mainly through manual labour. Ageing parents become less productive over time, so their power in the household declines. In our survey in Guangdong Province, we found that the headship rate declines with advancing age, signifying the transfer of economic decision power to the middle-aged children. A 1 per cent sample survey of old people in Hubei province, conducted by Wuhan University in early 1987, found the same inverse relationship between decision-making power and age.

Status of old people
In the official media, old people are stereotyped as kind, likeable, stable and mature; people who can be made fun of and whose wisdom and knowledge is sought after by the young. In reality, though, older people are treated according to their educational attainment and economic status more often than according to their less tangible human qualities. This cold reality, coupled with the urban 'inheritance' pattern noted above, often drives older urban residents to work even harder after retirement! 'For the children . . .', many say resignedly. This is particularly true among officials and well-trained staff members in ministries and educational institutions whose skills sometimes bring them a higher income than their preretirement jobs. No wonder the elderly people in the urban sector have on average a more authoritarian status.

In addition to a material basis, this seemingly anachronistic state of affairs has a historical basis unique to China. Those who are retiring now were educated in the late 1940s and early 1950s. Their technical expertise, superb human skills and extensive connections are sorely needed today in various institutions, especially those that have dealings with foreign firms and organizations. This is because there exists a 'vacuum layer' of manpower wrought by the devastating Great Proletariat Revolution (1966–1976) during which academic standards from primary school to postgraduate level suffered severely. Graduates of secondary and tertiary institutions in that tumultuous decade were generally ill-trained and quite a proportion of them might have personalities shaped by the Cultural Revolution. Many of the retirees on the other hand are survivors of political struggles and are professionally competent, and they are therefore welcomed by the joint ventures and the like.

According to the population census of 1982, 24 million retirement-age people continued to work either in their original organizations or as consultants to other organizations. Of these, over 300 000 took up 'leading roles' in the state, the Party, mass organizations, and industrial and business enterprises. In the 1987 national survey by CASS, the rate of re-employment after retirement was 15.6 per cent. In cities it was 18 per cent, whereas in towns it was 13.2 per cent. Among those elderly people who did not work, many said they were capable but did not want to work. Relatively few said they were refused jobs because of old age (Tian, 1988).

In the rural areas, on the other hand, ageing parents expressed a strong desire for economic security from their children. In our survey in Guangdong Province, we found that 70 per cent of middle-aged respondents stated that they would insist that their children 'provide them with sufficient living allowances', so they would 'receive money regularly'.

Inflation hurts urban elderly people more than their rural counterparts. In 1985, the per capita annual amount of money given to old residents in cities was RMB 889 per annum. But the average urban living expenses alone would be RMB 732. The difference of RMB 157 per annum is a very meagre disposable income. Low-rank employees with few or no working children have a hard time making ends meet, especially in an expensive city such as Canton. In that city, a survey was conducted in 1987 and it was found that 14.6 per cent of retired workers lived below the poverty line ('minimum living standard'). To survive, many had to seek employment even if it was against their wishes. In fact, 34 per cent of the retirees in cities and 33 per cent of those in towns who re-entered the labour force cited economic needs as their motive for working, according to the CASS survey. The same survey also detected sentiments against persons of advanced age (80 and above). They were regarded by the 'young old' as very dependent and a heavy burden; this is in stark contrast with the cultural 'ideal image'.

In brief, a gap exists between the cultural ideal image of the old and social attitudes to them. Elderly people today are nominally respected for their experience. To a certain extent the presence of young children helps to retain some of the traditional roles reserved for the aged. Yet in a fast-changing society such as China, especially among urbanites, the 'present value' of individuals is most esteemed, not the parental sacrifices of the past or the long-forsaken traditional virtues. In this respect, being old with either no economic role or only a weak economic role places people in a disadvantaged position. This is in spite of being in a supposedly Confucian society bolstered by a selfless socialist ethos.

POLICY TOWARDS OLD AGE

In view of the massive ageing process that is already underway in China, any feasible policy towards the aged must be long-term in nature and be involved with the major social, economic and fiscal policies of the whole country. It has been pointed out that the social security for old people in the rural areas will rest on three 'pillars' for a long time to come. In order of priority these are the family, the collectives and the state (Zhu, 1988; Yuan, 1988). Such a policy must call into question controversial issues such as radically altering the life-time guaranteed employment in the government and in tens of thousands of economically uncompetitive enterprises; instituting forced savings to establish superannuated pension schemes, and the like. All of these changes must be made as soon and as resolutely as possible during during the lenient 'period of grace' of some 30 years between now and the year 2020 when the tidal wave of retirement begins to hit the shore. The interim years are so-called because the age pyramid will be 'middle heavy', and there will be fewer children and elderly people per 100 working persons, a favourable condition for economic development.

During the next few decades there will still be a substantial number of people entering retirement age. As economic and social reforms deepen, the government at various administrative levels and in different regions is making the following adjustments with regard to ageing problems (Xiao and Tao, 1990).

Reform of the payment schemes for retirement benefits
To date, most retirement benefits have been parcelled out in a 'pay-as-you-go' fashion by enterprises. Many factories have already had to cease business because of ageing equipment and uncompetitive products on the one hand and, on the other, the crushing burden of the annual payment of retirement benefits. Storms loom in the old industrial towns of China over a hotly debated issue: namely, whether to 'socialize' the payment scheme for retirement benefits. In the name of socialism (with a human face), money-losing enterprises gladly support, and profitable ones strongly oppose, a scheme whereby a 'socialized' pool of retirement funds would be set up. Factories belonging to the same industry would have to contribute to it and retiring workers and officials could withdraw their entitled share of retirement benefits from it.

Since the decision makers of all enterprises (most of whom are officials nearing retirement) tend to support the scheme, it is accepted in many cities. A very interesting political-economy observation is to be made here: the class line is drawn not between the officials of profitable or unprofitable organizations who all support the scheme; but rather, the young and old employees are sharply divided! This is because the old officials in unprofitable enterprises stand to gain most, at the expense of the young workers of profitable enterprises.

This being the case, a further question is: if the efficient and profitable enterprises are drained of their much-needed capital for reinvestment and expansion, how long can this go on before they become obsolete and unprofitable? A likely answer is that this seemingly innocuous but ultimately harmful scheme would 'socialize' other sectors of the economy. A bigger pool would be created and it would draw in other more profitable sectors of the economy. The clear danger is that, for the sake of sustaining the welfare of the ever-growing cohorts of ageing cadres and workers in the 'pay-as-you-go' fashion, and by sustaining the sunset industries and expanding government bureaucracies, the whole society could one day be submerged, or hyperinflation will result.

Proposed establishment of funded social security systems in the rural areas
There are few funded social security systems in rural China. We found that even in a relatively wealthy rural county like Panyu, south of Canton, officials were well aware of the long-term benefits of the funded scheme, but concrete action had not been taken because there was no experience in setting up and running such a scheme. It is also said that rural folk are averse to the idea of life insurance – connoting death. Although different forms of mutual funds are being organized among the aged at the village level and xiang (formerly People's Commune) level to provide a degree of social security for the peasants, progress is slow. Life insurance companies have been 'revived' after decades of dormancy and they are trying to enrol more customers.

Reform of the medical and health system for the aged
The world-famous 'barefoot doctors' quietly faded from the scene with the demise of the People's Commune system around 1983–1985. Most changed jobs, and some moved to practise in rural towns rather than staying in the villages. Although progress has been made, for the most part, health care at the grass-roots level has basically returned to what it was before the commune system. One of the major reasons for the disintegration of the community health-care system was economic. After communes were abolished, the grass-roots organizations ('Brigades') that once managed the finance and personnel of the health stations ceased to function. Old people tend to suffer more under the

current system because many collectives cannot afford to pay the higher fees charged by the privatized doctors. Radical reform in the medical and health delivery system is therefore urgently needed.

Undertake gerontological and sociopsychological studies for policy making
Given limited economic and administrative resources, national policies for welfare provision must be based upon sound scientific bases. Carefully-designed social surveys must be conducted to ensure that the reformed schemes are acceptable to their target groups. Rigorous actuarial research must also be undertaken in order that an equitable and viable distribution of pension and social security payments can be achieved. The establishment of self-supporting funds generated from fee-charging services can finance these studies as well as basic research in the gerontological and geriatric fields. But the major thrust at present comes from the government; the 'China Aged Population Research Center' in Beijing was established under the auspices of the China National Committee on Ageing. Research is also conducted in other institutions, and there are now over 30 newspapers and journals on ageing published by various organizations. Research projects are also carried out in universities and in local branches of the Chinese Academies of Science and Social Sciences.

In addition to demographic and econometric projections of the pace of the rapid and massive wave of retirement anticipated in 2020, there should be studies on the psychological shock waves that will accompany the demise of the iron 'rice bowl' (life-time state employment). China seems to be moving towards a more individually rather than collectively-motivated incentive system. It therefore is imperative for researchers and officials alike to contemplate the implications of this movement. How psychologically prepared are individuals and how appropriate are their retirement plans?

Orientation to 'individual futures' and a competently-informed ability to undertake forward retirement planning are grossly lacking today in a wide spectrum of contemporary Chinese groups, and not just those in China. The exceptions are perhaps found in small pockets of Chinese middle-classes in Hong Kong, Singapore and Taiwan, who have had extensive exposure to Western living styles. The older generations have not, however, developed this orientation and many hold fatalistic attitudes about the future. The young are also confused.

If only because they will be the 'shock troops' of the retirement boom of the next century, middle-aged people in China are the most interesting subjects for gerontological and social psychological investigation. These people were exposed to socialist indoctrination in the 1950s which held that there is no need of an individualistic future, for the state will take care of the group. This of course has been debunked by the cruel events of the Great Leap Forward. After the Cultural Revolution, other extreme attitudes developed. First, for instance, since witnessing the horrifying experience that an individual (no matter how high the post that he holds) is very vulnerable to the state and the 'masses', a nihilistic and untrusting attitude has firmly taken root in the subconscious of millions of middle-aged officials and ordinary people. Secondly, as a corollary of these attitudes and in part due to wildly fluctuating official economic policies (the open door can be shut overnight), an 'immediate-gratification pattern' as opposed to a deferred-gratification pattern developed.

The net result is that many people are fundamentally insecure about the future and relatively few have personal plans outside the framework of planning for their children's future. They tend to have short-term economic behaviour, and accept corruption while vested personal power and influence last. They tend to sacrifice personal welfare in order to amass enough wealth and power for the benefit of their children. When making plans for children is no longer a concern, whatever assets they have at their disposal they tend to use for immediate satisfaction and material gain rather than saving. They are, in any case, commonly ignorant about life insurance, individual pension plans, and the like.

FUTURE PROSPECTS: UNCERTAINTIES AND DILEMMAS

When we look ahead into the next century, the need for high-technology therapeutics will rise as China prospers under the policies of reconstruction and open-door economics (if continued). The desire for high-tech services will be further accentuated by the rapid rise in the population aged 80 and above. The polarity between those who can afford and demand such services and those who cannot will increase. The arbitration role of the government will become crucial. It will have to mediate between the conflicting demands, balance equations of cost-benefits, and weigh up the social worthiness of advanced medical treatments. Ultimately, it will have to justify the ethics of all these assessments to the public in a democratic manner.

In following the current road of encouraging privatization, yet preserving a sizeable centrally-planned economic sector, there will be continual conflicts between the vibrant private sector and the stagnant public sector. Competition amongst the prosperous southern provinces and the more spartan northern provinces will also intensify. It also appears certain that the open coastal region will grow richer and socially more developed than the closed inland areas (Phillips and Yeh, 1989). Amidst all these competitions and conflicts, old people could easily become victims whose interests are the first to be sacrificed, yielding to the needs of the younger age groups. So, too, will the interests of the 'collective', which will yield to individual interests, be sacrificed. The health-care consequences of the abolition of the commune is but a harbinger of social developments which have yet to appear.

In the medium term, the Chinese government must squarely face many new dilemmas. The fact that the commune system failed, all things considered, does not guarantee that the privatized approach will necessarily succeed. In the fields of social gerontology and welfare provision for the elderly population, China has much to learn from Western and East Asian countries such as the Four Little Dragons. 'Capitalist' experiences are ironically becoming more and more relevant to Chinese society as the years go by.

CONCLUSIONS

China already has the largest population of old people in the world, and the Chinese people will, in about 30 years time, have to prepare for one of the most rapid and massive population-ageing processes in human history. This process is the result of the twin effects of the sustained fertility boom of the 1950s followed by unprecedented fertility control a generation later. The combined effect makes the second decade of the next century particularly worrying because the massive cohorts of 'baby boomers' will, by the time they retire, find much smaller cohorts of their children to support them.

The social ramifications of these broad-brush scenarios are beyond the scope of this chapter. At present, China is still seeking a delicate balance between the centrally-planned sector and the free-market sector of the economy. This chapter identifies two touchstones of the government's strategy to solving the perceived ageing problem. For the urban areas, the first is how the government will handle the debated issue of socializing the retirement payment schemes. In the rural areas, the second is how it will institute a viable social security system that is at the same time attractive to the peasantry.

A properly assessed and planned strategy to deal with the ageing problem in China should include not only the provision of essential goods and services, but also spiritual guidance for hundreds of millions of psychologically battered individuals. This provision is less discussed in the literature than institutional and social analyses. To the extent that the current economic reforms in China will broaden and deepen, individualism will also rise and the voice of freedom to choose will be applauded. So, researchers and planners must also include a psychological and spiritual counselling component in their strategy. A new ethic upon which this component will have to rest awaits cultivation. Among the desirable qualities of a culturally-transformed Chinese people, those appropriate to the long-term solution of the ageing problem may include the following: assertiveness, self-help and mutual-help, self-respect, and the respect of others' individuality and dignity.

REFERENCES

Banister J. (1988). *Implications of the Aging of China's Population.* CIS Staff Paper 44, Bureau of the Census, Center for International Research, Washington DC.

Chinese Academy of Social Sciences (CASS) (1988). *China, 1987. Aged Population over 60 Years [Old]. Sampling Survey Data (Computer Tabulation).* Beijing.

Davis-Friedmann, D. (1985). *Long Lives: China's Elderly and the Communist Revolution.* Harvard University Press, Cambridge, Massachusetts.

Di, Angzhao and Li, Xuezheng (1990). Zhongguo renkou laolinghua ji qi dui shehui jingji de yingxiang (Population ageing of China and its socio-economic effects). In B. Ma *et al.* (Eds) (1990), pp. 164–79.

Hu, R. (1988). Woguo chengshi laoling wenti ji duice chutan (The ageing problems of China and preliminary discussion on the strategies to deal with them). In *Collection of Essays on Sociology*, Nos. 1 and 2. pp. 27–34. Tianjin Academy of Social Sciences.

Hu, R. and Wang, L. (1988). Zhongguo chengshi laonianren canyu shehui fazhan de jiben fangshi (Basic patterns of participation of urban elderlies in social development). In *PISAP*, pp. 358–76.

Jiang Zhenghua and Zhu Chuzhu (1985). Zhongguo renkou de nianling jiegou (Age structure of China's population). *Almanac of China's Population*, Social Science Documentation Publishing House, Beijing, p. 235.

Kwong, P. (1991). The 1990 Census and the Fertility Policy Debate. In *China Review 1990*, H. Kuan and M. Brosseau (Eds). Chinese University Press, Hong Kong.

Liang, J., Tu, E.J. and Chen, X. (1986). Population aging in the People's Republic of China. *Social Science and Medicine*, **23**, 1353–62.

Ma, B., Kong, D. and Yu, J. (Eds) (1990). *Zhongguo renkou yu kongzhi: Shijian yu duice (Population Control in China: Practices and Strategies).* China International Broadcast Press, Beijing.

Martin, L.G. (1988). The Aging of Asia. *Journal of Gerontology: Social Sciences*, **34**, 99–113.

Parish, W.L. and Whyte, M.K. (1978). *Village and Family in Contemporary China*. Chicago University Press, Chicago.

Phillips, D.R. and Yeh, A.G.O. (1989). Special Economic Zones. In *China's Regional Development*, D.S.G. Goodman (Ed.), pp. 112–34. Routledge, London.

Proceedings of the International Seminar on Ageing Problems (PISAP) (1988). Laodong Renshi Chubanshe (The Labour and Personnel Press), Beijing.

Tian, S. (1988). *Zhongguo laoling wenti yanjiu (Studies on Aging Problems of China)*. Hangzhou, Zhejiang, Zhejiang Renmin Chubanshe (Zhejiang People's Press).

Tian, X. (1988). Zhongguo 1987 nian 60 sui yishang laonian renkou chouyang diaocha baogao (A report on the survey study of the elderly aged 60 and above in China, 1987). In CASS, pp. 13–34.

Wang, R. (1986). Zhongguo laonianren de jiaoyu he zai jiuye wenti (The problems of education and re-employment among the elderly of China). In *Almanac of China's Population*, pp. 82–6. Social Science Documentation Publishing House, Beijing.

Whyte, M.K. and Parish, W.L. (1983). *Urban Life in Contemporary China*. Chicago University Press, Chicago.

Wu, Y. and Xu, Q. (1988). Zhongguo renkou lao-hua dui shehui jingji fazhan he jiating de Yingxiang (The effects of China's aging upon the family and her socio-economic developments). In *PISAP*, pp. 24–42.

Xiao, Z. (1988). *An Overview of Research on Problems of Aging in China*. Personal communications and manuscript thus named.

Xiao, Z. and Tao, L. (1990). Zhongguo renkou laolinghua qushi ji duice (China's trends of population ageing and her strategies). In Ma, B. *et al.* (Eds) *op. cit.*, pp. 180–96.

Yao, S. (1986). Zhongguo laonian renkou fazhan yuce (Projections of China's future old age population). *Almanac of China's Population*, 78–82.

Yuan, J. (1988). Zhongguo laonian shehui baozhang tixi de gaige (The reform of China's system of social security for the old). In *PISAP* pp. 288–98.

Zeng, Y. and Vaupel, J.W. (1989). The impact of urbanization and delayed childbearing on population growth and aging in China. *Population and Development Review*, **15**, 425–45.

Zhongguo laodong gongzi tongji ziliao (Data on Labour and Wage Statistics of China) (1990). State Statistical Press, Beijing.

Zhongguo shehui tongji ziliao (Data on Social Statistics of China) (1990). China Statistical Press, Beijing.

Zhongguo tongji nianjian (Statistical Yearbook of China) (1990). China Statistical Press, Beijing.

Zhou, Y. (1988). Shi lun laonianren jiazhi guan wenti (The value system of old people: A preliminary discussion). In *PISAP*, pp. 129–38.

Zhu, C. (1988). Zhongguo nongcun xin xingshi xia laonian shehui baozhang de 'San gen Zhizhu' (The '3 pillars' of social security for old people in rural areas of China). In *PISAP*, pp. 242–47.

Hou-Sheng Chan

Department of Sociology,
National Taiwan University

8 AGEING IN TAIWAN

INTRODUCTION

With its great success of economic development, Taiwan has experienced a rapid industrialization and urbanization process in the past decades. As the process of modernization gained momentum in the 1970s in particular, the structure of Taiwan's society begun undergoing significant transformation. Extensive differences from the earlier situations are now evident in a variety of social dimensions, including changes in population structure, social mobility, political groupings, cultural interests, the range of economic pursuits, and institutionalized responses to alterations in the international economic and political order. As the pace and extent of social change continue to be rapid and pervasive as Taiwan moves into the 1990s, how to cope with the growing needs of different groups of people becomes a crucial issue faced by the government. Of various changes in Taiwan, the process of demographic transition has been particularly noticeable in the past decades, due to rapid decline in fertility rates and significant increase in life expectancy. The proportion of the elderly population aged 65 and over in Taiwan increased from 2.5 per cent in 1950 to 4 per cent in 1978, and then to 6 per cent in 1989. With the decline both in birth and death rates and the prolongation of life expectancy, it is projected that the proportion of those aged 65 and over in the total population will reach about 10 per cent in 2011. This figure may not be impressive in comparison with the figures of other developed nations, where over 10 per cent of the total population are now included in the aged groups. However, the rapid increase in the number of aged people in Taiwan, accompanied by changes in family structure, has indicated the increasing significance of problems related to the aged in Taiwanese society. Problems faced by the aged in the biggest metropolitan city of Taiwan (Taipei) have appeared more serious than those in many other places.

The main theme of this chapter is the exploration of the problems associated with the ageing of the population, which seem to be a common and perhaps inevitable consequence of the move toward an industrial and modern society. In the meantime, based on an interdisciplinary research project, Taipei Study of Gerontology (1986–87), this paper also intends to analyse the emerging social needs of elderly people in Taipei. In so doing, it starts with a brief introduction to major features of change in Taiwan's population structure. The focus will then move to the analysis of empirical findings concerning the needs of elderly people for social services, as well as an explanation of social welfare services provided for the elderly in Taiwan.

THE STRUCTURE OF TAIWAN'S SOCIETY

In general, as society moves towards industrialization and modernization, the age structure of its population often undergoes critical changes. The outcomes of modernization development, such as rising incomes, improved sanitation and advanced medical care have all contributed to the production of better health and longer life of the people. The rubric 'newly industrialized country' (NIC), sociologically speaking, has sympathetic resonances beyond trade balance sheets and foreign exchange accounts. Modernization includes, of course, economic growth with a concomitant sophistication of business, trade, banking and related micro- and macro-economic structure. But, for a deepening of the modernization process, that is, for the economic structure to take permanent root, there must also be associated changes in society. These alterations are crucial to the development of the society, for they appear to guarantee the long term endurance of modernization itself. In other words, the modernization process will not be complete if a society only achieves its success in economic terms, but leaves its societal and cultural features unchanged. This is because the latter transformation enables its new structure to be flexible enough to adjust to the faster changes associated with modern, international societies.

The remarkable economic achievement of Taiwan society in the 1970s has been widely cited as a 'miracle' in the world. During this major phase of societal change, economic development focused on expanding employment opportunities in order to increase per capita GNP. This orientation was indeed a great success, for the economy developed at an unprecedented speed, achieving an average growth rate of 8 per cent in the 15 years from 1970 to 1985. In 1986 this growth rate reached 15.0 per cent, then fell to 11.2 per cent and 7.8 per cent in 1987 and 1988 respectively, and then increased to 9.3 per cent in 1989. The increase in per capita GNP has also been great. It started at NT$2 019 in 1952, increased to NT$15 544 in 1970, and reached NT$198 036 in 1989 (US$1 = NT$28 (approx.) £1 = NT$45 (approx.)). This economic growth prompted upheavals in traditional social structure.

During the process of modernization, Taiwanese society underwent major changes in the way it organized itself. Such a process, which is characterized by a tumultuous atmosphere, consists of structural differentiation and functional specialization, both of which are intimately related to the processes of growth in terms of both personal and institutional change. From a sociological perspective, differentiation refers to a loosening of ascriptive bonds – primarily associated with a weakening of immediate and extended family ties – and a growing mobility of people, goods, and ideas. It therefore leads to extensive networks of exchange and greater disposable resources. As social differentiation becomes more pervasive, and as traditional forms of social integration break down, widespread problems may arise. The increasing population of elderly people, accompanied by a rapid growth in the number of the dependent population, results in a challenge to traditional social values, which gave a high respect to older people and placed a high value on seniority. People are forced to realign themselves with one another in new ways and with social institutions ranging from government agencies to neighbourhood or community organizations. Such problems may not come as a surprise to sociologists or other observers of society. However, the solution to the problems, at first needs accurate problem identification, for which a detailed explanation of the growth trends of the elderly population in Taiwan is required.

Growth trends of the elderly population

As mentioned above, a major phase of societal change in Taiwan occurred during the 1970s. In the past two decades Taiwan's society has been trans-

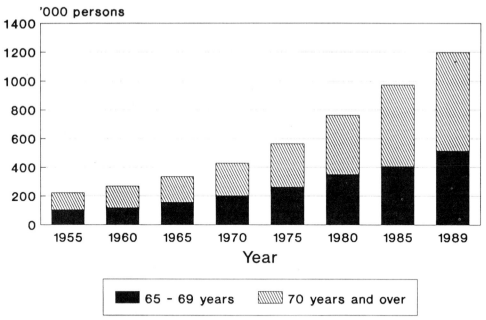

Fig. 8.1   Number of elderly persons in Taiwan.

Source: Council for Economic Planning and Development ROC (1990).

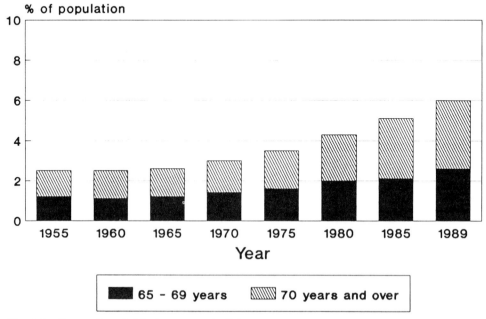

Fig. 8.2   Proportion of elderly persons in Taiwan.

Source: Council for Economic Planning and Development ROC (1990).

formed from one with a primarily rural and agricultural base to one that is increasingly urban and industrial. Rising standards of living throughout the island have increased life expectancy, and have raised the proportion of the elderly in the population.

The number of those aged 65 and over, as Fig. 8.1 shows, increased from 203 000 in 1952 to 1 197 000 in 1989. This nearly six-fold increase in the past 37 years was much greater than the 2.5 times increase in the total population from 8.1 million to 20.1 million in the same period. In addition to the difference in the extent of the growth, there is also a noticeable difference between the paces of growth rates of the elderly and the total population. There was a trend of increase in the growth rate of the total population in the 1950s, starting at 33.3 per cent in 1952 and falling to 3.9 per cent in 1959; a slow trend of decline followed after 1960 until, in 1989, the growth rate of the total population had dropped to only 1.0 per cent. Changes in the growth rate of the elderly show somewhat different patterns. Before 1958, the growth rate of the elderly population remained at 3 per cent every year. It rose steadily afterwards, and accelerated after 1970. After reaching a peak of 6 per cent in 1987, this growth rate dropped slightly and maintained a steady increase (at about 5 per cent) in 1988–89. Such a dramatic increase both in the number and the proportion of the elderly has made Taiwan move away from the 'young phase', defined by the United Nations, and enter into the 'mature phase' (Fig. 8.2). And since the proportion of the elderly in the total population will soon reach 7 per cent in the 1990s, Taiwan's society will step into the 'aged phase' along with most advanced countries. How effective people in Taiwan will be in adjusting to such a demographic change remains to be seen. However, the fact that the ageing process of Taiwan's population started later but proceeded faster, in comparison with many other advanced societies, has created pressure on the government and its people in the provision of care for aged dependents.

In general, the term 'dependents' refers to young people aged under 15 and old people aged 65 and over, who are normally viewed as not being economically active. In 1952, the dependency ratio (the proportion of the combined aged and young population to those of working age (15–64)), was as high as 81.3 per cent (Fig. 8.3). At that time, elderly people accounted for only a very small proportion of the dependent population (about 5 per cent). This dependency ratio rose steadily to reach 94.1 per cent in 1962. Thereafter it has steadily declined, and dropped to 50.2 per cent in 1989. It is worth noting that, because the dependency ratios of the aged and the young took different directions of change (i.e. the aged dependency increased while the young dependency declined), such a decrease in the total dependency ratio mainly resulted from a reduction of the proportion of young dependents. In other words, it is the young rather than the elderly who contributed to the reduced dependency of population. The ageing of the population deserves more attention in the adoption of expeditious means to solve problems brought about by demographic transformation.

THE CHARACTERISTICS OF AGED PEOPLE IN TAIWAN

In addition to examining the proportion of the aged in the total population, another way of exploring the ageing problem is to look at the characteristics of elderly people. According to a survey conducted by the DGBAS (Directorate-General of Budget, Accounting and Statistics, Executive Yuan, ROC) at the end of 1986, 98.9 per cent of the 1 031 000 sampled in the survey aged 65 and over were living in ordinary homes; those living in institutions accounted for only 0.8 per cent (Table 8.1). The government plays a very important role in

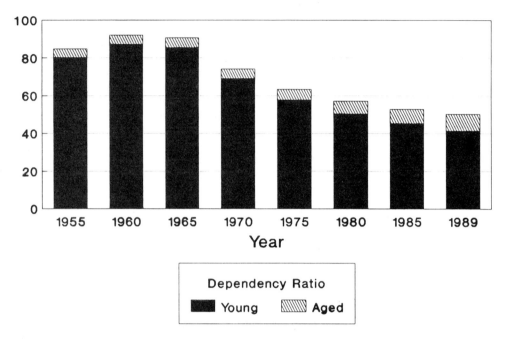

Fig. 8.3   Taiwan: dependency ratio.

Source: Council for Economic Planning and Development ROC (1990).

Table 8.1   The places of residence of elderly people in Taiwan.

	Total	Males	Females
Total (No. of cases, thousands)	1031	538	493
Ordinary homes	(%)	(%)	(%)
Subtotal	98.9	98.1	99.7
Living alone	11.6	14.4	8.5
With spouses	14.0	17.3	10.5
With children permanently	65.0	60.4	70.0
With children (take turns)	5.3	3.5	7.1
With relatives	2.5	1.7	3.4
With friends	0.5	0.8	0.2
Residential homes			
Subtotal	0.78	1.20	0.32
Public	0.66	1.11	0.17
Private	0.02	–	0.04
Religious	0.10	0.09	0.10
Others	0.36	0.66	0.04

Source: DGBAS (1987), pp. 78–85.

providing institutional care for the elderly. 87 per cent of the 8 000 living in residential homes were cared for by public institutions, and the rest were cared for by private, mostly religious, institutions. Of those living in ordinary homes, the majority (about 71.1 per cent) lived with their children, 14.2 per cent lived with their spouses only, 1.7 per cent lived alone, and 3 per cent lived with relatives or friends.

What is more interesting is that about 5.3 per cent of the elderly people were living with children but not on a permanent basis. They lived with their children by means of taking turns – staying with one child for a certain period of time and then moving to another child's home. And, as Tables 8.1 and 8.2 show, not only is this kind of residence pattern more frequently adopted by females (7.1 per cent) than males (3.5 per cent), but the educational background

Table 8.2 Education of elderly people living in ordinary homes.

	Total (%)	Primary education	Secondary education	Higher education
Total	100.0	100.0	100.0	100.0
Total	(100.0)	(85.6)	(9.1)	(5.3)
Living alone	11.7	11.5	16.1	10.0
With spouses	14.1	11.9	21.5	39.0
With children	71.1	73.4	62.3	50.0
With relatives and friends	3.0	3.2	3.1	1.0

Source: DGBAS (1987), pp. 78–85.

Table 8.3 Attitudes of elderly people towards their residential situation.

	Satisfied (%)	Dissatisfied (%)	Others (%)
Total	77.5	2.9	19.6
Illiterate	74.7	2.8	22.5
Self-taught	73.9	4.7	21.5
Primary school	80.8	3.1	16.1
Junior high school	81.6	4.0	14.4
Senior high school	85.1	1.2	13.8
Univ. and college	83.8	2.2	14.0
Males	76.6	2.6	20.8
Illiterate	70.7	2.1	27.1
Self-taught	73.5	3.9	22.6
Primary school	79.2	3.1	17.6
Junior high school	79.5	3.9	16.6
Senior high school	84.2	1.1	14.7
Univ. and college	83.4	1.8	14.8
Females	78.4	3.3	18.4
Illiterate	76.7	3.1	20.2
Self-taught	74.5	6.1	19.4
Primary school	85.6	3.0	11.5
Junior high school	89.5	4.4	6.1
Senior high school	87.5	1.6	11.0
Univ. and college	87.8	5.8	6.4

Sources: DGBAS (1987), pp. 86–89.

Table 8.4 The physical condition of elderly people in Taiwan.

Age	Total no. (1 000s)	Healthy (%)	Unhealthy but not very seriously ill (%)	Ill and in need of care (%)
Total	1 031	54.4	37.2	8.4
65–69	429	63.1	32.5	4.5
70–74	309	53.1	38.0	8.9
75–80	174	47.6	43.0	9.4
80+	118	36.8	43.4	19.9
Males	538	57.6	33.5	8.9
65–69	239	65.1	29.8	5.1
70–74	171	55.4	34.3	10.3
75–80	78	53.3	38.1	8.6
80+	50	36.1	41.1	22.8
Females	493	51.0	41.2	7.9
65–69	191	60.5	35.8	3.7
70–74	139	50.2	42.6	7.2
75–80	96	43.0	46.9	10.1
80+	68	37.2	45.1	17.7

Sources: DGBAS (1987), p. 90.

Table 8.5 Participation in insurance schemes by elderly people.

	Total no. (1 000s)	Insured (%)	Not insured (%)
Total	1 031	17.3	82.7
Illiterate	565	6.1	93.9
Self-taught	62	22.0	78.0
Primary school	250	18.6	81.4
Junior high school	48	46.3	53.7
Senior high school	50	49.2	50.8
Univ. and college	54	66.5	33.5
Males	538	27.2	72.8
Illiterate	186	11.6	88.4
Self-taught	41	27.8	72.2
Primary school	187	21.4	78.6
Junior high school	38	50.7	49.3
Senior high school	37	56.5	43.5
Univ. and college	49	67.6	32.4
Females	493	6.4	93.6
Illiterate	380	3.5	96.6
Self-taught	22	11.0	89.0
Primary school	63	10.4	89.6
Junior high school	10	29.9	70.1
Senior high school	13	28.5	71.6
Univ. and college	5	55.7	44.3

Sources: DGBAS (1987), p. 91.

of the elderly is also a factor influencing the adoption of their residential patterns. As for the attitudes of elderly people towards their current residential patterns, it can be observed from Table 8.3 that there was not much difference in attitudes of the elderly between the sexes. The majority of elderly people of both sexes were quite satisfied with the way they were living. Those who felt dissatisfied only accounted for about 3 per cent. However, attitudes towards residence varied with educational levels; the higher the educational qualifications of elderly people, the more they were satisfied with their current residence patterns.

The same survey also found that 54.4 per cent of the elderly people sampled were in good health. 37.2 per cent of the elderly answered that they were sometimes sick (but not very seriously ill), and 8.4 per cent were seriously ill and needed to be cared for by others. Looking at these figures in more detail, it can be seen from Table 8.4 that physical condition differed with age. The older the age group, the worse their physical condition. For example, only 36.8 per cent of elderly people aged 80 and over were in good health, while 63.1 per cent of those aged between 65 and 69 felt themselves to be 'healthy'.

In relation to the allocation of resources, it was also found that education plays a crucial role in the utilization of the existing welfare resources. As Table 8.5 shows, of these 1 031 000 sampled, only 17.3 per cent were insured. In other words, the vast majority of elderly people (82.7 per cent) did not take part in any insurance scheme. The participation in insurance schemes also varied with education and sex. Out of 493 000 elderly females, only 6.4 per cent had participated in insurance schemes, whereas 27.2 per cent of males had done so. For both sexes, well-educated people, especially those with higher education backgrounds, seemed to know better how to utilize existing welfare resources and protect themselves from risk by means of taking part in insurance schemes. Differences in the utilization of welfare services between people with different educational backgrounds is more noticeable among the female group than among males.

THE NEEDS OF ELDERLY PEOPLE IN TAIWAN

As the number and proportion of elderly people has grown, care for them has attracted a great deal of attention from both welfare policy makers and the general public in societies where aged people have been facing more and more problems in their lives. In most industrial societies, it is evident that changes in family structure have led to the transformation of the role played by the family in caring for old people. Although the functional relationship between change in family structure and industrialization or modernization has not yet been theoretically fully established, there is evidence that the responsibility for providing services or care for the elderly has gradually been shifted from the family to society. Based on the concept of risk-sharing, it is assumed that care for the elderly is better undertaken by institutions other than in their homes. However, there is also a substantial number of people holding different viewpoints. For example, it was once pointed out that 'the underlying principle of our services for the old should be this: that the best place for old people is their own homes, with help from home service if need be' (Shanas et al., 1968). Therefore, home help and home nursing have become the two most important domiciliary services for old people in many Western industrial societies. Domiciliary services for elderly people have been supplemented by health visiting and meals services available to small minorities of the elderly population. Only those old people who are physically handicapped and in need of special care will generally be accommodated in residential homes provided through public and non-profit agencies.

By observing the experiences of the care for elderly people in Western industrial societies, it seems that welfare provision has developed into two patterns. The first pattern is domiciliary services for those old people remaining in their homes. The second pattern is residential services for those old people who are unable to take care of themselves and are not cared for by home help provided by social workers and health visitors. These two patterns of welfare provision for elderly people can be seen as a reflection of state intervention into the supply of social services for the aged at a period when the function of the family has increasingly been dismantled on the one hand, and the role of the state in the provision of social services for old people has been enlarged on the other. These two patterns of welfare provision for elderly people in industrial societies have also been adopted in industrializing societies on the assumption that the structure and function of the family have begun to change as a result of industrialization and urbanization, as observed in Western societies earlier this century. It is accordingly assumed that the old people in today's industrializing societies are in need of the same patterns of social services developed in industrial societies.

As a society moving into the final stage of demographic transition, Taiwan has become an ideal crucible for testing the above theories about changes in family structure and suitable patterns of welfare services. In past decades, Taiwan has witnessed a sequence of changes in its societal, economic and political structure. It is often suggested that the family structure in Taiwan has undergone significant changes since 1950 – from a traditional extended family pattern into a nuclear one, in particular in view of the housing design in urban areas which appears to be more adequate for nuclear-sized families rather than extended ones. However, data presented in Table 8.1 give us a picture quite different from that normally assumed. More than 70 per cent of elderly people were living with their children. The adoption of such residence patterns is related to the level of education of elderly people; about three quarters of those with primary education (or less) living in ordinary homes were staying with their children, whereas only half of elderly people with higher education levels did so.

The same survey also found that, out of 2 180 000 people aged between 50 and 64, those who preferred to live with their children in old age accounted for 73.1 per cent, whereas those who wished to live in residential homes accounted only for 2.8 per cent. Again, level of education played an important role in determining the preferred residential pattern. The higher the education of the people, the more they preferred to live with their spouses only or live alone when growing old. For example, 18.2 per cent of illiterate people preferred to live with their spouses only or live alone when old, but 42.5 per cent of those with university or college education gave as their preference to stay with their spouses only or live alone.

With regard to the needs of elderly people for home services in Taiwan, in particular in urban areas, many empirical studies undertaken in past years in different cities of Taiwan have drawn quite similar conclusions (Chou, 1984; Chen, 1985; Hsu, 1986). These studies all indicate that over half of the elderly people in cities prefer to live with their children, more than one-third prefer to live near their children but in independent housing, and fewer than 15 per cent of elderly people prefer to live alone (Hsu, 1986). Similar findings are seen in the Taipei Study on Gerontology, which, in 1987, interviewed 1 519 people aged 65 and over in the Taipei metropolitan area (but excluded those elderly people in hospitals and institutions for the elderly). Whereas 73.8 per cent of sampled old people were staying with their children, 78.7 per cent of those sampled were willing to stay with their children (Chan, 1988a). More interestingly, it can be observed from studies of the DGBAS in the years between 1986 and 1989 that there is a declining trend in the willingness among people aged between 50 and 64 to live in residential homes. Data from studies of these four years show that of people aged between 50 and 64, the proportion of those willing to stay in residential homes dropped from 2.84 per cent in 1986, to 2.43 per cent in 1987, to 2.04 per cent in 1988, and then to 1.97 per cent in 1989 (DGBAS, 1990; Chan, 1991). Certainly, factors affecting the willingness of people to live in residential homes are many and complicated, but the tradition of strong family ties in Chinese society and people's reluctance to leave their own family may explain this phenomenon to some extent. Therefore, even though the modernization process has taken place over some time, the great majority of elderly people in Taiwan still prefer to stay with or close by their children. The proportion of elderly people who are willing to move into residential homes for care remains very small. That such a small proportion of elderly people receive institutional care is certainly different from Western countries.

The Taipei Study on Gerontology also found three main reasons which led elderly people not to live with their children. The first was that the elderly persons had no children or that their children were living abroad (40 per cent). The second was that children moved out of home after marriage (38.1 per cent). And the third reason was that housing was too small to accommodate two generations (21.9 per cent) (Chan, 1988a). However, it is also worth noting that with such housing arrangements, the proportion of elderly people who were dissatisfied with their current living arrangements was small (only 7 per cent), and 73.8 per cent of those interviewed were satisfied with their current living arrangements. This high degree of satisfaction is supported by the following finding. When the samples were asked whether they wished to change their current living arrangements, about three quarters of the elderly gave a negative answer, 17.5 per cent answered 'they do not mind', and fewer than 10 per cent expressed their wish to change their living arrangements. Based on the assumption that the preference for the living arrangements of elderly people reflects their need for welfare provisions, the study made a further investigation. It was found that most elderly people (67 per cent) preferred to live with their children, 6.5 per cent preferred to live near their children, 10 per cent preferred to stay alone, and 14.7 per cent preferred to stay in residential homes. Since the Taipei Study on Gerontology is a large-scale interdisciplinary research project, which provides fruitful data for the analysis of the ageing features in Taiwan, several features concerning the elderly in Taiwan may be summarized as follows:

The employment and health of elderly people
Elderly people interviewed in this study who are still in employment accounted for 18.3 per cent of the total sampled, and 81.7 per cent were not working. Table 8.6 indicates that the percentage of those elderly people who are still working declines with advancing age. With regard to health, about 30 per cent of those interviewed regarded themselves as being in a healthy condition, more than 40 per cent answered that their health was normal, and those who felt unhealthy accounted for 30 per cent. It is understandable that the older the respondents, the higher is the percentage of those who think their health is bad.

Table 8.6   Working and health conditions (self-evaluated) of elderly people.

	Total	Age		
		65–69	70–74	75+
Working	18.3	24.9	17.4	13.1
Not working	81.7	75.1	82.6	86.9
Total number	1 519	486	499	534
%	100.0	32.0	32.9	35.2
Unhealthy	27.9	23.6	29.3	30.7
Normal	42.3	44.6	40.9	41.6
Healthy	29.7	31.8	29.9	27.7
Total number	1 517	484	499	534
%	100.0	31.9	32.9	35.2

Source: Chan (1989).

Proportion of elderly people with health insurance
About 15 per cent of the interviewed elderly people were covered by various kinds of health insurance schemes, provided either by the government or by private agencies. The older the respondents, the smaller the proportion covered by health insurance. For instance, 21.8 per cent of those aged 65–69 were insured, while in the group aged 75 and over, the proportion of the insured was only 10.9 per cent.

Participation in community and social associations
It was found that only 10.8 per cent of the respondents had ever taken part in social and community associations for the aged. The participation rate for males (13.5 per cent) was higher than that for females (6.9 per cent). In order to understand the need of elderly people to join activities organized by these associations, several questions concerning the willingness of participation were asked. About 28.2 per cent of respondents replied positively, and there was a considerable difference in willingness to participate between sexes. The willingness to participate in community and social associations for males (35.4 per cent) was about twice of that for females (18.1 per cent).

Based on the assumption that the condition of health of elderly people has been improving over the past years due to the provision of health services for old people and their improving capability to work, this study also asked questions concerning the willingness of the aged to engage in social services even after retirement. About 23.2 per cent of the respondents expressed their willingness to provide social services for the community. But, differences between sexes are great, and the degree of willingness also varies with the age of the respondent. For example, while about one-third of the male respondents (32.3 per cent) replied that they were willing to contribute to society by providing services to the community, only 10.1 per cent of the females held a similar attitude. The older the respondents, the weaker the degree of willingness to provide social services to the community. In the group aged 65–69, 32.9 per cent of respondents were willing to provide services to the community; in the group aged 70–74, 22.7 per cent were, and in the group aged 75 and over, there were even fewer (15.2 per cent).

In response to asking whether they have any intention of finding a paid employment, about 81.1 per cent gave a negative answer. Differences between sexes in this respect are also noticeable: 90.5 per cent of the female respondents had no intention to do paid work, compared with 72.9 per cent for the males. The intention to find a paid job varied with educational level. For those who were educated in colleges, there were about 41.2 per cent wishing to do paid work. But for those who had never received any formal schooling, the proportion was only about 11.9 per cent.

The most serious problems faced and the most urgent needs
This study used open questions to explore the 'felt-needs' of elderly people. With regard to what matters worried elderly people the most when sick, about 61.3 per cent of respondents replied that they did not have any serious problem to worry about. Over one-fifth of respondents worried about their financial situation, 5 per cent worried about their families, and 3.8 per cent worried about their physical condition. More interestingly, about 6 per cent answered that the thing they worried about the most was the quality of doctors, and about 4 per cent were mostly concerned about medical facilities and the medical process. It was also found that the higher the education level of the elderly respondent, the higher the proportion of those who replied that there were no serious things to be worried about even while ill (Table 8.7). As to the question 'What is the most serious problem currently being faced in ordinary life?', 59.3 per cent of the elderly gave a negative reply, i.e., no difficulty at all. About one-fifth named economic problems as the most serious difficulty they were facing. Fewer than 10 per cent gave health problems as their answer (Table 8.8), and the proportion who named emotional comfort or leisure activity arrangements as the most serious problem was only about 3.7 per cent. With regard to the services most needed by elderly respondents, it was again found that about two-thirds replied 'no special need at all'. About 17.8 per cent of the respondents needed financial assistance, 4.5 per cent needed health and medical care, 2.4 per cent needed someone to help with housework, 2 per cent needed emotional support, and 1.6 per cent needed assistance for leisure activity arrangements (Table 8.9). Education again played a crucial role in the kind of the 'felt-need' of the elderly. The higher the education level of the respondents, the higher the proportion of respondents answering 'no special need'. Of more interest is the fact that the older the respondents, the higher is

Table 8.7 What most worried elderly people when sick.

	Education level			
	No schooling	Primary education	Secondary education	College
Do not worry	56.6	61.3	69.9	71.2
Economic	25.6	20.0	14.1	6.8
Quality of doctors	5.1	7.9	6.0	5.1
Medical facility	2.2	1.3	2.2	1.7
Physical condition	4.1	3.6	2.7	4.5
Medical process	0.9	1.5	1.6	2.3
Families	5.1	4.1	3.8	7.9
Job	0.4	0.3	0	0.6
Total number	684	390	184	177
%	47.7	27.2	12.8	12.3

Source: Chan (1989).

Table 8.8 The most serious problems currently faced by elderly people.

	Age			
	65–69	70–74	75+	Total
No difficulty	58.4	59.1	60.4	59.3
Health	8.1	7.7	11.0	9.0
Economic	23.0	22.5	17.1	20.8
Emotional problems	2.3	2.5	4.6	3.2
Housing	1.7	0.8	1.3	1.3
Leisure	0.4	0.8	0.2	0.5
Housework	1.1	1.7	1.7	1.5
Others	4.9	4.7	3.8	4.4
Total number	469	479	520	1 468

Source: Chan (1989).

Table 8.9 The services needed the most by elderly people.

	Age			
	65–69	70–74	75+	Total
No need	63.5	66.6	67.9	66.6
Health	4.6	3.0	6.0	4.5
Economic	18.1	18.6	16.9	17.8
Emotional support	2.6	1.5	1.8	2.0
Housing	1.5	1.3	0.4	1.0
Children	0.4	0.9	0.6	0.6
Leisure	2.6	1.7	0.6	1.6
Housework	1.7	2.4	3.0	2.4
Job	2.4	1.1	0.8	1.4
Residential care	0.2	0.6	0.6	0.5
Others	2.2	2.3	1.6	2.0
Total number	458	467	504	1 429

Source: Chan (1989).

the proportion answering 'no need', although the difference between different age groups is not so great as that between different education levels.

The need for welfare services
As mentioned above, about three-quarters of elderly people were living with their children or close kin. But, by asking closed questions about the services received and the need of elderly people for these services, it was found (Table 8.10) that over half replied that they needed services such as being taken care of by others, having a leisure activity centre nearby, and going to visit or chat with friends. At the same time, about 44.9 per cent of the elderly expressed their need for assistance with housework, while an even smaller proportion expressed their need for assistance to contact their families (including family members in mainland China). More importantly, it was found that the relation of the services received to the need for services was not consistent with the original assumption of this study, which was that those who did not receive the services named would have a greater need for them. For instance, among those elderly

people who did not have anyone to help with their housework, only one-fifth replied they had such a need, while 66.5 per cent of the elderly people receiving housework assistance expressed their need for this kind of service. This kind of finding is also applicable to other services, such as being cared for by others and having friends coming to visit or chat.

Asking about whether respondents thought that married children should live with their parents, it was found that 58.2 per cent of the elderly held a positive attitude towards this living pattern. Only about a quarter of the respondents gave a negative reply. Answers to this question varied greatly with the current living style of the respondents. As Table 8.11 shows, among respondents living with children, 62.1 per cent thought that children should live with their parents after marriage, while the corresponding proportion among respondents who were not living with their children was only 47.3 per cent. Interestingly, the proportion of the elderly who expressed their willingness to live with married children was about 20 percentage points higher than the figure holding the positive attitude noted above. The degree of willingness to live with married children varied greatly with current residence patterns. It can also be seen from Table 8.11 that about 86 per cent of the elderly living with their

Table 8.10 Services currently received and the need for services.

Needs	Services received		
	Received	Not received	Total
Housework assistance	66.5	20.2	44.9
Care by others	68.4	31.9	56.8
Leisure activity centre nearby	68.3	52.8	58.0
Visit of friends	78.0	41.4	64.1
Assistance to contact families	65.1	15.2	38.1

Source: Chan (1989).

Table 8.11 Opinions about whether married children should live with parents and willingness to live with married children by current residence pattern.

	Current residence pattern		
	With children	Not with children	Total
Certainly should live together	62.1	47.3	58.2
Not necessary	20.6	35.9	24.6
Depends	17.3	16.7	17.2
Total number	1 120	395	1 515
%	73.9	26.1	100.0
Willing to live with children	85.9	58.6	78.8
Unwilling	8.3	29.4	13.8
Depends	5.8	12.0	7.4
Total number	1 117	391	1 508
%	74.1	25.9	100.0

Source: Chan (1989).

Table 8.12 Satisfaction with current living patterns and desire for change.

		Current residence pattern			
	Single	Couple only	Two generation	Three generation	Total
Satisfied	54.2	73.7	70.0	78.2	73.7
No comment	22.9	18.9	19.5	18.2	19.0
Dissatisfied	22.9	7.4	10.5	3.6	7.3
Total number	131	175	343	867	1 516
%	8.6	11.5	22.6	57.3	100.0
Wish to change	22.5	12.1	11.8	6.6	9.8
Do not mind	23.3	14.9	9.1	16.6	17.5
No intention to change	54.3	73.0	69.1	76.8	72.7
Total number	129	174	340	862	1 505
%	8.6	11.6	22.6	57.3	100.0

Source: Chan (1989).

children were willing to live with their children, whereas only 58.6 per cent who were not living with their children expressed their willingness to live with their married children. Family structure was also found to have considerable influence on the satisfaction of the elderly respondents. On the whole, about three-quarters (73.7 per cent) were satisfied with their current residence pattern. But, if we divide the respondents into four groups in terms of their family structure, it is the group who are single who have the highest dissatisfaction with their current residence pattern, while the group who live in large families (especially three generations), have the highest degree of satisfaction. This kind of satisfaction is closely related to their intention to change their current residence patterns (Chan, 1989).

To summarize, the Taipei Study on Gerontology seems in some respects to support the thesis that with the growing number of old people and with rapid changes in family structure, the needs of elderly people will continue to be diversified and there is a growing need for more home services rather than residential care. And given the fact that there has been a tendency in Taiwan for young couples both to work, it is foreseeable that the need for home services in the form of health visiting and domiciliary care will continue to grow. Because most of the houses accommodating old people are not well designed, being without lifts, for instance, these elderly people, especially those who are physically handicapped or disabled, will have to be confined in a small living environment, in need of extra home care services, even though they are living with their children. Concerning attitudes of elderly people towards seeking health care, it was found that 18 per cent of the elderly perceived distance barriers, and 40 per cent perceived cost barriers (Chiang, 1989). Therefore, how to effectively provide elderly people with the welfare services needed should be the major concern of the decision makers in Taiwan.

WELFARE SERVICES FOR AGED PEOPLE IN TAIWAN

The rise and expansion of social welfare services in Taiwan is a consequence of a form of incrementalistic strategy through which social welfare services have been moulded in coverage and range. Despite its comparatively short history of implementation, the development of Taiwan's social welfare services has been a mixture of idealism and pragmatism. On the one hand, the idea of social welfare has been drawn mainly from traditional Chinese culture which rests upon Confucianism, whose main tenet is centred around the theme of the 'Great Harmonious World'. Social welfare services have therefore been instituted as a result of compromising the ideal of social welfare as a social virtue with the actual situations in society at the time. On the other hand, Taiwan's social security measures have also been largely influenced by the Western model of social security, and especially by the concept of the 'welfare state', which is in consonance with Chinese culture in pursuit of a prosperous and stable society.

At present, welfare provisions in Taiwan are basically available in the form of social welfare, which can be divided into two main patterns in terms of the nature of provision. The first pattern is the social insurance scheme which provides cash benefits as well as benefits in kind for its contributors. The second pattern is personal social services which mainly provide services in kind for special needy groups. The former was instituted and implemented as industrialization was about to develop in the 1950s, while the latter had been made available in a piecemeal fashion in the 1960s but it was not until the end of the 1970s that legislation emerged.

Basically, social welfare services for elderly people are not available universally for everyone; rather, they are provided in a piecemeal form and on a selective basis. Although there have been a few residential homes for the aged provided by the private sector in recent years, the contemporary welfare provisions for aged people in Taiwan are provided by central government's two insurance bureaux and social affairs departments (bureaux) of the provincial (municipal cities) government in the following schemes:

1. An old-age retirement lump-sum benefit for those elderly people insured under the schemes of labour insurance or government employees' insurance.
2. Residential welfare services for homeless retired veterans and elderly people without support from close kin.
3. Medical treatment for elderly people who are below the prescribed subsistence level (measured by a means-test): treatment — free or at a concessionary rate.

The first welfare scheme for elderly people is one involving cash and is available only to those who have been covered by labour insurance, or the government employees' insurance, before retirement. Under the government employees' insurance, old-age benefit is normally paid to those who have been working in governmental agencies for at least five years; the retirement age for government employees' insurance is generally 65 years. However, those who have paid their premium for five years and reached the age of 65 are entitled to old-age benefit upon retirement. Under this scheme, the old-age benefit is paid in a lump sum, but in addition to the old-age benefit paid by the GEI, all government employees are entitled to receive their occupational pensions either in lump-sum or monthly payments, or as a mixture of the above, which are earnings-related. As for labour insurance, the old-age retirement benefit is payable to males aged 60 and females aged 55 with a minimum of one year's contribution. But those with more than ten years of contributions are entitled to a reduced old-age benefit while reaching retirement age. These old-age benefits are paid as a lump sum which varies with the length of contribution, and are earnings-related. The amount paid and conditions of eligibility for these old-age retirement benefits under labour insurance and government employees' insurance are different, and may be explained as follows:

Labour insurance
The amount of old-age benefit stipulated by the Labour Insurance Act of 1988 varies according to the following conditions:

1. For those who reach the retirement age and have contributed to the scheme for more than one year but fewer than fifteen years, a lump-sum old-age benefit equivalent to one-month's salary per accumulated credit year is paid upon retirement.
2. For those aged 55 or over who have contributed to the scheme for more than fifteen years, a lump-sum old-age benefit equivalent to two-month's salary per accumulated credit year with a maximum of 45 months is paid upon retirement; a period exceeding half a year may be reckoned as one year.
3. For those who have been working for the same company and contributed to the scheme for more than 25 years, regardless of age, a lump-sum old-age benefit equivalent to two-month's salary per accumulated credit year with a maximum of 45 months is paid upon retirement, with any period exceeding half a year being reckoned as one year.
4. For those aged 55 or over who have been working in a post with special risks, or in physically hard labour, approved by the government, for more than five years, a lump-sum old-age benefit equivalent to one-month's salary of the insured is payable.

Claimants for the old-age retirement benefit under the labour insurance scheme have had a marked increase in the past decades. During the period 1950–60, the total number of claims for old-age benefit was 4 543. It increased to 21 355 in the 1960s, and then to 71 700 in the 1970s. After 1980, the number of claims has maintained a steady growth. After reaching its peak (27 911) in 1986, it fell slightly to 25 841 in 1988. Payments to the old-age benefit under the labour insurance scheme have grown steadily since 1950. During the period 1950–55, the proportion of old-age benefit payments to the total benefit payments was 1.26 per cent. It rose to 9.49 per cent in 1956–69, then to 13.19 per cent in 1970–78, and reached its highest level (18.3 per cent) in 1979. Since 1980, the proportion of old-age benefit payment to the total benefit payments fluctuated between 13 per cent and 17 per cent; it was 15.7 per cent in 1988.

Government employees' insurance
Under this scheme, only those who have contributed for at least five years are entitled to old-age benefit upon retirement. The criteria for the old-age benefit are prescribed by law as follows:

1. For those who have contributed to the scheme for up to five years but for fewer than six years, a lump-sum old-age benefit equivalent to five months' salary is payable.
2. For those who have contributed to the scheme for six to ten years, in addition to a lump-sum old-age benefit equivalent to five months' salary, an amount of one-month's salary is payable per accumulated service year from the sixth year.
3. For those who have contributed to the scheme for ten to fifteen years, in addition to a lump-sum old-age benefit equivalent to ten months' salary, an amount of two-months' salary is payable for accumulated service years from the eleventh years.

4. For those who have contributed to the scheme for more than fifteen years but for fewer than twenty years, in addition to the previous lump-sum old-age benefit, an additional amount of three months' salary is payable per accumulated service year from the sixteenth year.
5. For those who have contributed to the scheme for more than twenty years, a maximum amount of thirty-six months' salary is paid upon retirement.

The number of claimants in 1964 for this old-age retirement benefit under the government employees' insurance scheme was 1 074, or less than 0.5 per cent of total contributors. This number increased to 8 527, or 1.7 per cent of total contributors in 1987. The proportion of payments to this old-age benefit to the total government employees' insurance expenditure has increased dramatically from 0.1 per cent in 1963 to 15.6 per cent in 1970, 46.7 per cent in 1980, and 50.9 per cent in 1987. This rapid increase reveals that the old-age benefit has become the largest part of government employees' insurance expenditure, and it will continue to grow as the number of the insured reaching the eligible retirement age substantially increases.

Apart from the above two statutory insurance schemes, those employed in private firms receive a lump-sum retirement allowance from their employers, which varies from occupation to occupation without statutory regulations. There are also two other schemes for welfare services provided especially for elderly people. First, residential welfare services for homeless veterans are directly provided by the Commission for Veterans Training and Occupational Guidance which is a statutory body of the central government. Up to now (1991), the Commission has operated thirteen residential homes which accommodate about 70 000 aged veterans. Meanwhile, county authorities of Taiwan province operate 29 residential homes, accommodating about 546 homeless aged people. In addition, voluntary and private welfare agencies also run 35 residential homes for aged persons, in which about 8 000 people are cared for free of charge. Of these 35 residential homes, over half also provide accommodation for aged people charged with certain proportions of costs. Finally, there are two other private residential homes accommodating those elderly people who are able to pay fees themselves. Generally speaking, although the number of residents in both public and private residential institutions increased to over 10 000 in 1988, this still accounted for only a meagre proportion (less than 1 per cent) of the elderly population in Taiwan (Chan, 1991). Even if the number of elderly people living in the Homes for the Veterans is included, the number of aged people being cared for in residential institutions is low in both absolute and relative terms.

In addition to residential services for the aged, county authorities have also established the following services in kind. The quantity and quality of these services vary with the number of the elderly population and the availability of financial resources in each county authority.

1. Health and medical services for elderly people, which are restricted to free medical examination, a service started in 1981. The central government has, by means of giving financial support, asked professional nurses or related medical associations to provide aged people with home nursing services. The number of this kind of nursing services reached 762 in 1988.
2. With financial subsidy from the central government, a great variety of old people's clubs (often called 'evergreen clubs') began to be set up in 1980 at the community level. These clubs, associations or cultural centres for the aged numbered about 3 000 in 1988 and are designed to provide elderly people with leisure and recreational facilities.

3. Consultative services for elderly people are provided to address personal and family problems and to deal with other difficulties.
4. Free or reduced fares for public bus services or public exhibitions are provided upon proof of age for those aged over 70 years. In 1988, five cities (Taipei City, Taipei Hsien, Keelung City, Tainan City and Kaohsiung City) ran free bus services for aged people.
5. The Ministry of the Interior has since 1987 subsidized local governments to provide day-care services for their aged residents.
6. In order to take care of aged members of low-income families, Taipei and Kaohsiung cities and Taiwan province provide them with a cash allowance. In 1988 the amount of this monthly allowance in the above three administrative districts was NT$3 600, NT$1 900 and NT$2 100 respectively.

CONCLUSION

Taiwan is a nation enjoying rapid economic growth of economy, and welfare for needy groups, such as the poor, handicapped and elderly people, has begun to receive more attention from both the government and the general public. However, although the government sees itself as being responsible for the welfare of aged people, the fundamental principle underlying its welfare services for the aged is that the family should be responsible for caring for elderly people. The preference of the elderly to stay with their children clearly reflects the tradition of family ties in Chinese societies. But housing problems, especially in urban areas, make the ideal goal of 'living together' difficult to maintain. With the growth in the number of women working outside the home, elderly people who live with their children may be left in isolation or receive no care in the daytime. Therefore, if the family still retains its major role in providing support for the elderly, it is then necessary for the government to find alternative ways to take care of the aged as a group.

Undoubtedly, the trend of increase in the number and proportion of elderly people in the total population will continue to accelerate. The introduction of a national health insurance scheme and a pension scheme for labour in the near future, as announced by the government, may solve medical care and financial problems for aged people but the question of how to provide a well-designed and effective welfare programme for them should take into account the needs of elderly people, changes in family structure, and the prevalence of a traditional value system.

REFERENCES

Chan, Hou-sheng (1988a). A study on the relationship between welfare needs of the elderly and the family structure in Taipei metropolitan area. Paper presented to the Symposium on Taiwan's Social Phenomena. Sun Yat-sen Institute for Social Sciences and Philosophy, Academic Sinica, ROC, Taipei.
Chan, Hou-sheng (1988b). Needs of the elderly for home care services in a changing society: the case of Taipei metropolitan city. In National Association of Volunteers, Taiwan (1988) (Ed) *Social Service and Aging Policies*: pp. 28–36.
Chan, Hou-sheng (1989). The need of the elderly for social services in a rapidly changing city – the case of Taipei. Paper presented to the Symposium on Institutional Transition in Changing Societies: The Case of Taiwan and South

Africa. Sun Yat-sen Institute for Social Sciences and Philosophy, Academic Sinica, ROC, Taipei.

Chan, Hou-sheng (1991). *A Study on Residential Care Services in Taiwan.* Council for Research, Development and Evaluation, Executive Yuan, ROC, Taipei.

Chen, Y.C. (1985). *The Study of the Problem of Welfare for the Elderly in Kaohsiung City.* Social Welfare Research Centre, Tung-hai University, Taichung, Taiwan.

Chiang, Tung-liang (1989). Use of health services by the elderly in the Taipei area. In *Journal of the Formosan Medical Association*, **88**, 9, 919–25.

Chou, W.L. (1984). The study of welfare needs and living satisfaction of the elderly in Taipei City. M.A. thesis, National Taiwan University.

Council for Economic Planning and Development (1990). *Taiwan Statistical Data Book* CEPD, ROC, Taipei.

DGBAS (Directorate-General of Budget, Accounting & Statistics) (1987). *A Study on the Youth and the Elderly in Taiwan*, DGBAS, Executive Yuan, ROC, Taipei.

Hsieh, Kao-chiao (1986). Population aging and social policy in Taiwan. Paper presented in the International Conference on Social Service and Aging Policies, May 15, 1986, Taipei.

Hsu, James *et al.* (1986). *A Study on the Welfare Needs of the Elderly and Planning for Meeting Needs.* Soochow University, Taipei.

National Association of Volunteers, Taiwan (NAV) (Ed.) (1988). *Social Service and Aging Policies.* NAV, Taipei.

Qureshi, H. and Walker, A. (1986). Caring for elderly people: the family and the state. In *Aging and Social Policy: A Critical Assessment*, C. Phillipson and A. Walker (Eds), Gower, London.

Ross, R.B. *et al.* (1985). *Welfare Provision for the Elderly and the Role of the State.* Anglo-German Foundation for the Study of Industrial Society, London.

Shanas, E., Townsend, P., Wedderburn, D., Friis, H., Milhøj, P. and Stehower, J. (1968). *Old People in Three Industrial Societies.* Routledge and Kegan Paul, London.

Tinker, A. (1984). *The Elderly in Modern Society.* Longman, London.

Sung-Jae Choi
Department of Social Welfare
Seoul National University

9 AGEING AND SOCIAL WELFARE IN SOUTH KOREA

INTRODUCTION

The phenomenon of modernization, of which salient aspects are the development of health techniques, the development of economic technologies, urbanization, and the expansion of mass education, is supposed to contribute to the diminishing status of older people in society (Cowgill, 1974). Thus it appears that the diminished status of older people, in turn, ultimately contributes to the emergence of the problems often associated with ageing in industrial society.

Korea, previously a stable agricultural society, began to modernize with the influx of Western thought and the institution of modern mass education immediately after the end of World War II. This modernization has been accelerated by rapid industrialization since the early 1960s. In Korea's industrial structure, products from secondary and tertiary industry accounted for 89.8 per cent of the GNP in 1989 compared to 59 per cent in 1960, while employment in both sectors accounted for 80.5 per cent of the total employment in 1989 compared to 31.0 per cent in 1965. Per capita GNP increased to US $4 968 (all references are to US dollars) in 1989 from $87 in 1960. Urbanization advanced rapidly: the urban population increased from 28 per cent in 1966 to 72 per cent in 1989. As mass education expanded, the average number of years of education received increased from 5 in 1966 to 8.6 in 1985. In 1985, the average number of years of education that people between 20–49 years of age received was 9.9, while for people of 50 years and over it was only 4.6.

The phenomenon of modernization in Korea seems not only to diminish the status of older Koreans, but ultimately to contribute to the occurrence of the problem of ageing; a problem that has emerged as a social problem principally since the beginning of the 1970s. With an increasing elderly population, social problems are now becoming serious.

From the basic position of supporting the modernization theory of ageing and viewing ageing as a serious social problem in Korea, this paper will review the demographic aspects of ageing in Korea. It then examines the problems and needs of elderly Koreans, investigates existing social welfare provisions for the elderly, analyzes problems in current policies and, finally, makes recommendations for policy development.

DEMOGRAPHIC ASPECTS OF AGEING

As indicated in Table 9.1 the life expectancy of the Korean people has seen a great increase since the beginning of this century. In the early years of this

Table 9.1 Life expectancy of Korean people for selected years.

Year	Male	Female
1905–1910	22.6	24.4
1945–1950	45.6	50.7
1950–1955	48.3	53.9
1960–1965	54.9	61.0
1970–1975	59.8	66.7
1980–1985	64.9	71.3
1990–1995	68.2	75.0
2000–2005	69.3	76.2

Source: Adapted from C.K. Kim (1984); Economic Planning Board (1989).

century (1905–1910), life expectancy for male Koreans was 22.6 years and for females it was 24.4 years. After 40 years (1945–1950), it had doubled to 45.6 years for males and 50.7 years for females. Another 40 years later (1980–1985) it had tripled to 64.9 years for males and 71.3 years for females. It is expected to reach the level of industrial countries for both sexes by the year 2000. With the lengthening of life expectancy, the sheer number and proportion of the elderly population of 65 years and over has also increased. A more rapid increase in this and the next decade is expected, as shown in Table 9.2.

The number of elderly people aged 65 and over, 713 000 in 1955, doubled after 25 years (1980), and after another 25 years (2005) the number is expected to increase by more than four times that of the 1955 figure. The rate of increase in the number of older Koreans has far exceeded that of any other component of the Korean population. The proportion of the elderly population was 3.3 per cent in 1955; it increased to 3.9 per cent 25 years later (1980) and is expected to be more than 6.2 per cent in another 25 years (2005). Although the proportion of the elderly population has shown a great increase over the past 40 years, it is expected to increase even more rapidly after the year 2000 because the ageing rate of the Korean population is apparently far greater than that of industrial countries (Ministry of Foreign Affairs, 1978).

Industrialization and urbanization have both contributed to changes in the

Table 9.2 The number and percentage of the population by age groups for selected years.

Year	Total	0–14 Years	15–64 Years	65+ Years
1955	22 502 (100.0)	8 865 (41.2)	11 924 (55.5)	713 (3.3)
1960	24 989 (100.0)	10 731 (42.9)	13 435 (53.8)	823 (3.3)
1966	29 160 (100.0)	12 684 (43.5)	15 514 (53.2)	962 (3.4)
1970	31 435 (100.0)	13 242 (42.1)	17 154 (54.6)	1 039 (3.3)
1975	34 697 (100.0)	13 208 (38.1)	20 264 (58.4)	1 207 (3.5)
1980	37 407 (100.0)	12 656 (33.8)	23 305 (62.3)	1 446 (3.9)
1985	40 420 (100.0)	12 095 (29.9)	26 575 (65.8)	1 750 (4.3)
1990	43 601 (100.0)	11 868 (27.2)	29 709 (68.1)	2 025 (4.7)
1995	45 962 (100.0)	11 598 (25.2)	31 968 (69.6)	2 397 (5.2)
2000	48 017 (100.0)	11 078 (23.1)	33 969 (70.7)	2 972 (6.2)
2020	52 473 (100.0)	9 258 (17.6)	37 445 (71.4)	5 772 (11.0)

Source: Economic Planning Board (1986; 1987; 1989).
Unit: thousands.

demographic structure of the older Koreans living in both urban and rural areas. In 1985, 59 per cent of elderly people lived in urban areas. However, the proportion of the elderly population living in rural areas was more than twice the proportion of those living in urban areas. The proportion of the elderly population in all urban areas was 3.3 per cent, while that of those in all rural areas was 7.8 per cent in 1985. Such a disparity in the demographic structure is expected to be much greater in the early years of next century in the light of rapid industrialization and urbanization. This expedites the migration of the younger workforce from rural areas into urban areas, thus leaving an older rural population. This change in demographic structure appears to contribute to the occurrence of the problems of ageing in the rural areas.

As regards living arrangements, 99.7 per cent of Koreans aged 65 and over are living with their families or alone in the community, whereas only 0.3 per cent are living in institutions. A national survey (Rhee *et al.*, 1989) conducted in 1988 revealed the living arrangements of the elderly aged 60 and over who were living in the community (Table 9.3). Three out of four Koreans aged 60 and over live with their married or unmarried children, while one in four lives only with his or her spouse or alone, away from his or her children. It is notable that the proportion of single-generation elderly families, in which an elderly person lives with either his or her spouse or alone, is much greater in the urban areas. The proportion of single-generation elderly families is likely to increase rapidly because an increasing number of elderly people, as well as their married children, prefer to live apart from each other (Kong *et al.*, 1987).

Table 9.3 Living arrangements of elderly Koreans residing in the community (number = 3 050).

Living arrangements	Total	Large city	Medium and small city	Rural area
Live alone	9.6	6.9	7.8	12.1
With spouse	13.3	7.7	9.2	18.8
With married son	53.7	55.8	58.0	50.6
With married daughter	3.6	5.7	4.3	1.9
With unmarried children	18.4	22.1	19.3	15.5
With relatives	1.1	1.3	1.2	1.0
With the unrelated	0.3	0.5	0.2	0.1
Total	100.0	100.0	100.0	100.0

Source: Adapted from Rhee *et al.* (1989).
Unit: per cent.

PROBLEMS AND NEEDS OF ELDERLY KOREANS

As the modernization theory of ageing postulates, salient aspects of the phenomenon are ultimately contributing to the emergence of the ageing problem in contemporary Korean society. The major types of problems related to ageing in Korean society can be said to be: the sharp decline of income and economic dependence on children; difficulties in health care; role loss and difficulties in finding leisure activities; and social-psychological conflicts and feelings of alienation. These problems will be briefly examined below.

Sharp decline of income and economic dependence on children
The most serious type of ageing problem in Korea is that of economic insecurity. One of the major factors contributing to a sharp decline in the income of Koreans and their consequent economic dependence on children is the mandatory retirement system. This retirement system has been in practice in both the public and private sectors of employment since the early 1960s. Because the National Pension programme covering most workers only started in 1988, and cannot provide benefits for retirees, the most common and major source of income for those subject to the mandatory retirement system is currently the retirement benefits given under the provision of the Labour Standards Act. However, its benefit level is not sufficient to maintain a minimum living standard (Min, 1985). Other factors contributing to the financial insecurity of elderly people are lack of social security provisions, excessive and unnecessary support for their children, difficulties in re-employment after retirement, and unstable employment and wages (Kim, 1984).

Of all the households below the poverty level in 1989 (the level was set by the government), 10 per cent were headed by those aged 65 and over. Out of the total number of elderly people, 20.6 per cent were below the poverty level (Ministry of Health and Social Affairs, 1989). About half of the elderly people aged 60 and over were said to have financial difficulties (Korea Survey Polls, 1984), and even more than half of the elderly people who received retirement benefits or old age pensions (special pensions for government employees, military personnel, and private school teachers) said it was difficult to live within that income (Ha and Kim, 1986).

As shown in Table 9.4, about half of older Koreans aged 60 and over are dependent on their children for their living expenses while the other half are independent of their children (Rhee, 1989). Only about half of the elderly aged 60 and over have their own income, the major sources of which are their own work, profits from property, public and private pensions and charity (Lim *et al.*, 1985). Most elderly Koreans take for granted that they will receive economic support from their own children. However, contrary to this expectation, there are many instances where older Koreans are not supported by their children. An increasing number of elderly Koreans suffer from financial difficulties because of their children's avoidance of, or inability to provide, economic support. This is one of the emerging aspects of the ageing problem in Korea.

Difficulties in health care
It is well documented that the risk of illness and disability increases with

Table 9.4 Economic support of elderly Koreans by living arrangements (number = 19 246).

Living arrangements	Type of economic support	Proportion (%)
Live with children	Dependent on children	44.3
Live with children	Independent from children	32.0
Live separately from children	Dependent on children	6.9
Live separately from children	Independent from children	15.2
Total		100.0

Source: Adapted from Rhee (1989).

advancing age. This generates a high demand for health care services, which in turn requires very high personal and social costs. A national survey (Korea Survey Polls, 1984) indicated more than half the elderly people are not in good health, with poor health being the most common matter for concern. From several survey studies it could be inferred that about 6 per cent of elderly Koreans are bedridden, while about 80 per cent have no limitations in performing daily activities and some 10 per cent or more have some physical limitations (Lim *et al.*, 1985; Rhee and Huh, 1985).

The major health care problems relating to the elderly are difficulties in the payment of health care costs and caring for frail or disabled elderly people who need help with normal daily activities. Since the prevalence of disease and accidents among the elderly is two or three times that of the remaining population and the treatment period is much longer (Huh, 1983), their health care costs (the patient's share of the costs) are also higher. The Medical Insurance Statistical Yearbook of 1987 indicates that the medical costs of the population aged 60 and over are 1.6 times those of people over 60 (Federation of Korean Medical Insurance Societies, 1988).

As the aged population increases, the number of frail or disabled elderly Koreans who need assistance in normal daily life also increases. It is becoming more difficult to take care of such elderly people in the home. This may be due to several factors such as the changing values of family life, the nuclearization of the family, the decrease in family size, and women's increasing participation in the workforce and social activities. Contrary to this trend, the traditional value of filial piety that emphasizes the provision of personal care for one's parents seems to strongly discourage the family from accepting care services from non-family members. However, most elderly Koreans still want their sons and daughters-in-law to take care of them when they are not in good health (Lim *et al.*, 1985). Thus many elderly Koreans seem to have difficulties in receiving care services at home. This is becoming a new aspect of the problem of ageing in Korea.

Role loss and difficulties in leisure activities
Retirement is generally said to be a product of modernization or industrialization (Donahue, *et al.*, 1960). The loss of social roles, particularly the loss of the occupational role and its correlates in industrial societies, results mainly from the mandatory retirement system.

It is noticeable that while the mandatory retirement age in private sectors of employment, to which the overwhelming majority of workers belong, is generally 55 (Korea Employers' Federation, 1988), in public sectors it varies from 58 to 65. Retirement at an earlier age tends to make for a long period of later life without any particular work or activity. Roles appropriate to age are prescribed by social norms and values (Rosow, 1974). Korean society is caught between traditional and modern values in the process of rapid social change, without having developed new values that support the roles of elderly people in modern Korean society. Moreover, rigid age-grading norms that are relatively well preserved are likely to limit the development of new roles or activities for elderly people. This results in confusion as to the kinds of roles and activities that are appropriate for them. Elderly Koreans seem to be caught in 'roleless' roles.

Not only because of a lack of role models, but also due to a lack of socialization to leisure activities and a lack of organized leisure programmes, older Koreans often seem unable to enjoy leisure activities that are socially desirable as well as appropriate. A majority of older Koreans undertake simple informal activities such as visiting friends or relatives, listening to the radio and watching TV, housework, playing cards or chess and the like (Chang and Choi, 1987).

Social-psychological conflict and alienation
The social-psychological conflict with, and alienation from, children or family members is also an emerging aspect of the problem of ageing in Korea. Integration into the family is an important component of life satisfaction for older people (Liang *et al.*, 1980). In Korea, it appears that modernization is exerting a strong negative influence on the social integration of old people into the family. The factors of modernization, specifically work-role loss, differences in educational levels and in value orientation between elderly people and their children all seem to contribute to a psychological alienation of many Korean elderly people from their families (Choi, 1984).

The educational level of older Koreans is generally much lower than that of the younger generations. This difference in the level of education may result in differences of values between the generations (Choi, 1984). Most elderly Koreans seem to feel that there is a great difference in value orientation between them and their children. One study revealed that more than 50 per cent of the respondents expressed at least some degree of value difference between them and their children, and about 30 per cent of the respondents felt there was a great degree of difference (Lim *et al.*, 1985). In particular the value differences resulting from differences in educaticnal levels appear to have a strong effect on the alienation of the Korean elderly (Choi, 1984). Older Koreans and their married children increasingly want to live apart from each other in order to avoid conflict and the feeling of alienation (Kim *et al.* 1986; Kim and Kim, 1983; Kong *et al.*, 1987). Increasing instances of children avoiding care of older parents, parental abuse, elderly people seeking separate living accommodation (including homes for the aged), and elderly people running away from home, all seem to be related to the problems of conflict and alienation.

SOCIAL WELFARE PROVISION FOR ELDERLY KOREANS

Social welfare provision for elderly Koreans can be grouped into four categories according to the nature of the provision: income maintenance, health care, housing, and social services. The major programmes in each category will be examined around the four basic dimensions of policy issues: coverage and eligibility requirements, benefit provision, delivery, and financial system.

Income maintenance programmes
Currently there are five categories of income maintenance programmes for older Koreans (Table 9.5): public pensions, public assistance, retirement benefit, special treatment for the elderly, and job placement.

Public pension programmes
There are four public pension programmes, all designed as contributory social insurance schemes. Three are for people employed in particular occupations, such as civil servants, military personnel and private school teachers. The fourth, known as the National Pension (NP), is for people in general, those employed in industry, commerce, agriculture, fisheries and those who are

Table 9.5 Income maintenance programmes for elderly Koreans.

Category	Programme	Year instituted
● Public pension	Civil Service Pension (CSP)	1960
	Military Service Pension (MSP)	1963
	Private School Teachers Pension (PSTP)	1975
	National Pension (NP)	1988
● Public assistance	Livelihood Protection (LP)	1961
	Old Age Allowance (OAA)	1991
● Retirement benefits	Retirement Benefits (RB)	1953
● Special treatment	Elderly Discounts (ED)	1980
	Free Bus Coupon (FBC)	1990
● Job placement	Elderly Job Bank (EJB)	1981
	Elderly Workshop (EW)	1986
	Elderly Job Support (EJS)	1991

Table 9.6 Covered persons and recipients under income maintenance programmes in 1990.

	Covered persons (A) (thousands)	A/Total employees (%)	Recipients (B) (thousands)	B/Elderly population of 65+ (%)
Civil Service Pension (CSP)	828[1]	4.8	18	0.9
Military Service Pension (MSP)	132[2]	0.7	37	1.9
Private School Teachers Pension (PSTP)	152[3]	0.9	1	0.5
National Pension (NP)	4 594[4]	26.5	–	–
Livelihood Protection (LP)	2 251[5]	–	269	13.7
Retirement Benefits (RB)	4 828[6]	29.5	–	–
Total	8 196*	36.0	334†	17.0

Sources: [1] Civil Service Pension Administration Corporation
  [2] Ministry of National Defence
  [3] Private School Teachers Pension Corporation
  [4] National Pension Corporation
  [5] Ministry of Health and Social Affairs
  [6] Ministry of Labor

Notes: * The number of persons covered by the NP was excluded from the total because those covered by the NP are also covered by the RB.
  † The number of total recipients includes only those who are currently receiving benefits. Those who received a lump-sum refund in special pension programmes and retirement benefits are excluded from the total recipients.

self-employed. The persons covered and the recipients of income-maintenance programmes are shown in Table 9.6.

Pensions for people with special occupations (CSP, MSP, and PSTP), which currently cover 6.5 per cent of total employees, were instituted earlier than the NP. The CSP and MSP were instituted in the early 1960s and the PSTP in the mid-1970s, while the NP was instituted in the late 1980s. The special pension programmes provide 14–18 categories of benefits including old age, work-related injuries, disability, survivors' pension and others. Currently, 65 000 or 3.3 per cent of older Koreans aged 65 and over are receiving these special pensions. This is also the total number of pensioners in Korea in 1990.

The public pension programme for people in general was, in fact, created by the National Welfare Pension Act of 1973. However, its enforcement was delayed until 1988 for various reasons. In 1986, the Korean government entirely amended the National Welfare Pension Act, renaming it the National Pension Act. Based on this act, the National Pension (NP) programme covering most Korean workers was, at last, instituted in 1988. The NP system will eventually cover all workers aged 18–60 who are not covered by special pension systems. To help implement it at the beginning, only the employees and employers of workplaces with 10 or more full-time workers are currently covered.

Categories of benefits under the NP programme are: the old age pension; the invalidity pension; the survivor pension; and the lump-sum refund. Of these four categories the main one is the old age pension. To be eligible for an old age pension one should have been insured for 20 years or more and be 60 years old. There are some special categories in the old age pension which also warrant eligibility (reduced old age pension, incumbent old age pension, and advanced old age pension).

The NP plan is paid for by a contribution from the employee's wages and accumulated retirement benefits along with the employer's liability (from employee's wages and employer's liability until 1992, and from employee's wages and accumulated retirement benefits and employer's liability from 1993). The NP programme is administered by the regional offices of the National Pension Corporation, a semigovernmental organization under the supervision of the Ministry of Health and Social Affairs (MOHSA). Since the NP programme only began in 1988, the current elderly are not eligible for the benefits. As of 1990 about 4.6 million Korean workers, 26.5 per cent of all Korean workers, are compulsorily covered by the NP programme as indicated in Table 9.6, but, as yet, none of them are recipients of the NP. Therefore, today, pensioners in Korea are not recipients of the national pension but of special pensions.

Public Assistance Programmes
Livelihood protection programme   The Livelihood Protection (LP) programme was established by the Livelihood Protection Act in 1961. It was not until the enactment of this Act that the constitutional right to a minimum but decent living standard was substantiated. To be eligible for the LP programme an elderly person must meet three requirements: he must be judged to be poor by the standard of income and assets that are set by the government every year; he must be 65 or over; and there must be no-one legally responsible for supporting him or, if there is someone, that person has to be unable to work.

The LP programme stipulates four categories of benefits for elderly people: livelihood assistance; funeral assistance; medical assistance; and self-reliance assistance. The level and types of benefits vary according to the status of the

Table 9.7 Number of Livelihood Protection recipients for selected years.

Year	Total recipients (A) (thousands)	Elderly recipients (B) (thousands)	A/Total population (%)	B/Total elderly population (%)	B/A (%)
1965	3 922	–	13.8	–	–
1970	2 116	–	7.9	–	–
1975	1 331	–	3.8	–	–
1980	1 829	–	4.8	–	–
1981	2 090	196	5.4	13.1	9.4
1982	3 420	–	8.7	–	–
1983	2 954	259	7.4	16.0	8.8
1984	2 556	–	6.3	–	–
1985	2 273	–	5.5	–	–
1986	2 174	–	5.2	–	–
1987	2 354	222	5.6	12.0	9.5
1988	2 310	245	5.4	12.9	10.6
1989	2 196	269	5.2	13.7	12.2

Source: Ministry of Health and Social Affairs.
Note: – indicates that data are not available.

recipient which can be classed as domiciliary protection, institutional protection, or self-reliance protection.

As noted in Table 9.7, the number of elderly recipients of the LP has been around 200 000–270 000, or 12–16 per cent of the total elderly population aged 65 and over, or 9–14 per cent of the total LP recipients. It is notable that the proportion of elderly recipients has shown an increase in recent years.

The central government contributes 80 per cent of the programme costs, with the remaining 20 per cent shared by local government. The programme is administered under the responsibility of the Ministry of Health and Social Affairs (MOHSA), but assistance is actually delivered through agencies of local governments under the direction of MOHSA.

Old age allowance
This provision was created by an amendment of the Elderly Welfare Act in 1989 and came into force from 1991. This programme was designed to solve the problems that arose when the NP programme was instituted without any interim provision for those who have already reached the pensionable age of 60 and who cannot benefit from the NP programme. Eligible persons are limited to those who cannot be covered by any kind of public pension, who are 65 years old and over, and who are of low income judged by a means test. This programme is financed by the central government and administered by the same delivery system as the LP programme.

Retirement Benefits Programme
The Retirement Benefits (RB) system was introduced by the Labor Standards Act of 1953. The Act stipulates that workplaces with 10 or more full-time workers should reserve retirement benefits which are paid to workers upon retirement. This programme could be regarded as a public income maintenance programme in that it is compulsorily applicable to all workplaces with 10 or more full-time workers by the provision of law, even though it is not rigidly applied. Any full-time worker who has worked for more than 1 year in a workplace with 10 or more full-time workers is eligible for the RB. The RB is

paid as a lump sum when the worker leaves the workplace because of having reached retirement age or for other reasons. Currently, this programme is the principal income maintenance programme for most retirees in Korea, covering some 4.8 million, or 29.5 per cent, of Korean workers.

Special Treatment Programme
The Special Treatment (ST) programme for the elderly was started for those aged 70 or over in 1980 by a government ordinance, and it was expanded to those aged 65 and over from 1982 by the provision of the Elderly Welfare Act of 1981. This programme provides elderly people with discounts on public transport (operated by the government) and on admission to public facilities such as parks and museums. In addition to these discounts, this programme provides elderly people with 12 free bus coupons that can be used on city buses operated by private enterprises.

Job Placement Programmes
There are three job placement programmes that provide elderly people with an opportunity to earn income by making good use of their free time. They are the Elderly Job Bank (EJB), the Elderly Workshop (EW) and the Elderly Job Support (EJS). The EJB is operated by local branch offices of the National Association of Older Koreans. This programme started in 1981, and now operates with government assistance in 14 cities. The EW helps set up workshops where elderly people can work together and receive remuneration for their work. This programme was started in 1986 and is operated by voluntary organizations with government assistance. The EJS began in 1991 to give priority to elderly people in granting permission to install stalls that sell daily necessities in public facilities such as parks, and permission to sell government monopoly goods.

Health care programmes
Another essential aspect of the constitutional right to a decent living standard was substantiated by the institutionalization of medical insurance and medical assistance programmes in the latter part of the 1970s. As of 1989, all Koreans have been covered by these health care programmes as indicated in Table 9.8: 90 per cent by the medical insurance programme and 10 per cent by the medical assistance programme.

There are three kinds of health care programme for elderly people: medical insurance; medical assistance; and health examinations.

Medical Insurance programmes
There are two medical insurance programmes for elderly people. One is Medical Insurance (MI) for people in general, and the other is Civil Servant and Private School Employee Medical Insurance (CSPSEMI) for those employed in special occupations. In fact, the MI scheme was created by the enactment of the Medical Insurance Act of 1963, but it covered only a limited number of people on an experimental basis until 1976. This act was entirely revised in 1976 and enforced from 1977.

The MI scheme is designed to cover all Korean residents, including the elderly, except for those covered by special medical insurance (CSPSEMI) and the Medical Assistance (MA) scheme. For convenience of implementation, the coverage has been gradually expanded since its inception. However, until 1989, it covered all Koreans except for those covered by both the MI and the MA schemes.

Table 9.8 Beneficiaries of health care programmes for selected years.

Year	Medical Insurance (%)	Medical Assistance (%)	Total (%)
1977	3 203 (8.8)	2 095 (5.7)	5 298 (14.5)
1978	3 878 (10.5)	2 095 (5.6)	5 973 (16.1)
1979	7 789 (20.7)	2 134 (5.7)	9 923 (26.4)
1980	9 113 (23.9)	2 142 (5.6)	11 255 (29.0)
1981	11 407 (29.5)	3 728 (9.4)	15 135 (39.1)
1982	13 513 (34.3)	3 728 (9.4)	17 241 (43.7)
1983	15 577 (39.0)	3 728 (9.4)	19 305 (48.3)
1984	17 050 (42.1)	3 259 (8.0)	20 309 (50.1)
1985	17 995 (43.9)	3 259 (7.9)	21 259 (51.8)
1986	19 361 (46.6)	4 386 (10.5)	23 747 (57.1)
1987	21 257 (50.6)	4 356 (10.4)	25 643 (61.0)
1988	28 383 (66.6)	4 290 (10.1)	32 674 (76.7)
1989	38 134 (90.0)	4 246 (10.0)	42 380 (100.0)

Source: Ministry of Health and Social Affairs.
Note: The number in parentheses indicates the percentage of the total population.
Unit: thousand persons.

To be eligible for the MI scheme, a person should be either the insuree or a dependent family member of the insuree. The MI pays for diagnosis, inpatient and outpatient treatment, operations, nursing, medications, and transport for treatment. The payment level varies with the medical care system and the kind of treatment. The MI pays 50–70 per cent of the fees for outpatient care and 80 per cent for inpatient care, while the patients themselves have to pay 20 per cent or more of the total medical fees.

The MI scheme is financed by equal contributions from both employee and employer for those in workplaces with more than five full-time workers, but by equal contributions from both the insuree and the government for farmers, fishermen, and self-employed people including employers in workplaces with fewer than five workers. The MI scheme is administered by the medical insurance societies and their federation (Federation of Korean Medical Insurance Societies), an organization under the supervision of the Ministry of Health and Social Affairs (MOHSA). Government assistance is provided only for the administration costs of the societies and the federation.

The special medical insurance scheme (CSPSEMI) covers 10.6 per cent of the total population. The eligibility requirements, benefit categories and benefit levels of the CSPSEMI scheme are similar to those of the MI scheme.

Medical Assistance programme
The Medical Assistance programme (MA) had been a benefit category under the Livelihood Protection (LP) programme until a separate programme was established by the enactment of the Medical Assistance Act of 1977. With the establishment of MA, its coverage was expanded to include not only LP recipients but also veterans, human cultural treasures, disaster-stricken people, and the medically needy whose income level is slightly higher than the poverty line but who would drop below the poverty line should they pay medical bills.

As indicated in Table 9.8, as of 1989, 10 per cent of all Koreans and 20.6 per cent of all those aged 65 and over were covered by this programme.

The MA scheme pays for the same categories of benefits as the MI scheme, but its payment level varies with the status of the recipient and the medical care system (primary or secondary). Deductible amounts are imposed on those who are under self-reliance protection and on the medically needy. When they are unable to make payments, the state makes loans without interest with a reimbursement period of from 1 to 3 years. This programme is financed by the contributions of central and local governments and medical fees paid by recipients (specifically those under the self-reliance protection of the LP and the medically needy), and administered under the auspices of local government.

Elderly Health Examination programme
The Elderly Health Examination (EHE) programme was established in 1983 by the Elderly Welfare Act of 1981 for the detection and prevention of diseases. The state's provision of health examinations is not compulsory but is subject to budget constraints. Hence, so far, the provision has been limited to low-income elderly people with the number of elderly eligible for the EHE fixed since its inception to 230 000.

Housing service programmes
There is no explicit housing policy for older Koreans, for neither those living with their children nor for those living separately from their children. One provision of the Elderly Welfare Act stipulates that the state or local government should facilitate the construction of houses appropriate for elderly people. The provision is ambiguous in terms of the government's responsibilities, and consequently housing programmes in accordance with this provision have rarely been created. Besides the ambiguity of the provision, there are several other reasons for the underdevelopment of a housing policy for the elderly. The housing shortage has been so serious nationally that there is little room to consider a housing policy aimed particularly at the elderly population. Since the social welfare policy for elderly people has focused on institutional care, the government has not paid attention to the housing problems of elderly people living in homes. The spirit of 'family responsibility' for taking care of the elderly in a co-residential arrangement, which is still relatively well preserved, is also hindering the development of a housing policy specifically for the elderly. Because housing prices are unprecedently high, few older Koreans can afford to buy or rent, even though housing for elderly people should be supplied.

The only housing project for the elderly in accordance with the provision of the Elderly Welfare Law, was the supply of 360 units of three-generation family housing by the Korea Housing Corporation (KHC) in 1987 on an experimental basis. The KHC is likely to supply more three-generation family housing given the positive response of the occupants (Korea Housing Corporation, 1990).

Regarding the institutional accommodation programme, there are four kinds of institutions: free homes, fee-charging homes, free nursing homes, and fee-charging nursing homes. In 1989, there were 69 free homes for the aged accommodating 4 962 elderly persons, while there were 2 fee-charging homes for the aged accommodating 54 persons. There were 18 free nursing homes accommodating 1 324 persons, while there were 4 fee-charging nursing homes accommodating 37 elderly persons in 1989.

Social service programmes

The meaning and scope of social services differs according to political and cultural contexts. In this chapter, social services are taken to mean 'programmes that protect or restore family life, help individuals cope with external or internal problems, enhance development and facilitate access through information, guidance, advocacy, and concrete help of several kinds' (Kahn, 1979).

Along with the improvements in living standards, the needs of the Korean elderly have been elevated to higher levels and have been diversified (to include, for example, personal help needs, social-psychological developmental needs and others). In spite of these changing needs, the number of social service programmes directed to meet the needs of the elderly population are few in number. There are six social service programmes stipulated in the Elderly Welfare Act: elderly counselling; elderly welfare centres; elderly club houses; elderly schools; home-help programmes; and elderly resting facility programmes.

Elderly counselling is designed to provide counselling services for elderly people; the counsellors are employed by the local government. Elderly Welfare Centres are designed to provide a range of services concerning health improvement, adult education, recreation, counselling, information and guidance, amongst other things. By 1989 there were only two such elderly welfare centres.

The elderly club houses began to be established in the early 1950s by voluntary donations from local people. These are the most generalized elderly welfare facility in both urban and rural areas. By 1989 there were 17 140 club houses with members comprising more than one-third of those aged 60 and over. Organized programmes are seldom offered in the club houses, with most of the activities being casual: chatting with friends, playing cards and chess, watching TV, listening to the radio, or just sitting around. Elderly schools are the second most generalized welfare facility provided for elderly Koreans. They have become popular since the middle of the 1970s (Chung and Kim, 1984) and are operated by voluntary organizations. By 1987, the number of schools was 756 with 52 876 elderly persons attending. Government financial assistance to elderly club houses and elderly schools is meagre and nominal.

The home help programme was introduced in 1987 by a voluntary organization affiliated with a British social service agency (HelpAge International). Home help services are currently provided on a free-of-charge basis exclusively for elderly people in domiciliary protection under the Livelihood Protection Programme. It is provided by volunteers under the supervision of the service organizations. In 1988, about 400 volunteer home helpers worked with four voluntary organizations, and provided home help services to 400 elderly persons.

PROBLEMS ASSOCIATED WITH CURRENT POLICIES; AND RECOMMENDATIONS FOR THE FUTURE

This chapter has reviewed the demographic aspects of ageing in Korea, the problems and needs of elderly Koreans, and current social welfare programmes for elderly Koreans. It is now appropriate to discuss the problems of current policies for the elderly and to make recommendations aimed at solving them.

First, it may be said that the government holds an erroneous perspective on the problem of ageing which acts as one of the barriers to policy development. If we define a problem as social, its causes are much more related to societal factors such as social change, modernization, industrialization and urbanization, and social structure than to other factors (Merton, 1971; Etzioni, 1976). Since the main causes of the problem of ageing in Korea are more related to societal factors than to personal or familial factors, the efforts directed towards finding a solution should be initiated by society or the state (Horton and Leslie, 1955). This means that the fundamental solution of the problem cannot be undertaken by individuals or families.

However, the Korean government's policy on solving the problem of ageing has been generally based on a premise that ageing is a personal or family problem rather than a social problem, and thus solvable through family efforts. This position had been strongly supported by the traditional value of filial piety that emphasizes family responsibility in taking care of the elderly. The general guiding principle of government policies for the elderly is 'care by the family first, social security second'; this reflects a perspective which assumes that the problem of ageing may be solved by the age-old principle of family responsibility. Unless the Korean government abandons such an erroneous perspective on the problem of ageing and its means of solving it, it may take a long time before fundamental measures will or can be instituted.

Secondly, the Korean government's measures for social welfare in general have been almost exclusively focused on poor or low-income groups and based on the residual perspective of the social welfare system. Although this perspective may be unavoidable in the early stages of welfare states, the persistent holding of this perspective has meant that the concept and scope of social welfare in Korea has been limited to the provision of government benefits free of charge to the poor.

The problem of ageing has many facets as discussed earlier in this chapter and these types of problems are not limited to the elderly poor. Modernization, a gigantic social change, affects all elderly people to some degree at least, regardless of their socio-economic status. Problems of health care, social-psychological conflict and alienation, role loss and difficulties in leisure activities are common to many elderly Koreans. Social services that can address these problems and needs have emerged as social welfare provisions for all elderly people in welfare states (Tinker, 1984). Therefore, policy concerns currently focused on the elderly poor should be directed more towards the elderly in general, with particular attention being paid to developing more varied social services.

Thirdly, an institutional-care-orientated policy has hindered social welfare provisions for the elderly in general, who reside at home. In almost all countries social welfare measures for elderly people have developed which are focused on institutional care, still the most important area of policy concern. The same phenomenon can be observed in Korea, but since even institutional care programmes have not been well developed, there still remains much room for the development of institutional care itself. However, at the same time, negative effects that may result from the emphasis on institutional care should be addressed as well.

The welfare state was introduced to buttress the family as the basic unit of welfare provision, and thus the welfare services should have been provided to strengthen the functions of the family. In most welfare states, welfare benefits tend to have been provided to individuals after a breakdown in family functions rather than to support the family before breakdown. Such a policy has resulted in an increase in the institutionalized population and ineffective and inefficient care services. The experiences of advanced welfare states suggest that Korean society should develop more domiciliary care programmes while expanding institutional care programmes. That is, policy making should pay greater attention to developing social services such as home health care and home help services in order to prevent unnecessary or premature institutionalization, as well as to ensure more effective and efficient care of elderly people in a majority of cases.

Fourthly, an emphasis on family responsibility for supporting elderly people is deterring policy development for elderly Koreans. In supporting or taking care of the elderly the emphasis is on family responsibility because it is an age-old principle that has been supported by the traditional value of filial piety in Korea. In a modern welfare state, the emphasis on family responsibility can make the state's responsibility minimal, and thus deter the development of welfare provisions. As discussed earlier, it is held that the causes of the problems of ageing in modern society are much more related to societal than other factors, particularly in the economic aspect of the problem.

Income maintenance and health care for elderly Koreans should at least be assumed as a responsibility of the state. This does not mean that the state should assume all the responsibility for the support of elderly people, but it does mean that the state should take the initiative to prepare institutional programmes for economic and medical security for elderly people. The responsibility for taking care of frail or sick elderly people needs to be shared between the family and the state with the main role of the state being that of strengthening the care function of the family with social services. Hence, the principle 'care by the family first, social security second', which has to date guided social policies for elderly Koreans, should be changed to 'family and state share joint or complementary responsibility' in the support and care of elderly people.

Fifthly, the traditional value of filial piety, which emphasizes family responsibility for the economic support of elderly people and the provision of care services to them by their own family members, is also hampering the development of a social welfare policy for the elderly. Filial piety, according to its original meaning, can be dealt with at both the familial level and the societal level. One of the most important reasons for filial piety is to repay one's parents for their love and care (Choi, 1982). The role of filial piety at the familial level is to provide economic support and direct care services to parents in order to repay them for their love and care, whereas filial piety at the societal level is the state's welfare provision to the elderly in order to repay their contributions to society. Filial piety has traditionally emphasized the familial level, but not the societal level.

For this value to be preserved as a social value appropriate to modern familial and social conditions, new ways of putting this value into practice at both levels should be developed. At the familial level, a new way of conducting this value would be to complement home care services with social services provided by non-familial persons, for example by home health care persons and home helpers. To promote this value at the societal level would emphasize the duty of society to compensate elderly people for their contributions to the development of that society. The conduct of filial piety at the societal level is consistent with the position justifying the state's welfare provision for elderly people in modern society (Kutza, 1981). This value should not be emphasized solely as a basis for supporting family responsibility for looking after the elderly. Efforts to preserve and develop the value of filial piety could be justified in the sense that it can slow down the pace of family disorganization and the disruption of the community. The tradition of filial piety can never be justified as grounds for making the family assume sole responsibility for taking care of elderly people.

Sixthly, the delivery system for social welfare services for the elderly is retarding policy development. The current delivery system for social welfare in general, including the delivery system for the elderly, is that policies made by the Ministry of Health and Social Affairs are implemented through the general administrative agencies of the central and local governments under the control of the Ministry of Home Affairs. That is, the delivery system of social welfare services is fused with the general administrative system. With this present system, it is very hard for policy planning and service delivery to be professional or to utilize people with professional expertise and knowledge of social welfare. A recommendation for establishing an independent delivery system under the direct control or supervision of the Ministry of Health and Social Affairs has been made many times during the past 10 years or so, but it has not yet been accepted at the central governmental level. Without improvements in the delivery system, neither efficiency nor effectiveness in the social welfare system in general can be expected.

Seventhly, since the government budget for elderly welfare has been very small compared to GNP (the total national budget) and the national budget for social welfare in general, it should be increased considerably. Most policy problems and recommendations are ultimately related to the size of the social welfare budget, particularly the welfare budget for the elderly. It must be recognized, of course, that a welfare state can never be achieved without substantial financial expenditure. As indicated in Table 9.9, the budget for social welfare has increased but it has still remained less than 5 per cent of the national budget and less than 1 per cent of GNP in 1989. Although the elderly

Table 9.9 Indicators related to social welfare in Korea for selected years.

Year	Per capita GNP ($)	BSW /NB (%)	BSW /GNP (%)	BEW /BSW (%)	60+ /TP (%)	65+ /TP (%)	ANFM (per-sons)
1965	115	3.39	0.39	–	5.3	3.3	5.5
1970	288	1.95	0.34	–	5.4	3.3	5.2
1975	590	2.42	0.44	–	5.6	3.5	5.0
1980	1 589	2.30	0.48	0.07	5.9	3.8	4.6
1981	1 719	2.40	0.42	0.04	6.1	3.9	4.5*
1982	1 773	2.67	0.49	0.28	6.3	4.0	4.5*
1983	1 914	2.88	0.51	0.43	6.4	4.0	4.4*
1984	2 044	2.79	0.46	0.54	6.5	4.1	4.3*
1985	2 047	2.87	0.49	0.59	6.7	4.3	4.3*
1986	2 300	3.30	0.50	0.61	6.8	4.4	4.2*
1987	3 098	2.93	0.50	0.69	6.9	4.4	4.1*
1988	4 127	3.80	0.62	0.59	7.0	4.5	4.0
1989	4 968	4.50	0.66	0.69	7.2	4.6	3.9

Sources: Ministry of Health and Social Affairs, Ministry of Finance, and Economic Planning Board.
Note: NB: Total National Budget
   BSW: Total National Budget for Social Welfare
   BEW: Total National Budget for Elderly Welfare
   GNP: Gross National Product
   TP: Total Population
   ANFM: Average Number of Family Members
   * Indicates estimated data.

welfare budget has also steadily increased, it remains at less than 1 per cent of the social welfare budget.

As we know from the experience of advanced welfare states, the major factor in deciding the size of social welfare costs on the supply side is national economic prosperity, while the major factors on the demand side are the proportion of the elderly population and the nuclearization of the family (Konuma et al., 1984; Wilensky, 1975). It should be noted that the greatest proportion of the increase in social welfare costs is that of welfare for the elderly.

It is proper to define elderly people as those aged 60 and over in the current Korean situation, since the mandatory retirement age for most employees is generally between 55 and 60, and the eligible age for an old age pension is set to be 60 and over. If we define the elderly as those aged 60 and over, the proportion of the elderly population was 7.2 per cent in 1989, not much lower than in many advanced countries. The average size of the family has also been steadily decreasing, and was estimated to be 3.9 in 1989. With an unprecedented high rate of economic growth, the per capita GNP greatly increased during the 1980s and reached almost US $5 000 in 1989. In the light of these indicators, the government's budget for elderly welfare, as well as social welfare in general, has been too small when compared to GNP and the national budget. It has also been too small in comparison with developing countries, even taking national defence expenditure into consideration. Therefore, the government's budget for social welfare, particularly elderly welfare, should be substantially increased.

CONCLUSIONS

The problems of ageing have become such a social issue in Korean society that it has emerged as a new concern that has never been experienced before. It is becoming a new challenge in that the multifaceted problem requires the state to deal with it and this is testing the state's capability to develop an appropriate social welfare system as a solution. The problems of ageing that challenge contemporary Korean society could act as an accelerator to building up the welfare state, if the government would remove its old way of thinking that up to has now acted as a safeguard for economic development but which has built barriers to the development of social welfare. The Korean government, benefiting from the experience of advanced countries, should now take positive steps to develop social welfare policies for elderly people; this will be one of the most significant components for building up the Korean welfare state. The Korean welfare state should build, of course, on efforts to develop the values of a modern sense of filial piety and of citizens' collective responsibility towards people in general.

REFERENCES

Chang, I.H. and Choi, S.J. (1987). Welfare of the Elderly. Seoul National University Press, Seoul.

Choi, S.J. (1982). A Study on Korean Family. Ilji-Sa, Seoul.

Choi, S.J. (1984). Modernization and Social Integration of the Aged into the Family in Korea. PhD dissertation, Case Western Reserve University.

Chung, J.W. and Kim, D.I. (1984). Present state and needs of adult education for the elderly. In Problems of the Elderly and Their Adult Education, UNESCO of Korea (Ed.), pp. 167–208. UNESCO of Korea, Seoul.

Cowgill, D.O. (1974). Aging and modernization: A revision of the theory. In *Late Life: Communities and Environmental Policy*, J.F. Gubrium (Ed.), pp. 123–46. Charles C. Thomas, Springfield.

Donahue, W., Orbach, H.L. and Pollak, O. (1960). Retirement: The emerging social pattern. In *Handbook of Social Gerontology*, C. Tibbits (Ed.), pp. 330–406. University of Chicago Press, Chicago.

Economic Planning Board, the Republic of Korea (1986). *Population Estimates: Long-Term Estimates of Population Based on the Results of Population and Housing Census of 1985*. Economic Planning Board, Seoul.

Economic Planning Board, the Republic of Korea (1987). *Summary Report of Analysis of Population and Housing Census of 1985*. Economic Planning Board, Seoul.

Economic Planning Board, the Republic of Korea (1989). *Population Statistics and Future Population Estimates*. Economic Planning Board, Seoul.

Etzioni, A. (1976). *Social Problems*. Prentice-Hall, Englewood Cliffs, New Jersey.

Federation of Korean Medical Insurance Societies (1988). *Medical Insurance Statistical Yearbook*. Federation of Korean Medical Insurance Societies, Seoul.

Ha, S.N. and Kim, S.Y. (1986). *Actual Living Conditions of Retirees: Focused on Pensioners*. Korea Association of Retirees, Seoul.

Horton, P.B. and Leslie, G.R. (1955). *The Sociology of Social Problems*. Appleton-Century-Croft, New York.

Huh, J. (1983). The elderly and health: Physical health. In *Modern Society and Welfare Services for the Aged*, Asan Foundation (Ed.), pp. 97–108. Asan Foundation, Seoul.

Kahn, A.J. (1979). *Social Policy & Social Services*, 2nd edition. Random House, New York.

Kim, C.K. (1984). Current health status and future prospects of the aged. *Journal of Korea Gerontological Society*, **4**, 60–72.

Kim, H.C., Han, N.J., Choi, S.J. and Ryu, I.H. (1986). *A Study on the Development of Standard Model of Korean Family*. Institute of Korean Studies, Seoul.

Kim, S.S. (1984). *A Study on the Welfare of the Elderly in Industrial Society*. PhD dissertation, Hanyang University, Seoul.

Kim, T.H. and Kim, E.S. (1983). Preparation consciousness of young adults and the middle-aged for successful aging. *Journal of Korea Gerontological Society*, **3**, 16–25.

Kong, S.K., Park, I.H., Cho, A.I., Kim, J.S. and Chang, H.S. (1987). *Family Transition in Korea*. Korea Institute for Population and Health, Seoul.

Konuma, M., Jinusi, S.S. and Hosaka, D.S. (1984). *Introduction to Social Security*. Kawasima Publishing Co., Tokyo.

Korea Employers' Federation (1988). *A Survey Research on Retirement Systems of Enterprises*. Korea Employers' Federation, Seoul.

Korea Housing Corporation (1990). *Post Occupancy Evaluation*. Korea Housing Corporation, Seoul.

Korea Survey Polls Ltd. (1984). *Life Style and Value System of the Aged in Korea*. Korea Survey Polls Ltd., Seoul.

Kutza, E.A. (1981). *The Benefits of Old Age: Social Welfare Policy for the Elderly*. University of Chicago Press, Chicago.

Liang, J., Dvorkin, L., Kahana, E. and Mazian, F. (1980). Social integration and morale: A re-examination. *Journal of Gerontology*, **35**, 746–57.

Lim, J.K., Kong, S.K., Kim, J.S., Nam, J.J. and Ryu, J.S. (1985). *A Study on Aged*

Population in Korea. Korea Institute for Population and Health, Seoul.

Merton, R.K. (1971). Social problems and social theory. In *Contemporary Social Problems*, 3rd edition, R.K. Merton and R. Nisbet (Eds), pp. 793–845. Harcourt Brace Jovanovich, New York.

Min, J.S. (1985). Retirement benefits and pension system. *Korean Social Security Studies*, **1**, 61–9.

Ministry of Foreign Affairs, Japan (1978). *Demographic Yearbook of 1977.* Ministry of Foreign Affairs, Tokyo.

Ministry of Health and Social Affairs (MOHSA), the Republic of Korea (1988). *Health and Social Affairs 1988.* MOHSA, Seoul.

Ministry of Health and Social Affairs (MOHSA), the Republic of Korea (1989). *The State of Recipients of Livelihood Protection.* MOHSA, Seoul.

Rhee, K.O. (1989). Changes in family structure and problems of supporting the elderly. In *A Study on Policy Direction for the Welfare of the Elderly.* Y.S. Park (Ed.) pp. 4–41, Korea Institute for Population and Health, Seoul.

Rhee, K.O., Kim, H.S., Kwon, J.D., Kwon, S.J., Ahn, H.Y. and Chung, Y.J. (1989). *A Study on Actual Conditions of Elderly Households.* Korea Institute for Population and Health, Seoul.

Rhee, S.J. and Huh, J. (1985). A study on health status of the elderly in Korea. *Journal of Korea Gerontological Society*, **5**, 103–26.

Rosow, I. (1974). *Socialization to Old Age.* University of California Press, Berkeley.

Tinker, A. (1984). *The Elderly in Modern Society.* Longman, London.

Wilensky, H. (1975). *The Welfare State and Equality.* University of California Press, Berkeley.

10 HEALTH AND WELFARE SERVICES FOR ELDERLY PEOPLE IN MALAYSIA

INTRODUCTION

There is sufficient demographic evidence to indicate that the Malaysian population is ageing and within the next decade or two, elderly people will constitute a relatively large component of the population. They are now viewed, not as a distinct group, but as individuals. Families do play an important role in their care, and the social services that have been established provide some support for them. The growth in their numbers will increase the pressure for services especially as the responsibility for the care of elderly people can no longer be expected to be completely in the hands of the family. Stock must be taken of what exists as a preliminary step towards meeting future demands.

This chapter outlines the available health and welfare services as provided by government and non-government organizations. Note is taken of studies already conducted so as to develop an understanding of the people and the situation, and to ascertain the needs of the elderly. Finally, possible directions for future service developments are considered.

THE ELDERLY DEFINED

Most industrialized and economically advanced countries classify individuals as being elderly on attaining 65 years of age, with further distinctions being made between early elderly and advanced elderly persons. Where elderly people are already a sizable proportion of the population and where a range of support services have been established, these distinctions often serve to differentiate between those who manage to live independently and those who do not. It is generally accepted that many of the advanced elderly may require assistance to a greater or lesser degree over time. In the present context, the term elderly is defined as persons who are 60 years and older.

In Malaysia, this cut-off at 60 years seems appropriate for more than one reason. This is the age used by many countries in the region to categorize elderly people (Singh, 1983). The official age of retirement is 55 years although advisory positions and special concessions are made available on a personal basis to some older individuals. However, such instances are more the exception than the rule. But, except where poor health is an issue, all those at the mandatory age of retirement cannot be automatically classified as non-productive. A proportion of those being withdrawn from the workforce remain capable of making a sound contribution and they do often strive to find parallel or alternative employment in the private sector, not for remuneration alone, but because they wish to remain active.

It seems wholly inappropriate to utilize the official retirement age as the basis for categorizing elderly people when they can remain gainfully employed, if they are given the opportunity. The Malaysian government is considering raising the retirement age to 60 years (*New Straits Times*, 1988). Another factor taken into account is the provision of welfare services on the basis of age. An individual who is indigent, or in need of shelter, becomes eligible for assistance under schemes for the aged on becoming 60 years old. It is also generally accepted among two out of the three ethnic groups that comprise the Malaysian community that entry into the sixth decade has particular significance. The Indians and Chinese mark this as a special event. At the same time, it must be stated that courtesy and respect for the older person has always been a way of life for the Malay. It is because of these factors that the age of 60 has been identified as the point at which individuals are to be classified as elderly in this study.

THE DEMOGRAPHIC BACKGROUND

Malaysia is a federation of 13 states and 2 federal territories. Kuala Lumpur, which is a federal territory, and 11 states are in Peninsular Malaysia. The other two states of Sabah and Sarawak, often jointly referred to as East Malaysia, are on the Island of Borneo. Labuan which was part of Sabah is the second federal territory. Malaysia is multiethnic in character with the Malays, Chinese and Indians constituting the main racial groups. Approximately 83 per cent of the population live in Peninsular Malaysia with about 8 per cent and 9 per cent in Sabah and Sarawak respectively. The population growth rate for the country as a whole is given at about 2.5 per cent per annum, with an estimated population of 17.9 million in 1990. Approximately 63 per cent live in the rural areas. The life expectancy is 68 years for males and 73 years for females and the overall age dependency ratio is 72 to every 100 persons of working age (Hamid *et al.*, 1986). Per capita income is given as M$5 550 per annum (Far Eastern Economic Review, 1991).

Figures from the 1980 census and the estimated population figures for 1985 indicate the growing number of people aged 60 years and over. Table 10.1 also gives projections until the year 2000.

Countries are known as young, mature or aged based on the proportion of those defined as elderly in the total population. The United Nations categorizes a country as young when the population includes fewer than 4 per cent aged 65 years and above. Where a total of 4 to 7 per cent are included in this category, it is seen as a mature country. A total of more than 7 per cent defines it as aged. In Asia ageing is measured at an earlier point and the Association of South-east Asian Nations (ASEAN) has adopted slightly different criteria to describe a country, using 60 years as the cut-off point in defining 'elderly'. Fewer than 6 per cent of the population aged 60 years and over earns a place as a young country. Similarly, aged would mean that the same category comprises at least 15 per cent. Further categorizations of youthful and mature describe countries where percentages are in between 6 to 10 per cent and 11 to 14 per cent respectively (Masitah, 1985). Using the ASEAN categorization, Malaysia remains a young country at present with approximately 5.7 per cent of its population aged 60 years and over.

It is important to note that a major population policy shift was initiated in 1983 to attain a national target population of 70 million by the year 2100. The impact of this new policy has yet to be evaluated in real terms. However, given

Table 10.1 Malaysia: population projections: 1980 to 2000.

Summary of age groups	1980			1985			1990			1995			2000		
	M	F	Total	M	F	Total	M	F	Total	M	F	Total	M	F	Total
0–15	2 834.1	2 708.3	5 542.4	3 093.4	2 948.4	6 041.8	3 381.4	3 219.3	6 600.7	3 686.1	3 510.2	7 196.3	3 957.4	3 765.7	7 723.1
15–49	3 401.7	3 408.6	6 810.3	3 993.8	3 975.4	7 969.2	4 599.5	4 560.2	9 159.7	5 212.6	5 150.2	10 362.8	5 876.3	5 776.5	11 652.8
50–59	380.0	387.1	767.1	446.2	456.1	902.3	531.3	531.4	1 062.7	633.8	621.7	1 255.5	764.6	757.6	1 522.2
60+	376.3	383.2	759.5	416.1	458.4	874.5	480.3	557.2	1 037.5	575.1	681.2	1 256.3	704.7	825.0	1 529.7
Total	6 992.1	6 887.2	13 879.3	7 949.5	7 838.3	15 787.8	8 992.5	8 868.1	17 860.6	10 107.6	9 963.3	20 070.9	11 303.0	11 124.8	22 427.8

Source: Department of Statistics (1987).
Units: thousands.

the trends already stated, it is clear that institutional changes will have to be implemented.

A DEFICIT OF CONCERN

The Malaysian who is 60 years or older can claim, and usually is accorded, a position of respect within the family and community. Traditionally, the family is expected to care for the older members of its unit but, with many changes in the country, this expectation can no longer be taken for granted.

Industrialization in Malaysia is part of the major thrust being made to develop the nation. The basic services and personal consumption requirements of people, both as producers and consumers, have to be taken into account in development activity and the human resource component is viewed as a vital factor in nation building. Consideration is given to the health and welfare of people. However, it is evident that the sectors of the population seen as providing manpower needs, or having the potential for doing so, have first priority. Those within the working age group of 15 to 55 years and the young have services established for their benefit, but elderly persons have yet to be seen as a category with special needs. Nevertheless, in the 1990s there is a definite increasing interest in Malaysia becoming a more caring society generally, and elderly people should benefit as part of this drive.

It would be incorrect to maintain that the elderly are not currently given any consideration as a group. However, at the same time, it can be said that the benefits now available to them have developed mainly as an offshoot of the earlier work-related stage in their lives. Reference is made here to pensions and payments from the Employees Provident Fund on retirement. Concessions, such as travel at half the normal fare by rail or air within the country, are accorded to elderly people in Malaysia.

These are, however, meagre acknowledgements of the needs of elderly people when compared with the other sectors of the population. For instance, workers have various schemes and organizations to safeguard their interests, with the Ministry of Labour and Manpower administering the Labour Code and providing general supervision in all matters pertaining to the workforce. Technical training schemes are mounted by the same ministry to augment skilled labour requirements. Statutory organizations such as the Employees Provident Fund Board and the Social Security Organization (SOCSO), also have special responsibility for workers. Protective legislation in the form of the Workmen's Compensation Act of 1952 and the Social Security Act of 1961 provide a safety net for the employee who suffers injury, or is disadvantaged in the course of duty. Health and welfare aspects are incorporated in the measures already adopted. Equally important is the fact that unionization of labour is seen as legitimate, with unions having a role in enhancing terms and conditions of service.

Similarly, in the case of the young, their vulnerability is accepted and protected. In the matter of health, for instance, the emphasis of the services provided by the Ministry of Health is towards the maintenance of maternal and child health. This is true both for urban and rural parts of the country. Indeed, the rural health care system, with its infrastructure of health centres and midwifery clinics, is a direct response to meet grave health problems among mothers and infants. Certain immunization programmes are mandatory. The nutritional status of infants and children receives special consideration, both through health education and through projects jointly sponsored with agencies other than health.

The Ministry of Education plays an equally significant role in the lives of the young, in preparing them for a productive life. In the priorities that exist, education occupies an important position and this is reflected in budget allocations. Primary education is free although not compulsory and an added incentive is provided through a massive textbook-loan scheme, administered for children from families with limited means. Direct financial support in the form of scholarships, subsidies for examination fees and uniforms is also available for selected children. This is again based on need. Attempts have been made to introduce meals in schools in order to raise the nutritional status of children in areas where health problems are known to exist. However, this is not a fully-fledged scheme that covers all children. Pupils who show promise are given place allocations in premier schools, with transfers usually taking place from rural to urban centres, in order to nurture and maximize academic potential. There are vocational schools for the non-academically inclined. There is also legislation to protect the young, as in the case of children who are transferred or adopted, or where there is employment of minors or possible exposure to moral danger.

CHANGES IN FAMILY CARE AND THEIR IMPLICATIONS FOR ELDERLY PEOPLE

Socio-economic development has affected the life style of many people, particularly those in the urban areas. The trend is towards nuclear families (Chan, 1984), and neither the extended family system nor the traditional role of the woman in the household can be taken for granted any longer. It is now the norm rather than the exception for women to go out to work. It follows, then, that in the nuclear family where the wife works, the possibility of care for an elderly parent or relative becomes less likely or practical. The sense of responsibility is not always diminished, but it may take the form of paid help for the incapacitated member in the family, sometimes at considerable financial cost.

Another factor, and one which pertains particularly to the rural situation, is the loss of young women to factory employment. Industrialization has opened the door to paid work for large numbers of young women and they are recruited mainly from the villages. The multinational firms utilizing unskilled labour are usually established on the periphery of major towns. The movement of women from the villages to these areas has compounded the urban drift. The phenomenon of young men seeking employment opportunities in the towns has been evident for a long time and the older generation is often left behind now, bereft of support, to manage as best they can.

Yet another facet of the changing family picture with its implications for the care of elderly people is the emigration of many professionals to countries such as Australia and Canada in the last two decades or so. It is the nuclear family that usually seeks employment and educational opportunities abroad, leaving the first generation parents behind. While contact is maintained with short visits from time to time and although affectionate ties are not necessarily severed by distance, the question of emotional support and physical caring, particularly in times of illness, cannot be dismissed as unimportant.

SOCIAL SERVICES

Of the two main services under discussion, health and welfare services, welfare can be described as being more specifically orientated towards making provision for the elderly. However, until recently, any mention of welfare services in this context only brought two things to mind. These were financial assistance and institutional care. Both were principally for people who were indigent, without family for the most part, and almost exclusively for individuals who had been manual workers. This perception no longer holds true and today there is also a growing demand for services from people of different social situations, as is evidenced by the establishment of commercially-run homes for elderly people, catering for a range of middle-class clients.

The health and welfare services for elderly people have to be viewed within the context of the social services available in the country. Government priorities are quite clear. In the budget allocations under social services, the sections usually listed are: education, health, housing, and others. The last-named item includes allocations for welfare. In the 1989 budget, for example, an estimated total of M$6 367 million was allocated for the social services under operating expenditure. Of this, 69 per cent was earmarked for education, and health was apportioned 19 per cent, leaving only 12 per cent for housing and other services. Government concern for education and health is reflected here. The development expenditure for the same period reaffirms education as the biggest item in this sector, with it receiving 64 per cent of the allocation and health receiving 11 per cent (Ministry of Finance, 1988). The Budget estimates for the Ministry of Welfare from 1984 to 1988 are given in Table 10.2.

Table 10.2 Ministry of Social Welfare: Malaysia. Federal Budget Allocations.

	1984	1985	1986	1987	1988
Operating (M$)	44 693 300	47 264 100	50 115 800	49 145 000	49 364 000
Development (M$)	204 810	157 410	837 150	100	1 700 000
Total (M$)	44 898 110	47 421 510	50 952 950	49 145 100	51 064 000

Source: Government of Malaysia: Budget Estimates Programmes and Performance (1984, 1985, 1986, 1987, 1988).

HEALTH

Three divisions within the Ministry of Health have direct relevance when considering services for elderly people. One is the division of Health, in which promotive activities and activities pertaining to the prevention of disease are the main objectives, with the rural population as the target group. The vehicle for the delivery of services is the Family Health Programme, which encompasses all aspects of primary health care. However, given the composition and distribution of the Malaysian population, the overriding concern in maintaining health is focused on mothers and children. The elderly population are but part of the general adult population which comes within the ambit of the Family Health Programme.

The network of rural health facilities forms the infrastructure for the delivery of services that come under this programme. The 1985 Annual Report of the Ministry of Health Malaysia notes that there is a network of 399 health centres and 1 950 midwife clinics in the country. Within this, Peninsular Malaysia accounts for 373 health centres and 1 629 midwife clinics. Sarawak is the least well served, though it has the largest land area of the three components that constitute Malaysia. It has 8 health centres and 75 midwife clinics. Sabah has 18 and 246 respectively.

The second Ministry of Health division with a service component that is utilized by elderly people is designated as Medical Services. Both the inpatient and outpatient services of the Ministry of Health come under this division. The Inpatient or Hospital Programme has as its objective the provision of diagnostic, curative, and rehabilitative services to all people who need institutional medical care. Elderly people have access to all inpatient facilities as their needs are manifested, but there are as yet no specially designated geriatric services as such.

The Inpatient Programme of the Ministry of Health is undertaken through a system of hospitals that have been established to span the country. There are four different types of hospital. District hospitals are found in small towns and are without resident specialists. They vary in size from 24 to 350 beds and are manned by a small staff of medical and nursing personnel who provide basic diagnostic, curative, and nursing services. Regular visits are made by specialists from larger hospitals. They are also expected to provide a back-up service to the health centres in the district. There is a second category of district hospital found in the larger districts and again established in towns. These have a range of specialist services based on their size, with anything from 1 to 6 resident specialists. Patients from the smaller district hospitals requiring constant specialist attention are referred to them. General practitioners in the private sector also refer patients in need of specialist outpatient or inpatient care.

General hospitals located in each state capital are at the next level of the hierarchy. Their sizes vary but a full range of specialist services are available. They serve as centres to which referrals can be made from the other hospitals in the state, as well as from the health centres and general practitioners of the district in which they are located.

The general hospital in Kuala Lumpur is in a category of its own. It is not only the biggest hospital in the country with regular general and district hospital functions, but it also serves as the final national referral centre because of the establishment of highly specialized units (nephrology, urology, neurology, neurosurgery, plastic surgery, cardiology, cardiothoracic surgery, oncology, nuclear medicine and radiotherapy) within its complex. It also serves as a teaching hospital and a training centre for doctors, nurses, radiographers, physiotherapists and occupational therapists.

The Outpatient Programme is part of the patient care services and is provided from many points, both from within and outside hospitals. The health centres, midwife clinics, static dispensaries, travelling dispensaries, and mobile health teams cover the rural areas. The urban service is centred around the various hospitals and specially built polyclinics sited strategically in the larger towns. General outpatient clinics are available in all hospitals but specialist outpatient clinics are dependent on the availability of such personnel in these institutions. Table 10.3 shows the number of outpatient facilities available nationally. It should also be noted here that both Sabah and Sarawak have a Flying Doctor Service that carries patient care to remote areas, thereby expanding the coverage.

The Ministry of Health is not the sole provider of health care facilities. Non-government enterprise in the health sector is not new in Malaysia. Hospitals on estates and mines, and private hospitals, play a complementary role by providing both inpatient and outpatient services. Hospitals on estates and mines, by the very fact of their location, often have close links with the

Table 10.3 Number of outpatient facilities in Malaysia: 1985.

	Hospitals	Satellite centres	Health centres	Klinik desa	Static dispensaries	Travelling dispensaries	Sub- dispensaries	Total
Peninsular Malaysia	68	37	363	786	28	266	–	1 548
Sabah	16	1	18	180	66	5	–	286
Sarawak	17	3	8	75	17	123	61	304
Total	101	41	389	1 041	111	394	61	12 138

Source: Ministry of Health (1986).

rural health units and the smaller district hospitals in their vicinity. The private hospitals are almost exclusively urban based. There are 133 private hospitals and maternity hospitals/nursing homes in Malaysia, with a total number of 3 666 beds.

Government hospitals run by ministries other than the Ministry of Health also have patient care facilities accessible to elderly people. These are the two university hospitals that come under the Ministry of Education and the special hospital for the Aborigines which comes under the Department for Aboriginal Affairs. There are also two hospitals for military personnel but these are not taken into account within the context of the present discussion because the public have no right of access to them. Table 10.4 gives the total number of hospital beds available in the country.

The third division of the Ministry of Health identified as being specifically relevant in the context of this chapter is the Dental Health Programme. Services in dental care started with school children as their target, and clinical aspects were emphasized initially. Oral hygiene and the improvement of the dental health status of the population as a whole now receive equal attention and the services have been expanded. Dental clinics are sited in both the urban and rural areas. There are hospital-based dental units for surgical treatment and specialist care, as well as purpose-built dental clinics in the larger towns. Dental clinics also form part of the facilities and service provided by health centres. School dental clinics, mobile clinics, and dental squads work towards providing a service for at least half the primary and secondary school enrolment. Dental patients are categorized as: preschool, primary school and secondary school, as well as antenatal and adults. The elderly people fit into the last category and adults are now the major consumers of hospital-based specialist care.

From the outline provided above, it is evident that the general population is served by a comprehensive health care system. However, availability alone does not guarantee use of services and facilities, and elderly people are rarely specifically targeted. There are other factors to be considered in the case of elderly people than availability alone. For instance, incapacity, with attendant access problems and other difficulties, may cause delay in seeking treatment. Confusion of symptoms with a wrongly perceived understanding of the ageing process may also make individuals ignore the need for attention, until the condition becomes acute.

Interest in the health and also in the social needs of elderly people began to emerge in the late 1970s. A Society for the Welfare of the Elderly was proposed

Table 10.4 Sectoral distribution of hospitals and beds.

	Ministry of Health		Non-MOH		Private		Estates and mines		Total	
	Hospital	Beds	Hospital	Beds	Hospital	Beds	Hospital	Beds	Hospital	Beds
Peninsular Malaysia	68	26 491	5	2 170	119	3 559	65	1 820	257	34 040
Sabah	16	2 809	–	–	3	30	–	–	19	2 839
Sarawak	17	3 195	–	–	11	77	–	–	28	3 272
Total	101	32 495	5	2 170	133	3 666	65	1 820	304	40 151

Source: Ministry of Health (1986).
Note: Beds include those in special institutions, i.e. leprosarium, mental health and tuberculosis hospitals.

(Sandosham, 1977) but there was no response until much later. The World Assembly of Ageing in 1982 marked the turning point and provided the impetus to examine the issues involved (see Chapter 2). Clearly defined studies have begun to build a data-base, on which policy initiatives can be built.

Attempts are being made to identify the health needs of the elderly Malaysian. It was one of the aspects studied in a 4-year (1985–88) population project by ASEAN entitled *The Socio-Economic Consequences of Ageing of the Population.* The World Health Organization (WHO) also undertook a more specific health related study in 1984–85 reported in *Aging in the Western Pacific: A Four Country Study.* Andrews discusses these studies, their participants and their objectives in Chapter 2.

The Malaysian component of the findings was reported in a paper *Health and Ageing in Malaysia.* Of the 1 001 elderly individuals interviewed, 67 per cent had visual problems. Difficulty in chewing food was cited by 47 per cent, and 15 per cent indicated difficulty in walking 300 metres (Chen *et al.,* 1986). In the month prior to the interview, 41 per cent had sought treatment for a health problem and had chosen to see a doctor, instead of a nurse or a pharmacist. Only 2 per cent were hospitalized during the same period. The need for more health care was indicated by 9 per cent, while 72 per cent reported feeling healthy (Chen *et al.,* 1986). A positive inference can be drawn from these findings, but some caution will have to be exercised, as it is not known how the remainder were served, other than those feeling healthy.

There is clear evidence that elderly people have an increased burden of cardiovascular and cerebrovascular diseases, malignancies, diseases affecting the locomotor system, mental illnesses and accidents. Other sources of disability in old age are auditory and visual disorders (WHO, 1974). In comparing this list with the common causes for hospital admission, some overlap can be noted. It is therefore possible to surmise that a certain proportion of the inpatients constitute the elderly. The exact numbers involved can, however, only be accurately known when the medical record system is able to provide the necessary information by age.

Note must also be taken of the fact that little information is currently available on the main causes of admission into hospital among elderly people in Malaysia. Data are collated for all admissions, but it is not possible to locate specific causes, because the categorization is only between children and adults and it is not broken down by age. The 1985 Annual Report (Ministry of Health, 1986) lists the ten most common causes for hospital admissions. Of these only seven are relevant in so far as the elderly are concerned; these are accidents, diseases of the digestive system, the circulatory system, respiratory system and the urinary system, mental disorders and ill-defined conditions.

A National Health and Morbidity Survey conducted in Peninsular Malaysia reports that the incidence of sickness is more common among young children and elderly people (Pathmanathan and Lawson, 1988). Children are already identified as a category that needs special attention, but the elderly are not.

WELFARE

The provision of welfare services in the country has been a joint enterprise, undertaken by the government, voluntary organizations and sections of the community. On becoming directly involved in meeting the needs of disadvantaged people, the government has assumed a pivotal role. Most voluntary organizations have been established to meet a particular need and therefore only play a complementary role at certain times or for certain people. Special interest groups such as Service Clubs do not have welfare as their main focus, but they do provide a community service from time to time, and elderly people are often identified on special occasions by such clubs. This combination of government and voluntary activity is important in that it enlarges the coverage.

The Ministry of Welfare has evolved from being a temporary department concerned with purely residual and rehabilitative services, to being one with a role in national development. This has been possible with the acceptance that welfare as a concept does encompass more than financial assistance and shelter for the destitute. National development, it is now recognized, requires high levels of productivity not only from the workforce, but from all people. With the stress placed on the development of personal potential, the vulnerable groups (the elderly being identified as one such group) are not exempt from contributing to the total effort, to the best of their ability. This does not mean services are to be denied them, rather that support services will come into play only when needed. The emphasis is to encourage elderly people, as much as members of any other group who may require assistance, to maintain their independence. The active involvement of the family in their care, and that of the community, is implicit. This stance is enunciated in the Fifth Malaysia Plan 1986–1990 (Government of Malaysia, 1986). The contribution of the voluntary sector and of the community at large to every sphere of welfare activity is seen as vital in achieving the satisfactory coverage of welfare services.

The elderly are clearly identified as a vulnerable group and the Ministry of Social Welfare has responsibility for their care, with funding for services being allocated under state and federal votes. Elderly people come under the division designated as Family and Child Care Services, and the implementation of the relevant programmes is undertaken through the various Departments of Social Welfare at the district level in each state or in the federal territories.

Persons who are 60 years and older can apply to the Department of Social Welfare for financial assistance if they are without means of maintenance and have no family to support them. Institutional care is considered if the applicant is without a home. Assistance is also provided when an elderly person is unable to purchase appliances or prostheses necessary to carry out daily activities. Grants for glasses after an operation for cataracts, wheelchairs, hearing aids and the like, all come under this category. Details of financial assistance as provided under federal and state allocations are given in Table 10.5.

Every effort is made currently to maintain the old person within the community. In cases where relief is sought by an elderly person who is part of an extended family experiencing hardship, steps are taken to improve the family situation. For example, a capital grant can be considered for such a family to allow them to embark on a small-scale business, such as a food stall, where financial constraints have previously precluded such a venture. Assistance towards placement in employment for a member of the family who is in the working age group is another alternative. Fostering of elderly persons with families willing to take them into care because of long association is also considered as a substitute for institutional care, especially if the individual is in need of some supervision. The foster family is paid by the department, but it is safe to state that the reimbursement is more often a token than full payment for the service rendered.

Cataract glasses are a common request entertained by the Department of Welfare, and in 1987 some 333 old persons were assisted with the purchase of these. The officers of the department who have responsibility for elderly people work closely with the ophthalmologists in government hospitals to provide the

Table 10.5 Financial assistance for the elderly.

Source of funds	1983		1984		1985		1986		1987	
	No. of elderly	Amount allocated M$	No. of elderly	Amount allocated M$	No. of elderly	Amount allocated M$	No. of elderly	Amount allocated M$	No. of elderly	Amount allocated M$
Federal	8 672	4 641 858	8 917	4 998 772	8 892	5 714 643	10 851	5 579 918	10 884	6 101 750
State	17 231	5 918 057	15 656	5 542 861	16 123	6 737 279	15 909	7 075 056	16 323	6 967 069
Total	25 903	10 559 915	24 573	10 541 633	25 095	12 451 922	26 760	12 654 974	27 207	13 068 819

Source: Personal communication with Ministry of Welfare Officials (9.12.88).

necessary service and to purchase the required glasses. Less common are applications for other appliances, but they are nevertheless considered and efforts are made to supply them, particularly if the ability to act independently is dependent on the use of a particular appliance.

Institutional care for elderly people is the last resort and the Ministry of Welfare administers eight homes in Peninsular Malaysia with places for 2 450 individuals. These homes admit persons of both sexes and the largest home has a capacity for 350 people. It must be noted, however, that of the 2 087 persons resident in these homes at the end of 1987, only 1 460 were 60 years or older (Ministry of Welfare, 1988).

The presence of persons below the age of 60 years has arisen partly because of the implementation of the Vagrancy Act of 1977. The department mounts drives against beggars and vagrants from time to time. These take place all over the country and individuals who are brought in from these operations are often housed in the nearest home for the elderly, pending a court decision as to what should be done. There is in fact a special institution for the rehabilitation of beggars and, usually, those below the age of 60 are sent to this centre. If the person picked up in one of the drives is over 60 years, the chances are the person will be left in one of the homes for the aged and not transferred to the special institution. Admission to a home is not always seen as the best solution by an old person who prefers complete freedom of movement, and some do leave. Younger people are also admitted for reasons other than vagrancy. This happens when, for example, a medical problem precludes work and the person is without family support. Therefore, it can be said that expediency sometimes makes the homes for the elderly multipurpose institutions. This may often not be a satisfactory state of affairs for staff or residents, as the needs and care of the different people are not always compatible.

In the normal course of events, applicants for admission into these homes are required to be able to look after their personal needs, be free from infectious diseases, and be without the support of their family. There is usually a time lapse between application and actual admission because of the need to investigate the circumstances of each applicant. Once admitted, there is no question of turning a person out should health problems arise, and appropriate medical care is provided through the outpatient and inpatient facilities within reach of the institution.

In 1986, a study on Issues of the Aged was conducted among selected recipients of welfare assistance. This study was undertaken jointly by the Institute of Technology MARA and the Ministry of Welfare. MARA is an acronym for an institution, known in the official language of Malaysia as Majlis Amanah Rakyat (MARA). A loose translation would be: Amanah: A Trust for the People. Residents of departmental homes and elderly persons in receipt of public assistance from selected states in Malaysia but who continued to live in the community were interviewed. It was found that the Chinese form the biggest group in institutions for the elderly and that the Malays are the least likely to seek admission into a home (Normah et al., 1986).

This is not surprising because care of the aged still remains a strongly ingrained responsibility in the Malay community. It was found that most residents were single, or their spouse had died. Those who sought public assistance had invariably earned less than M$200 per month prior to seeking assistance, and few had had education in the formal sense (Normah et al., 1986). Only a small proportion kept themselves occupied in part-time work which augmented the allowance of M$50 provided by welfare. Social activities appeared to be limited to television viewing and visiting with friends. The inability to move around confidently does make it difficult for such elderly people to venture out of their homes more often and this has implications for health care. The lack of someone to accompany them to a source of care was cited as one reason for not going to see a doctor when ill. Transport difficulties to get to the hospital or clinic was the other main reason for non-attendance (Normah *et al.*, 1986).

Several non-government organizations also provide services to elderly people and various interests are represented by these organizations. They usually offer shelter and financial assistance. The Central Welfare Council (CWC) of Peninsular Malaysia has a special interest in the aged and it administers 140 homes, with a capacity to accommodate 2 094 elderly persons. There is close liaison with the Department of Welfare at all levels, but the CWC confines itself to the rural areas. The special features of these homes are their size and the fact that community participation is encouraged. They are almost always custom-built homes, because they serve old people in the locality they choose to live. The homes vary in size according to need, with the smallest accommodating one or two persons and the largest taking in 20. The materials are supplied by the CWC and the local residents undertake the construction. The sharing involved in each project makes it a particularly satisfactory manner of achieving objectives and, furthermore, the natural reluctance of the elderly to move away to a more distant institution is overcome.

The Malays are the biggest ethnic group in the rural areas and the fact that they form the smallest group among the residents in homes run by the welfare department may partly be attributed to the presence of these small village homes. In addition to providing shelter, the CWC also makes payments of cash grants amounting to M$30 per person per month. Problems of double payment from welfare and CWC are avoided by using welfare staff to assess the eligibility of all applications for such assistance.

In addition to the CWC, there are at least nine other organizations that offer shelter to the elderly, but almost always in the urban areas. These offer places for 800 residents. Only five of the nine organizations receive grants from the government. Clan associations also exist which look after their own members.

All the institutions mentioned so far are catering for those elderly people who cannot provide for themselves or who are willing to accept minimal service. In the last 10 years, a different kind of home has begun to appear which is being run on a commercial basis. They are registered as business concerns and only need to fulfil safety requirements in accordance with municipal, or local government regulations before beginning to operate. The Ministry of Welfare has no jurisdiction over them but is monitoring the situation, in order to decide whether conditions will have to be imposed for such homes. Nurses seem to have taken the initiative in this sector and the homes are an urban phenomenon, with units varying in size. The cost per person also varies from home to home and is dependent on the level of care that is expected. A charge of M$500 per month appears to be the minimum for an elderly person who is able to move about and look after his or her own personal needs. The bedridden are also accepted and standing arrangements are made with doctors to visit and prescribe treatment where this is necessary. The patient or families meet such costs. The more successful homes run their own vans to ferry the patients to clinics, hospitals or for outings.

The fact that more of these commercially-based homes are being established indicates that there is a need for the service they provide and that it is not just a matter of cost. The need to pay, however, and the lack of public support for these costs, restricts such facilities to those who can afford the charges. The private sector involvement in homes may be compared with the situations in Hong Kong, discussed in Chapter 4, and Singapore, Chapter 6.

Another development worthy of note is the establishment of clubs for senior citizens which began in the early to mid-1980s. They are active in the larger towns throughout the country. The largest has approximately 750 members and the membership is now frozen in this particular club. The majority of those who join are healthy and vigorous. The focus of interest is mainly directed towards health and recreational activities, although a caring element is integrated through services to other elderly people in the community.

AN APPRAISAL

Elderly people do merit greater attention and a more responsive stance to meet their needs is beginning to emerge in Malaysia. Several initiatives have been triggered in the 1980s and studies on the impact of ageing have been undertaken. Many will continue or expand in the 1990s. Attention is increasingly being focused on measures that will need to be adopted as the composition of the population changes. It is encouraging to note the multidisciplinary approach adopted in examining the issues involved, for it indicates a broader perspective in viewing the future of elderly people rather than merely viewing them as, say, economic or medical problems.

Given the rising numbers of elderly people in Malaysia, as elsewhere in the region, it is clear that services for them will have to be planned. There are several aspects to be considered and without doubt health is a key issue. While ageing does not necessarily imply sickness and disability, a proportion of elderly people will require a range of services and special facilities. Geriatric medicine is not an area of specialization as yet in Malaysia, but the need for special attention for elderly patients cannot be denied, as the ageing process is known to alter the presentation of symptoms and also responses to treatment. Unless medical personnel are appropriately trained for work with elderly people, the management of this growing group of patients will be less than is their right. Therefore, gerontology, geriatric medicine and knowledge about common illnesses in old age will need to be incorporated, with greater emphasis, into the medical curriculum. Importantly, in addition to doctors, other members of the medical team will have to be suitably prepared, so as to provide appropriate geriatric care and support for Malaysia's growing elderly population.

Some elderly people are known to become confused in unfamiliar surroundings and hospitalization can be a frightening experience even to younger patients. Therefore, the development of home nursing within the health care system could provide families with the necessary resources and support to care for elderly relatives in the home. Such a move is often a preferred alternative, provided of course it is not counter to medical advice. Where hospitalization is indicated, home nursing can also shorten the length of inpatient treatment. The Family Health Care programme, already functioning in the rural areas, focuses specifically on the whole family in providing care. With appropriate training, the staff in the health centres should be able to upgrade their skills and serve their elderly patients more effectively.

Health education is also an important aspect of health care and it is expected that in future both mental and physical health will receive increasing attention. Such educational activity would be generally beneficial not only to elderly people, but also to families and the community as a whole. The long-term effect would be to have within the community people who are aware of the process of, and consequently better prepared for, healthy ageing.

When discussing welfare, the issue of adequacy of services is pertinent, as neither the government nor voluntary organizations have yet been able to meet requirements in a wholly satisfactory manner. The person in need cannot turn to either source with confidence for an immediate response. Furthermore, welfare needs have, until recently, been seen in limited terms. In the absence of a universal old-age allowance scheme, public assistance is not only inadequate but varies and is not readily available. Institutional care remains basic for the most part. Once accepted into a facility, conformity rather than individuality is expected in the daily activities of individuals. A need to re-think the provision of financial help and shelter is indicated if there is to be improvement. It would appear that the varying nature of needs among the elderly is yet to be recognized.

Some needs require immediate attention. An intermediate facility that lies between hospital care and family responsibility would serve the community as a whole. Elderly patients often continue to remain in hospital after a bout of illness because there is no one at home who can provide care and supervision. Such people can pose a real problem and families are known to abandon them. A day-care centre offering the necessary service would be useful under such circumstances. Hospital beds are for the acutely ill and the pressure on them could be reduced if there were no blockage. At the same time, families would be able to retain responsibility and the elderly person in turn is able to maintain important personal links with family and friends. A day-care centre is not necessarily only for convalescing sick people, but could serve other elderly people in the community by acting as a point of social contact, provided it is planned to meet different kinds of needs.

A recent proposal by the Department of Welfare, following the practice of the CWC, to provide small units in familiar surroundings for the elderly when accommodation is requested, seems a step in the right direction. Such units would serve active people, or perhaps even the mildly incapacitated, better than the large institutions, especially if a home-nursing facility is available. Large institutions, even for those who need a great deal of attention can be unsatisfactory and, of course, have been abandoned in many developed countries. Again, appropriate training for staff in the welfare services, like those in health, is of paramount importance.

Note should also be taken of the variety among elderly people themselves. There are many in the community who are healthy, active, wishing to extend their involvement in gainful employment, participating in community affairs, and anxious to live full lives as long as possible. Among these are the individuals who have formed themselves into senior citizens clubs. Insights and contributions provided by this group could be invaluable when planning to improve the services for elderly people as a whole.

The responsibility for action does not rest with any one sector of the community. Representatives from communities, families who have experience in caring for aged relatives, the authorities, interested individuals, organizations, professional groups and academics, all need to work together. Each one has a role to play in making the lives of elderly people more satisfactory and fulfilling.

CONCLUSION

The review of services and the foregoing discussion make it clear that the elderly are an underserved section of the population. Whilst a caring society may be desired and might be evolving in Malaysia, established services indicate an extremely narrow view of the needs of elderly people. A more specific focus, developing from careful studies of the issues involved, must precede the planning and implementation of programmes. Elderly people can form a vulnerable group, who deserve more services and a better quality of care.

REFERENCES

Anderson, F. (1987). Education in geriatric medicine. *Anals: Academy of Medicine Singapore*, **16**, 146–50.

Andrews, G.R., Esterman, A.J., Braunack-Mayer, A.J. and Rungie, C.M. (1986). *Aging in the Western Pacific: A Four Country Study.* Manila, Western Pacific Reports and Studies No. 1: World Health Organization.

Chan, K.E. (1982). *The Elderly in Malaysia: A neglected group? Some socio-economic implications.* Faculty of Economics and Administration, University of Malaya, Kuala Lumpur.

Chan, K.E. (1983). *Socio-Economic Implications of Population Ageing in a Developing Country: The Malaysian Case.* Second regional congress proceedings. Singapore: International Association of Gerontology Asia/Oceania Region, 39–43.

Chan, K.E. (1984). *Population Ageing and the Family: Perspective and Prospective, with Special Reference to Malaysia.* International seminar on the family in the eighties, Kuala Lumpur.

Chen, C.Y.P., Andrews, G.R., Josef, R., Chan, K.E. and Arokiasamy, J.T. (1986). *Health and Ageing in Malaysia: A Study Sponsored by the World Health Organization.* Faculty of Medicine, University of Malaysia, Kuala Lumpur.

Chen, C.Y.P. (1987). Ageing in Malaysia. *Medical Journal Malaysia*, **42**, 144–5.

Department of Statistics (1987). *Population Projections: Malaysia 1980–2000*, Kuala Lumpur.

Dixon, J. and Hyung, S.K. (Eds) (1985). *Social Welfare in Asia*, pp. 214–45. Croom Helm, London.

Far Eastern Economic Review (1991). *Asia 1991 Yearbook*, Far Eastern Economic Review, Hong Kong.

Government of Malaysia (1984). *Mid-Term Review of the Fourth Malaysia Plan 1981–1985.* National Printing Department, Kuala Lumpur.

Government of Malaysia (1986). *Fifth Malaysia Plan 1986–1990.* National Printing Department, Kuala Lumpur.

Government of Malaysia (1984–7). *Budget Estimate Programmes and Performance, 1984; 1985; 1986; 1987; 1988.* National Printing Department, Kuala Lumpur.

Hamid, A., Ghandhi, A.D. and Ramasamy, A. (1986). *Population and Family Development.* National Population and Family Development Board, Kuala Lumpur.

Masitah, M.Y. (1985). The prospects of ageing, of the population in Malaysia. *Seminar Proceedings: Socio-Economic Consequences of the Ageing Population in Malaysia*, pp. 27–51. National Population and Family Development Board, Kuala Lumpur.

Ministry of Finance (1988). *Economic Report 1988/89.* National Printing Department, Kuala Lumpur.

Ministry of Health (1986). *Annual Report 1985*, Kuala Lumpur.

Ministry of Welfare (1988). *Annual Report 1987.* Family and Child Care Services, Kuala Lumpur.

New Straits Times, 15 November 1988, p. 5.

Normah, M.D., Lau, J.K. and Bakar, W. (1986). *Issues of the Aged: A Study on Welfare Recipients in Selected States in Malaysia.* MARA Institute of Technology and the Ministry of Welfare Services, Kuala Lumpur.

Pathmanathan, I. and Lawson, J. (1988). *National Health and Morbidity Survey in Peninsular Malaysia.* Public Health Institute, Ministry of Health, Kuala Lumpur.

Sandosham, A.A. (1977). The Welfare of the Elderly. *Medical Journal Malaysia,* **31**, 168–9.

Singh, G. (1983). *The Future of Gerontology in Malaysia*, Second regional congress proceedings. Singapore: International Association of Gerontology Asia/Oceania Region, pp. 57–60.

World Health Organization (WHO) (1974). *Planning and Organization of Geriatric Services.* Technical Report Series: 548. WHO, Geneva.

Anthony Warnes

Department of Geography
Age Concern Institute of Gerontology
King's College London

11 POPULATION AGEING IN THAILAND: PERSONAL AND SERVICE IMPLICATIONS

INTRODUCTION

This chapter discusses the ageing of Thailand's population and the consequences for the kingdom's people and institutions. The author, a British gerontologist, wishes to avoid simplistic statements about the burden of ageing, or over-selective prognoses of a rising prevalence of privation, incapacity or distress among old people. The educational, economic and health status of the people of Thailand is improving rapidly. These will be manifested by marked improvements in the living situation of the elderly population of future decades. But, at the same time, the nation has to adapt to an unprecedented pace and range of social, economic and experiential changes. The government's first priorities are understandably with the economy and in the social sphere with education and health services. It is not yet persuaded that it should take a significant role in the income or social support of elderly people.

In any country, however, it is wise occasionally to stand back from today's pressing problems and to consider longer-term issues. This article examines the interactions between an increasing elderly population and the social forms associated with the spread of urban-industrial, waged employment. Throughout the world, old people are excluded by regulation or convention from the expanding and most remunerative and productive sectors of employment, with profound implications for their economic and social roles. They are therefore vulnerable to social changes which disrupt the traditional forms of their support. Poverty is a condition and threat among large proportions of elderly people, even in the richest nations of the world. The general aim of this paper is to assess the implications of the nation's current sociodemographic trends for the welfare of elderly people in Thailand.

An inevitable outcome of a substantial fall in both fertility and mortality in a human population is an increase of the average age. This process has been underway in many European countries throughout this century, raising the share of the population aged 60 years and over from around one in twenty in 1900 to one in seven by the 1980s (Warnes, 1989). European and other developed countries have successfully adapted to this change: demographic ageing has prevented neither a high rate of economic growth nor a considerable improvement in the material and health standards of old people. There is some perversity, therefore, in the recently common opinion among Western élite groups that ageing is a societal problem and that elderly people are an economic burden.

Many nations in Latin America and South-east Asia have recently experienced a combination of substantial falls in mortality and lesser declines in fertility. Consequently demographic ageing has begun, and it is likely to proceed more rapidly than in Europe. In Asia the process is most advanced in the 'city states' of Hong Kong and Singapore: Thailand is among a second, major group of nations in which mortality began to fall substantially during 1950–55 and fertility began to fall a decade later (Kinsella, 1988; UNO, 1985; USA Bureau of the Census, 1988). These changes represent success in combating premature deaths and 'unwanted' births and it is both irresponsible and false to respond in a dominantly alarmist way or to take a problematic view of the changes. In nations such as Thailand, however, both macroeconomic and humanitarian reasons require that attention should be paid to the likely age-structure change and its implications. There will in the future be fewer adult children for each elderly person, there may be widening differences between successive generations in their educational levels, occupational experience and attitudes, and there may be much greater demands from elderly people for health and social services. The prevalence of childlessness or of adult children living abroad or many kilometres from their parents will increase. It is possible that altered social forms will first be revealed among relatively affluent elderly people in Bangkok and other towns, and then spread more widely.

Each newly industrializing country will need to develop its own responses to ageing, to enable old people to participate in the rising standards of living and to develop new roles. Mechanistic projections of the numbers of people in different age groups or of the ratios of the working to the non-working population are only the starting point for a continuing debate. Careful evaluations of changing family and household forms, of changing sources of income and support, and of the means of developing services and roles are required to guide a society's responses to demographic ageing and socio-economic change. This chapter reviews the recent demographic history of Thailand, with particular reference to ageing effects and with various projections for Thailand and Bangkok. It then examines the households, living circumstances, sources of income and health of the present elderly population, and concludes with a review of the provision of services and facilities, and the national policies for improving the living conditions of old people in Thailand.

THAILAND'S CHANGING POPULATION STRUCTURE

Thailand has strong intellectual, cultural, civil administrative and educational resources. It is one of the few less-developed nations for which alternative sources are available to study fertility and mortality, which enables confidence to be placed in the demographic record. This study builds upon a substantial foundation of evidence and analysis by Thai and visiting demographers (Chayovan et al., 1990; Knodel et al., 1985; Goldstein and Goldstein, 1986). During the last 30 years, the many changes in Thailand's society and economy have been closely interlinked with its demographic experience. Falls in mortality from the late 1940s, particularly among infants, have brought about a very high rate of population growth. Each decade, until very recently, has seen a greater total of births, and this alone will generate an increasing population of old people well into the next century. Since the mid-1960s there has been a decline in fertility, with uneven regional patterns, which has begun to increase the elderly population as a share of the national total. These changes in the vital rates of fertility and mortality have interacted with social and economic phenomena. The spread of modern-sector occupations, the expansion of primary education and the rising standard of living have all encouraged lower fertility and, in association with the pronounced urban-rural differentials in levels of living and life opportunities, rapid urbanization.

The first national population census was conducted in 1909 and the National Statistical Office (NSO, 1983a) has carried out decennial enquiries since 1960. Thailand's population increased from 11.5 million in 1929 to 22 million in 1954, and to 44.8 million in 1980 (Table 11.1). The average annual growth rate increased to 3 per cent during the 1950s. It has since moderated, to 2 per cent during the early 1980s and 1.5 per cent during 1985–90. The Thai government estimates that by the end of June 1986, the population had reached 52.5 million (Royal Thai Embassy, London, 1987). The population of the Bangkok Metropolitan Area (BMA) has increased more rapidly than that of the kingdom as a whole. In 1947 it had little more than 1 million inhabitants, but by 1986 there were 5.45 million residents (Table 11.1). The BMA now has lower fertility and mortality than Thailand. It receives substantial net-inmigration, enabling its share of the national population to increase from about 6.6 per cent in 1947 to 10 per cent in 1980. The estimates for 1986 suggest a reversal of this trend, with the share dropping to 10.4 per cent, but the 'outer-suburban' *changwats* contiguous to the BMA have high population growth rates.

The proportion of Thailand's population aged over 60 years has been growing slowly since 1947 and only recently has exceeded one in twenty. The annual growth rate of the elderly population is greater than that of the general population, and it rose from the 1960s to the 1970s. Until 1960, the proportion of elderly in BMA was higher than in the remainder of Thailand, but it has since fallen behind. None the less the growth rate of the city's elderly population has been in excess of that for the nation as a whole ever since 1947. The 1970s have marked a noticeable acceleration in the relative growth of the elderly population, as a direct result of the fall in the birth rate.

Trends in fertility and mortality: 1960–90

Authoritative studies are available on the trends in Thailand's vital statistics since the early 1960s. The Total Fertility Rate (TFR) at a specific date is the

Table 11.1 The population of Thailand and Bangkok (millions).

	1929	1937	1947	1960	1970	1980
Thailand						
Population	11.5	14.5	18.0	26.4	34.4	44.8
growth rate[1]		2.9	2.2	3.0	2.7	2.7
Aged 60+ yrs			0.7	1.2	1.7	2.4
share (%)			4.2	4.6	4.9	5.5
growth rate[1]				3.9	3.4	3.8
Bangkok[2]						
Population	0.7	0.9	1.1	2.1	3.1	4.7
national share (%)	6.4	6.2	6.6	8.1	8.9	10.5
growth rate[1]		2.4	2.6	4.9	3.7	4.3
Aged 60+ yrs			0.056	0.10	0.14	0.24
share (%)			4.7	4.7	4.6	5.1
growth rate[1]				4.6	3.5	5.4

Sources: NSO, Thailand Statistical Yearbook (various years).
Notes: 1 Average annual growth rate (%) since previous census.
   2 The changwats of Phranakhorn and Thornburi, termed in 1980 the Bangkok Metropolitan Area.

number of children that would be born to the average female who survived throughout the reproductive age span, assuming that date's age-specific fertility rates operate. The TFR has declined from 6.3–6.6 (as estimated from different data) in the early 1960s to 4.5–4.9 in 1975 and 2.6 in 1985–90 (UNO, 1989; USA National Research Council, 1980). 'Although it is difficult to date precisely when the decline began, most evidence indicates that (it started) during the 1960s and, for the rural population probably dates largely from the latter part of the decade' (Knodel *et al.*, 1985). Detailed studies of the regional variations in fertility change are available (Pardthaisong, 1978; Shevasunt and Hogan, 1979). The crude birth rate per 1 000 decreased from 46.6 in the early 1950s, through 35.1 in the early 1970s, to 28.0 in the early 1980s (Table 11.2).

Various estimates of recent trends in mortality are less consistent. One problem is that there is still serious underregistration of deaths, amounting to one-quarter of the total in 1985–86 (National Statistical Office, 1989). It is clear, however, that death rates have been falling over a longer period than birth rates and declined particularly strongly during the 1950s. The crude death rate per 1 000 fell from 19.2 in the early 1950s to 13.4 during the 1960s: it then fell to 9.3 in the early 1970s and to 8.0 in the early 1980s. As also estimated by the United Nations, life expectancy at birth has increased from about 47 years in the early 1950s, to 65 years in the late 1980s (UNO, 1989). Other sources suggest that infant mortality, or the probability of dying before 5 years of age, declined by about 15 per cent from the mid-1960s to the mid-1970s. In terms of overall mortality, expectation of life at birth probably increased by 2–3 years over the same period, reaching about 58 years for males and 64 years for females by the mid-1970s (USA National Research Committee, 1980). Estimates from the National Surveys of Population Change and from models developed by the US Census Bureau suggest that life expectancy at birth had attained 64 years for males and 69 years for females by 1985/86 (Chayovan *et al.*, 1990).

In South-east Asian countries there is considerable internal variation in mortality levels (Ruzicka, 1984). In most instances this is attributable to the social and economic conditions in which people live and work, such as variations in access to health services, sterile drinking water and efficient sanitation. Data from the World Fertility Survey reveals that in the late 1970s in Thailand, the mortality rate of children aged 1 month to 5 years of a metropolitan 'élite' population was 3 per 1 000, whereas the rate for traditional rural populations was 56 per 1 000 (Hobcraft *et al.*, 1985). The urban élite were defined as couples with 7 or more years of education, the wife working for others and the husband in clerical or professional occupations: traditional rural couples were uneducated with the wife engaged in family work and the husband in agriculture. Thailand's differential (18.7) exceeded that in Malaysia (12.5), the Philippines (8.3) and 9 other nations. This suggests that, as is true in affluent Western countries, there are pronounced variations in survival to old

Table 11.2 Crude birth and death rates and natural change, 1950–85.

	1950–55	1960–65	1970	1975	1975–80	1980–85
CBR	46.6	43–46	36–38	32–36	31.6	28.0
CDR	19.2	10–11	9–10	9–10	8.3	8.0
Nat. Inc. R	27.4	32–34	26–29	23–26	23.3	20.0

Sources: Figures for 1950–55, 1975–80 and 1980–85 are drawn from UNO (1986).
Other figures are drawn from USA National Research Council (1980).
Notes: The rates (crude birth rate, crude death rate, natural increase rate) are per 1 000 per year.

age dependent on income and socio-economic status. It is obvious that in the early stages of demographic ageing, the increase in old people over-represents the privileged strata of a nation.

Internal migration to and from Bangkok

The 1960, 1970 and 1980 censuses in Thailand established the place of residence of each respondent 5 years before the census. These data, the commentaries which have accompanied the census migration reports, the birthplace data and specific studies of migrants to the BMA have all built up an unusually full record of internal migration (Arnold and Piampiti, 1984; Goldstein, 1978; Goldstein and Goldstein, 1986; Goldstein et al., 1981; Piampiti, 1984; Sternstein, 1976; NSO, 1978, 1985).

Thailand's migration patterns are structured by the considerable disparities in regional economic development, and by the dynamism of urban areas, particularly Bangkok. Goldstein suggested that during the 1950s, urban population growth in Thailand was attributable equally to natural increase and to net-inmigration. By the early 1970s, however, urban natural increase accounted for approximately 60 per cent of growth. 'This change, common to many South-east Asian countries, reflected the accumulation in the towns (of the) reproductive age span ... through migration and the maturation of children born in the urban areas to natives and to earlier migrants' (Goldstein, 1978). This accumulation will be shown to have particular consequences for the ageing of Bangkok and other urban populations.

The interregional migration flow pattern within Thailand during 1975–80 was dominated by two features: substantial net attraction towards the BMA, and considerable net losses from the North-eastern region, the poorest and most rural part of the nation. Only 4.1 per cent of the region's population resided in municipal areas in 1980. The comparative prosperity of Bangkok and the North-eastern regions is indicated by the inbalanced flows between them. The net flow towards the city represented 84 per cent of the gross movement of 116 500 persons. In contrast the movements between the BMA and the Central region which surrounds it were more balanced: the net flow towards the city constituted 41 per cent of the gross flow of 174 900 persons.

The age and sex-specific structure of migration between Bangkok and the remainder of the nation shows many features characteristic of movements towards primate Third-World cities. The dominant flow is of young people aged 15–24 years moving towards the capital city, with females, particularly among teenagers, predominating (Fig. 11.1). The imbalance of flow is exceptional, with the net movement into the BMA of females aged 15–19 years being 85 per cent of the gross flow. Out-movements from the city are relatively greater among those aged 20–39 years but still far less than in-movements. Males predominate among the young out-migrants and among in-migrants aged 25–39 years. Among older people, the flow of migrants is much lower, and there is a net out-movement from the BMA among those aged 50–59 years.

Population of Thailand and Bangkok in 1980

The age structure of Thailand was surprisingly stable from 1947 to 1980 (Fig. 11.2). A small decrease in the relative population aged less than 10 years and a small increase of the share aged over 70 years occurred. The greatest changes have been in the proportion aged 20–24 years, with males increasing more than females by 1980, possibly reflecting a recovery after the Second World War losses. Changes in the age structure of the BMA are described for 1960–80 (Fig. 11.2). The recent decline in fertility and the age-specific patterns

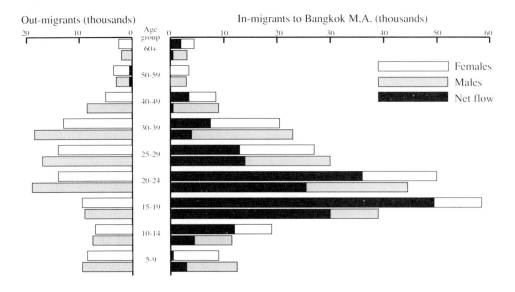

Fig. 11.1 Migrants between the Bangkok Metropolitan Area and the remainder of Thailand by age and sex, 1975–80.

of internal migration during the 1960s and 1970s have resulted in a declining relative presence of children and increases in the proportion aged 20–29 years. The annual growth rate of the population aged over 60 years increased from 3.4 per cent in Thailand and 3.5 per cent in the BMA during the 1960s, to 3.8 per cent and 5.4 per cent respectively during the 1970s. The population aged over 60 years exceeded 1 in 20 for the first time (Table 11.1).

POPULATION PROJECTIONS AND AGEING IN THAILAND AND BANGKOK

The United Nations has published population projections for Thailand with a base year of 1984 (UNO, DIESA 1986). Three variant projections are employed with different fertility assumptions, all based on the date at which the TFR falls to 2. For high-fertility countries like Thailand, the UN demographers assume that once a decline in fertility has begun, it proceeds sinusoidally. The high-growth projection assumes that the crude birth rate (CBR) was 29.2 per 1 000 in 1980–85 and that it will fall at a declining rate to 26.2 in 1990–95 and to 18.2 by 2020–25, a 38 per cent fall. The medium-growth projection assumes a 45 per cent decline, and the low variant a 49 per cent decline (Table 11.3). The assumption concerning mortality is that infant mortality rates will decline from 48 per 1 000 in 1980–85 to 13 by 2025. For each of the three variant growth models, the CDR falls from 1980 until the earliest years of the next century but rises thereafter in response to the ageing of the national population. The high-growth projection assumes a 19 per cent decline in the CDR from 1980 until 2015 and a 15 per cent decline over the 40 year projection period to 2025. The medium-variant projection assumes only a 7.5 per cent fall in the CDR during 1980–2025 and the low variant projects an increase of 1.3 per cent. Finally it should be noted that the UN projections assume no external migration.

A) Thailand

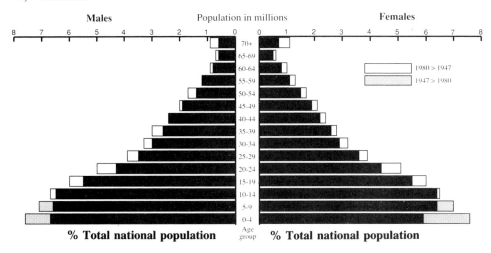

Males   Population in millions   Females

% Total national population   Age group   % Total national population

B) Bangkok

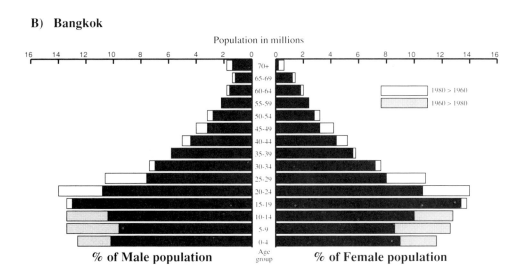

Population in millions

% of Male population   Age group   % of Female population

Fig. 11.2 Age/sex structure of Thailand and Bangkok, 1947, 1960 and 1980.

These assumptions generate projections of Thailand's population which range from 62.9 to 68.3 million by the end of this century, and from 77.3 to 95.9 million by 2025 (Table 11.3). The elderly, represented by the population aged over 65 years, increase in all three variant models from 1.65 million in 1980 (3.5 per cent of the population) to 3.11 million in 2000 and 7.80 million in 2025. The elderly proportion of the total population diverges according to the fertility assumptions of the three projections. By 2000 the divergence is between 4.5 per cent in the high-growth projection and 4.9 per cent in the low-variant projection, and by 2025 the divergence is between 8.1 and 10.1 per cent.

To examine the prospective ageing of Bangkok's population, a further series of population projections have been prepared for the entire kingdom and for two regions: the BMA and the remainder of Thailand (Warnes and Horsey, 1988). The projections employ 1980 census population totals (lower than the UN figures) and 1980 actual age and sex-specific fertility, mortality, and migration schedules, i.e. migration between the BMA and the rest of the nation. Variant assumptions concerning fertility do not affect the absolute size of the elderly population for the next 6 decades, although they do control the proportion of elderly people. The critical assumptions are therefore those relating to trends in mortality and migration between Bangkok and the rest of the kingdom. The figures presented here assume either constant mortality or declines at 1 per cent per annum and, for migration, either age and sex-specific rates which decrease at 1.5 per cent per annum, or stay constant, or increase at 1.5 per cent per annum.

Table 11.3   United Nations' 1984 population projections for Thailand.

	1980–85	1990–95	2000–05	2010–15	2020–25	1980–2025 % change
Crude birth rate						
High	29.2	26.2		19.9	18.2	−37.7
Medium	28.0	23.7	21.2	17.3	15.5	−44.6
Low	26.7	21.4		14.9	13.5	−49.4
Crude death rate						
High	8.0	7.2		6.5	6.8	−15.0
Medium	8.0	7.2	6.9	6.8	7.4	−7.5
Low	7.9	7.2		7.2	8.0	+1.3

	1980	1990	2000	2010	2025	1980–2025 % change
Population (millions)						
High	46.5	56.8	68.3	79.6	95.9	106.2
Medium	46.5	55.7	65.5	74.8	85.9	84.7
Low	46.5	54.8	62.9	70.2	77.3	66.2
Population 65+ years (millions)						
All variants	1.65	2.17	3.11	4.26	7.80	372.7
Population 65+ years (% of total)						
High	3.5	3.8	4.5	5.3	8.1	131.4
Medium	3.5	3.9	4.7	5.7	9.1	160.0
Low	3.5	4.0	4.9	6.1	10.1	188.6

Source: UNO (1986).

A summary and selected results from the projections are given in Table 11.4. The model which assumes constant fertility, mortality and migration schedules projects a BMA population in 2020 of 11.8 million. The model which assumes that fertility is declining at 1.5 per cent annum projects a population of 10.5 million, or, if mortality rates fall, 10.9 million. The influence of internal migration transfers on the growth of Bangkok's elderly population is intricate. Within the range of the present migration-trend assumptions, until the year 2000, population mobility has little influence on the size of the elderly population. Somewhat surprisingly, migration transfers reduce the population of elderly males in the year 2000, because of the net losses among those aged 45–59 years and the lower net gains of elderly men compared to elderly women (4.13 per 1 000 over 5 years compared to 13.56). Rising migration rates would increase this effect.

After the year 2000, however, migration transfers produce different effects. A substantial net gain of people in their early forties, or younger after 1980 increases the population which, after the end of this century, ages *in situ* into the over-60-years age group. Migration transfers at the 1975–80 age-specific rates increase the elderly population of Bangkok by 10 per cent in 2020 over the projection which ignores migration. The supplementation is greater for females than males: it also becomes stronger as the migration rates increase or if mortality rates fall. Over the 40 year period of these projections, future changes in fertility have no effect on the absolute size of the elderly population. All those who will be over 60 years of age in 2020 were born before 1960. It is all the more remarkable that the migration transfers into Bangkok of young adults (under 45 years) are likely to produce a 11.3 per cent increase of the elderly population in 2020 to 1.52 million. If Thailand experiences further mortality improvements at 1 per cent each year, the elderly population of Bangkok could be increased by 13.6 per cent to 1.7 million by 2020.

Another clear demonstration from these projections is that the recent decline of fertility in Thailand and the present high rates of net inmigration to the BMA, as well as any future fluctuations in fertility, mortality and migrations, will have a much stronger effect on the relative presence than the absolute number of elderly people in the capital (Table 11.4). For example, constant age-specific fertility, mortality and net migration rates will result in the elderly forming 12.8 per cent of Bangkok's total by 2020. This compares with a proportion of 15.5 per cent if migration ceases, showing the rejuvenescent effect of migration into Bangkok. If migration slows down, the city's population growth will moderate but it will age more rapidly.

A similar effect occurs should fertility continue to fall. If fertility rates fall by 1 per cent a year, Bangkok's elderly population will form 14.4 per cent of the total by 2020: if they fall by 1.5 per cent each year, the elderly will become 15.2 per cent of the population. Ageing will also intensify with further improvements in mortality. The United Nations' medium-growth variant assumptions have been approximated by declines in the death rates of 1 per cent each year and in birth rates of 1.5 per cent per annum. These result in a projection for 2020 that the elderly will form 16.4 per cent of Bangkok's population. Of the city's female population, 18.3 per cent would be over 60 years. If migration rates also fell, 19 per cent would be elderly. The continuation or mild modification of the present vital and migration rates will therefore result in at least one in seven of Bangkok's population being aged over 60 years within 30 years. This is a direct result of the city's recent rapid growth and will produce situations comparable to those presently found not only in Hong Kong and Singapore but also in many European cities.

Table 11.4 Projections of Bangkok Metropolitan Area's elderly population incorporating net migration between the city and the rest of Thailand.

Model	1990 m	1990 f	2000 m	2000 f	2010 m	2010 f	2020 m	2020 f
• *Constant mortality*								
Total population								
decreasing	3.08	3.23	3.94	4.11	4.66	4.87	5.53	5.79
constant	3.08	3.23	3.97	4.15	4.75	5.00	5.75	6.06
increasing	3.09	3.24	4.01	4.20	4.87	5.15	6.06	6.42
Population aged 60+ years								
decreasing	1.56	2.04	2.40	3.20	3.50	4.86	6.27	8.80
constant	1.56	2.04	2.40	3.21	3.49	4.87	6.28	8.86
increasing	1.56	2.04	2.39	3.21	3.49	4.89	6.29	8.95
Population 60+ years as percentage of total								
decreasing	5.1	6.3	6.1	7.8	7.5	9.9	11.3	15.2
constant	5.1	6.3	6.0	7.7	7.4	9.7	10.9	14.6
increasing	5.0	6.3	6.0	7.7	7.2	9.5	10.4	13.9
• *Mortality decreasing 1% p.a.*								
Total population[1]								
decreasing	3.06	3.21	3.84	4.02	4.44	4.67	5.07	5.34
constant	3.06	3.22	3.87	4.06	4.53	4.79	5.27	5.58
increasing	3.07	3.22	3.91	4.10	4.64	4.92	5.53	5.90
Population aged 60+ years[2]								
decreasing	1.57	2.06	2.51	3.31	3.84	5.19	7.16	9.65
constant	1.57	2.06	2.51	3.31	3.84	5.21	7.17	9.73
increasing	1.57	2.06	2.51	3.32	3.84	5.22	7.18	9.81
Population 60+ years as percentage of total[3]								
decreasing	5.2	6.4	6.6	8.4	8.9	11.4	14.9	19.0
constant	5.1	6.4	6.6	8.3	8.7	11.2	14.4	18.3
increasing	5.1	6.4	6.5	8.2	8.5	10.9	13.7	17.5

Source: Warnes and Horsey (1988).
Notes: 1 Millions. 2 Hundred thousands. 3 Also assumes that fertility rates fall by 1.5 per cent per annum. The variant projections assume that age/sex specific migraton rates either decrease at 1.5% p.a., remain constant, or increase at 1.5% p.a.

THE CIRCUMSTANCES OF ELDERLY PEOPLE IN THAILAND

Despite the rapid rate of urbanization in Thailand, most people live in rural areas and depend on agriculture for their living. Throughout the kingdom, elderly people receive little or no pension income, have little wealth, live in large households, and either continue to work or are supported by the members of their household and by other children. Only 1.7 per cent of the population aged over 60 years live in 'collective households', of whom the vast majority are male, 99.7 per cent of whom are monks. For all practical purposes, the collective household is synonymous with temples and is the only significant alternative to private households (Chayovan *et al.*, 1990). Very few elderly people receive formal social services. Access to medical services has improved vastly in recent decades but remains limited, particularly in rural areas. The prospective welfare of elderly people will depend upon the interaction between societal ageing and the spread of family-planning programmes, primary education, urbanization, modern-sector occupations and Western material values. Thai government officials have already questioned whether multi-generational living arrangements will survive the reduction of family size and the increase of childlessness that accompanies family planning. Will traditional support arrangements be difficult to sustain in modern urban housing and among families dependent upon waged employment? Will improving late-age survival increase the prevalence of chronic physical and mental disorders among the elderly population? Will this, in turn, generate demands for support and care beyond the capacity of the informal caring system that is so effective and valued in the country at the present time, even if it is bolstered by peripatetic formal support? These are difficult questions to evaluate. This appraisal begins with the present living conditions of elderly people in the nation.

Household and living arrangements
In Thailand's towns and cities, people live in large households. In 1980 only 2.9 per cent of all households consisted of one person while 27.7 per cent had at least seven persons. Household size increases with the age of the head of the household in all areas, most strongly in Bangkok (Table 11.5). It is rare in Thailand for other than the most affluent of old people to maintain separate households. Chiswick (1982) has described the characteristic evolution of the large household and, in particular, the transition from the two to the three-generation household as the senior members reach old age. After the children of a marriage reach adulthood and leave a nuclear family household, often one daughter and her husband will remain. As time passes, grandchildren are born, three generations become co-resident, and the recognized head may change from the grandparent to a parent. This change can be influenced by the health, the personality and the comparative earnings of the older and younger household members. Where the younger generation supports the older, the former is most likely to be the head, and *vice versa*. One result is that in households with older heads, both generations are likely to be contributing to the household income producing a relatively high per capita income (Chiswick, 1982).

Comparative data from the early 1970s and the 1980 census suggest a marked decline in household size, little of which is attributable to the reduction in the presence of children. While care is necessary in the interpretation of data from different kinds of enquiry, including sample surveys, it does appear that the urbanization of the nation, the increasing contribution to the housing stock of Western-type dwellings, and the rising standard of living of the country, are encouraging a reduction in household size. This must raise questions about the durability and cultural roots of Thailand's large, multigenerational household structures. As has been the experience in many other parts of the world, a rise in disposable income has enabled the population to reduce the sharing of dwellings, for instance by newly married couples. Sharing arrangements are in many situations forced upon people by economic necessity and are not always an expression of preference. The dynamics of household formation and change are intricate in any country: they are an expression of both cultural and social norms and the microeconomics of housing demand. On the one hand, individuals desire privacy, personal space and control of their own homes; on the other hand, preferences are moderated by effective purchasing power and the local cost of housing space.

Table 11.5 Household size in Thailand: 1971/73 and 1980.

	1971/73	1980	1971/3–80 % decrease	1980 Extended family
Rural areas	5.86	5.18	−11.6	0.68
Provincial towns	5.51	4.87	−11.6	0.78
Bangkok MA	6.15	5.01	−18.5	0.96

Source: NSO (1980); Chiswick (1982).
Notes: Adults are persons aged over 16 years. Extended family members include spouse of child, grandchildren, parents and other relatives.

Elderly people's sources of income

State old-age income support is less developed in Thailand than in any other ASEAN nation. The few people receiving state pensions are mainly retired government employees, although the number increased by 50 per cent between 1980 and 1985 to 123 000 and entailed expenditure of 3 036 million baht (NSO, 1987). For high-ranking public servants, university professors, medical specialists, and key personnel in large businesses a retirement age of 60 years applies, but many work beyond this age (UNO, 1985). The number of retirees from such positions is not known. For most people in Thailand, retirement and pensions do not exist. A Social Insurance Bill was announced in 1982 but is not enacted: more recent revisions of the proposals have included an old-age pension. Elderly people continue to earn, or to work in unpaid family enterprises, notably rice farming in rural areas, or they are supported by their families and household. In 1980 it was estimated that 60 per cent of men and 33 per cent of women aged over 60 years were economically active (UNO, 1985). A 1986 ASEAN Ageing Survey found that for almost all elderly people in Thailand, the principal sources of financial support were either their own earnings or businesses, or their children or grandchildren (Table 11.6) (Hugo, 1988, citing Jones, 1988).

Chiswick (1982) describes an equilibrating mechanism whereby low earners are incorporated into households with economically stronger individuals, and relatively high earners are dispersed as the supporters of separate households. The well known Thai flexibility and pragmatism as to household membership has an equalizing tendency, the extended family household being an important internal mechanism for raising the consumption opportunities of low earning individuals. It is difficult to disentangle individual from household income: some of the best evidence compares the sources of income in households headed by young and old heads. In the early 1970s incomes were at least 2.5 times higher in provincial urban areas, and over 4 times higher in Bangkok, than in rural areas (Table 11.7). Per capita incomes rise moderately with the age of the household head. In all regions of the country, wages and other earnings accounted for at least 88 per cent of the income in households headed by persons aged over 50 years (Table 11.8). This is a few percentage points lower than in households headed by younger persons, the difference being partly accounted for by the greater contributions first from interest, dividends and rent, which is expected towards the end of the earnings cycle (for most wealth is accumulated during a family's life time rather than inherited); secondly from pensions, annuities and assistance (direct income and in-kind transfers from other households), which accounted for 8 per cent of BMA household income.

In traditional agricultural households and in urban households having their own business, able-bodied elderly people are often productive members. In the towns, 'approximately two-thirds of wage earners live in households with no other type of earnings, whereas in rural areas at least half of wage earners live in households reporting self-employment income' (Chiswick, 1982). More than half of the rural labour force was unpaid in the early 1970s and 78 per cent worked in enterprises using unpaid family labour, while fewer than 20 per cent of the urban labour force was unpaid and only 31 per cent worked in household enterprises using unpaid family labour. These contracts highlight the implications of the spread of modern, corporate wage labour. At some point the availability in Bangkok and other towns of paid work or self-employment (and their earning capacity in relation to urban living costs) will place considerable strains on the traditional pooling of household resources and the exchange reciprocity arrangements whereby elderly people are supported.

Health and nutrition

Reliable information on the health of the elderly people of Thailand is relatively scarce but special tabulations from the 1986 Survey of Health, Welfare and Traditional Medicine provide valuable self-reported indicators (Chayovan et al., 1990). Although death rates have been falling, the substantial falls in infant, child and young adult mortality have not been matched by the rates for those aged over 55 years (Fig. 11.3). Cause-of-death data help little in understanding this rigidity, partly because 'old age and other ill-defined conditions constitute most of the "others" category' which accounts for two-thirds of all deaths (Krongkaew, 1982). Through the early 1970s, heart and cancer conditions were diagnosed for less than 6 per cent of all deaths. Even allowing for undiagnosed cases, the degenerative disorders, which predominate among the causes of death among elderly people in Western countries, are probably rare. On the other hand, there is still much avoidable ill health and mortality from infectious diseases, with leading causes being respiratory and digestive tract conditions. These could be controlled by changing habits, immunization and improved sanitation (Krongkaew, 1982).

Avitaminosis and malnutrition are significant causes of ill health and mortality producing a 91 per 1 000 rate of outpatient visits throughout Thailand in 1972, but they are mainly identified with infants and pregnant and nursing women. The average calorie deficiency has been estimated at about 9 per cent, but there are more substantial deficiencies for vitamins B_1 and B_2. Actual food expenditure in 1975 was 31 per cent lower than the level required for a well-balanced diet. Regional differentials were pronounced, with a shortfall of 42 per cent in the North-east region but only a 10 per cent deficiency in

Table 11.6 Main and subsidiary sources of support of elderly people (65+ years) in Thailand, Malaysia, Singapore and Indonesia: 1985.

	Their own earnings or businesses (%)				Children or grandchildren (%)				Pensions (%)			
	Main		Some		Main		Some		Main		Some	
Country	m	f	m	f	m	f	m	f	m	f	m	f
Indonesia	56	30	61	34	22	47	56	70	13	4	16	5
Malaysia	36	12	49	21	38	67	76	90	16	6	21	8
Singapore	25	7	30	9	53	80	80	91	9	1	29	7
Thailand	40	21	n.a.	n.a.	38	54	n.a.	n.a.	5	1	n.a.	n.a.

Source: Hugo (1988); Jones (1988).

Table 11.7 Average income for households of different ages: 1971/73.

	Age of h'hold head	Household size			Mean household income			Index numbers		
		Total	Adults	Labour force members	Per h'hold	Per capita	Per adult	Per h'hold	Per capita	Per adult
Rural areas	All	5.86	4.81	3.07	9 138	1 560	1 901	98	107	103
	50+	5.55	4.88	3.54	9 715	1 751	1 992	105	121	108
Provincial towns	All	5.51	4.63	2.18	24 366	4 422	5 257	262	304	256
	50+	5.74	5.11	2.72	26 726	4 656	5 224	288	320	284
Bangkok MA	All	6.15	5.25	2.38	40 933	6 656	7 812	441	458	425
	50+	6.61	6.00	2.99	47 721	7 220	7 969	514	497	433

Source: Chiswick (1982); based on NSO (1974).
Notes: Total income (baht) adjusted for regional and urban-rural differences in the cost of living and expressed in Bangkok prices. The index numbers are expressed relative to the income of rural middle-aged households (100).

Table 11.8 Sources of household income by age of head: 1971/73.

Area	Age of h'hold head	Money income as % of all income	Sources of money income (%)			
			Wages, salaries, earnings	Pensions, annuities, assistance	Interest, dividends, and rent	Other
Rural areas	All	82	94	4	2	1
	50+	82	91	5	3	1
Towns	All	98	93	4	3	1
	50+	98	90	6	4	0
Bangkok MA	All	99	92	5	2	2
	50+	99	88	8	4	1

Source: Selected details from Chiswick (1982).

Bangkok (Krongkaew, 1982; citing NESDB, 1979). The significance of malnutrition among elderly people is that it debilitates the immune system, which increases the lethality of infectious disorders. A universal syndrome among elderly people is the presence of multiple disorders. Even if malnutrition is not unusually prevalent among elderly people, its combination with unhygienic food preparation and eating practices produces high late-age mortality. Recognition of this causal sequence underlies the importance attached by the Ministry of Public Health to preventive health-education programmes, especially in the fields of nutrition, hygiene and environmental sanitation. These are particularly important in rural areas. As late as 1976 fewer than 3 per cent of rural dwellings had piped water supplies (compared to 80 per cent in urban areas), and 87 per cent had 'improvised or unknown' types of toilet facility (compared to 27 per cent in urban areas) (Tanphiphat and Singhasakeres, 1982).

Access to health facilities and medical services
Since 1961 public health policies have been developed within the framework of Thailand's 5-year national socioeconomic-development plans. The first two (1961–66 and 1967–71) placed emphasis on the expansion of health facilities, while the following (1972–76 and 1977–81) stressed the importance of more effective birth-control programmes (Bowornwathana, 1984). The fifth plan for 1982–86, however, is principally aimed at strengthening primary health care through the expansion of health facilities at the district, sub-district and village levels. This includes (as the fifth objective), the provision of free medical-care services to low-income groups and old persons. After a lengthy period of gestation, and a pilot USAID-supported programme in the Lampang district, 'the Ministry of Public Health decided that the best strategy for providing rural health care is ... to elicit community participation by mobilizing local resources in the categories of village health communicators, village health volunteers, sub-district doctors and traditional birth attendants' (Bowornwathana, 1984). A National Health Care Plan for the Aging 1982–86 has also been developed: it places great emphasis on both in-service training programmes for professional and paraprofessional health workers and the development of primary health care, including mobile health units, to enable the majority of elderly people to have access to preventive and curative services in their communities.

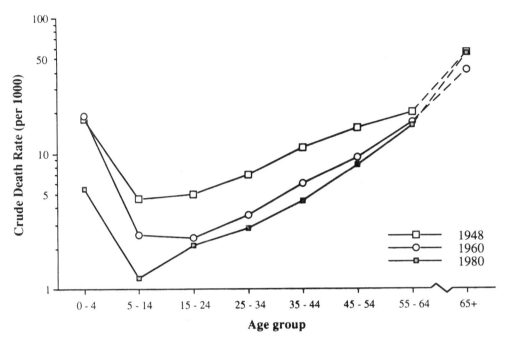

Fig. 11.3   Thailand: age specific death rates.

Thailand's rapidly developing medical services, facilities and personnel are diverse and include Western and traditional practices. Several government departments and enterprises, local government bodies from the provincial (regional) to the village level, private hospitals, clinics, pharmacies, and traditional doctors and midwives all provide services. A strong effort is being made to spread medical facilities to rural areas and to reduce the regional differentials. From 1977 to 1984, physicians increased from 5 846 to 8 058, nurses from 15 208 to 31 827, and pharmacists from 2 235 to 3 312. The number of beds in all types of facility increased from 39 729 to 79 000 in the same period (Krongkaew, 1982; NSO, 1987). By 1987 98 per cent of all local districts were equipped with a health centre, and primary health-care services had been extended to nine out of ten villages (NESDB, 1987). A Geriatric Health Service was established in Bangkok in 1980 to provide specialized training to health personnel in the care of older patients. By 1985, 12 general hospitals had established geriatric units and they are planned for all such hospitals (UNO, 1985).

A 1981 National Health and Welfare Survey collected data on the age, sex and duration of hospital admissions (NSO, 1983b). Tabulations are provided for public and private-sector facilities, for hospitals in municipal and non-municipal areas and for each region. Of 2,408 million patient admissions in 1981, 85 per cent were in government facilities, 10.6 per cent in Bangkok and 7.2 per cent in other urban areas. Of these admissions 55.7 per cent were female, one-fifth were children aged less than 7 years, and a high proportion (36.8 per cent) of the female patients were in the peak child-bearing ages (20–34 years). An interesting feature is the over-representation of old people: 8 per cent of all patients were aged over 60 years, and 16.2 per cent were aged over 50 years.

Further information concerning the high demand for medical services from elderly people is gained from an analysis of the utilization of bed-nights. These have been calculated by assuming mean durations for the published periods of admission. Missing information means that the following estimates are approximations. In 1981 there were 182.9 million patient bed-nights in Thailand's hospitals (Table 11.9). Of these, 88.6 per cent were in the public sector and 19.4 per cent in urban hospitals. Young children stayed briefly, accounting for only 12.9 per cent of the bed-nights, and women aged 20–34 years claimed 33.6 per cent of the female total, indicating that child bearing generated admissions of average duration. Elderly people made high demands: they represented 5.5 per cent of the population in 1980 but accounted for 13.8 per cent of the bed-nights. As many as 31.6 per cent of the adult (16+ years) bed-nights were occupied by people aged over 50 years.

A multiplicative relationship exists between urban/non-urban and public/private-sector facilities and the length of admission. Whereas 72 per cent of patients in public-sector urban hospitals remained less than a week, in non-municipal private hospitals the comparable figure was 87.6 per cent. Rural private-sector hospitals were least engaged with the relatively long-stay care of elderly people, whereas in urban areas the average duration of admission of an old person was 17 days, more than double the national average. Generally, elderly men were admitted for longer periods than women (Table 11.9).

Social services
The UN World Assembly on Ageing in 1982 caused the government of Thailand to review the situation of elderly people in the nation and its relevant policies. One priority which emerged from the resulting documents was to promote the development of family and community-based welfare services. It was emphasized that the care of elderly people must be primarily in their own homes. 'The strategy . . . was to use traditional gathering places as focal points for organizing social services' (UNO, 1985). Mobile units are being used to provide care for frail elderly people in their own homes. Some social welfare centres offering more comprehensive facilities, such as treatment, rehabilitation, day care, family assistance, counselling services, and the organization of social events, were first developed in the 1970s in conjunction with homes for the elderly. But the plan in the early 1980s was to establish these in future as free-standing units in both urban and rural areas (UNO, 1985). Another aspect of the government's approach is to provide financial and technical assistance to voluntary agencies which care for elderly people.

Residential care is limited, targeted towards poor, neglected and socially isolated old people, and considered a last resort when needs are unmet by other means. At the 1982 World Assembly, Thai officials argued that institutional care was an option only for old people without family or requiring constant nursing care. They did recognize, however, that to meet increasing demand nursing-home beds would have to be substantially increased (UNO, 1985).

The Sixth National Plan 1987–1991
The preamble to the 1987–91 plan makes it clear that economic difficulties and reduced enthusiasm for a welfare-state approach are likely to slow the development of public-sector social facilities (NESDB, 1987). Emphasis is to be shifted from the expansion of basic social services, principally primary education and primary health care services, to 'increasing the development of the basic components of society: individuals, families and communities'. Specific aims are to reduce the annual population growth rate to 1.3 per cent by

Table 11.9 Hospital patients and bed-nights in Thailand: 1981.

Sector of provision	Patients thousands	%	female	aged 0–6	aged 50+	aged 60+	days of stay <8	>8
● Municipal hospitals and facilities								
Public	311.2	72.8	59.6	18.5	15.5	8.3	72.0	8.2
Private	116.1	27.2	61.6	19.6	16.9	9.6	78.7	3.8
Total	427.3	100.0	60.1	18.8	16.0	8.8	73.8	7.0
● Non-municipal hospitals and facilities								
Public	1 736.0	87.6	54.7	20.1	15.6	7.8	75.8	5.5
Private	245.1	12.4	54.5	17.1	20.9	8.2	87.6	2.3
Total	1 981.1	100.0	54.7	19.7	16.3	7.9	77.3	5.1
● All facilities								
Total	2 408.4		55.7	19.5	16.2	8.0	76.7	5.5

Source: NSO (1983b).
Notes. The published data uses the following categories of admission duration. Figures in parenthesis are the assumed category means: 1–7 days (3 days); 8–14 (11); 15–28 (21); 29–42 (35); and 43+ (60).

1991, to improve education, preserve peace and security, and alleviate unemployment and labour problems, e.g. with child labour. The plan makes frequent reference to the encouragement that will be given to private organizations, communities and families to take a greater role in preventing and solving social problems. References are made to the duties and roles of families, the government's willingness to provide support to community organizations, and a policy of raising fees for public-sector services.

One of the Plan's shortest and least prescriptive chapters concerns 'improving social development mechanisms'. Its analytical core is that the government has had the prime responsibility for providing social services and solving social problems, and the role of the private sector and the general public has been limited. 'During the sixth plan period, it is expected that the national monetary and fiscal condition will prevent the government from . . . increasing the budget allocation for expanding social services and solving social problems. At the same time, growth in private-sector income and population size will give rise to increased demand for social services. . . . Rather than taking sole responsibility for providing and administering social services, the government should take a supporting role'. The principal concrete proposals are to establish national agencies and budgets to promote widespread information and educational campaigns for these ends. The government will 'encourage social institutions, especially families, to recognize their role and responsibility in preventing and solving social problems by teaching children morality and discipline, providing health care for the elderly and other family members (and) promote the participating role of women in decision making at the family, community and national levels.

DISCUSSION AND CONCLUSIONS

Thailand's recent demographic history means that its elderly population will increase rapidly in forthcoming decades. Recent declines in the birth rate, and the spreading effectiveness of the nation's family planning programme, mean additionally that elderly people will increase as a share of the total population.

d-nights ·usands	%	Percentage share: female	aged 0–6	aged 50+	aged 60+	Mean length of stay (days) all	male	female	male 60+	female 60+
2 771	78.1	49.0	10.9	28.0	15.7	8.9	11.2	7.3	17.5	14.9
776	21.9	52.9	15.3	26.6	16.7	6.7	8.2	5.7	16.2	9.2
3 547	100.0	49.8	11.8	27.7	15.9	8.3	10.4	6.9	17.2	12.7
3 429	91.1	50.9	13.2	24.3	13.6	7.7	8.4	7.2	13.8	13.0
1 318	8.9	60.5	11.8	21.0	10.6	5.4	4.7	6.0	4.0	9.5
4 747	100.0	51.8	13.1	24.0	13.3	7.4	7.9	7.0	12.7	12.5
8 294		51.4	12.9	24.7	13.8	7.6	8.3	7.0	13.6	12.6

The ageing process will be particularly rapid in Bangkok, because of its over-representation of young and middle-aged adults and its relatively low fertility. If there is success in reducing the economic differentials between Bangkok and the nation's provinces, and if this slows net migration into the capital, a faster rate of change of the capital's age structure will occur.

To go beyond the demographic prospects and to consider the social geronto-logical implications, the salient influences are associated with the rapid modernization of the country. In the fields of employment, income, housing, education, health care and family life, a host of changes will manifest the rising standard of living of the country, new ambitions, life opportunities and expressions of familial affection, loyalty and support. The likely changes may follow those of neighbouring and culturally similar countries. Traditional households and support arrangements have altered to a greater extent in Malaysia, and signs of adaptation to modernization and ageing are evident in many parts of Asia (Andrews *et al.*, 1986; Cain, 1990). The immediate prospects for Thailand are indicated elsewhere in Asia, and the questions which are being raised throughout the continent are relevant. What should the roles of the family and the government be in caring for elderly people who cannot care for themselves? Should eligibility for public support be based on age or need? (Martin, 1988).

It does seem unlikely that as high a proportion of elderly people as hitherto will be supported by their families. The factors that will place increasing strain on traditional forms of accommodation and income support include: increasing childlessness, increasing geographical separation, and progressively improving survival into and through old age. Over time this greater longevity may well be associated with a greater ability, and indeed determination, to live indepen-dently and be self-reliant, but the prevalence of frailty will also increase, at least for a short period towards the end of many people's lives. Chronic physical and mental disorders, widowhood, the absence of close relatives, and the erosion through a long old age of savings and assets, must all be likely to increase. Looking several decades ahead, there may be particular difficulties for those born in the 1960s and early 1970s – the cohort which preceded the downturn in fertility – when they reach old age. 'This cohort will produce relatively few children itself (and) as it enters old age it will cause a rapid jump in the proportion of the elderly in the total population, which will put a strain on the capacity (and even willingness) of society as a whole to finance (their) needs' (Jones, 1988).

It is hardly ever suggested that the parents or family should take all the responsibility for 'social reproduction' or for preparing a nation's children for the new patterns of work and life opportunity brought about by the transformations associated with modernization. It is surely no more appropriate in transformed societies to place all responsibility for the care of dependent and frail elderly people on their relatives. As Thailand's economy modernizes, its people will become better educated and they will work increasingly in modern sector waged occupations. Simultaneously, their health status will improve and life expectancy will increase. Smaller families and smaller dwellings will become more common. Almost inevitably, more and more people will experience 'retirement' in the sense of exclusion from their accustomed paid employment. Some retired elderly people will then be supported within traditional family enterprises or in the households of their children, and others will earn some income from secondary and informal occupations. But the process of modernization will create a substantial number of old people who have no income and no family framework of support. Humanitarian concerns and political pressures will demand attention to old-age destitution and distress. Each modernizing country articulates a system of welfare protection and support appropriate to its own cultural, economic and political realities. This is a task that the far-sighted leaders of Thailand will address.

Acknowledgements

The research for this paper was undertaken with a grant from the Simon Population Trust. Their encouragement and support is greatly appreciated. I also wish to thank Ashley Horsey who was particularly responsible for producing the population projections.

REFERENCES

Andrews, G.R., Esterman, A.J., Braunack-Mayer, A.J. and Rungie, C.M. (1986). *Aging in the Western Pacific*. World Health Organisation, Manila.

Arnold, F. and Piampiti, S. (1984). Female migration in Thailand. In *Women in the Cities of Asia*, J.T. Fawcett, S.-E. Khoo and P.C. Smith (Eds), pp. 143–64. Westview, Boulder, Colorado.

Bowornwathana, B. (1984). *Public Health Bureaucrats in Rural Thailand*, pp. 177–82. Faculty of Political Science, Chulalongkorn University, Bangkok.

Cain, M.T. (1990). The activities of the elderly in rural Bangladesh. *Population Studies*, **45**, 189–202.

Chayovan, N., Knodel, J. and Siriboon, S. (1990). *Thailand's Elderly Population: A Demographic and Social Profile Based on Official Sources*, pp. 10–24. Research Report 90–2, Population Studies Center, University of Michigan, Ann Arbor.

Chiswick, C.U. (1982). The distribution of income in Thailand. In *Basic Needs and Government Policies in Thailand*, P. Richards (Ed.), pp. 19–66. Singapore, Maruzen Asia.

Goldstein, S. (1978). Thailand's urban population reconsidered. *Demography*, **13**, 238–58.

Goldstein, S. and Goldstein, A. (1986). Migration in Thailand: a 25 year review. *Papers East-West Population Institute*, **100**, 54.

Goldstein, S., Goldstein, A. and Limanonda, B. (1981). *Migration and Fertility Related Attitudes and Behavior in Urban Thailand*. Research Paper 38, Institute of Population Studies, Chulalongkorn University, Bangkok.

Hobcraft, J., MacDonald, J. and Rutstein, S. (1984). Socioeconomic factors in infant and child mortality: a cross-national comparison. *Population Studies*, **39**, 363–85.

Hugo, G. (1988). *The changing urban situation in south east Asia and Australia: some implications for the elderly*. UN Conference on Aging Populations in the Context of Urbanisation, Sendai, Japan.

Jones, G.W. (1988). *Consequences of rapid fertility decline for old age security*. Fertility transition in Asia: diversity and change. Seminar, Institute of Population Studies, Chulalongkorn University, Bangkok.

Kinsella, K.G. (1988). *Aging in the Third World*. Staff Paper 35, Center for International Research, US Bureau of the Census, Washington DC.

Knodel, J., Debavalya, N. and Kamnuansilpa, P. (1985). *Thailand's Continuing Fertility Decline*. Paper 40, Institute of Population Studies, Chulalongkorn University, Bangkok.

Krongkaew, M. (1982). The distribution of and access to basic health services in Thailand. In *Basic Needs and Government Policies in Thailand*, P. Richards (Ed.), pp. 67–104. Maruzen Asia, Singapore.

Martin, L.G. (1988). The aging of Asia. *Journal of Gerontology*, **43**, S99–113.

NESDB (National Economic and Social Development Board) (1987). *The Sixth National Economic and Social Development Plan, 1987–91*. Office of the Prime Minister, Bangkok.

NSO (National Statistical Office) (1978). *1970 Population and Housing Census*, Migration Subject Report 2, Office of the Prime Minister, Bangkok.

NSO (1983a). *1980 Population and Housing Census: Whole Kingdom*. Office of the Prime Minister, Bangkok.

NSO (1983b). *Health and Welfare Survey 1981*. Office of the Prime Minister, Bangkok.

NSO (1985). *1980 Population Census. Household Structure and Factors Affecting the Size of Households*, C. Pejaranonda and S. Santipaporn (Eds). Office of the Prime Minister, Bangkok.

NSO (1987). *Statistical Yearbook 34, 1985–86*. Office of the Prime Minister, Bangkok.

NSO (1989). *The Survey of Population Change 1985–86*. Office of the Prime Minister, Bangkok.

Pardthaisong, T. (1978). The recent fertility decline in the Chiang Mai area of Thailand. *Papers of the East-West Population Institute*, **47**, Honolulu, Hawaii.

Piampiti, S. (1984). Female migrants in Bangkok metropolis. In *Women in the Cities of Asia*, J.T. Fawcett, S.-E. Khoo and P.C. Smith (Eds), pp. 143–64. Westview, Boulder, Colorado.

Royal Thai Embassy, London (1987). Thailand's Population as of 30 June 1986, personal communication.

Ruzicka, L.T. (1984). Mortality transition in Asia: technology confronts poverty. In *Demographic Transition in Asia*, G.W. Jones (Ed.), pp. 31–56. Maruzen Asia, Singapore.

Shevasunt, S. and Hogan, D.P. (1979). *Family and Family Planning in Rural Northern Thailand*. Community and Family Studies Center, University of Chicago, Chicago.

Sternstein, L. (1976). Migration and development in Thailand. *Geographical Review*, **66**, 401–19.

Tanphiphat, S. and Singhasakeres, S. (1982). Housing in Thailand. In *Basic Needs and Government Policies in Thailand*, P. Richards (Ed.), pp. 127–60. Maruzen Asia, Singapore.

United Nations Organisation (UNO) Department of International Economic and Social Affairs (1985). *The World Ageing Situation*, pp. 158–72. UNO, Vienna.

UNO (1986). *World Population Prospects: Estimates and Projections as Estimated in 1984*. UNO, New York.

UNO (1989). *World Population Prospects: Estimates and Projections as Estimated in 1988*. UNO, New York.

USA Bureau of the Census (1988). *Aging in the Third World*. International Population reports P-95, No. 79, Bureau of the Census, US Government Printing Office, Washington DC.

USA National Research Council, Committee on Population and Demography (1980). *Fertility and Mortality Changes in Thailand, 1950–75*. National Academy of Sciences, Washington DC.

Warnes, A.M. (1986). The elderly in less developed countries. *Ageing and Society*, **7**, 373–80.

Warnes, A.M. (1987) Geographical locations and social relationships among the elderly in developing and developed countries. In *Progress in Social Geography*, M. Pacione (Ed.), pp. 252–93. Croom Helm, Beckenham, Kent.

Warnes, A.M. (1989). The ageing of populations. In *Human Ageing and Later Life*, A.M. Warnes (Ed.), pp. 47–66. Edward Arnold, London.

Warnes, A.M. and Horsey, A. (1988). *The Elderly Population of Third World Cities: Projections for Selected Metropolitan Areas*. Department of Geography, King's College, London.

Graeme Hugo
Department of Geography
University of Adelaide

12 AGEING IN INDONESIA: A NEGLECTED AREA OF POLICY CONCERN

INTRODUCTION

In 1985, 5.57 million Indonesians were aged 65 years or more giving it the tenth largest elderly population among the world's nations (Torrey *et al.*, 1987). Yet, although Indonesia is one of the few countries to have a Ministry focusing specifically upon population (and environmental) issues, ageing is not high on the national agenda of population concerns. This partly derives from a preoccupation with other issues, especially the following:

- Overall annual population growth rates – these remain high (2.1 per cent in the mid-1980s) despite substantial fertility decline (Hugo *et al.*, 1987).
- Population distribution – Java-Bali has 62.5 per cent of the national population compared to 6.9 per cent of the land area. There is also increasing concern about the burgeoning growth of Jakarta which may have a population of 30 million by the end of the century (Douglass, 1988).
- Underemployment and unemployment – while the problem here is usually considered to be one of underemployment (which is estimated to affect between 20 and 40 per cent of the workforce) the incidence of open unemployment is increasing so that some 62 per cent of high school graduates aged 15–19 are unemployed (Vatikiotis, 1988). Moreover, the workforce is increasing at 3 per cent per annum, nearly half as fast again as the total population.

It also has its origin partly in the fact that aged people, despite their substantial numbers, comprised only 3.4 per cent of the total population in 1985. However, as I have argued elsewhere (Hugo, 1985), social planning is for people not percentages and the burgeoning numbers of aged Indonesians is a matter for policy concern. The other issue which has militated against ageing being considered a significant population policy issue is the belief, which takes on the aura of conventional wisdom among policy makers, that the Indonesian traditional extended family will take care of the elderly population as it has in the past.

Hence, in the GBHN (the broad outline of state policy), which serves as the basis for national development planning, scant mention is made of ageing except to reinforce the traditional stereotype:

> 'The Indonesian culture and the existing value systems regarding the aged for their protection against the hazards of old age, socially, economically, etc., is inherently based on the extended family system and the community. Therefore, the policy and the approaches of the Indonesian government for the protection and making the aged more responsive to their needs and requirements, i.e., to obtain a fair and

equitable share in the national development, is to strengthen the existing value systems. Through those systems are the aged integrated into the community, in which they belong, rather than being segregated to an alien setting in which they will only feel a sense of isolation and lack of belongingness.' (quoted in Adi, 1982)

However, as will be shown later in this paper, the assumption that traditional family systems supporting the elderly are intact in Indonesia is, at the very best, an arguable one.

Partly reflecting the low priority given to ageing issues by the government, the literature on the aged in Indonesia is limited. The major sources employed here are the decennial national censuses and intercensal surveys, and a handful of specialized surveys and studies. The most important of these was a 1986 survey attached to the Intercensal Survey. It covered some 4 000 households with at least one person aged 60 years or over but was limited to only ten Kabupaten in Java (Fig. 12.1) of which two were urban (Chen and Jones, 1988). In addition, in 1982/83 special questions were asked of 37 346 older people in almost all provinces (Irian Jaya and East Timor were excluded) as part of the Indonesian Bureau of Statistics' ongoing SUSENAS (socio-economic) surveys (Biro Pusat Statistik, 1984). There are also a small number of case studies of Indonesia's elderly population available, such as one by Adi (1982) carried out in aged homes in Jakarta and another by Evans (1985) in the Solo area of Central Java.

The aims of this chapter are twofold. First, it summarizes the contemporary demography of the elderly in Indonesia and analyses impending changes in the older population. Secondly, it discusses some important issues relating to the present and likely future well-being of elderly people in Indonesia.

THE CONTEXT

Indonesia is the world's fifth most populous country, and its 164 million people (1985) make up more than half of the total population living in the South-east Asian region. It consists of an archipelago of more than 13 000 islands, although 62.5 per cent live on the three islands of Java, Bali and Madura (Fig. 12.1) which account for only 6.9 per cent for the national land area. This concentration is even more marked for the population aged 65 years with over 68 per cent of them living in 'inner Indonesia' in 1985 (Fig. 12.1). The enormous geographical diversity within and between the islands is more than matched by Indonesia's social, economic, religious and ethnic complexity, with more than 300 distinct ethnolinguistic groups being identified, all of the world's major religions being significantly represented and major regional variations in average levels of well-being in the population (Hugo et al., 1987).

During the 1970s and 1980s Indonesia has experienced rapid and sweeping social and economic change. For most of this period economic growth has exceeded 5 per cent per annum, self-sufficiency in the staple food, rice, has been achieved as has universal attendance at elementary school. Whereas fewer than 5 per cent of eligible women were practising modern contraceptive methods two decades ago in many parts of Indonesia, more than 50 per cent of such women are now doing so and the proliferation of transport and com-munication systems has greatly reduced the isolation of even the remotest villages (Hugo, 1988a). While Indonesia remains a predominantly rural nation with 74 per cent of the national population living in communities so desig-nated, urbanization is occurring at a very rapid pace with the growth of the

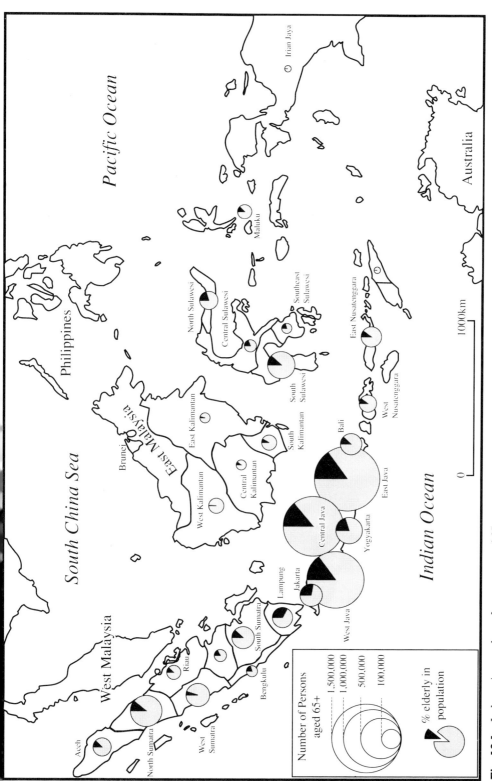

Fig. 12.1 Indonesia: number of persons aged 65 years or over.

Source: Indonesia: Biro Pusat Statistik, 1985 Intercensal Survey.

urban population being 5.5 per cent per annum over the 1980–85 period compared to 1.2 per cent for the rural population (Hugo, forthcoming).

In spite of the enormous changes of the last two decades, Indonesia remains squarely within the echelons of those countries designated as 'less developed'. Per capita GNP remains low at US$490 as does life expectancy at 57 years (World Bank, 1988). Among the ASEAN nations only the Philippines rivals Indonesia as the poorest country in the region. The implications of this poverty, and especially the major changes of recent years, for elderly Indonesians are not the subject of much concern in Indonesia. The other issues referred to earlier are viewed as overwhelmingly pressing by both policy makers and researchers in population, whereas ageing is not.

THE DEMOGRAPHY OF AGEING IN INDONESIA

Table 12.1 shows that even by regional standards the level of ageing in Indonesia is low. In 1985 only 3.4 per cent of the national population were aged 65 years and above. However, some qualifications have to be made to this observation. First, as pointed out earlier, while analyses of percentage age distributions have an important role, it should not be forgotten that social and economic planning is concerned with people, and change in the actual numbers of people in particular age groups should thus be a significant consideration in that planning (Hugo, 1985). Second, there is some evidence to suggest that 65 may not be too advanced an age to use as a cut-off point in defining the elderly in less-developed countries (LDCs) (Hugo, 1985), so that the data presented here may understate the two dimensions of ageing in the society.

The rapidity of recent growth of the elderly population in Indonesia, depicted in Table 12.2, must be stressed. The population aged over 65 has grown more than twice as fast over the 1971–85 period as the total population. However, even more rapid growth is in store for the next four decades. As Table 12.1 indicates, the aged population of Indonesia will almost treble in the last two decades of this century. Indeed, over this period Indonesia will have the fourth fastest growing aged population among the world's nations (Hugo, 1985). It should also be noted from Table 12.2 that the proportional representation of the aged has increased substantially in the last 15 years from 2.51 per cent aged 65 years and over, to 3.4 per cent in 1985. Moreover, Table 12.1 shows that this pattern of increase will continue such that by the end of the

Table 12.1 ASEAN countries: aged populations in 1980 and projection of percentage of population aged 65 and over.

| | Numbers aged 65 and over (thousands) | | Percentage aged 65 and over | | | | |
	1980	2000	1980	1990	2000	2010	2020
Indonesia	3 761	9 521	3.3	3.8	4.9	6.1	7.4
Malaysia	500	924	3.7	3.9	4.4	5.6	7.8
Philippines	1 400	3 000	3.4	3.5	3.8	4.7	6.3
Singapore	199	213	4.7	5.6	7.1	9.2	14.5
Thailand	1 432	2 991	3.5	3.9	4.7	5.7	7.5

Source: Jones (1988); Population Reference Bureau (1988).

Table 12.2   Indonesia: growth of the elderly population 1971–85.

	1971	1980	1985	% change 1971–85
Total population	118.4 m	146.8 m	164 m	38.5
Population aged 65+	2 968 377	4 769 916	5 572 948	87.7
Per cent aged 65+	2.5	3.25	3.40	35.4
Population aged 75+	786 858	1 525 373	1 645 818	109.2
Per cent aged 75+	0.67	1.31	1.00	49.2
Sex ratio 65+	94.2	84.8	88.7	−5.8
Sex ratio 75+	93.6	82.3	79.5	−15.1
Sex ratio total pop.	97.2	98.8	99.1	−2.0

Source: Biro Pusat Statistik, Indonesian Censuses of 1971 and 1980, Intercensal Survey of 1985.

century they will comprise nearly 5 per cent of the population and by 2020, 7.4 per cent.

The demographic explanation for the increased tempo of ageing and the growth of the aged population in Indonesia is fairly clear. Declining levels of mortality have been important in two respects:

• As in many LDCs a decline in infant and child mortality, together with continued high fertility in the 1950s and 1960s, created a 'bulge' in the Indonesian age structure (Fig. 12.2) similar to those characteristic of many more-developed countries (MDCs) which experienced a post-World War II 'baby boom'. This bulge will, of course, lead to a substantial increase in the number of elderly Indonesians in the early years of the next century.
• There has been an overall improvement in mortality in recent years which has seen life expectancy at birth increase from 37.5 in 1955–60 to 57 in the mid-1980s (Hugo *et al.*, 1987). This reflects an increase in the longevity of Indonesians which has contributed to the rapid growth in the number of elderly people.

The major factor influencing the ageing of the Indonesian population, however, is the unexpected and rapid decline in fertility which has seen the Total Fertility Rate decline from 5.61 in 1967–70 to 4.27 in 1980 and 3.26 in 1985 (Hull and Dasvarma, 1987). This unprecedentedly rapid fertility decline will inevitably produce an accelerated process of ageing of the population, especially beyond the year 2000 when the increase in the proportion of old people will increase much faster than was the case in Western countries in the post-World War II period. As Jones (1988), stresses in discussing ageing in all ASEAN countries, 'What is to come is crucial, not what has already happened'.

Turning to some aspects of the demographic structure of the elderly population of Indonesia, Table 12.3 indicates that the growth rate of the 'old-old' population over the last 15 years has been faster than that of the aged population overall. Moreover, Table 12.3 shows that the representation of those over 75 years among the total population aged 60 years and over, will increase over the next few decades such that more than one in five will be in the 'old-old' category by the year 2010. Hence, not only is there an overall ageing of population but there is an ageing within the aged population. Although this latter trend is not as marked as in contemporary MDCs, it does have important implications in terms of demand for health and specialized age-care services.

Table 12.4 shows the universally recognized pattern of sex ratios decreasing

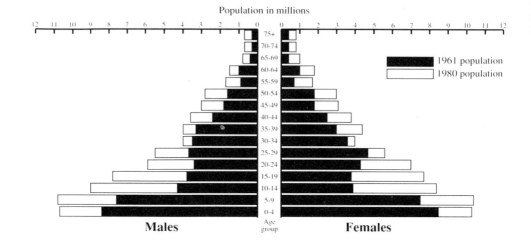

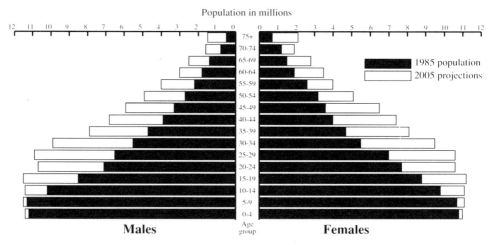

Fig. 12.2 Indonesia: Age/sex distribution 1961, 1980 and 1985 and projected distribution 2005.

Source: Biro Pusat Statistik, Indonesian Censuses of 1961 and 1980, Intercensal Survey of 1985.

Table 12.3 Indonesia: actual and projected ratios of the population aged 60+ 1980–2020.

Year	Ratio 75+ : 60+
1980	0.151
1990	0.166
2000	0.172
2010	0.214
2020	0.216

Source: Chen and Jones (1988).

Table 12.4 Indonesia: sex ratios among the elderly population 1980–2020.

Sex ratios in 1980		Projected sex ratios among 60+	
60–64	93	1990	88
65–69	90	2000	88
70–74	84	2010	85
75–79	77	2020	85
80+	72		

Source: Biro Pusat Statistik, Indonesian Census of 1980; Chen and Jones (1988).

Table 12.5 Indonesia: actual and projected dependency ratios 1971–85.

	Number of persons per 100 aged 15–64				
	1971	1980	1985	1995	2005
Total dependency ratio (less than 15 and more than 64 years)	86.82	79.07	74.68	61.33	52.57
Child dependency ratio (less than 15 years)	82.13	73.25	68.73	54.25	44.53
Aged dependency ratio (more than 64 years)	4.69	5.82	5.93	7.08	8.04

Source: Biro Pusat Statistik, Indonesian Censuses of 1971 and 1980, Intercensal Survey of 1985.

with age although this pattern is not as great as in most MDCs. However, it is interesting to note in Table 12.2 that the excess of females among the elderly has increased since 1971 and Table 12.4 shows that this trend is likely to continue in the latter part of this century.

In both MDCs and LDCs, one of the major issues or areas of concern as the population ages is the changing 'balance' between various age groups. Much attention has been focused upon the so-called 'dependency ratio' – defined as the ratio of the population under 15 and 65 years and older to those between the ages of 15 and 64. It has been feared that over the next 20 to 30 years the economically active age groups (generally taken as those aged 15–64) will not be able to support the dependent age groups, especially the elderly. Ageing, however, does not mean the total burden of dependency will necessarily increase; in fact, Table 12.5 shows that the total dependency ratio has fallen sharply since 1971. However it is also clear that there are different tendencies within the young and old components of the 'dependent' population. Table 12.6 shows that the rate of growth of the number of children aged under 15

Table 12.6 Indonesia: average annual population growth rates of the 'dependent' age groups 1971–1985.

Age group	1971–80	1980–85
0–14	1.60	1.46
55–64	4.22	5.43
65+	5.41	3.16
75+	7.63	1.53
Total	2.42	2.25

Source: Biro Pusat Statistik, Indonesian Censuses of 1971 and 1980, Intercensal Survey of 1985.

years has been substantially slower than that of the older age groups. As a result, the child dependency ratio has declined even more substantially than the total dependency ratio. On the other hand, the aged dependency ratio has increased, although it is still very low by MDC standards. Moreover, official projections in Table 12.5 show these patterns continuing for the next two decades with the aged-dependency burden in 2005 being almost double that in 1971 while that of the young will be almost half that of 1971. Moreover, it is likely that these tendencies will continue during the early part of the twenty-first century. Chen and Jones (1988) project the total dependency ratio will fall to 45 in the year 2020 and thereafter increase due to the rapid increase in the aged dependency ratio, finally returning to 1980 levels by around 2050. They identify 2045 as the critical year when there is the important crossover when the aged dependency ratio will be greater than the child dependency ratio.

In MDCs, one of the major problems associated with the sex imbalance of older age has been that 'associated with widowhood, one-parent families (female headed) or one-person (female) households, reduced income and increased poverty of older women and greater risks of ill health and institutionalization of women' (Siegel and Hoover, 1984). To this could be added the problems of loneliness of single older women which, although well documented in MDCs, are scarcely referred to in the LDC literature. Yet in village-based fieldwork in West Java, the present writer (Hugo, 1975; 1978) found that one of the most significant social problems in these rural communities was the loneliness, poverty and deprivation of older widows and never-married women who lived on their own and often had to rely upon the charity of the community to survive. In fact Figure 12.3 shows that a greater proportion of older women in Indonesia were not married in 1980 than was the case among their Australian counterparts in 1981. Hence, we must guard against lower overall sex ratios among the aged in LDCs being interpreted as indicating a lower incidence of problems and need among ageing women. Moreover, Heisel (1985) points out that the situation of aged women in many LDCs deserves special attention due to the 'dependent and lower status' of such women which 'has least prepared them to confront changing social structures' so that 'few have, or are even able to take advantage of, existing benefits'. Table 12.7 shows that fewer than a third of Indonesian women aged over 60 years are currently married compared to 85 per cent of men in that age group.

THE SPATIAL DISTRIBUTION OF ELDERLY PEOPLE IN INDONESIA

Whereas the changing spatial segregation of the elderly is a major area of

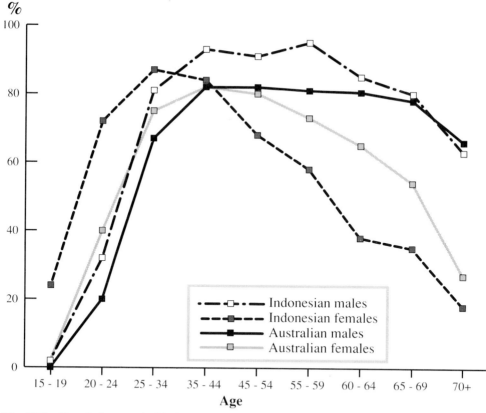

Fig. 12.3 Population married in Australia (1981) and Indonesia (1980).

Source: Hugo (1985).

Table 12.7 Indonesia: marital status of the population aged 60 years and over (percentage distribution) 1980.

	Single (%)	Married (%)	Widowed (%)	Divorced (%)
Males	0.8	85.2	12.2	1.8
Females	1.0	31.0	62.4	5.6
Total	0.9	56.4	38.9	3.8

Source: Biro Pusat Statistik, Indonesian Census (1980).

geographical and social gerontological research in MDCs, it is an almost totally neglected area in LDCs like Indonesia. In general, however, there is a substantially lower degree of spatial concentration of elderly people in LDCs than MDCs (Hugo, 1988b). This is, of course, associated with the fact that the majority of elderly persons in LDCs live with or very near their children and grandchildren which inevitably produces a greater age mixing in communities and local areas than in MDCs. Table 12.8 shows that, as in most LDCs (Hugo, 1985), the aged are less urbanized than the total population. The proportion of the urban population aged 65 years and over increased significantly over the 1971–85 period but not as much as the proportion of the rural population in

Table 12.8 Indonesia: rural-urban distribution of older population 1971–85.

	1971	1980	1985
Percent of urban population aged 65+	2.16	2.63	2.92
Percent of rural population aged 65+	2.58	3.43	3.57
Per cent of 65+ population in urban areas	14.8	18.1	22.5
Per cent of total population in urban areas	17.3	22.4	26.2

Source: Biro Pusat Statistik, Indonesian Censuses of 1971 and 1980, Intercensal Survey of 1985.

that age group. Hence, while the aged are becoming more urbanized, this is not occurring as fast as it is for the total population. This is due to:

- The selective outmigration from rural areas of the young working-age population which produces an ageing of the origin areas (Hugo, 1981a).
- A well-developed pattern of urban-to-rural return migration, often associated with retirement from the public or private sector (Hugo, 1978). This applies particularly to government, police and army employees who are usually compulsorily retired at around the age of 45 when most are still physically able to work. For many the small pension they receive makes it necessary for them to have an additional source of income. In fact, this is recognized in the institution of the 'pre-pension period' whereby both civil and military employees of the Indonesian government are released from duty before the actual period of retirement begins expressly to enable them to find other employment.

Despite the rural bias in the distribution of aged people as compared to the total population, the urban aged population is increasing twice as fast as the rural aged. This raises some important planning issues. For example, it is apparent that while there is little difference between male and female urbanization levels at other ages, levels are significantly higher for older women than men. In this context, Neysmith and Edward (1984) observed in reference to LDCs generally that 'the limited data suggest that a considerable proportion of these women live in slums and squatter communities where they are engaged in roles as house and/or child caretakers. It appears that the urban areas attract and retain more older females than males. Unlike widowers, widows remain in or migrate towards urban areas'. The latter pattern has been observed in an analysis of migration to and from Indonesia's larger urban centres (Hugo, 1981a, 1981b) where, following the death of their husbands, many older women migrate from rural to urban areas to join their children and/or to take advantage of greater access to amenities and services. For the period 1971–85 the following consistent trends were evident in Indonesian census and intercensal survey data:

- Males and females in all age groups became more urbanized.
- Male/female differentials in urbanization increase consistently with age.
- For individual years the overall urban proportion decreases with age for males but not for females; in fact there is an increase at the oldest ages for females.

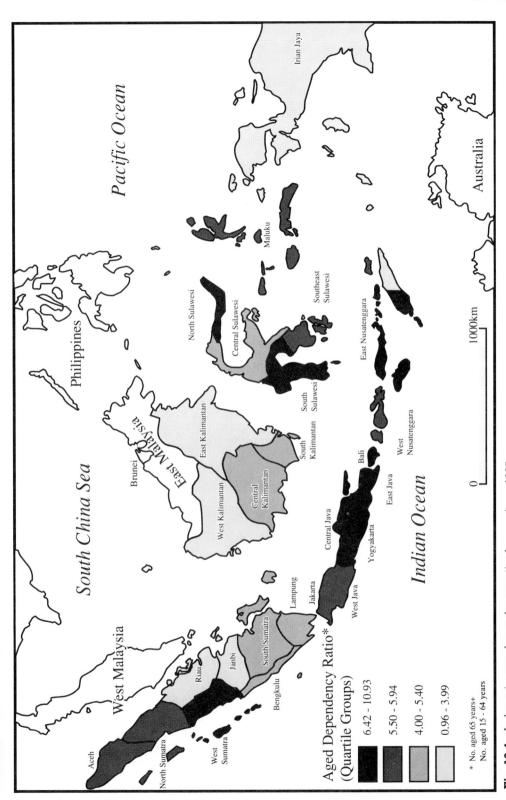

Fig. 12.4 Indonesia: age dependency ratios by province, 1985.

Source: Calculated from Indonesia Intercensal Survey.

Another aspect of the spatial distribution of elderly people is evident in Figure 12.1, namely considerable variations between regions. Two provinces (East and Central Java) had more than 1 million residents aged 65 years and over in 1988, while West Java almost reached this level. The underdeveloped provinces of Eastern Indonesia had the smallest numbers of elderly residents (e.g. Irian Jaya had 7 218 and East Timor 11 170). Although there is a disproportionate concentration in Java, North Sumatra and South Sulawesi, each had around a quarter of a million elderly residents.

Some of the most interesting regional variations are depicted in Figure 12.4 which shows variations in the aged dependency ratio between Indonesia's provinces. In 1985 this ratio varied between 0.96 (Irian Jaya) and 10.93 (Yogyakarta). The highest age dependency ratios are in provinces which either have experienced major declines in fertility (e.g. Bali, Yogyakarta, East and Central Java, North Sulawesi) and/or heavy outmigration (West Sumatra, Nusa Tenggara, Timor, South Sulawesi). On the other hand, the regions of very high inmigration (Jakarta, Irian Jaya) and frontier or natural resource exploitation regions (East Kalimantan, Jambi, Riau) had very low aged dependency levels. It is interesting to note that that major destinations of 'transmigrants', persons moving under government auspices from Inner to Outer Indonesia, do not have especially low ratios, indicating that much of this inmigration is of extended families, including older people, whereas the movement to natural resource exploitation areas is very selective of young adults.

THE WELL-BEING OF ELDERLY PEOPLE IN INDONESIA

The well-being of the aged population is influenced by a complex set of interacting factors – their income, living conditions and arrangements, social contacts and above all their physical and mental health. Ageing often involves individuals being more vulnerable to poverty, physical disability and emotional problems such as loneliness. In the traditional context the family provided the support necessary to cope with these difficulties. There is insufficient data currently available to determine definitely whether or not the well-being of the elderly has deteriorated over recent years. Indeed, there is a lack of information concerning their contemporary situation vis-à-vis other age groups, let alone how this has changed over time. There are certainly scattered indications of a worsening of the situation of elderly people but how representative such reports are cannot be established. In this section we will examine some dimensions of the well-being of the elderly in Indonesia.

Living arrangements
As is the case in most LDCs, few Indonesian elderly persons live alone. Table 12.9 shows that fewer than a tenth live alone and 15 per cent live only with their spouse. In Australia on the other hand, at the 1986 census, 23 per cent of elderly people lived alone while a further 23.2 per cent lived only with their spouse. There are some substantial differences between the living arrangements of males and females among elderly Indonesians. This is largely a function of the fact that most Indonesian women outsurvive their husbands due to their greater longevity and especially the fact that women tend to be younger than their husbands. Hence 8 out of every 10 Indonesian aged men live with their spouses compared to fewer than 3 out of 10 aged women. Most remaining aged men live with other family members while of the remaining women, 57

Table 12.9 Indonesia: living arrangements of the aged (percentage distribution) 1986.

Living arrangements	Males	Females	Total
Alone	1.9	13.5	8.0
With spouse only	20.0	10.5	15.0
With spouse and other family	60.3	16.9	37.6
With other family	17.2	56.8	37.9
With non-family	0.7	2.2	1.5
Total	100.0	100.0	100.0

Source: Chen and Jones (1988).

per cent live with other family members and 13.5 per cent live alone.

There are also some interesting differences between urban and rural areas in the living arrangements of elderly people in Indonesia. Indonesia's large urban centres face a major housing crisis with housing completions barely keeping up with population growth let alone making up the huge backlog of demand (Hugo *et al.*, 1987). The housing crisis in these cities results in most people living in structures 'which are hardly big enough for a nuclear family and which they cannot even hope to change for a bigger one to accommodate an elderly parent' (Fadel-Girgis, 1985). Consequently, housing costs militate against the urban elderly living independently and the incidence of the elderly living with their children tends to be greater than in rural areas. For example, the Indonesian census of 1980 included a question on the relationship of each person enumerated to the head of the household. Of course, in many multigenerational households tradition will have resulted in the oldest person being designated the head even though he or she was not the main breadwinner. Nevertheless, Table 12.10 shows that a high proportion of older Indonesians reported that they were living in a household in which a child, child-in-law, or relative other than a wife, husband or parent was the designated head. It is interesting to note that there is a higher incidence of old people reporting themselves as the parent of the head of the household in urban than rural areas. These findings would appear to contradict the conventional wisdom of family support for the aged being eroded more quickly in urban areas, but it is clearly a function of the differential availability and cost of housing in rural and urban areas. Andrews *et al.* (1986) explain it thus '... co-residency may be explained better by necessity than by cultural orientation. Parents in urban areas may have no

Table 12.10 Indonesia: relationship of aged persons to head of household, 1980.

Age	Urban (%)		Rural (%)		Total (%)	
	Parent	Other	Parent	Other	Parent	Other
50–54	6.5	3.9	6.7	2.3	6.6	2.6
55–59	10.9	3.8	10.0	2.4	10.2	2.7
60–64	20.2	4.5	17.7	2.2	18.2	3.4
65–69	27.3	4.8	22.3	3.4	23.2	3.7
70–74	32.6	7.7	31.3	5.0	31.5	5.5
75+	39.3	10.3	38.6	6.4	38.7	7.1

Source: Biro Pusat Statistik, Indonesian Census of 1980.

choice but to live with their children or vice versa. Elderly rural inhabitants would not suffer necessarily because they did not live with their children. Family support can be experienced just as fully by parents who live near, but not with, their children. Secondly, the trend away from rural and towards urban living may affect younger people selectively, so that aged parents remain in villages while their children move to cities'.

Workforce participation

It is clear from Table 12.11 that workforce-participation rates among the elderly in Indonesia are higher than in most MDCs. Indeed, it may be that there is an under reporting of elderly workforce participation in the Indonesian census since the ASEAN Ageing Survey (Chen and Jones, 1988) found somewhat higher levels of workforce participation among the Indonesian elderly of 61 per cent for males and 34 per cent for females. As would be expected, there is a decline in workforce participation with age among the older population but a third of Indonesian males aged 75 years and over were still in the workforce in 1980. Moreover, Chen and Jones (1988) show that in Indonesia there is a reduction in hours worked per day with advancing age, especially in urban areas.

In Indonesia the mandatory retirement age for civil servants and military personnel is 55 years and this is also adopted by many formal-sector private employees. There are variations such as 65 years for higher-level educators and 60 years for lower levels, but the fixed retirement ages are generally lower than in MDCs. However, for the vast majority of Indonesian workers, the concept of retirement and the dependency it implies has little applicability. Most farm workers and those involved in the urban informal sector continue to work until disability prevents them from doing so, although there are usually changes in both the type and intensity of work undertaken with increasing age.

With the growing significance of the formal sector in the Indonesian economy, the proportion of aged persons in the workforce is beginning to decline. Table 12.12, for example, shows that there has been substantial decline, especially in the oldest age group.

Family support

The high workforce participation notwithstanding, there is still a high degree of reliance on the family for economic and social support among Indonesia's elderly population. The ASEAN Ageing Survey, for example, found that 22 per cent of males and 47 per cent of females indicated that their major source of support was their children or grandchildren, while 50 and 70 per cent respectively relied upon them for at least some income.

There is some concern that the social, economic and demographic changes which are currently occurring in LDCs like Indonesia are undermining the

Table 12.11 Indonesia: labour force participation among the elderly 1980.

Age	Males	Females
60+	48.5	21.6
60–64	76.5	31.5
65–69	48.8	19.2
75+	34.0	9.9

Source: Biro Pusat Statistik, Indonesian Census of 1980.
Unit: %.

Table 12.12 Indonesia: labour force participation rates by sex and age 1971–80.

Age	1971 Males	1971 Females	1980 Males	1980 Females
25–44	94.2	39.9	94.3	40.5
45–49	93.4	45.9	94.1	46.8
50–54	90.6	43.5	90.0	44.3
55–59	86.0	40.5	84.6	40.8
60–64	79.3	35.2	76.7	32.9
65+	62.9	24.5	53.4	19.0

Source: Torrey *et al.* (1987).

basis of this family support. One of the most striking transformations in Indonesia in recent years has been the fertility decline referred to earlier. Demographers suggest that this has been associated with significant changes in family structure and intergenerational relationships within families. Caldwell (1976; 1982), for example, demonstrates that in pretransitional (i.e. societies with high stable fertility), essentially rural societies, the economic benefits of children far outweigh their economic costs over the lifetime of the parents. The fundamental issue in the transition from high to low fertility, he argues, is a change in the direction and magnitude of net intergenerational wealth transfers. The critical factor is the net balance of the two flows (one from parents to children and the other from children to parents) over the period from when people become parents until they die. In traditional societies, the net flow of wealth is from children to parents, and fertility will not begin to decline until there is a reversal of the net flow of wealth. Caldwell argues that the primary cause of this reversal is social – that is, changes in the traditional system of family relationships. This involves a gradual change from an extended family in which one's primary responsibilities and relationships are towards one's parents, to one which is economically and emotionally nucleated and in which relationships with one's spouse and children assume much greater significance. In the West these changes in family structure were caused by a social revolution encompassing a number of developments, especially the introduction of compulsory mass schooling. In the Third World, Caldwell argues that a major cause of the initiation of fertility decline is the importing of European concepts of family relationships and obligations, with mass education and the mass media being major vehicles of that importation. Caldwell says that from a demographic viewpoint the most important 'social exports' from Europe have been the predominance of the nuclear family with the strong husband-wife ties and concentration of concern and expenditure on one's children rather than one's parents. That such changes in family structure have occurred in Indonesia and have been a fundamental factor in the fertility decline is generally accepted (Jones, 1988).

The changing pattern of intergenerational linkages is usually considered by demographers in terms of its impact on fertility. However, the strengthening of the ties between economically active adults and their spouses and children, and the reduction in the importance of the upward ties to their parents has major implications for the welfare of older persons. The net intergenerational transfer of not only wealth but caring and attention upwards in favour of older people in traditional society, has meant that older people in such societies could count on their children for security in old age. However, intrafamilial changes such as those discussed above and the reversal of net intergenerational wealth flows associated with it, would suggest that in such circumstances the older generation may no longer be able to count on the degree of support in their old age that has been the case previously.

Two aspects of traditional families favoured aged people being given strong support:

- First, the intrinsic normative structure which placed major significance upon caring for one's parents.
- Secondly, having a large number of progeny meant that the burden of care of the elderly was shared among a large number of children and grandchildren.

The contemporary changes in family structure and fertility in ASEAN countries, potentially at least, threaten to weaken both of these buttresses of support for the elderly.

An important question which has not been adequately addressed in the literature is that of how far the traditionally strong tendency to care for the aged within the family is a function of the burden being shared among a large number of kin for very few old people, and how far it is a function of intrinsic respect and veneration of the elderly. The assumption has been that it is largely the latter and the former has been little investigated. With the decline in fertility in Indonesia and the increased longevity, the ratio of kin carers to old people is being drastically reduced and this may well be a factor in reducing the strength and effectiveness of informal support systems for the aged. Clearly, this implication of fertility decline needs further research. Moreover, to suggest that children will care for their aged parents is to assume that all older persons have children to care for them in old age. Yet it is recognized that subfecundity and childlessness are substantial in many LDC contexts. Hull and Tukiran (1976) reported that the incidence of apparent primary sterility in Indonesian women in 1971 was 11.6 per cent in urban centres and 14.2 per cent in rural areas, and a further 2.2 per cent of older women were childless due to all of their children predeceasing them. These data are especially significant when it is recalled that women usually outsurvive their husbands. Clearly large numbers of Indonesian elderly persons, especially women, do not have children to call upon to care for them in old age. Moreover, the greatly increased mobility of Indonesians (Hugo, 1988a) means that the probability of an older person with only one or two children, having at least one living nearby has been reduced.

A further element is the increased participation of younger Indonesian women in the workforce outside the home, especially in urban areas. Heisel (1985) points out that this may interfere with women being able to perform a traditional role of providing intensive continuous care for the frail elderly at home.

The economic situation of elderly people

The economic situation of the elderly is very difficult to establish in any context and almost impossible in a 'data-poor' situation such as in Indonesia. Nevertheless, there are some indications that the elderly are less well off economically than the rest of the adult population due to inability to earn. In Indonesia it is officially estimated that around 30 per cent of the population aged 60 and over, or 2.65 million persons, are living in the poorest of the poor conditions (Adi, 1982). This proportion is substantially higher than for the population as a whole (Hugo et al., 1987).

Elsewhere, a number of developments in the Indonesian economy which may have had detrimental effects upon the aged have been identified (Hugo, 1988b).

- The increased importance of the formal sector in the economy is resulting in an increasing exclusion of the aged from economic production processes. In the rural and urban informal sectors, in which the extended family is often the unit of production, there is no concept of a mandatory retirement age and elderly people are readily incorporated into such processes, although their specific roles in that process may change as their physical capabilities decline.
- Related to the above is the fact that older workers find it especially difficult to compete in the formal sector of the labour market because they are generally less well educated than the younger generations who reached school-going age during the post-war expansion of education. This resulted in much higher proportions proceeding to later high school and tertiary education than had been the case with the cohorts educated in the 1920s, 1930s and 1940s.
- The rapidly increasing cost of living in urban areas in Indonesia, associated with the immense pressure being placed upon housing, land, services, food, etc., is especially hardfelt by the aged. This is because such a high proportion of them do not have the independent power to compensate for such increases through obtaining increases in wages.

Literacy and education

The elderly people in Indonesia have very low levels of formal education, having passed through their childhood and young adult years during the colonial occupation when educational opportunities for indigenous people were very limited. Hence the ASEAN Ageing Survey found that only 7 per cent of males aged 60 years and over and 2 per cent of females had any secondary or postsecondary education, while only 44 per cent of males and 14 per cent of females were literate (Chen and Jones, 1988). The levels of education and literacy decrease consistently with increased age and are substantially lower in rural than in urban areas. Clearly as each successive cohort enters the older age groups there will be an improvement in average literacy and education levels. However the fact that the majority of elderly Indonesians (and in the case of women, the vast majority) are illiterate has important implications for service provision and dissemination of information to the elderly. Kinsella (1988) has pointed out 'the accomplishment of literacy affords persons in developing societies a smoother relationship with the socio-economic transition now engulfing many nations. Formal educational attainment greatly enhances economic prospects and permits younger persons to prepare for the economics of old age'.

Health

Very little is known about morbidity among Indonesia's older population and it has not been established that the health of the elderly in LDCs is worse than that of their younger counterparts. Indeed, the higher levels of mortality at younger ages in nations like Indonesia may select out those more prone to illness so that the survivors may on average be healthier than those in MDCs. Indeed a comparative study of Indonesia and Australia by Evans (1985) found that 'the age-specific prevalence of handicap at 55 and over is 4.3 times greater on average in Australia than it is in Indonesia. Prevalence of handicap increases exponentially with age in both countries, but approximately twice as fast in Indonesia, while the familiar cross-over between the sexes appears to occur 7–15 years earlier in Indonesia. Discussion of these findings in demographic terms suggests that the process of ageing advances more rapidly in Indonesia than in Australia but that the population of handicapped people in the former country is maintained at a lower level by higher group-specific mortality rates'.

The 1980 Indonesian census asked a question on health status and Table 12.13 shows that there is a decline with age in the proportion of Indonesians reporting that they are in good health. The ASEAN Ageing Survey included several questions on health and disability and found (Chen and Jones, 1988):

- Some 60 per cent of elderly persons reported that they had experienced a major illness or injury which affected their activities of daily living.
- Among married persons 74 per cent of those aged 60–64, 65 per cent of those aged 65–69 and 47 per cent of those aged 70 and over reported themselves in good health. The percentages were slightly lower for unmarried persons.
- More than half (58 per cent) of older persons could not see well and 26 per cent could not hear well. Some 21 per cent wore glasses.
- Nearly two-thirds had difficulty chewing.
- Most (86.5 per cent) were sufficiently mobile to get around the home without help.

Table 12.13 Indonesia: proportion of older population reporting they are in good health 1980.

Age group	Proportion reporting themselves in good health
55–59	85
60–64	80
65–69	75
70+	64

Source: Biro Pusat Statistik, Indonesian Census of 1980.

Social security
Where pension schemes exist in LDCs they are generally:

- Only available to persons who have worked in the formal sector for a particular period.
- Based upon the level of contributions made while employed.

Table 12.14 shows that pensions are the main source of income for only a very small proportion of Indonesia's elderly population. Moreover, it should be pointed out that:

- The bulk of pension recipients are urban dwellers since 'social security legislation does not usually provide old-age pensions to agricultural workers' (Heisel, 1985).
- Pensions are rarely sufficient to meet the needs of the full living costs of elderly persons (Jones, 1988).

It is apparent from Table 12.14 that the average number receiving social security in Indonesia is very low, even in comparison to other ASEAN

Table 12.14 ASEAN countries: proportion of respondents in the ASEAN Ageing Survey whose main source of support is a pension and the proportion receiving some form of pension 1985.

	Main source of support (%)		Per cent receiving some income	
	Males	Females	Males	Females
Singapore	9	1	29	7
Malaysia	16	6	21	8
Philippines	n.a.	n.a.	18	9
Thailand	5	1	n.a.	n.a.
Indonesia	13	4	16	5

Source: Jones (1988).

countries. Jones (1988) reports that some 11.5 per cent of Indonesia's current workforce (about 6 million persons) are presently covered by pension or old-age assurance provisions. These are almost all civil servants, army personnel and city-based industrial workers.

SERVICE PROVISION FOR ELDERLY PEOPLE

With the changes in intrafamily relationships referred to earlier, the same degree of family support may not now be available so that there will be a greater reliance on services provided externally. There is, however, little aged service infrastructure available in Indonesia. For example, there are very few specialized institutions for the aged and the level of institutionalization of the aged is very low. Adi (1982) reports that the city of Jakarta (1985 population 7.9 million) has only 9 institutions for the aged, with a total of 420 resident elderly people. In Repelita IV, Indonesia's fourth five-year plan which covered the period 1984–1989, it was stated that there was a need to make provision for the approximately 630 000 very poor elderly persons who were lacking family support, and the objectives shown in Table 12.15 were set (Adi, 1982). Data were not available at the time of writing to establish whether or not these very ambitious targets were met but interviews with government officials suggest that the realization fell far below the target.

It is clear that in Indonesia, as is the case in most LDCs, there is almost total reliance upon the family and, to a lesser extent, the local community to care for the elderly. As Chen and Jones (1988) point out, Indonesian policy makers '. . . whether of necessity or from philosophical conviction, seek to maintain the existing systems of family care and concern for the elderly. The family is seen

Table 12.15 Indonesia: actual and target provision of support for the elderly, 1981 and 1989.

Type of support	Number of persons covered	
	1981 (Actual)	1989 (Target)
Institution places	4 713	30 000
Non-institutional support	86 700	500 000
Social security	0	100 000

Source: Adi (1982).

as ultimately responsible for its elderly dependants, and institutionalization to be used only as a last resort. The aim is to obtain as much community participation as possible. This philosophy is reflected in the kinds of income maintenance, health care, recreational programmes and publicly-funded institutional care available to the elderly. Governments provide limited special services for particular groups of the aged, and rely on private and charitable groups to assist in providing for the needy. Social security programmes are typically limited to employed individuals with complementary special welfare programmes for the impoverished and the impaired'.

The ASEAN Ageing Survey found that 24 per cent of their aged respondents belonged to old people's organizations and some 20 per cent participate in educational programmes for the elderly (Chen and Jones, 1988). When compared to MDCs, these indicate very high rates of participation in such social organizations. Nevertheless, although there is not enough information to allow an evaluation of the adequacy of provision of services, it is clear that there is a lack of non-institutionalized services for aged people in Indonesia. Chen and Jones (1988) identify a number of areas of service provision which need to be given urgent attention in Indonesia and other ASEAN nations.

- The needs of the most vulnerable elderly, namely those without families or living alone, need to be thoroughly assessed and provision made for them.
- There is a need for more services to assist the home-based elderly, such as day-care centres, respite centres, home nursing services, 'meals on wheels' and befrienders.
- There is a particular need to establish the needs of the rural elderly since the few services which exist already are mainly in urban areas.
- There needs to be attention given to ways of assisting and encouraging families who care for their elderly members within the traditional system.

In Indonesia, the rapid growth of population is placing great strain on the provision of all types of public services and utilities. In such a situation it is difficult to persuade city, regional and national governments to move into what are largely new areas of spending to provide specialized services for aged people. The need for such services, especially those which mesh with, support and encourage family-based systems, is considerable though. There is a need to provide the elderly (especially the handicapped) with greater opportunities for community-based social activities. In this context the conclusions of a WHO sponsored four-country survey are especially relevant. The study specifically stresses the 'need to explore the appropriateness and effectiveness of day-centre programmes, particularly in urban settings in countries where the growing numbers of the ageing in the population and limitations on extended family activities mean that opportunities for social interaction among the elderly are necessarily restricted ... it is important that urban planning policies, public housing and community development activities take proper account of the special needs of the growing minority of the elderly. Housing policies in the past, for instance, have too often not responded to the needs of the extended family and have resulted in diminished opportunities for family interaction and support' (Andrews et al., 1986).

It is undoubtedly true that the provision of many services for aged people is facilitated by the greater accessibility and economies of scale afforded by the concentration of population in urban centres, rather than in scattered rural communities. As a result current levels of provision are greater in urban areas. However, it should be pointed out that, unlike the situation in MDC urban areas, the aged population in large Indonesian cities is not spatially concentrated to a significant degree. Thus there is not as much scope as in MDC cities for targeting of services to particular sections of the city.

CONCLUSION

This chapter has discussed a number of issues which constitute, or potentially constitute, areas of concern for the maintenance and enhancement of the well-being of elderly people in Indonesia. It should be stressed that most of these problems are largely predicated upon beliefs that:

- Traditional support systems are changing in character and that the family's direct role in the care and support of aged people will be reduced.
- The resources available to the Indonesian government are insufficient to compensate for this loss of support.
- The resources accumulated by the old people themselves during their working lifetimes are not sufficient to compensate for the loss of support.

None of these assertions can be substantiated definitely with empirical data. First, with respect to reduction in family support for the aged in ASEAN cities, Jones (1988) has pointed out:

Many would argue that, even if the Asian countries under consideration were to become as urbanized and industrialized as the West, this does not mean that the aged would be accorded the same roles as in Western societies . . . the earnestly expressed belief (or hope?) of spokesmen from many Asian countries [is] that what is good in their family traditions will be durable enough to avoid a creeping Westernization (one aspect of which is perceived to be neglect of the aged) in the face of forces of economic and social change.

However there are strong indications that there are changes occurring in intergenerational relationships and that many policy makers are aware of them. Heisel (1985) has reviewed the perceptions and policies on ageing of LDC governments articulated in documents submitted to the World Assembly on Aging and to the Fifth Population Inquiry of the United Nations. She concluded that the issues most widely felt and commented upon were as follows:

. . . values of the traditional family system are still very important and the aged command respect and attention from the young members of the family, who have the responsibility for caring for their elders. However recent economic and social changes, particularly migration, have pro- duced a decline in the traditional system of assigning responsibility in the family and in its capacity to cope with some of the fundamental needs of its aged members.

With respect to the second and third propositions there is also a degree of uncertainty as Jones (1988) has expressed:

It is difficult to prognosticate about the old-age security implications of aging trends in Asian countries because many of the factors which will be altering the traditional role of the aged in their family as aging occurs will at the same time be altering their work patterns and independent sources of income in old age. The social and economic changes which underlie sustained fertility decline and aging are at the same time leading to basic changes in the structure of employment, including a shift towards non-agricultural jobs, located in urban areas, requiring higher average levels of education than previously. This will inevitably have implications for the patterns of retirement and income earning capacity for the aged, which will in turn influence their role and status within the family and the community.

Hence, many Indonesians prepare for their old age much as the bulk of their MDC counterparts do, by accumulating assets (especially housing) during their working lives and contributing to pension or superannuation schemes. However, two points need to be made regarding this:

- The generation making these preparations, by and large, is in the early or middle years of their career cycle. Most of the population currently aged or about to enter those age groups are not so fortunate. They represent a 'transitional generation' whereby they may have suffered a decline in family support but not benefited from the social and economic development which occurred late in their working lives, or from increased coverage of pensions.
- Secondly, it is clear that the proportion of the population able to make such preparations for old age is still limited to those most able to benefit from the changes which are occurring, and by no means all of the current working-age population are able to make extrafamilial arrangements for their later years.

Clearly, there is much room for speculation about the impact of the urban transition on the well-being of elderly people in Indonesia. What does appear certain is that change is occurring in family structures, that the aged population is growing at an unprecedentedly rapid rate and that there is at least potential for a substantial determination of well-being over the remaining years of this category.

Ageing represents a challenge to Indonesia's planners but it is one which is by no means insurmountable. However, it will take a judicious blending of policies and programmes which combine aspects of traditional systems of care and support of elderly people with new initiatives which bolster and enhance those systems, if the well-being of Indonesia's elderly population is to be improved.

REFERENCES

Adi, R. (1982). *The Aged in the Homes for the Aged in Jakarta: Status and Perceptions.* Pusat Penelitian, Universitas Katolik Indonesia Atma Jaya, Jakarta.

Andrews, G.R., Esterman, A.J., Braunak-Mayer, A.J. and Rungie, C.M. (1986). *Aging in the Western Pacific.* World Health Organisation Regional Office for the Western Pacific, Manila.

Biro Pusat Statistik (1984). *Penelitian Tentang Masalah Kesejahteraan Sosial Lanjut Usia 1982/1983.* Biro Pusat Statistik, Jakarta.

Biro Pusat Statistik (1987). *Proyeksi Penduduk Indonesia 1985–2005 Berdasarkan Hasil Survei Penduduk Antar Sensus 1985*, Seri Supas Nomor 33, Biro Pusat Statistik, Jakarta.

Caldwell, J.C. (1976). Toward a Restatement of Demographic Transition Theory. *Population and Development Review*, **2**, 3–4, 321–66.

Caldwell, J.C. (1982). *Theory of Fertility Decline.* Academic Press, London.

Chen, A.J. and Jones, G.W. (1988). *Ageing In ASEAN; Its Socio-Economic Consequences.* Institute of Southeast Asian Studies, Singapore.

Douglass, M. (1988). *Urbanization and National Urban Development Strategies in Asia: Indonesia, Korea and Thailand.* Department of Urban and Regional Planning Division, Paper No. 9, University of Hawaii.

Evans, J. (1985). *The Development of Handicap with Ageing in Australia and Indonesia*, pp. 27–33. Proceedings of the 20th Annual Conference of the Australian Association of Gerontology, 1985.

Fadel-Girgis, M. (1985). *Family Support of the Ageing in Developing Countries.* Paper presented at International Congress of Gerontology, New York.

Heisel, M.A. (1985). *Population Policies and Ageing in Developing Countries*, pp. 58–9. Presented at International Congress of Gerontology, New York.

Hugo, G.J. (1975). *Population Mobility in West Java, Indonesia.* Unpublished PhD dissertation, Department of Demography, Australian National University, Canberra.

Hugo, G.J. (1978). *Population Mobility in West Java.* Gadjah Mada University Press, Yogyakarta.

Hugo, G.J. (1981a). Implications of the imbalance in age and sex composition of sub areas as a consequence of migration: the case of a rural developing nation – Indonesia, pp. 387–415. International Union for the Scientific Study of Population. *International Population Conference Manila 1981, Solicited Papers*, **2**.

Hugo, G.J. (1981b). Patterns of interprovincial migration, pp. 81–110. ESCAP, *Migration, Urbanization and Development in Indonesia*, Country Reports. United Nations, New York.

Hugo, G.J. (1985). *Population Ageing: Some Demographic Issues in Developing Countries.* Background paper prepared for the Program for Developing Country Participants, International Congress of Gerontology, New York, July 12th–17th.

Hugo, G.J. (1988a). Population movement, economic development and social change in Indonesia since 1971. *Tijdschrift voor Economische en Sociale Geografie*, **79**, 4.

Hugo, G.J. (1988b). *The Changing Urban Situation in Southeast Asia and Australia: Some Implications for the Elderly.* Prepared for International Conference of Aging Populations in the Context of Urbanization, Sendai, Japan.

Hugo, G.J. (forthcoming). Population distribution and urbanization in Indonesia: recent trends and some policy issues for the Fifth Five Year Plan. In *Mobilitas Penduduk dan Pembangunan Daerah*, K. Wirosuhardjo (Ed.). University of Indonesia Press, Jakarta.

Hugo, G.J., Hull, T.H., Hull, V.J. and Jones, G.W. (1987). *The Demographic Dimension in Indonesian Development.* Oxford University Press, Kuala Lumpur.

Hull, T.H. and Tukiran (1976). Regional variations in the prevalence of childlessness in Indonesia. *The Indonesian Journal of Geography*, **6**, 32: 1–25.

Hull, T.H. and Dasvarma, G.L. (1987). The 1985 Intercensal Survey of Indonesia: **3**. Evidence of Continuing Fertility Decline. *International Population Dynamics Program Research Note* No. 77, Department of Demography, Australian National University. Canberra.

Jones, G.W. (1988). Urbanization trends in Southeast Asia: some issues for policy. *Journal of Southeast Asian Studies* **XIX**, 1: 137–54.

Kinsella, K.G. (1988). *Aging in the Third World.* Center for International Research, US Bureau of Census, International Population Reports, series P-95, No. 79, Washington DC.

Neysmith, S.M. and Edward, J. (1984). Economic dependency in the 1980s: its impact on Third World elderly. *Aging and Society*, **4**, 1, 21–44.

Population Reference Bureau (1988). *World Population Data Sheet.* Population Reference Bureau, Washington.

Siegel, J.S. and Hoover, S.L. (1984). *International Trends and Perspectives: Aging.* US Department of Commerce, Bureau of the Census, International Research Document No. 12, Washington DC.

Streatfield, K. and Larson, A. (1987). The 1985 Intercensal Survey of Indonesia: 4. Infant and Child Mortality Levels. *International Population Dynamics Program Research Note on Child Survival* No. 14CS, Department of Demography, Australian National University, Canberra.

Torrey, B.B., Kinsella, K. and Taeuber, C.M. (1987). *An Aging World.* US Bureau of the Census, International Population Reports Series P95 No. 78, Washington DC.

Vatikiotis, M. (1988). Worrying about idle minds. *Far Eastern Economic Review*, 13 October, 39.

World Bank (1988). *World Development Report, 1988.* Oxford University Press, New York.

Mark Cleary

and

Hairuni H.M. Ali Maricar

Department of Geography
University of Brunei Darussalam

13 AGEING, ISLAM AND THE PROVISION OF SERVICES FOR ELDERLY PEOPLE IN BRUNEI DARUSSALAM

INTRODUCTION

Brunei Darussalam is a small, independent, Islamic state on the north-west coast of Borneo (Leake, 1989). Located between the Malaysian states of Sabah and Sarawak, the country is of particular interest to demographers and planners for at least two reasons. First, the country is one of the richest in the world: the oilfields around Seria in the south-east of the state provide massive revenues for this state of only some 249 000 people. The per capita GDP in 1989 was, at over $21 000 per year, one of the highest in the world (Brunei Darussalam, 1989). A second feature worthy of emphasis is the importance of Islam in the state. It is the state religion (66.5 per cent of the population was Muslim in 1989) and Islamic codes of behaviour and social welfare colour all aspects of daily life. Recent developments seem likely to accentuate the importance of Islam as the guiding principle of daily life (Far Eastern Economic Review, 1990). Both because of its wealth and its distinctive religious culture, the ways in which the elderly are provided for in this society are of particular interest. This chapter will trace first the demographic background to the question of ageing; secondly, the place that Islam occupies in concepts of caring for the elderly; and thirdly, the ways in which these concepts of care are reflected in the provision of services for these groups.

THE DEMOGRAPHY OF BRUNEI DARUSSALAM

Between 1921 and 1981, the date of the last full census in the country (the next census is planned for 1991), the population of Brunei Darussalam increased nine-fold, from 25 451 to 192 832 (Census of Population, 1981). The partial 1986 Demographic Report indicated a further sharp increase to 226 300, as Table 13.1 shows. The sustained high rates of growth in the country can be attributed to both natural increases and to migration, for the economy continues to rely heavily on an expatriate labour force both from the ASEAN region and from further afield (New, 1989; Hairuni Ali Maricar, 1987). Much of this labour is employed in the booming construction sector – in the oil industry the size of the expatriate labour force has fallen as localization programmes take effect.

Ethnically, Malays comprised 68.8 per cent of the population in 1989. The Chinese formed the next major group at about 17.7 per cent of the population whilst 'other indigenous groups' (such as Iban, Melanau and Punan) comprised

Table 13.1 Population growth of Brunei Darussalam 1911–1986.

Year	Total population	Annual % increase
1911	21 718	
1921	25 451	1.6
1931	30 135	1.7
1947	40 657	1.9
1960	83 877	5.7
1971	136 256	4.5
1981	192 832	3.5
1986	226 300	3.1

Source: Census of Population (1981; 1986).
Note: The population figure for 1911 is an estimate.

about 5.2 per cent of the total (Brunei Darussalam, 1989). The population is concentrated in two areas: in and around the capital, Bandar Seri Begawan, where most of the government offices, commercial outlets and light industry are concentrated; and around the oilfields at Seria and Kuala Belait. Malays comprise about 75 per cent of the population in the Brunei/Muara district; in the Kuala Belait area, around the oilfields, the Chinese are proportionately more important. The other two districts of the state, Tutong and Temburong, are more sparsely populated and are predominantly Malay. The Chinese are overwhelmingly an urban population – the Malay population is more evenly divided between urban and rural locations. In the interior jungle areas (81 per cent of the country remains covered by primary rainforest) the population is thin and scattered.

The rapid growth in the population of the country has given it a predominantly youthful age profile and demographers consider the country to be entering a third stage of the demographic transition with a decline in crude birth rates and a more moderate population growth (Hairuni Ali Maricar, 1987). But the population remains a young one and the proportion of young adults in the population increased from 29.4 per cent in 1960 to 40.4 per cent in 1989. The elderly population, which is defined as those over 60, the age at which old-age pensions are payable by the state, has a different position, for the size of this cohort has fallen in relative terms from 5.6 per cent of the population in 1960 to 4.1 per cent in 1989 (Table 13.2).

It is thus in the context of an essentially young population structure that provision for elderly people needs to be considered. This becomes even clearer when demographic projections are taken into account. As Table 13.3 indicates, the proportion of the population aged 15–24 and over 55 is unlikely to alter markedly over the next decade. It is also important to note ethnic differences in the size of the elderly population cohort. The proportion of Malays was highest in 1986 with 4.7 per cent aged over 60. The Chinese follow closely behind at 4.5 per cent whilst 'other indigenous groups' are much lower at 3 per cent (Census of Population, 1986).

In the light of the above demographic features, it is perhaps not surprising that, in common with many other countries in the region (with the exception, perhaps, of Singapore), it is the size and growth of the young population that is of most immediate concern to planners and government departments. The problems of youth unemployment, the need for economic diversification and heavy resource inputs into all sectors of the education infrastructure form a dominant theme in the planning forecasts of government departments. The

Table 13.2 Age Cohorts 1947–89.

Age groups	1947	1960	1971	1981	1989
Under 15	39.6	46.6	43.4	38.6	36.1
15–34	33.6	29.4	34.1	40.1	40.4
35–59	21.9	18.4	17.7	17.0	19.4
60+	4.9	5.6	4.6	4.3	4.1

Source: Brunei Darussalam (1989).
Note: The date for 1989 is based on mid-year estimates.

Table 13.3 Population projections by age cohort.

	1986		1991		1996		2001	
	No. (thousands)	%	No.	%	No.	%	No.	%
Age cohort								
15–24	51.5	22	57.1	21	61	20	66.6	19
55+	13.4	6	16.4	6	20	6	23.6	6.6

Source: Niew (1989).

relatively small size of the elderly population, coupled with its slow growth rate, largely relegates the issue to a secondary place in considerations of future economic and social provision.

When longer-term projections are taken into consideration, however, a rather different picture emerges. In 1986, as part of the 20-year Brunei Darussalam Master Plan, a consultant's report indicated a number of likely scenarios for future age-cohorts in the population (Brunei Darussalam Master Plan, 1986). There are, of course, particular difficulties in estimating the total projected population for a country like Brunei because it employs considerable expatriate labour (in 1989 some 32 per cent of the workforce was expatriate). Their future numbers are bound to reflect fluctuations in the state of the economy linked, as it is, to oil and gas revenues. Projections based on the continued employment of a large migrant labour force suggest, as was noted in Table 13.2, that the proportionate size of the elderly population is likely to remain stable. If, however, attention is focused solely on the permanent population (that is, citizens and permanent residents of the state), a rather different scenario is apparent.

Assuming a fall in expatriate labour, the country will move towards an increasingly ageing population by the year 2005 with the number of people aged 60 and over increasing from 9 700 in 1985 to 18 500 by 2005, an increase of 90.7 per cent (Niew, 1989). Improvements in life expectancy from 42.6 years and 42.7 years for male and female respectively in 1947, to 70.1 years and 72.7 years in 1989, underpin this evolution (Brunei Darussalam, 1989). The youngest age group is likely to grow by only 39 per cent over the same period. 'These changes', notes Niew, 'would mean a gradual shift from the burden of child dependency to old-age dependency, which will bring with it certain social and economic implications' (Niew, 1989). Pension costs, medical and other welfare expenditure and patterns of demand are all likely to be influenced by these demographic changes.

In the short term, then, financial and welfare provisions for the elderly would not appear to be as central a problem as providing for the large, youthful-population cohort in the country. But, if population projections are taken into account, a steady increase in the elderly population is certain to take place, although estimating the proportionate importance of that group is complicated by the uncertainties surrounding the size of the expatriate labour force in the country.

ISLAM AND CARE FOR ELDERLY PEOPLE

Islamic precepts of behaviour govern all aspects of social life in Brunei Darussalam and, in this respect, the care and welfare of elderly people is no exception. Three sources in particular reveal the importance and character of such precepts: the Koran itself; that body of traditions relating to the Prophet Muhammad known as the Hadith; and the concept of Melayu Islam Beraja (Malay, Muslim, Monarchy or MIB) which is increasingly seen as the guiding philosophy of social life in Brunei Darussalam. What then, do these sources indicate about care for elderly people?

In various chapters of the Koran, emphasis is laid on the need for children to accept responsibility for the care of their elderly relatives. One can note, for example, the following verses:

> 'And that ye be kind to parents. Whether one or both of them attain old age in thy life, Say not to them a word of contempt, nor repel them, but address them in terms of honour. And out of kindness lower to them the wing of humility and say: My Lord! bestow on them Thy Mercy even as they Cherished me in childhood.'
> (Sura VXII, Al-Isra, verse 23–24; Abdullah, 1975, 700–701)

> 'And we have enjoined on man (to be good) to his parents; In travail upon travail did his mother bear him, And in years twain Was his weaning: (Hear Thy Command); show gratitude to Me and thy parents.'
> (Sura XXXI, Luqman, verse 14; Abdullah, 1083)

Such views are central to the social and religious philosophy of Islam taught in school and mosque and they are reinforced in the Hadith. Here, the body of traditions of the Prophet Muhammad are collected. In many of these Hadith, it is made clear that obligations towards elderly relatives are to be taken very seriously, for attitudes towards the elderly are a touchstone of religious adherence. The Hadith also enjoins upon children to care for their parents since, by so doing, they will then set a good example for their own children. The Hadith accords a particular place to the mother of the family. Children are seen as having a particular responsibility for her care.

Given the strength of such religious dictates on caring for elderly people, it is perhaps not surprising that the state has seen provision for the elderly as being first and foremost the responsibility of the family. From the Islamic perspective children are required (not simply encouraged) to provide financial assistance for their parents in old age. Islam is strong in its condemnation of children who fail in this duty and whose parents are required to carry on working into old age simply in order to support themselves. Children are also enjoined to show a continued concern for their parents' welfare, if necessary by living together with them in the extended family. The concept of placing family members in a special home for the elderly would be regarded as an abrogation of religious duty. If parental love for their children is in some way undermined (perhaps by their children's failure to care for them) this is regarded by Islam as degrading and dishonourable (Hasyim, 1985). Such is the significance of elderly people in Muslim society, that to fail to care for one's parents is to compromise the chances of a place in heaven.

Added to these strong religious dictates, there is no doubt that elderly people occupy a significant place in Malay–Muslim culture generally. Malay culture emphasizes that children should care for and obey their parents, all the more so when they are elderly or infirm. It is tantamount to social disgrace for children to neglect the welfare of their parents – a disgrace both to Malay culture and to Islam. Respect for the elderly is regarded as a central component of the MIB philosophy which is becoming increasingly prominent in Bruneian life (Far Eastern Economic Review, 1990).

In theory, then, the strictures governing the care of elderly people are clear and unequivocal. It is the responsibility of children, and the family is the unit within which care for the elderly must take place. The strength of these dictates comes from both the Koran and from the cultural mainspring of the Malay identity. Of course, a gap between theory and reality, between the rhetoric and the practice is inevitable, and it would be absurd to pretend that these precepts mean that there are no problems facing elderly people in Brunei Darussalam. Inevitably, changes in the family such as the erosion of the extended family, the increasing numbers of women in the workforce and the pressures of material-ism mean that some form of provision has to be made for those elderly people who escape the 'net' of family responsibility. But the religious and cultural foundations of care for the elderly have meant that the role of the state is considered secondary to that of the family, and this undoubtedly colours service provision in the country.

THE PROVISION AND TAKE-UP OF SERVICES

For the state, ultimate responsibility for elderly people rests squarely with the family, a view considered consistent with the tenets of Islamic social mores. There is thus no formal legislation setting out a framework for caring for the elderly and no social welfare legislation regarding community or domiciliary help for families with elderly members. The absence of such provisions, perhaps strange to Western observers, is seen as consistent with the Malay–Islamic culture of Brunei Darussalam. The care and support of elderly people, whether they be Malay, Chinese or other groups, remains unformalized and pragmatic. That said, however, it should be emphasized that there are provi-sions for a variety of informal types of assistance to be given to families facing difficulties in looking after their elderly relatives.

All citizens and permanent residents as well as individuals who have lived and worked in Brunei Darussalam for a minimum of 30 years have, since 1955, been entitled to a monthly pension, currently fixed at $100, in addition to any other entitlements they may have accrued. In addition, elderly people receive additional allowances if they have any dependants below working age. Overall, the maximum entitlement from the Pensions Office is fixed at $500 a month. Some elderly people are in receipt of occupational pensions and, with time, the numbers in receipt of such pensions, whether through work in the private or public sector, are likely to increase. The stipend is paid through the Pensions Section of the Ministry of Welfare, Youth and Culture and is channelled through the mukim (groups of villages) or kampung (village) headman who pays it directly to the elderly persons of the village. In addition, small pensions are payable for the blind, disabled, lepers and mentally infirm through the same system. It should be noted that, given the high cost of living in the country, the

Table 13.4 Distribution of old-age pensions by district and ethnic group.

Ethnic group	Total (T)	%	Malay T	%	Chinese T	%	Other indigenes T	%
District:								
Brunei-Muara	4 536	55	3 893	86	638	14	4	–
Belait	1 882	23	821	44	943	50	114	6
Tutong	1 481	18	1 345	91	88	6	48	3
Temburong	313	4	264	84	16	5	33	11
Total	8 212	100%	6 323	77%	1 685	21%	193	2%

Source: Jabatan Pencen-Pencen Negara (1990).

sum is not sufficient to maintain an elderly person, reinforcing the importance of family help. A recent initiative of the Pensions Section has been to encourage small-scale handicraft production by those recently retired to help supplement personal incomes.

The size of the pensions budget has increased steadily as the numbers of pensioners and the monthly stipend has grown. From a figure of about 2 000 pensions in 1955, the current total is 8 212. This represents about 80 per cent of all those entitled to receive such pensions. Table 13.4 indicates the geographical and ethnic breakdown of the pensions statistics for 1989/1990, and illustrates how ethnic distributions vary between different parts of the state, with a strong concentration of Malays in Brunei/Muara, Tutong and Temburong and of Chinese in Belait. The current pensions budget is about $11 million per year. Should the need arise, the Pensions Department can increase this budgeted amount through direct application to the Treasury (Jabatan Pencen–Pencen Negara, 1988).

Alongside these mandatory pension provisions, other discretionary grants are available through two ministries, the Ministry of Culture, Youth and Sports and the Ministry of Religious Affairs. The latter, in particular, has considerable sums to disburse through its accumulated fund of religious tithes, the zakat and fitrah. The former is essentially a tax on wealth whilst the latter is paid by all muslims just before the celebration of Hari Raya. The religious funds are intended mainly for five major categories of people with the 'poverty stricken' (fakir) and 'poor' (miskin) receiving the majority of monies, as Figure 13.1 indicates. Elderly people form a majority of those receiving such hardship monies. In 1989, the sum disbursed from the zakat and fitrah funds was around $1.65 million and about 4 000 people in the fakir and miskin were helped. The procedures for gaining access to either pensions or to these discretionary grants are outlined in Figure 13.2.

The role of the ketua kampung or village headman in this process is particularly significant. Families whose elderly relatives are facing difficulties will amost invariably take their problems in the first place to the ketua kampung who is appointed because of the respect he can command in the community. The headman may subsequently approach the mukim head (the penghulu mukim) or he may make direct representation to the district office. Alternatively, he may simply point the applicant along the right administrative corridors. It is, furthermore, the headman who is responsible for paying the

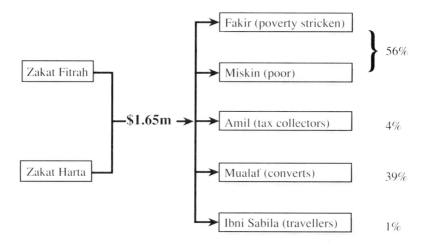

Source: Zakat dan Fitrah di-Negeri Brunei
          Data from Ministry of Religious Affairs

Fig. 13.1   Brunei: Destination of Zakat Fitrah funds 1989–90.

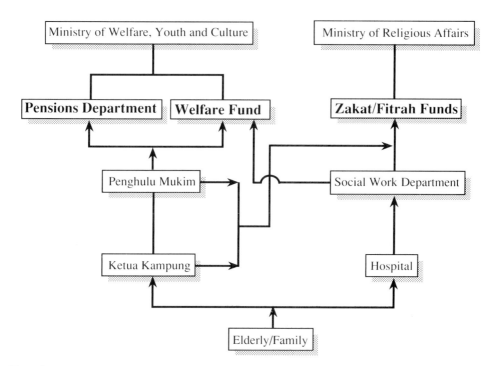

Fig. 13.2   Brunei: access to pensions and discretionary funds.

monthly pension directly to elderly people. He is thus in an important position
to assess the conditions and needs of the elderly population in the kampung. In
the absence of any kind of regular domiciliary help, his role can take on
particular importance. For the Chinese, charitable help can also be obtained
from the Chinese Chamber of Commerce which plays an active charitable role.

The central importance of care within the family and the kampung has meant that old people's homes are virtually unknown in the country and, indeed, are actively discouraged. Only one such home exists, at Seria. It caters for a small number of elderly Chinese (currently 18 of the 60 places are occupied) who have no family to care for them, and receives a government grant of $10 000 per year towards running costs. It was opened in 1957 and is now known as the Community Service Council Centre. The bulk of its costs are covered by charitable donations. The government, emphasizing its policy of family care, decided in December 1986 that no new clients would be admitted and, in time, the home will close. There are no private homes for elderly people, nor, it is imagined, would the authorities look favourably on applications for developing such facilities.

Probably the most frequent way in which elderly people come into contact with the welfare authorities is through the medical services. A brief outline of medical provision is perhaps worthwhile. There are large, modern hospital facilities in the capital, Bandar Seri Begawan, in the larger towns of Seria and Kuala Belait as well as in the smaller towns of Tutong and Bangar in the Temburong district (see Fig. 13.3). At local level, a network of primary health care clinics has also been established in both the urban district of Bandar and the rural areas of the country. These are staffed by nurses and, whilst their role is primarily focused on children and mothers, in the more rural areas they do see elderly patients for emergency treatment. The problems of primary health care in the remoter rural areas are tackled by a system of travelling dispensaries based at Bandar Seri Begawan and Bangar, and by larger rural clinics in Lamunin and Labi. Finally, the Flying Medical Service provides health care in the remote interior on a monthly schedule of visits to 14 rural centres. All medical care, consultations and hospitalization are free of charge in the state (Ministry of Health, 1988).

It is largely through the hospital doctors that access to forms of welfare and psychogeriatric care is obtained, for, at present, no system of community care through regular domiciliary visits has been established. Whilst such a system might be feasible in the capital, in the more isolated rural areas it would be logistically very difficult and expensive. It is clear, then, that the hospital and welfare authorities will come into contact with elderly people only when medical needs require a visit to one of the main hospitals. As a result a system of crisis management rather than preventive care has tended to develop. Doctors can thus refer their elderly patients (and their relatives) to a range of counselling and social services which are organized through the main hospital (the Raja Isteri Pengiran Anak Saleha Hospital or RIPAS) in the capital.

A medical social work department, established in 1983, operates from the RIPAS hospital and, as one of its main functions, provides counselling for the elderly and their families on the particular social and medical needs of their relatives. Thus, for example, the families of elderly patients who have suffered bone breakages are advised on the types of changes needed to make the home environment a safer one. Similarly, advice to families experiencing difficulty in looking after their infirm relatives can be given. But although the social work department cannot offer any financial help for such works, it can at least help process applications for help from the various discretionary funds available. Such procedures can however be slow and cumbersome. Furthermore, the scope of activity of the department is limited since it has only a small staff and has a wide range of other functions to fulfil. The department admits that its role is primarily one of 'first aid' for elderly people and that preventive activity and advice is, at present, beyond its scope. Nevertheless, it estimates that perhaps

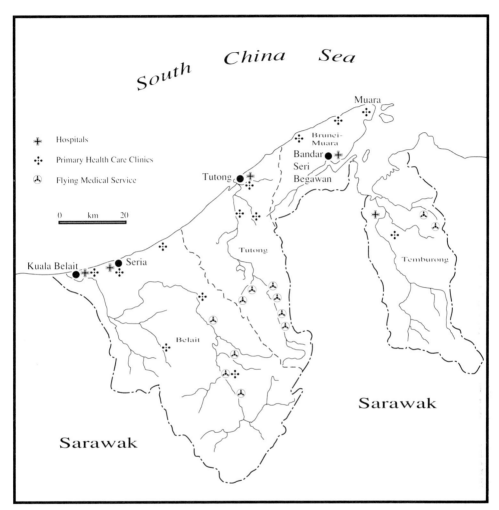

Fig. 13.3 Location of health facilities in Brunei.

around 10 per cent of the elderly population comes into contact with the hospital administration each year and can therefore potentially be counselled. In reality, of course, the numbers of elderly people dealt with by the social work department are much lower.

CONCLUSION

One of the objectives of this chapter has been to emphasize that the provision of services for elderly people in Brunei Darussalam flows directly from the precepts of the Malay–Islamic way of life. Indeed, it is this, the authors argue, which makes the case of Brunei Darussalam of particular interest. As the section on demography has shown, the numbers of elderly permanent residents and citizens will increase considerably over the next two decades, although present social and economic policy focuses more on the younger age groups.

Arising from the nature of Islam, planners in the country have made a conscious decision to place responsibility for the elderly with the family, not the state. Whilst in many respects (such as the availability of free medical care, free education and pensions), the country displays elements of a welfare state (a product, no doubt of the large oil and investment revenues available for a small population), care for elderly people is regarded differently. Much of the provision has been geared towards providing a 'safety net' for those elderly people who, for one reason or another, face problems. The view that there might be an alternative to care within the family (through, for example, state or commercial old people's homes) is seen as anathema. Whilst the cynic might argue that such a view conveniently reduces demands on the Treasury, a consideration of Islamic precepts on caring for elderly people suggests rather more deep-seated roots for the family-centred nature of elderly care.

Focusing responsibility clearly on the family does, not surprisingly, carry risks. It would be naïve to suggest that there are no problems with elderly care in Brunei Darussalam. Hospital and social work personnel are having to cope with a number of cases of neglect and ill-health brought on by the failure of family care (Medical Social Work Unit, RIPAS, 1990). The very existence of facilities to back up family care points to potential problems that exist. Indeed, it may be that these problems are likely to increase. Brunei Darussalam is a rich country with a high GDP and high levels of personal consumption by many of its inhabitants. Such materialism may well threaten to erode the importance of the family as a caring unit, a danger that planners and ministers are increasingly conscious of. This typifies the dangers of elements of 'Westernization' discussed in other chapters in this book. Likewise, it has been argued that an increase in the number of women in the workforce (from 20.1 per cent of the workforce in 1960 to 31.3 per cent in 1981) poses potential threats to the stability of the family. These general debates about the nature of social and family life in Brunei Darussalam have important implications for elderly care both now and in the future.

Acknowledgements
The authors would like to thank the Medical Social Work Unit; the Departments of the Ministry of Welfare, Youth and Culture; the Religious Council of Brunei Darussalam; and Aliudin Mahjudin of Universiti Brunei Darussalam for their help in providing information for this chapter.

REFERENCES

Brunei Darussalam Master Plan (1987). *Final Report.*

Brunei Darussalam (1989). *Statistical Yearbook.* Economic Planning Unit, Brunei Darussalam.

Census of Population (1981). Economic Planning Unit, Brunei Darussalam.

Census of Population (1986). Partial Report. Economic Planning Unit, Brunei Darussalam.

Far Eastern Economic Review (1990). The Malay Monarchy, 15 November.

Hairuni Hj Mohamed Ali Maricar (1987). *Population Change in Brunei Darussalam.* MA Thesis, University of Durham.

Hasyim, U. (1985). *Anak Yang Saleh.* Pustaka Nasional, Singapore.

Jabatan Pencen-Pencen Negara (1988). Brunei Darussalam.

Leake, D. (1990). *Brunei: The Modern Southeast Asian Sultanate.* Forum, Selangor.

Medical Social Work Unit, RIPAS (1990). Interview material, October–November.

Ministry of Health (1988). *The Report.* Brunei Darussalam.

Niew Shong Tong (1989). *Demographic Trends in Negara Brunei Darussalam.* Universiti Brunei Darussalam.

SUBJECT INDEX

Thailand   3, 25, 27, 185–206
  age structure   186, 189, 193
  average income   198, 199
  birth control in   203
  birth rate   192, 203
  circumstances of elderly   195
  day care in   202
  demographic aspects   185, 186
  elderly population   193, 194, 210
  employment of elderly in   15, 197
  family care in   197, 204
  fertility in   185, 186, 187, 193, 194
  health and nutrition in   199
  health care in   200, 204
  hospitals in   201, 202, 203
  household size in   196
  housing in   204
  internal migration   189, 190, 193, 194
  life expectancy   6, 188, 204
  living arrangements   195
  medical services in   195, 200
  mortality rates   185, 186, 187, 188, 192,
    193, 194, 199
  population   189, 190, 191
  poverty in   185
  private sector in   201
  residential care in   202
  social services   202, 203
  source of elderly income   196

  water supply   200
Three generation households   40, 43, 195

United Nations
  studies of developmental implications   27
  World Assembly on Ageing 2, 176, 202
United Nations University Study   26
Urbanization
  China   112
  Indonesia   228

Vietnam   3
  age structure   9
  life expectancy   6, 8
Voluntary agencies   14

Welfare systems   12–14
  Hong Kong   45
  Malaysia   176
  public   15
  Taiwan   140, 141, 142
Welfare to Hardship Households
  in China   114
Western diseases   11, 47
Western Pacific Four-country Study   25, 176
Workforce, elderly in   81, 100, 102
  See also separate countries
World Health Organization (WHO)
  South-east Asian Studies   26, 176

AUTHOR INDEX

Page numbers in *italic* indicate references

Management and Co-ordination Agency   38, 39, *43*
Manton, K.   25, *35*
Maricar, H.M.   viii, 231, 232, *241*
Martin, L.G.   5, 11, 16, 17, *20*, 22, 23, 25, *35*, 36, 38, 41, *43*, 66, *76*, 113, *126*, 204, *205*
Maruo, N.   41, *44*
Masitah, M.Y.   168, *183*
Matsuzaki, T.   32, *34*
Mazian, F.   153, *165*
Medical Social Work Unit   240, *241*
Merton, R.K.   161, *166*
Min, J.S.   151, *166*
Ministry of Community Development, Singapore   89, *103*
Ministry of Finance, Malaysia   172, *183*
Ministry of Foreign Affairs, Japan   149, *166*
Ministry of Health, Brunei   238, *241*
Ministry of Health, Korea   151, 156, *166*
Ministry of Health, Malaysia   174, 175, 176, *183*
Ministry of Health, Singapore   78, 88, 89, *103*
Ministry of Health and Welfare   36, 37, *43*, *44*
Ministry of Labour, Singapore   *104*
Ministry of Welfare, Malaysia   *183*
Mishra, R.   12, *20*
Montgomery, R.J.V.   66, *76*
Myers, G.   23, 25, *35*

Nakai Town Administration   40, *44*
Nam, J.J.   151, 152, 153, *165*
National Association of Volunteers   *147*
National Statistical Office, Bangkok   188, 196, 201, 202, *205*, *206*
National University of Singapore   100, *104*
NESDB, Bangkok   199, 201, 202, *205*
New Straits Times   168, *183*
Neysmith, S.M.   216, *230*
Ng, Y.Y.   46, *63*
Ngan, R.   69, *76*
Niew Shong Tong   231, 233, *241*
Normah, M.D.   179, 180, *183*

Okuyama, S.   37, 38, 40, *44*
Olshansky, S.J.   11, *20*
Omran, A.R.   11, *20*
Orbach, H.L.   152, *165*

Palmore, E.B.   4, *20*
Pamphiphat, S.   200, *206*
Pardthiasong, T.   188, *205*
Parish, W.L.   105, *127*
Park, I.H.   150, 153, *165*
Pathmanathan, I.   176, *184*
Payne, M.   70, *76*
Peng, S.   17, *21*
Phillips, D.R.   vi, 1, 4, 11, 14, *20*, 45, 46, 47, 49, 53, *63*, *64*, 66, *76*, 125, *127*
Phillipson, C.   73, *76*
Piampiti, S.   189, 204, 205
Pollak, O.   152, *165*
Population Reference Bureau   7, *20*, 210, *230*
Powell, M.   5, *20*

Quadagno, J.   65, *76*
Qureshi, H.   *147*

Race, D.   46, *64*
Reif, L.   13, *19*

Rhee, K.O.   150, 151, *166*
Rhee, S.J.   152, *166*
Rigg, J.   3, *20*
Rosow, I.   152, *166*
Ross, R.B.   *147*
Royal Thai Embassy   187, *205*
Rungie, C.M.   2, 6, 10, 14, *19*, 25, *34*, 176, *183*, 204, *205*, 219, 226, *228*
Rutstein, S.   188, *205*
Ruzicka, L.T.   188, *205*
Ryu, I.H.   153, *165*
Ryu, J.S.   151, 152, 153, *165*

Sanborn, B.   13, *19*
Sandosham, A.A.   176, *184*
Sangl, J.   72, *76*
Sankar, A.   32, *35*
Schulz, J.H.   77, *103*
Secretaries of State (U.K.)   72, *76*
Seebohm Report (U.K.)   65, *76*
Sepulveda, J.   11, *19*
Shanas, E.   135, *147*
Shevasunt, S.   188, *205*
Shibita, H.   32, *34*
Shichita, K.   32, *34*
Shimonka, Y.   32, *34*
Shore, B.K.   65, *75*
Siegel, J.S.   23, *35*, 214, *230*
Sims, C.   65, *76*
Singapore Council of Social Service   78, 87, 88, 94, 95, *104*
Singh, G.   167, *184*
Singhasakeres, S.   200, *206*
Sittitrai, W.   27, *35*
Social Welfare Department, Hong Kong   58, 60, *64*, 71, 72, *76*
Squier, D.A.   65, *76*
State Statistical Press, Beijing   110, *127*
Sternstein, L.   189, *206*
Stones, R.   72, *76*
Streatfield, K.   *230*
Stull, R.E.   66, *76*
Sung-jae Choi   14
Sushama, P.C.   vii, 167
Swift, C.   49, *64*

Taeuber, C.M.   207, 221, *230*
Tan, B.H.   61, *64*, 90, *104*
Tanphiphat, S.   200, *206*
Tao, L.   122, *127*
Tian, S.   119, *127*
Tian, X.   105, 111, 121, *127*
Tinker, A.   *147*, 161, *166*
Titmuss, R.   12, *20*
Topley, M.   50, *64*
Torrey, B.B.   207, 221, *230*
Tout, K.   1, *21*
Treas, J.   18, *21*
Trowell, H.C.   47, *64*
Tu, E.J.   116, *126*
Tukiran   222, *229*

United Nations   9, *21*, 23, *35*, 186, 188, 192, 197, 200–1, 202, *206*
United States Bureau of the Census   *206*
United States National Research Council   188, *206*

Vatikiotis, M.   207, *230*